GOD AND THE OTHER

INDIANA SERIES IN THE PHILOSOPHY OF RELIGION

Merold Westphal, *editor*

GOD

AND THE

OTHER

ETHICS AND POLITICS AFTER
THE THEOLOGICAL TURN

J. AARON SIMMONS

Indiana University Press
Bloomington and Indianapolis

This book is a publication of

Indiana University Press
601 North Morton Street
Bloomington, Indiana 47404-3797 USA

www.iupress.indiana.edu

Telephone orders   800-842-6796
Fax orders   812-855-7931
Orders by e-mail   iuporder@indiana.edu

♾ The paper used in this publication meets the minimum requirements of the American National Standard for Information Sciences—Permanence of Paper for Printed Library Materials, ANSI Z39.48-1992.

Manufactured in the United States of America

Library of Congress Cataloging-in-Publication Data

Simmons, J. Aaron, [date]
   God and the other : ethics and politics after the theological turn / J. Aaron Simmons.
     p. cm. — (Indiana series in the philosophy of religion)
   Includes bibliographical references (p.   ) and index.
   ISBN 978-0-253-35592-8 (cloth : alk. paper) — ISBN 978-0-253-22284-8 (pbk. : alk. paper) 1.
Religion—Philosophy. 2. Continental philosophy. 3. Ethics. 4. Political science—Philosophy.
I. Title.
   BL51.S5435 2011
   210—dc22

                                                                        2010034440

          1 2 3 4 5 16 15 14 13 12 11

To my family, with appreciation

More than any other form of democracy, more than social democracy or popular democracy, a Christian democracy should be welcoming to the enemies of democracy; it should turn them the other cheek, offer hospitality, grant freedom of expression and the right to vote to antidemocrats, something in conformity with a certain hyperbolic essence, an essence more autoimmune than ever, of democracy itself, if "itself" there ever is, if ever there is a democracy and thus a Christian democracy worthy of its name.

—Jacques Derrida, *Rogues*

CONTENTS

Contents

ACKNOWLEDGMENTS

This book is the result of much more than long hours spent in libraries and late nights at the office. Were it not for the support of many others, I would never have been able to complete this project (which seems appropriate, given its substantial focus on the Other). I want to express my appreciation to my family (to whom I have dedicated this book): my dad, John, my mom, Kathy, my brothers, Evan and Nathan, my sister, Merinda, and especially my wife, Vanessa, and new son, Atticus.

I want to thank Dee Mortensen at Indiana University Press for her efforts on behalf of this project and Merold Westphal for welcoming it into the Indiana Series in the Philosophy of Religion. I am also very appreciative of the extremely careful copyediting done by David L. Dusenbury. I have greatly benefited from the work of Peggy Morrison in the interlibrary loan office at Hendrix College and the many people who have read parts of this manuscript and offered extremely helpful criticisms and suggestions. I am grateful to them all: David Wood, John Lachs, Merold Westphal, Jeff Dudiak, Robert B. Talisse, Mason Marshall, Bruce Ellis Benson, Stephen Minister, John D. Caputo, J. Caleb Clanton, Kevin Carnahan, Diane Perpich, William Edelglass, John Sanders, Fred Ablondi, Chris Campolo, Lawrence Schmidt, Chad Maxson, David Dault, Burt Fulmer, Joshua B. Davis, Nathan R. Kerr, Scott F. Aikin, Michael Hodges, Jeffrey Tlumak, and Clayton Crockett.

Finally, I would like to thank my research assistant, Lana Allen, and extend a note of appreciation to several people who probably don't know I have been writing this book, but who nevertheless played a significant role in its completion: the staff at the Starbucks coffee shop on Harkrider Street in Conway, Arkansas.

Earlier versions of several of the chapters in this book have appeared in print elsewhere. I list them below, and thank the various editors and publishers for permission to use these essays here:

- Large portions of chapter 2 first appeared as "What About Isaac? Re-Reading *Fear and Trembling* and Re-Thinking Kierkegaardian Ethics," *Journal of Religious Ethics* 35, no. 2 (Spring 2007): 319–45.

℞ Chapter 6 first appeared as "God in Recent French Phenomenology," *Philosophy Compass* 3, no. 5 (Fall 2008): 910–32.

℞ An expanded version of chapter 7 first appeared as "Continuing to Look for *God in France:* On the Relationship Between Phenomenology and Theology," in *Words of Life: New Theological Turns in French Phenomenology,* ed. Bruce Ellis Benson and Norman Wirzba (New York: Fordham University Press, 2010), 15–29.

℞ Chapter 8 first appeared as "Is Continental Philosophy Just Catholicism for Atheists? On the Political Relevance of *Kenosis,*" *Philosophy in the Contemporary World* 15, no. 1 (Spring 2008): 94–111.

℞ Chapter 10 first appeared as "Politics as an Ethico-Religious Task: Kierkegaard and Levinas on Religion in the Public Square," *Soundings: An Interdisciplinary Journal* 89, no. 1–2 (Spring/Summer 2006): 1001–18.

Kierkegaard

CA   *The Concept of Anxiety: A Simple Psychologically Orienting Deliberation on the Dogmatic Issue of Hereditary Sin*. Ed. and trans. Reidar Thomte and Albert B. Anderson. Princeton, N.J.: Princeton University Press, 1980.

CUP   *Concluding Unscientific Postscript to Philosophical Fragments, Vol. I: Text*. Ed. and trans. Howard V. Hong and Edna H. Hong. Princeton, N.J.: Princeton University Press, 1992.

EO I&II   *Either/Or*, 2 vols. Ed. and trans. Howard V. Hong and Edna H. Hong. Princeton, N.J.: Princeton University Press, 1987.

EUD   *Eighteen Upbuilding Discourses*. Ed. and trans. Howard V. Hong and Edna H. Hong. Princeton, N.J.: Princeton University Press, 1990.

FSE/JFY   *For Self-Examination / Judge For Yourself!* Ed. and trans. Howard V. Hong and Edna H. Hong. Princeton, N.J.: Princeton University Press, 1990.

FT   *Fear and Trembling / Repetition*. Ed. and trans. Howard V. Hong and Edna H. Hong. Princeton, N.J.: Princeton University Press, 1983.

JP   *Søren Kierkegaard's Journals and Papers*. Ed. and trans. Howard V. Hong and Edna H. Hong. Princeton, N.J.: Princeton University Press, 1967–1978. Citations are by volume and entry number.

PA   *The Present Age / Of the Difference Between a Genius and an Apostle*. Trans. Alexander Dru. New York: Harper & Row, 1962.

PC   *Practice in Christianity*. Ed. and trans. Howard V. Hong and Edna H. Hong. Princeton, N.J.: Princeton University Press, 1991.

PF   *Philosophical Fragments / Johannes Climacus*. Ed. and trans. Howard V. Hong and Edna H. Hong. Princeton, N.J.: Princeton University Press, 1985.

PV   *The Point of View for My Work as an Author: A Report to History*. Trans. Walter Lowrie. Ed. Benjamin Nelson. New York: Harper & Row, 1962.

SLW   *Stages on Life's Way*. Ed. and trans. Howard V. Hong and Edna H. Hong. Princeton, N.J.: Princeton University Press, 1988.

SUD   *The Sickness Unto Death: A Christian Psychological Exposition for Upbuilding and Awakening*. Ed. and trans. Howard V. Hong and Edna H. Hong. Princeton, N.J.: Princeton University Press, 1980.

| UDVS | *Upbuilding Discourses in Various Spirits.* Ed. and trans. Howard V. Hong and Edna H. Hong. Princeton, N.J.: Princeton University Press, 1993. |
| WL | *Works of Love.* Ed. and trans. Howard V. Hong and Edna H. Hong. Princeton, N.J.: Princeton University Press, 1995. |

Levinas

AT	*Alterity and Transcendence.* Trans. Michael B. Smith. New York: Columbia University Press, 1999.
BPW	*Basic Philosophical Writings.* Ed. Adriaan T. Peperzak, Simon Critchley, and Robert Bernasconi. Bloomington: Indiana University Press, 1995.
CPP	*Collected Philosophical Papers.* Trans. Alphonso Lingis. Pittsburgh: Duquesne University Press, 1987.
DF	*Difficult Freedom: Essays on Judaism.* Trans. Seán Hand. Baltimore, Md.: Johns Hopkins University Press, 1990.
EI	*Ethics and Infinity: Conversations with Philippe Nemo.* Trans. Richard A. Cohen. Pittsburgh: Duquesne University Press, 1985.
GDT	*God, Death, and Time.* Trans. Bettina Bergo. Stanford, Calif.: Stanford University Press, 2000.
GWCM	*Of God Who Comes to Mind.* Trans. Bettina Bergo. Stanford, Calif.: Stanford University Press, 1998.
OE	*On Escape.* Trans. Bettina Bergo. Stanford, Calif.: Stanford University Press, 2003.
OTB	*Otherwise Than Being, Or Beyond Essence.* Trans. Alphonso Lingis. Pittsburgh: Duquesne University Press, 1997.
PM	"The Paradox of Morality: An Interview with Emmanuel Levinas." With Tamara Wright, Peter Hughes, and Alison Ainley, in *The Provocation of Levinas: Rethinking the Other.* Ed. Robert Bernasconi and David Wood. London: Routledge, 1988, 168–80.
PN	*Proper Names.* Trans. Michael B. Smith. Stanford, Calif.: Stanford University Press, 1996.
RTB	*Is It Righteous to Be? Interviews with Emmanuel Levinas.* Ed. Jill Robbins. Stanford, Calif.: Stanford University Press, 2001.
TI	*Totality and Infinity: An Essay on Exteriority.* Trans. Alphonso Lingis. Pittsburgh: Duquesne University Press, 1969.
TO	*Time and the Other.* Trans. Richard A. Cohen. Pittsburgh: Duquesne University Press, 1987.

GOD AND THE OTHER

God . . . *Again*—Again . . . *God*

The thesis of this book is that Continental philosophy of religion, especially in the wake of Søren Kierkegaard and Emmanuel Levinas, serves as a critical interlocutor for Anglo-American philosophy of religion and contemporary post-Rawlsian political theory. Specifically, I argue for three claims: (1) Behind the recent debates surrounding the "theological turn" of French phenomenology stands an alternative ontology found in the works of Kierkegaard and Levinas. Namely, these two thinkers can jointly be read as advocating an ontology of constitutive responsibility in which the self is defined by a bi-directional obligation to God and to the Other. (2) "New phenomenology" is properly considered phenomenology—that is, there has not been a "theological turn" but a deepening of the phenomenological impulse in the direction of the philosophy of religion. (3) The alternative ontology advocated by Kierkegaard and Levinas, and echoed in new phenomenology, offers profound resources for both philosophical inquiry and social justice. These three claims map onto the three parts of the book.

Accordingly, this book is an attempt to think productively at the intersection of three questions.

Question One

God seems to be having trouble in contemporary society—well, at least among some intellectuals. While this may be a matter of simply not having a good press secretary, it could also be that God has become (or is perceived to have become) outdated in the twenty-first century. For example, in the perspective of the "new atheism" proposed in the works of such popular writers as Daniel Dennett and Richard Dawkins, God continues to be "an unnecessary hypothesis" in the light of progress in evolutionary theory (see Dawkins 2006; Dennett 2007). Extending the general trajectory of Freud's designation of religion as an "illusion," other popular writers such as Christopher Hitchens and Sam Harris are convinced that people who believe in God require an "education into reality." As Hitchens writes:

> God did not create man in his own image. Evidently, it was the other way about, which is the painless explanation for the profusion of gods and religions, and the fratricide both between and among faiths, that

we see all about us and that has so retarded the development of civilization. (2007, 8)

In a similar vein, Harris laments the fact that people who "believe that dinosaurs lived two by two upon Noah's ark" are the same people "with the power to elect our presidents and congressmen" (2006, xi). He proceeds to decry the prominence of religious belief (of a particular kind) in America: "Our country now appears, as at no other time in her history, like a lumbering, bellicose, dim-witted giant. Anyone who cares about the fate of civilization would do well to recognize that the combination of great power and great stupidity is simply terrifying, even to one's friends" (2006, xi; see also 2004).

On the ethical front, violence "in the name of God" continues to occur across the globe. The time of "religious wars" does not appear to be safely confined to the past, but is a topic of current conversation on the nightly news shows. Politically, the notion that religious belief should be kept private—that is, out of the public square—has been a prominent position in political philosophy in the wake of John Rawls's political liberalism, although such views certainly extend back much further in the history of political philosophy.[1] Given much in the history of the twentieth century, one might surmise that the notion of God is offensive to good taste and stands in opposition to progressive politics.

Nonetheless, recent Continental philosophy (largely in the phenomenological and deconstructive veins) has been increasingly turning its attention to questions in the philosophy of religion. For French thinkers such as Jean-Luc Marion, Emmanuel Levinas, Jacques Derrida, Michel Henry, Jean-Louis Chrétien, Jean-Yves Lacoste, and Paul Ricœur, "God-talk" is not something that philosophy has rightfully moved beyond, but rather requires substantial rethinking in the light of postmodern insights. The "postmodern God" that is considered (and even defended) by these thinkers, along with others working in various contexts, provides a new frame in which to consider beliefs, practices, and perspectives that appear to warrant the label "religious." This turn has caused some philosophers to claim that the work of these thinkers is nothing more than thinly veiled theology. For example, Dominique Janicaud (1991) (who will be considered in detail in part 2) famously claimed that recent French phenomenology has taken a "theological turn." Similarly, Hent de Vries (1999), while contesting the "theological" dimension of this trajectory, also refers to the "turn to religion" that has occurred in European philosophy in the wake of Heidegger.[2]

Of course, one might find this espousal of God-talk to be rather odd in Continental philosophy, not only because of the resistance to religion among large sections of Western academia, but because of the major voices in the tradition itself. Wasn't it Nietzsche who claimed that "God is dead"? Doesn't Husserl, the father of phenomenology, explicitly "bracket" God from phenomenological inquiry? Didn't Heidegger say that for philosophy really to make progress it needed to be atheistic? It seems that the God of recent French philosophy stands as something of an enigma within the very discursive community in which the notion continues to be developed.

This "turn to religion" also occurs in the wider context of a world in which "God" is often viewed as more of an obstacle to social progress and living a moral life *as an adult* (as psychoanalysis might say) than an "ever present help in time of trouble" (Psalms 46: 1). Accordingly, the first guiding question of this book can best be presented as having two components: (A) *Is this postmodern God adequate to the challenges we face in a time in which a history of genocide and the horrors of technological encroachment couple with a potential future of ecological disaster and economic collapse?* In times like these, turning to God might make a lot of sense—but it could also indicate a refusal to deal with the realities of ethico-political existence. (B) *Is the expanding literature on the postmodern God a turn away from philosophy and toward something like "revealed" theological discourse?* In a political context in which "philosophy" (read as secular, universal reasoning) might have traction in public discourse in a way that "theology" might not, getting clear on (B) is important for more than esoteric debates of interest to specialists. And taken in tandem, (A) and (B) lead us to see that it is a *profoundly ethical and political concern* that we face when we question the role of "God" in our present situation and our philosophical discourse.

Question Two

For too long, Continental ethical and political philosophy have been largely disconnected from the thorny issues that attend the move from theory to practice. Scholars working in these fields have, for the most part, failed to adequately consider whether the complicated relations to the "Other" that are articulated in the work of Levinas and Derrida, for instance, actually offer a better model for social engagement than do relevant contenders. Indeed, for many in Continental philosophy, applicability to present circumstances is not even viewed as a valid concern. The brilliance of the Continental ethical gesture, they might suggest, is that it eradicates the distinction between theory and practice that has been prominent through much of the history of moral philosophy. The worry here is that to hold too tightly to what we might call *the necessity of practical application* would be to continue operating within a notion of ethics as a guidebook for right action, which Continental ethicists have rightly resisted. There is something sensible about taking this view seriously. For example, those working in a decidedly Levinasian vein might protest that the distinction between theory and practice is one that is always "too late" for the actual ethical encounter, which is itself a matter of how the self is constituted from the outset and not how a constituted self decides to move forward in the world. Nevertheless, I contend that we should be attentive to the insights of Hilary Putnam—a philosopher who has recently become quite amenable to a Levinasian perspective—when he claims that:

> The primary aim of the ethicist, in Dewey's view and in the view I defend, should not be to produce a "system," but to contribute to the solution of practical problems—as, indeed, Aristotle already knew. Although we can often be *guided* by universal principles . . . in the solution of practical problems, few real problems can be solved by treating them as mere instances of a universal generalization, and few practical problems are such that when we *have* resolved them—and Dewey held that the solution to a problem is always provisional and fallible—we are rarely able to express what we learned in the course of our encounter with a "problematic situation" in the form of a universal generalization that can be unproblematically applied to other situations. Even Kant, who is often considered to be *the* great representative of the sort of ethical theory that seeks to lay down universal moral rules, was well aware that what he called "the moral law" cannot be applied to concrete situations without the aid of what he himself calls "mother wit," and that "mother wit" or "good judgment" is not something that can be reduced to an algorithm. (2004, 4)

Putnam encourages philosophers not to allow ethics, regardless of which philosophical tradition one is working in, to become a merely speculative enterprise. Now, surely one could take issue with the notion that ethics, as such, should operate according to the necessity of practical application. By this I simply mean to say that there is no *prima facie* rationale for why ethics (as a branch of philosophy) needs to be specifically relevant to one's existence. Perhaps it is rightly defined as a particular domain of inquiry that falls under a more general rubric of "intellectual exercise." To say that ethics is somehow not able to be considered as theory for theory's sake would be to beg the question of one's own practice. However, internal to a discourse that is deeply marked by Kierkegaard's critique of Hegel's speculative philosophy, Nietzsche's genealogical fury at the history of Western moral theorizing, the historicity of Simone de Beauvoir's "ethics of ambiguity" and Jean-Paul Sartre's "existential humanism," and more recently Derrida's commitment to the importance of embodiment for ethics, it seems problematic to affirm such an esoteric and abstract view of moral (and political) philosophizing. That is, all of these thinkers encourage a move *away* from ethics understood as abstraction from the concrete and, alternatively, advocate a thoroughly *situational* conception of moral philosophy which is focused on the historical realities of existing individuals.

God and the Other

For these Continental philosophers, ethics is an activity to be conducted because we face real problems in a messy world. And so: in Kierkegaard we find an emphasis on the singular, historical, and risky decision of the individual as the condition for lived-obligation; in Nietzsche there emerges a focus on the particular histories in which we are able to become the selves that we are and according to which we understand "morality"; in de Beauvoir and Sartre it is the actuality of ethical tension that constitutes one's existential condition (i.e., there are many "good" ways forward and ethics is not something that can shine a light on the best path, but simply helps one to understand the stakes of this existential investment that one must make); and in Derrida (as in Levinas) we run up against the constant temptation to allow the "Other" to become a category instead of a "being [who] counts as such" (BPW, 6). For all of these thinkers, ethics is about a *transformation of worldly existence*. Those of us working in the wake of this existential/phenomenological tradition should always ask ourselves the question: does Continental ethics help make tomorrow better than today for the Other(s) that inhabit our communities as well as occupy our philosophical imaginations? Putnam describes Levinas's philosophy as an "extreme" version of situational ethics because it is not about a "system" of thought from which one then *engages the world*, but a specific way of being opened to the singularity of each and every other (whether human or non-human) with whom one *shares the world*.

Nonetheless, "there are tensions between the concern of Levinasian ethics, which is situational in the extreme, and the concerns of Kant and Aristotle," Putnam notes. He continues:

> Levinas's thought experiment is always to imagine myself confronted with *one* single suffering human being, ignoring for the moment the likelihood that I am already under obligation to many other human beings. I am supposed to feel the obligation to help *this* human being, an obligation which I am to experience not as the obligation to obey a *principle*, as a Kantian would, but as an obligation *to that human being*. Kant's concern, that I have at least one universal *principle*— the principle of always treating the humanity in another person as an end, and not merely as a means—a principle which I am not willing to allow to be overridden by considerations of utility, obviously pulls in a different direction, and both the Levinasian concern with the immediate recognition of the other and the Kantian concern with principle have been seen as being in conflict with the Aristotelian concern with human flourishing. But that is not the way I see things. The tension is real, but so is the mutual support. Kantian ethics, I have argued (as Hegel already argued) is, in fact, empty and formal unless we sup-

ply it with content precisely from Aristotelian and Levinasian and yet other directions. (Among those other directions, one might mention today concerns with democracy, concerns with toleration, concerns with pluralism, and, of course, still many others.) And Levinas is right to remind us that even if the ethical person acts in accordance with the Categorical Imperative, her focus is not on the Kantian principle as an abstract rule, but on the particular other person she is trying to help. (2004, 26–27; original emphasis)

Again we find Putnam asserting the importance of "trying to help" other people as a requirement of ethical theorizing if our theory is not to be "empty and formal" (see also Putnam 2008). As I will suggest in chapter 1, if we allow Continental ethics—and in particular Levinasian ethics—to become detached from the attempt to help bring justice to the marginalized and oppressed of the world, then we have weakened the rationale for advocating a specifically Continental approach to ethics (which is decidedly committed to the concretization of obligation and the singularity of responsibility). If such advocacy is not simply to be about philosophical one-upmanship, the claim that Levinas, or Derrida, or John Caputo, or Simon Critchley offers a better way forward in ethics and politics must be linked to some sort of argument that their approaches could really serve to bring about a more just world. If such an argument is not forthcoming, then we run headlong into a situation in which we advocate Continental ethics "in the name of the Other," but then fail to demonstrate how such a perspective actually meets the needs of the Other(s) we claim to care so much about. In such a case, a real concern for the Other (as advocated by our theory) would seem to require that we abandon our theory in order that this concern motivate a transformed praxis. Ethics may indeed be "first philosophy," but unless I put the Other "first" and work to make the world better for her, then this "firstness" risks becoming only a theoretical perspective and not a way of life.

Hence, the second question is one of practical efficacy: *does Continental ethics actually lead to a transformed world in which works of love and acts of justice are encouraged?* If not, then it seems like we should move on precisely in the name of the Other that Continental thinkers continue to speak of with such frequency. Importantly, the "new phenomenology" of Henry, Chrétien, Levinas, Lacoste, Derrida, and Marion demonstrates the complicated relationship between selfhood, obligation, alterity, and transcendence. To be concerned about justice in postmodernity is to wrestle with the intersection of all of these notions—i.e., none can stand in isolation. But these thinkers also contend that such an intersection is essentially "religiously" invested. As Levinas so profoundly suggests, working for justice in the world is not detached from the question of what living a holy life before God could mean *after* onto-theology; and as Derrida reminds us, something like "abso-lute hospitality" requires an openness to the radically other—an openness which is *perhaps* indistinguishable from a receptivity to the call of God.

Following from these first two questions, I assert that the situation in which Continental philosophy of religion and Continental political philosophy find them-selves, or, rather, *should* find themselves can be expressed thusly: *Religion must be considered as an ethico-political reality and ethics/politics must be understood as impli-cated in decidedly "religious" issues.*

Question Three

The third question does not require any elaborate setup. Simply put: *can the insights of Continental philosophy of religion and Continental ethico-political philosophy be brought into a productive conversation with "mainstream" debates in Anglo-American philosophy?* If the answer is "no" then we face the specter of what could rightly be called "cliquism" in Continental thought. That is, if only those of us with "deep" backgrounds in Heidegger, Foucault, and Derrida are able to see how viable these thinkers are for our continued social existence and professional philosophical ac-tivities, then we are faced with a question of how one is to convince one's inter-locutor that a Continental perspective is the best option. The problem here is that either this viability is something that can be supported by argument or it cannot. If it cannot, then we are dangerously close to inscribing into Continental philosophy a notion of in-crowd group-think. And more problematically, it may even run the risk of recognizing "force," in Simone Weil's sense of the term (see Weil and Be-spaloff 2005), as the only way of moving the Continental viewpoint(s) forward. When "force" becomes "legitimate" in such a way, problems arise at the level of being continually open to the call of one's non-Continental Other.

But if, alternatively, Continental philosophy *can* support the viability of cer-tain philosophical trajectories with argument, then we should be able to express these arguments with the requisite clarity and lucidity to make that trajectory ac-cessible to those who are not already counted among the "converted," as it were. Merold Westphal's encouragement to Christian philosophers applies more gener-ally, and perhaps more pointedly, to Continental philosophers: "I think we should be known for our lucidity and not our density" (1999b, 175). Accordingly, then, it seems that the answer to Question Three is at least the following: *Those working in Continental philosophy should, at the very minimum, try to become conversation partners with those in non-Continental philosophy who are also working on issues of obligation, normativity, justice, personhood, governance, economics, and policy.* It would be sadly ironic if our constant touting of the importance of the Other only served to ex-clude from conversation all those others who are not already convinced by Hei-degger, Levinas, and Derrida. In such a situation, the philosophical conversation would now be more appropriately labeled "our" conversation. The obvious difficulty of holding such a position while being committed to a "hospitality without condition" (as Derrida says) should be clear.

Now, I want to emphasize that my comments here should not be understood as advocating a one-way street of philosophical engagement. The burden of responsibility for creating a meaningful dialogue between various philosophical traditions does not lie solely on the shoulders of Continentalists. However, within Continental circles one often hears of the marginalization that occurs at the hands of unreceptive analytic colleagues; and similarly, one frequently finds analytic calls for greater clarity and rigor from exponents of the Continental perspective. What is far more difficult to find are these calls for clarity from *within* the Continental tradition. So while I recognize that there can be no productive discourse if peace is only declared on one side, as it were, my question (and goal) here is meant to articulate the need for substantive rethinking of how Continental philosophy understands itself as a partner in the philosophical conversation that extends beyond the pages of Heidegger, et al. Moreover, as I will suggest in chapter 1, it is precisely the "Otherism," as I will term it, of much of Continental philosophy that internally challenges the possible cliquishness of Continental discourse.

Thinking at Intersections: The Current Project

Thinking at the intersection of these three questions could take many different shapes, and many important voices are beginning to emerge at this juncture.[3] One of the most pressing areas in which there is need for continued work, I believe, is in "applied" Continental/deconstructive ethics and politics. For example: extended considerations of how Levinasian-Derridean hospitality can be deployed for rethinking immigration policy; how conceptions of "alterity" can be articulated to allow for a sustainable approach to not only environmental philosophy, but environmental legislation; how a democracy "to come" stands in relationship to legislative procedure; how discussions of the complex linguistic frames in which gendered, raced, sexed identities are performed can translate into governmental practices, grassroots movements, and personal behaviors that bring about societies that are more free, equal, and charitable to the "least of these our brethren" (Matthew 25: 40). The problem is that those of us working in Continental ethics and philosophy of religion tend to talk quite a bit about the "Other," but don't consistently allow this discussion to motivate substantive ethical norm-activation and engaged political activism. Problematically, our practice often stands in contrast to our theory.

In a controversial review essay on the work of Judith Butler, Martha Nussbaum does a nice job of exposing the problems that *can* accompany such inconsistencies between thought and practice. Nussbaum worries that when we turn away "from the material side of life, toward a type of verbal and symbolic politics that makes only the flimsiest of connections with the real situation of real women," or the oppressed of any identity group,[4] we fail to really enact the justice that we continue to call for, anticipate, and expect in our philosophy (1999, 38). Even if one rightly has objections to Nussbaum's overall reading of Butler, this specific worry is surely one worth taking seriously.[5] Following from Questions Two and Three above and Nussbaum's claim here, I contend that *if* Continental ethics in general faces a lack of existential traction, *then* it potentially stands as a threat to a better tomorrow, rather than a step toward such a future. These "applied" considerations must demonstrate that the deconstructive vision of justice is not simply a dream-state, but instead includes a radical agenda for social change. Given the way in which new phenomenology brings the question of God and the Other together, such applied ethico-political concerns are inherently "religious" in their trajectory (at least internal to this tradition).

As such, I believe that it is of utmost importance that we begin to ask whether Continental God-talk contributes to or distracts from ethical, political, and philosophical practice. This book is meant to be a step in the direction of thinking about Continental ethics, philosophy of religion, and political philosophy at the intersection of theory and practice. That said, it is problematic to merely assume that the relation between God and the Other is one that should be granted as legitimate in contemporary philosophy. Indeed, as Question One outlined, it might be best to simply move past God-talk altogether—and such a move might be called for precisely in the name of ever-increasing justice for our social contexts. The neo-Pragmatic philosopher Richard Rorty advocates just such an abandonment of Continental ethics due to its "religious" baggage.

In claims that are scattered throughout his oeuvre, Rorty presents a sustained challenge to Levinas (and, by extension, to Continental ethics in general) by contending that Levinas's understanding of ethics is unnecessarily abstract, detached from practice, and embedded in a hyperbolic rhetoric. Far from being a clear example for the future of postmodern politics, it is itself *un*-ethical—or, to be more consistent with Rorty's charge, *un-helpful*. For Rorty, as we will see in chapter 1, the abstract character of Continental ethics is largely due to the "religious" gesture that occurs in references to "infinity," "absolute alterity," "the command," "the face," "the trace," "election," and "absolute height." And if these gestures were not bad enough, Levinas even refers to the responsible relation to other people as "religion," suggests that truth is best understood as "testimony," and that "prophecy" has a role in ethical life. Viewing religion as a "conversation stopper" (at least at one point in his authorship), Rorty finds such language often to be an impediment to the task of helping the Other that Putnam locates as the essence of Levinasian ethics.

In light of Rorty's critique, I will think at the intersection of our three guiding questions by asking: *Is the "turn to religion" within recent Continental philosophy something that stands as an* obstacle *for those who want to defend a deconstructive political theory, or as an* opportunity *for rethinking important issues in light of new arguments (now making reference to the theological "archive")?* Simply put, *can a philosophical concern for the question of God actually enrich and undergird an ethico-political concern for others in the world—while also opening spaces for Continental thought to participate in debates in the larger philosophical literature?* I hope that this book will open productive spaces for further work in applied Continental ethics/politics by discussing both the background issues in the contemporary debates surrounding the "theological turn," and by also showing how these debates can provide productive ways forward in such areas as environmental ethics, political philosophy, epistemology, and philosophy of religion. Admittedly, it is still a book on/of theory, but as Question Two makes clear, we should not *abandon* theory, but instead do theory (at least in this particular tradition and in this specific area) *with an eye toward a transformed world*.

In part 1, I ask what is at stake in deciding in favor of the priority of the God-relation or the priority of the Other-relation? In order to be able to articulate how to move forward from the intersection of Continental philosophy of religion and political philosophy that I have identified, I take this question of priority to be urgently pressing. I propose that the best way to work through this question is to bring together two thinkers who seemingly advocate alternative notions of how to conceive this priority: Kierkegaard and Levinas. Hence, in chapters 2 through 5, I bring these thinkers into conversation regarding the issue of how to understand the relation between self, God, and the Other, and argue that when we read these figures together we should advocate an *ontology of constitutive responsibility*. Importantly, the self that is described in such an ontology is not defined *solely* in reference to God *or* to the Other. Instead, what emerges is a notion of selfhood as *bi-directionally responsible* to God *and* to the Other. The ethico-religious task undertaken by such a self, I argue, yields an important conception of democratic political critique in the name of an ever-increasing justice.

In part 2, I move from the background of the debates between Kierkegaard and Levinas to the more contemporary concerns arising from the "theological turn in French phenomenology." Chapter 6 is meant to be a general introduction to this philosophical trajectory. There, I work through the resistance to "God-talk" in Husserl and Heidegger and then defend the philosophical legitimacy of such discourse in the work of thinkers ranging from Levinas and Henry to Chrétien and Marion. I put forward several important unifying characteristics of this "new phenomenology," and then show how these stand as contributions to such issues as religion in the public square and post-foundationalist notions of justification. Chapter 7 builds upon this basic introduction by exploring in more detail Dominique Janicaud's famous resistance to the "theological turn." In the light of Janicaud's critique, I consider a recent book titled *God in France* as an example of the way the debate has developed. I suggest that the possible options of how to understand this phenomenological God-talk have tended toward either "separatism" (i.e., keep God out of phenomenology) or "reconstructivism" (i.e., let God in as long as "God" simply means something like "the hope for justice"). My thesis in chapter 7 is that separatism falls back into a problematic notion of a "worldless subject" that postmodernism attempts to overcome, while reconstructivism is potentially patronizing to religious believers, which in certain cases amounts to a failure to listen to the Other in the first place. Therefore, one is objectionable on logical grounds and the other on ethical grounds. I conclude by proposing an alternative, "reconstructive separatism," that avoids both of these problems.

In chapter 8, I follow Hent de Vries and contend that the "theological turn" is not really a turn toward theology and away from philosophy, but a decidedly philosophical movement that recognizes the importance of being open to the possibility of receiving inspiration from the history of religious communities. I offer a defense of a particular sort of God-talk within Continental philosophy that centers on the notion of *kenosis* (self-emptying) by demonstrating (1) that the so-called theological turn is not a *turn away* from philosophy toward theology, but instead a *deepening* of the specific philosophical impulses of phenomenology, and (2) that this deepening yields profound political, and specifically democratic, consequences that we should seriously consider.

Part 3 targets four areas in which I find the ontology of constitutive responsibility to be particularly relevant. The first four chapters here attempt to show that when thinking in light of the "theological turn," one is not limited to critique, but can also begin to envision positive alternatives. Chapter 9 argues that the project of a decidedly postmodern Christianity is viable, but requires a rethinking of what a "belief in God" might look like after the postmodern turn. My suggestion is that rather than primarily arguing for the "existence of God," we instead argue for living one's life invested in the reality of bi-directional responsibility while historically located in a determinate religious tradition. This then leads to chapter 10, where I defend a model of religion in the public square according to which "politics" names the multiplicity of infinite obligations and not a space in which we need to abandon comprehensive doctrines. Accordingly, the debate concerning the availability of public reason moves from an epistemological register to one of an ethico-religious sociality.

In chapter 11, I bring new phenomenology into conversation with contemporary debates in epistemology and ask the following question: Must Continental philosophy abandon justification and display, as Simon Critchley (2007) and John

Caputo (1993) seem to contend, nothing but "commitment"? I argue that we need not make such concessions. Instead, by bringing together figures in Continental ethics and contemporary epistemologists such as Robert Audi, William Alston, Nicholas Wolterstorff, and Alvin Plantinga, what we actually see is a profound model of a post-foundationalist (or *modest* foundationalist) epistemology of trust that allows for more than mere commitment while maintaining a profound humility about what this "more" entails.

Attempting to respond to my own call for more "applied" demonstrations of Continental ethics, in chapter 12 I consider what a possible approach to the ethics of climate change might entail in light of the ontology of constitutive responsibility. My argument is that climate change presents a "meta-ethical emergency" to the contemporary world, and as such, we need to find an ethical theory that will be able to respond to what I term the epistemic and ethico-political challenges raised by this emergency situation. A particularly promising option, I contend, is what I term a "relational model of anthropocentrism" (which I draw from the moral philosophy of Levinas). The key to this relational model is the way in which it allows for a complex relationship between temporality and obligation and also for an expansive notion of contextual ethico-political communities of discourse.

In chapter 13, I conclude the book by bringing together the various concerns discussed in part 3, and suggesting that we need to articulate a notion of "ethico-political exemplars" in order to address the problem of how to understand "moral guidance" after the death of God. Rather than a deontological conception of universal rational principles or a narrowly consequentialist conception of utility, for example, in light of the theological turn we cannot look for instruction anywhere other than in our histories. Within these histories, I contend, we find "exemplars" who demonstrate the tension between infinite obligation and the demand for finite decision and action. Drawing on the work of Edith Wyschogrod and Susan Wolf, I argue that these persons should function in our lives as *"postmodern* saints." I look at four possible examples of such "saints"—Corrie and Betsy Ten Boom, Dietrich Bonhoeffer, and the filmic representation of Oskar Schindler.

In conclusion, then, while recognizing the weight of Rorty's charge that the "religious" gestures of Continental ethics are politically disastrous, this book seeks to demonstrate the ways in which the theological turn of new phenomenology stands as a profound resource for mainstream philosophy of religion, contemporary ethics, and democratic politics not *despite* the "God-talk" found therein, but perhaps precisely *because of it.*

As a final note to the reader, this book is intentionally constructed to be something of a "choose your own adventure" narrative. That is, the chapters can be read in order if one wishes to follow my argument from the historical stakes of an alternative theory of ontology (namely, an "ontology of constitutive responsibility"), to the contemporary debates surrounding the theological turn, and finally to questions of application and intersection with mainstream philosophical issues. However, the chapters in parts 2 and 3 are all written in such a way as to invite being read individually as well. The arguments in each, while drawing on and referencing other parts of the book, are for the most part self-contained. So, for readers without much background in contemporary Continental philosophy of religion, I encourage them to read chapter 1 in order to understand the specifics of the ethico-political critique provided by Richard Rorty and then move on to part 2, which will raise the phenomenological objections to the "theological turn." At that point, part 1 will become more accessible in its demonstration of how it is that Kierkegaard and Levinas open spaces for considering the stakes of subjectivity as constituted according to an alternative ontology (an ontology that runs implicitly throughout much of the discussions in parts 2 and 3). Alternatively, for readers unconcerned with the more technical issues of relevance to contemporary Continental philosophy, part 3 can be read on its own as a model of how new phenomenology is a resource for ethics, politics, epistemology, and religion.

ONE

The Problem: Richard Rorty's Critique of Emmanuel Levinas—or, Why Continental Ethics and Philosophy of Religion Face Political Challenges

Contesting Levinas in the Name of Ethics

The neo-Pragmatism of Richard Rorty and the phenomenologically inspired ethics of Emmanuel Levinas are not often brought into conversation with each other. However, Rorty offers a pressing objection to Levinas (and Continental ethics and philosophy of religion more generally) that demands serious consideration. Consider the following claim that Rorty offers in an exchange with Simon Critchley:

> I don't find Levinas's Other any more useful than Heidegger's Being— both strike me as gawky, awkward, and unenlightening. I see ethics as what we have to start creating when we face a choice between two irreconcilable actions, each of which would, in other circumstances, have been equally natural and proper. Neither my child nor my country is very much like a Levinasian Other, but when I face a choice between incriminating my child or breaking my country's laws by committing perjury, I start looking around for some ethical principles. I may not find any that help, but that is another question. My failure to do so is not satisfactorily explained by reference to an Abyss that separates me from an Other. (1996b, 41)

Rorty's critique that Levinasian ethics are not useful for ethical and political life requires a defensible answer, I believe, because it offers something of an immanent critique to Levinas from the foremost commitment of Levinas's own thought. Simply put, *Rorty contests Levinas in the name of ethics.*

For if Rorty is right, and Levinas is not doing ethics, then what *is* he doing? Why all the ethical language? Moreover, what would the practical value of Levinas be if not an overriding concern for rethinking ethics? This chapter takes a crucial first step toward addressing not only these specific questions of technical Levinasian scholarship, but more importantly the larger issues of political theory and praxis that follow from the so-called theological turn of French phenomenology. Namely, if the complicated discourse about the "call" (Chrétien), the "face" of the Other (Levinas), the (im)possibility of the "gift" (Marion), and the need for "absolute hospitality" (Derrida), to mention just a few examples, is unable to move from speculative philosophical gestures to practical visions and concrete proposals for how to make things better for all the "others" with whom we share the world, then all this discourse about the "Other" threatens to become not much more than empty rhetoric.

One might ask, then: Is Levinas's account of the ethical helpful in everyday situations that demand a specific and instructive way forward? If the answer is *"no,"* then it seems like the new phenomenology that largely occurs in concert with his thought might signal a disastrous political trend in philosophy.[1] Nonetheless, in light of this worry I will contend throughout the present work that I think the answer to this question is a strong, although qualified, *"yes."* In the attempt to set the stage for an extended consideration of the way in which the recent intersection of Continental ethics and Continental philosophy of religion provides critical resources for mainstream philosophical debate and even applied public policy, within this chapter I will sketch a picture of Rorty's reading of Levinas and demonstrate what is at issue in it.[2] I propose that Rorty asks legitimate questions of Levinas, and that he ultimately points to a dangerous type of formalism that can emerge if Levinas is unable to speak to his concerns.

My suggestion is that Rorty and Levinas—and as we will see in later chapters, such figures as Kierkegaard; proponents of the "new phenomenology" including Michel Henry, Jean-Luc Marion, Jean-Louis Chrétien, and Jean-Yves Lacoste; as well as other figures in Continental philosophy of religion such as Gianni Vattimo—share a common, and robust, vision for the future of human social interaction, which should give us pause in dismissing them as conversation partners in contemporary dialogues regarding political theory and social justice. However, this common vision calls for a rethinking of the significance of such thinkers in light of Rorty's charges. Ultimately, Rorty's critique of Levinas opens key lines of interrogation that those working in contemporary Continental ethics and philosophy of religion would be wrong to simply dismiss.

Missing the Other and Missing the Point: Rorty's Reading of Derrida

Despite Rorty's rather encyclopedic appreciation of the humanities, only briefly does he speak about or even gesture toward Levinas. His comments are usually contained within his readings of Derrida, and therein, Levinas emerges as something of a dark-spot in the Derridean heritage. While offering praise for Derrida as being one of the best examples of a "private ironist," Rorty contends that what is worst about Derrida is his dependence on and continued ties to Levinas. As he comments in "Remarks on Deconstruction and Pragmatism": "I have trouble with the specifically Levinasian strains in his [Derrida's] thought" (Rorty 1996a, 17). Hence, I will initially provide some context by looking briefly at how it is that he interprets Derrida.[3] Rorty's reading of Derrida will open the space in which to then consider his fragmented and scattered direct references to Levinas.

The specific way Rorty reads Derrida hearkens back to Rorty's famous split between "private ironists" and "public liberals" developed in *Contingency, Irony, and Solidarity*. Though presented as the sort of thing that any good liberal ought to affirm, Rorty's distinction between the private and public should not be confused with the public/private distinction that occurs in Rawls, for example. For Rawls, the split between the two spheres is primarily a matter of limiting governmental power and establishing norms for certain kinds of discourse (i.e., some speech must operate according to "public reason" and some need not). Though certainly appropriating some of the Rawlsian tendencies, Rorty's version of the public/private dichotomy is best understood not as being primarily a matter of (the limits of) the political, but as a matter of how to continue thinking after having abandoned dreams of unified metaphysical theories. "A postmetaphysical culture," Rorty writes, "seems to me no more impossible than a postreligious one, and equally desirable" (1989, xvi). In such a culture, one would no longer need to explain the different aspects of human existence according to some universally applicable criterion. The distinction between the private and the public is really a matter of recognizing the difference between one's relationship to one's own view of fulfilled selfhood and one's relationship to the task of social progress. For Rorty, these two relationships need not overlap or intersect and the sooner we realize this, the sooner we will be able to look to the right sorts of sources for improvement in the respective areas.

This distinction between the public and private applies both to thinkers and texts:

> Authors like Kierkegaard, Nietzsche, Baudelaire, Proust, Heidegger, and Nabokov are useful as exemplars, as illustrations of what private perfection—a self-created, autonomous, human life—can be like. Authors such as Marx, Mill, Dewey, Habermas, and Rawls are fellow citizens rather than exemplars. They are engaged in a shared, social effort—the effort to make our institutions and practices more just and less cruel. (Rorty 1989, xiv)

On the one hand, then, there are those texts which serve to enrich our personal imagination, and on the other hand there are those which serve to affect the policies and practices of shared public life. Rorty suggests that we don't need to "choose between" these groups of thinkers and texts, but instead contends that we "give them equal weight and then use them for different purposes" (1989, xiv). For Rorty, the "demands of self-creation and of human solidarity" are "equally valid" while remaining "forever incommensurable" (1989, xv). That is, while we might read Dewey for encouragement on how to improve social conditions, we might read Kierkegaard as an example of how to understand one's singularity. Trouble occurs when we apply to public life narratives that are primarily useful in the private sphere, and vice versa. Rorty is not exactly clear *why* such trouble occurs, but it seems that the best explanation for this is that when we forget the distinction we tend to fall back into all-too-religious metaphysical schemas that stand in the way of social progress. For example, Rorty claims that although the ironist is "invaluable in our attempt to form a private self-image," she is "pretty much useless when it comes to politics" (1989, 83).

Now, before moving on, I should note that Rorty's distinction between social hope and private irony is rather slippery, which complicates both comprehension and appropriation. For example, in chapter 4 of *Contingency, Irony, and Solidarity,* Rorty offers his most explicit claims regarding the political uselessness of private irony and yet also deploys the notion of the "liberal ironist," which seems to walk between the private/public distinction and instead stand in contrast to those advocates of "common sense" who "take for granted that statements formulated in that final vocabulary suffice to describe and judge the beliefs, actions, and lives of those who employ alternative final vocabularies" (1989, 74). Though Rorty has been moving in this direction throughout his book, by this point he is clearly using irony as not only a "private" matter, but as a different way of being publicly engaged. Moreover, when Rorty provides the three criteria for someone's being an "ironist," they have nothing immediately to do with the public/private split at all, and are not obviously located in the private sphere.[4] Instead, these criteria are primarily directed at resisting "final vocabularies," which could operate in either domain.

Further, Rorty's notion of a "liberal utopia," which he claims will be achieved "not by inquiry but by imagination," is clearly presented as a project of human solidarity in light of a shared hope that we begin to see "strange people as fellow sufferers" (1989, xvi). However, such an imaginative expansion is, it would seem, best achieved through the "ironic" task of "continual redescription" in which we "make the best selves for ourselves that we can" (1989, 80). But this project of self-making, presented here as the means by which we achieve a transformed public sphere, is what Rorty so pervasively claims is a private venture that is useless for attaining public goals. Eventually, Rorty does seem to recognize this problem and reconsider his account of the definitive *lack* of impact that private matters have on public life:

I don't think private beliefs can be fenced off (from the public sphere); they leak through, so to speak, and influence the way one behaves toward other people. What I had in mind in making the distinction was this: the language of citizenship, of public responsibility, of participation in the affairs of the state, is not going to be an original, self-created language. Some people, the ones we think of as poets or makers, want to invent a new language—because they want to invent a new self. And there's a tendency to try to see that poetic effort as synthesizable with the activity of taking part in public discourse. I don't think the two are synthesizable; but that doesn't mean that the one doesn't eventually interact with the other. (2006, 50)

These difficulties and confusions notwithstanding, the public/private distinction is crucial to understanding why Rorty evidences a resistance to the "Levinasian strains" in Derrida's thought. Solidly identifying Derrida as a private "ironist theorist" who shares this position with such thinkers as "Hegel, Nietzsche . . . and Foucault" (1989, 83),[5] Rorty's point here is key: he neither resists the "Levinasian strains" in Derrida due to their being "Levinasian," nor due to their being "private," but because they are the places where *Derrida the ironist* crosses the incommensurable boundaries of discourse and practice. Instead of becoming *Derrida the liberal*, which would be fine, Derrida becomes an ironist operating in a sphere where *private* irony is of minimal use. "Whereas Habermas sees the line of ironist thinking which runs from Hegel through Foucault and Derrida as destructive of social hope," Rorty claims, "I see this line of thought as largely irrelevant to public life and to political questions" (1989, 83).

Underlying all of *Contingency, Irony, and Solidarity* is the thesis that the "liberal utopia" is not "discovered by reflection" but must be, rather, "created" (1989, xv–xvi). Rorty's articulation of the public/private distinction is, therefore, a consequence of the anti-foundationalist leanings of his formulation of Pragmatism—leanings that he draws from his reading of Dewey.[6] After Dewey, philosophy is able to separate the questions of one realm from questions of the other, and thereby separate "the domain of the liberal from the domain of the ironist" (1989, 198). Although Rorty concedes that it is "possible for a single person to be both," she can only do so by keeping them apart, by recognizing these tasks and domains as being rightfully disparate (1989, 198). The payoff of this distinction is that Derrida, and indeed all "private ironists," are not to be viewed as helpful for questions occurring in the alternate domain.

Thus, the ironist can be spared the task of developing an ethics and/or politics. Expecting all branches of philosophy to in some way provide ethical insight that is applicable to interpersonal relationships is nothing, Rorty says, but a "result of a metaphysical upbringing" (1989, 94). Rorty attributes the demand that every philosopher produce an ethics to our not having overcome the desire for a unified theory of truth that obtains across every domain of human existence. Derrida's value lies, Rorty concludes, neither in raising ethical questions nor in addressing political issues, but in helping to further the case and cause of the singular individual along her path toward inner development and personal growth (though certainly not directed by a determinate teleology; see Simmons and Kerr 2009). Thus, Rorty proclaims, the public-private distinction "suggests that we distinguish books which help us become autonomous from books which help us become less cruel" (1989, 141). Derrida's books are of the former sort. Accordingly, the division between public and private is perhaps best understood as a distinction between the divisions of various types of questions we are trying to answer and various concerns we are attempting to address.

Given the above considerations, it is easy to see Rorty's frustration with the philosophy of Levinas. Rorty defines "ethics" indirectly as follows:

> What matters for pragmatists is devising ways of diminishing human suffering and increasing human equality, increasing the ability of all human children to start life with an equal chance of happiness. This goal is not written in the stars, and is no more an expression of what Kant called "pure practical reason" than it is the Will of God. It is a goal worth dying for, but it does not require backup from supernatural forces. (1999, xxix)

Guiding Rorty's vision of pragmatic ethics, then, is not some great "religious" authority (whether understood as God, Reason, Human Nature, or the Other) to which one appeals in a given situation, but instead, simply the goal of specific progress toward the betterment of humanity. This is not a utilitarianism based upon fundamental givens in the human psyche regarding the intrinsic desire for happiness. Further, due to his particular understanding of a pragmatic theory of truth,[7] Rorty offers a vision of ethics that is not concerned with bringing action and belief in line with a metaphysical conception of the Good, but of owning up to the inescapable "contingency" of human existence (see Rorty 1989, part 1). Ethics is, for Rorty, the decidedly historical task of attempting to make tomorrow better than today for those who are victimized and marginalized by current power structures. Yet, one is not under some sort of absolute obligation to be committed to such a task. When asked by Derek Nystrom and Kent Puckett about how we should respond to the historical oppression of various groups in America, Rorty says: "You can remember that suffering, or you can do your best to ignore it—it's up to you. Whatever a left politics is, it shouldn't have views on which choice a person should make in that situation" (Rorty, Nystrom, and Puckett 2002, 23).

At stake in Rorty's conception of ethics is his commitment to what we might term a *pragmatic consequentialism* (see Voparil 2004, 229). It is this commitment that repeatedly serves as Rorty's explanation of why the charge of relativism makes no sense regarding his thinking.[8] According to Rorty, relativism presupposes a theory of truth that is *not* relativistic against which the charge of relativism is already an indictment rather than a value-free observation. Ethical choice does not, he contends, evaporate due to its situational necessity. Instead, it is all the more crucial that we weigh and consider our actions since we do not have some absolute standard ready-to-hand and ready-to-apply. As Rorty will often say, borrowing from Daniel Dennett, we are without a "skyhook" to pull us out of our situations and our dilemmas, or according to which we can morally define ourselves (1991a, 13).

To exist in society is, he thinks, to be faced with extremely difficult decisions that demand responses. Put simply, everyone has a choice of how to respond—either by taking into account the situation of the other person and suppressing one's own will, or refusing to be bothered by the demands of the other person and instead privileging one's own voice and desires.[9] However, this choice, as Rorty rightly recognizes, is anything but simple. "I think of justice as muddling through," he says, "in the way judges do when deciding hard cases, and parents do when trying to figure out whether to inform the police about what their children are up to" (1996b, 42).[10]

Readers frustrated by the elusive discussion of *"différance"* in Derrida or the complicated meaning of the "here I am" (*me voici*) in Levinas might find Rorty's practical focus and pragmatic vocabulary refreshing. Replacing such Continental formulations are ways of articulating human relationships that appear to be decidedly engaged with the other person and not with a minor alteration of French orthography in *différance* or an alternation between *L'Autrui* and *L'Autre*. When faced with the difficulties of human existence, Rorty's account can seem quite attractive. Therein, ethics and politics are presented as tangible arenas where someone is existentially and historically affected and either brought into a better situation than she was before or not.

Given Derrida's deconstructive approach, Rorty views Derrida as someone who is "not . . . politically consequential, except in a very indirect and long-term way" (1996a, 16). In contrast, Rorty urges a focus on historical problems that confront people here and now and that require immediate responses. Despite what I take to be some quite beneficial aspects of Rorty's thought, in what follows I will argue that his own refusal to allow for a distinction between ethics and politics—i.e., between a realm of normative obligation which is separate from its practical application—quite substantially limits the political consequences of his own thought.[11] For Rorty, there is nothing other than a political logic that operates within our social conversation; politics goes *all the way down,* as it were. The result, I contend, is that for Rorty, there is no possibility of any real normativity because *everything* is in some sense normative.[12] Due to Rorty's deep historical nominalism, the differentiation between the "is" and the "ought" only amounts to a difference between competing descriptive accounts. Reminiscent of Sartre, he contends that our actions are the only way to demonstrate how others "ought" to act as well: "normativity" is nothing but a term that is given to the social implications of what we in fact do. Without being able to offer any suggestions as to why one given way is *better* than another, except that it reflects the general identifying characteristics of who "we" are, it becomes difficult to see how Rorty's own thought is "useful" for moving society toward the better tomorrow that he envisions.

Labor Unions, Congress, and Moral Entrepreneurs: From Theory to Narrative

Rorty resists treating Derrida and Levinas as ethico-political thinkers because they are part of a much larger group of thinkers which Rorty is concerned about—namely, those who feel that practice requires some sort of theoretical (and we might say especially "theological") underpinning. Thus, he continues to urge a move away from speculative inquiry and toward "imagination" and "narrative" (1989, xvi). By understanding Rorty's resistance to the political efficacy of theory, we will be in a better position to make sense of his opposition to the "religious" tendencies in Continental ethics.

In an interview, Rorty makes this point clear in his typical combination of seriousness and frivolity.[13] Regarding the suggestion that patriotism requires support from moral principles, he retorts that "moral principles are terrific in Ethics 101, but not as spurs to political action" (Rorty, Nystrom, and Puckett 2002, 16). He then goes on to say that it "seems a cheap thrill to have readers in both English and Political Science." "Now," he continues, "if you had readers both in labor unions and in Congress . . ." (Rorty, Nystrom, and Puckett 2002, 20).[14] Rorty's hope is that philosophers will stop trying to be relevant to various "disciplines," all of which are solidly located in a disengaged academy, and instead begin to focus on turning the ear of the people who are directly involved in social transformation and political reform.

Put simply, Rorty finds theory to be a luxury of political detachment that should be avoided in favor of messy involvement in the practical issues of human existence. However, he recognizes that his critique of theory is offered from within his own particular context in relation to the contemporary academic "left," which he sees as having made itself politically irrelevant in recent decades. Rorty brings both of these aspects into view when, referring to Richard Posner's distinction between "academic moralists" and "moral entrepreneurs," he says: "Most of the good is done by opportunistic moral entrepreneurs, who have a very specific target, call attention to a very specific set of instances of unnecessary suffering." It is only "later on," he continues, that "the academic moralists and social theorists come along and tie everything up in a neat package. But this later activity usually doesn't lead to political results" (Rorty, Nystrom, and Puckett 2002, 47–48). As Rorty writes in *Achieving Our Country*, "disengagement from practice produces theoretical hallucinations" (1998a, 94). Thus, Rorty suspects that when the "political left" of the early and mid-twentieth century became the "cultural left" of the last several decades, there was a disastrous move away from reformist politics toward reactionary theorizing.[15]

For Rorty, there are two problems in particular with this move. First, it represents a lessening of the role of the left in general. By this Rorty suggests that, with the transition from politics to culture, there has been a genuine loss of the left's political voice. This is itself a political problem for Rorty due to the simultaneous rise of the political right. And second, the establishment of the cultural left, although professing anti-foundational commitments, actually exposes a regression to what Rorty finds to be old-time metaphysical, and importantly, *religious* foundations. He makes this point clear in the essay "A Cultural Left," which is included in *Achieving Our Country*. There he states:

> I argued in my first lecture that the repudiation of the concept of sin was at the heart of Dewey and Whitman's civic religion. I also claimed that the American Left, in its horror at the Vietnam War, reinvented sin. It reinvented the old religious idea that some stains are ineradicable. I now wish to say that, in committing itself to what it calls "theory," this Left *has gotten something which is entirely too much like religion*. For the cultural Left has come to believe that we must place our country within a theoretical frame of reference, situate it within a vast quasi-cosmological perspective. (1998a, 95; emphasis added)

That Rorty links theory with religion is not unimportant. It shows that for him the critique of theory as politically irrelevant has deeper stakes: even to argue that theory is politically efficacious is to do so at the cost of re-entrenching what we should happily have left behind. The move toward theoretical coherence and the quest for a non-question-begging account of justification, for Rorty, involves a latent commitment to some sort of objective universality and theological appeal.[16] His insistence that we move toward imagination and narrative is itself an account of how to transform social practice. The problem that Rorty encounters is that this is hard to pull off without some sort of recourse to theoretical positions—regardless of their being anti-foundational, non-essentialist, and neo-Pragmatist. A theory of anti-foundationalist epistemology that is deeply rooted in naturalism and committed to the inescapability of Deweyan conceptions of human social interaction, say, remains a theory nonetheless.

To demonstrate Rorty's ambiguous relation to theory, despite his continued resistance to it, I will briefly consider his reading of John Rawls and Michael Walzer as examples of why we should not see Rorty's critique of Levinas as attributable, for example, to a distaste for Continental perspectives and vocabulary as such, but instead as a specific instance of his much broader approach to theory in general. Recognizing the influence and importance of Rawls, Rorty consistently uses Rawls as support for his own ideas. In an important 1984 essay, "The Priority of Democracy to Philosophy" (in Rorty 1991a), Rorty offers a sustained reading of Rawls in which he suggests that Rawls is more Deweyan than is often recognized. On Rorty's account, this "priority" neither entails metaphysical nor ontological status; it merely indicates a practical, i.e., a political, necessity. Rorty attributes to Rawls a political position that is completely disengaged from a "thick" theory of subjectivity. In other words, political liberalism gets divorced from not only Kantian, but all ontology. "On the Deweyan view I am attributing to Rawls," he concludes, "no such discipline as 'philosophical anthropology' is required as a preface to politics, but only history and sociology" (1991a, 181). Rorty's reading of Rawls stands in stark contrast to those interpretations of Rawls, as offered by Sandel (1998; 1984), Nagel (1975), and Barber (1975), for example, that find an all-too-transcendental notion of the self to underlie Rawlsian liberalism—at least as it was presented in *A Theory of Justice*. Rorty himself admits that it was only after earlier "misreadings" of Rawls in which he took him to be advocating a philosophical foundation for human rights and democratic politics that he arrived at his more Deweyan interpretation (1991a, 183n21, 184–85).

Although Rorty's rejection of theory is ostensibly intended to be applied to the political uselessness of theory as such, I contend that it is better understood as directed at those thinkers who offer a certain type of theory—namely, ones that are metaphysically, ontologically, or religiously committed. This clarification allows for a better account of why Rorty initially found Rawls's thought to be so problematic. Rorty's early rejection of Rawls, later followed by an embrace, is not explained by differences in Rawls's practical political framework but rather by Rorty's initial sense that *A Theory of Justice* advocated a *metaphysical support* for social justice; he later decided that this was not the case. This shift in Rorty's reading of Rawls would be neo-pragmatically understandable if Rorty initially took Rawls to inspire dangerous political consequences and then later came to realize that these dangers do not exist. However, what changes is neither Rorty's rejection of Rawls for being too theoretical, nor his recognition of Rawls's political utility, but instead Rorty's understanding of what *type* of theory Rawls advocated. As such, Rorty's championing of this "Deweyan" account of Rawls illustrates the problem with his claim to dismiss theory altogether: in order to reject theory, he draws support from theorists who contest the legitimacy of a certain notion of philosophical justification. In the end, Rorty uses theory, albeit of a particular narrowly defined sort, in order to make his own rejection of theory plausible. Moreover, it would seem that theory is quite useful at least internally to his own philosophical project and political vision. But importantly, there is a big difference between those who argue for non-theoretical approaches to the sources of epistemic justification and those who, like Rorty, argue for *theories* of why theory is useless. While there are certainly cases in which the former might be quite sensible, the latter will always face problems of self-refutation.

As another example of Rorty's tendency to pick and choose theory when it suits his purposes, consider his use of Michael Walzer's book *Thick and Thin* in his essay "Justice as a Larger Loyalty" (Rorty 1998b). Here, he attempts to describe how the idea of universal moral obligation can be replaced by loyalty to a larger group (viz., the human species). In trying to offer a non-Kantian account of morality, Rorty deploys a theoretical apparatus that articulates how we might understand morality outside the context of Enlightenment rationalism. Indeed, Rorty's own version of such a historical and completely socially constructed account of morality makes reference to Walzer's distinction between "thick" and "thin" obligations, as well as Rawls's distinction between a *"concept of justice"* and *"conceptions of justice"* (1998b, 49). Again, it is not the case that Rorty does not allow for theory at all, but just that he doesn't allow for theories that make room for what might best be termed "transcendence."

Now, in order to anticipate the discussion of a deconstructive approach to justification in chapter 11, I want to note here that the argument could be made that Rorty's particular *use of* theory is different from a perspective that would allow for justification *on the basis of* such theory. Further, one might say that what Rorty rejects is not a political narrative that has a theoretical tone, but only the claim that political activity *requires* theoretical justification. Whereas the second is a statement about epistemological warrant, the first is simply a matter of style. Although I feel confident that this is how Rorty would chose to frame the issue, the claim that narrative strategy does not require justificatory weight is still problematically tied to persuasive force. That it contains such force is accounted for by Rorty's descriptive account of political life. The claim that humans do not often act because of the best argument might indeed be true, but when Rorty makes such an assertion he offers it as a *reason* why we should abandon argumentative rigor in favor of narrative imagination. The move from philosophy to literature is not one that is made blindly. Rorty is not a weak thinker and his encouragement toward an expanded imagination and away from theoretical speculation is itself "grounded" upon his commitments to anti-foundational epistemology and a certain version of pragmatic truth. That there is no appearance/reality distinction, and no "mirror of nature," may not be offered as justification for Rorty's account to be true, but it is implicitly deployed as a reason why we should move past any metaphysical, theological, or political accounts that continue to operate in light of a "first philosophy."

When we admit that Rorty's political rejection of theory is more specifically a rejection of a certain kind of theory—namely, that which is laden with "religious" commitments—we begin to understand why it is that Levinas, Derrida, and much of the work being done in new phenomenology would seem to Rorty to be political nonstarters. Further, we can now understand why Christopher Voparil claims that Rorty is rightly understood as a *political theorist*. In his essay "The Problem with Getting it Right: Richard Rorty and the Politics of Antirepresentationalism," Voparil opens by rehearsing Rorty's claim that he does not offer arguments, but only "redescriptions." Voparil rightly admits that "it is hard to form a coherent idea of what a philosophical tract without argumentation or validity-claims would look like" (2004, 222).[17] Nonetheless, he continues on to say that Rorty's notion of redescription has an enormous "political value" in that it has the "power to change minds" (2004, 222). That Rorty is primarily concerned with doing to others what writers like Nabokov and Orwell have done to him (i.e., deeply move him toward a more engaged moral position) is for Voparil what is truly important about Rorty's authorship. Voparil recognizes that Rorty turns to redescription because of a deeply felt desire to actually change the world.

Along with Voparil, I applaud this desire for social transformation. Unfortunately, that Rorty has this desire does not entail that he succeeds in providing a framework according to which such transformation is likely to be encouraged. Drawing on parallels between Rorty's notion of redescription and Sheldon Wolin's notion of "political theory as a kind of 'vision,'" Voparil argues that we would not be amiss to view Rorty as a political theorist. Rorty's theory offers an account of political reality as being shaped by our ability to envision different futures rather than argue for the Good or the True. As Voparil writes, "the critique of foundationalism opens the door to political theory, as a discourse aimed not at truth but at persuasion" (2004, 228). This will become important in part 3 when I consider religion in the public square, epistemic justification, and political critique.

As I suggested above, much of Rorty's move away from theory is offered as a critique of the political irrelevance of the "cultural left." Voparil makes a similar claim and postulates that Rorty's value as a political theorist lies in his ability to offer such criticisms and, hence, challenge people to be better citizens tomorrow than they are today. Nonetheless, Voparil proceeds to offer various lines of criticism to Rorty as a newly inducted "political *theorist*." Voparil suggests that "giving up the idea of getting it right severs Rorty's redescriptions from reality and spells a loss of critical purchase." Driving this point home, he announces: "Where Rorty seeks to alter our vocabularies, the great political theorists sought to alter the world" (2004, 223). Here it would seem that Rorty is subject to the very sort of formalism of which he accuses Levinas.

A second version of the same critique is offered as a statement about abstraction. Voparil contends that Rorty's writings are as abstract and unhelpful for the specific issues of everyday life as are those of the theorists that he criticizes. In the attempt to shift our vocabulary in the direction of the "banal and familiar," Rorty simply replaces one level of abstraction with another. In agreement with Voparil, I want to suggest that in Rorty's description of ethics, although he attempts to strip it of the esoteric speculations and difficult language of more Continental philosophers, he remains a philosopher and continues to speak as one: he is still theorizing in a philosophical vocabulary about why we should not be philosophical theorists.

Rorty would likely find all this to be too much of an argument and not enough of a redescription, but the upshot of my position is that a good redescription of Rorty would be one that demonstrates the political difficulties his own thought faces.[18]

"Gawky, Awkward, and Unenlightening": Levinas and the Charge of Formalism

Earlier it was pointed out that Rorty is most unsatisfied with Derrida when Derrida is "Levinasian." As I have suggested, this amounts to the places where Derrida lapses into a certain *religious* longing and *theologico-metaphysical* legacy. Given that Rorty does not see any *"automatic* priority" (1989, 194; original emphasis) of ethics over the private realm of self-creation, it is important to realize that if he displays resistance to Derrida it is not due to Derrida's privatization. Indeed, Rorty thinks that Derrida's value is precisely *due* to his brilliance in the private realm, but runs into problems when his thought is applied to public discourse. Accordingly, Rorty's rather thoroughgoing disregard for Levinas, I contend, is due to the fact that Rorty does not see in Levinas the more promising and helpful private discussions that are so common in Derrida.[19] Whereas Derrida and Levinas might both be quite useless for politics, Derrida is at least useful for what Rorty terms the private task of self-creation.

Without instruction, or we might say, imagination, directed primarily toward the realm of "self-overcoming," Levinas is valuable neither for private individuals in the process of self-creation (because of his ostensibly ethical and political focus), nor to public citizens trying to become less cruel (because of his frequently hyperbolic, "religious" vocabulary and speculative conceptual apparatus). Hence, Levinas's obsessive concern with ethics just misunderstands ethics. Rorty's encouragement is simply to move past Levinas and attempt to interpretively disengage the Levinasian remnants often found in Derrida's otherwise valuable texts.[20] It is Levinas that we must *lose* if we are to *find* Derrida's real importance. Rorty sees Levinas as not being a private ironist who is occasionally guilty of unnecessary and unhelpful forays into the public domain, but instead as someone who fundamentally (and unnecessarily) sees ethics as a complicated non-ontological relation to the absolutely Other. Reminiscent of his initial frustration with Rawls, Rorty's critique of Levinas primarily stems from the way that Levinas defines ethics as constitutive of subjectivity: this is regarded by Rorty as basically a theological move. In contrast, Rorty suggests that we see ethics as the difficult business of trying to steer clearly through the treacherous waters of everyday decision-making. The move to metaphysical frameworks and abstract talk of absolute alterity is simply superfluous to the real business of making ethical decisions. Moreover, it can be detrimental to such an endeavor, either because it distracts us from the business at hand or because it causes us to obscure the real goal of ethics: a better tomorrow.[21] Mark Dooley nicely summarizes the neo-Pragmatist problem with Levinasian ethics:

> For a pragmatist, Levinas's Judaically charged ethics is at best idealistic. This is so because pragmatists in the mode of Rorty believe that ethics ought to take the form of concrete responses to pressing dilemmas. In suggesting that "the word of God speaks through the glory of the face and calls for an ethical conversion or reversal of our nature," Levinas, on a pragmatist reading, is simply indulging in hyperbolic rhetoric. Ethics demands practical projects which aim at relieving unjustifiable misery and suffering, and this is achieved through a manipulation of sentiment in which we come to see strange people as fellow-sufferers. (Dooley 2001b, 36–37)

This way of viewing the Rorty-Levinas relationship is made explicit in the few places where Rorty does directly address Levinas and his particular way of understanding ethics. Because such passages are so rare, I want to offer several of them in an attempt to demonstrate the consistency of Rorty's reading across his authorship (the following is not meant to be exhaustive).

> ✧ I am unable to connect Levinas's pathos of the infinite with ethics or politics. I see ethics and politics . . . as a matter of reaching accommodation between competing interests, and as something to be deliberated about in banal, familiar terms—terms which do not need philosophical dissection and do not have philosophical presuppositions. . . . Levinas's pathos of the infinite chimes with radical, revolutionary politics, but not with reformist, democratic

politics—which is, I think, the only sort of politics needed in rich constitutional democracies such as Britain, France and the US. (1996a, 17)[22]

↜ Levinas and Critchley are not in the same line of business as Dewey and I. . . . We should just thank our lucky stars that there are quite a lot of people nowadays who are pretty consistently appalled by human beings suffering unnecessarily. (1996b, 42)

↜ It seems to me pointless hype to dramatize our difficulties in knowing what to do by labeling our goal "indescribable," "unexperiencable," "unintelligible," or "infinitely distant." (1996b, 42)

↜ Maybe the only way to move still further away from "the philosophical language of the Greek *logos*" is to turn one's back on Levinas and his ubiquitous Other at the same time one turns one's back on Heidegger and his attempt to remember what the Greeks thought about Being. (1998c, 342)

↜ The notion of "infinite responsibility," formulated by Emmanuel Levinas and sometimes deployed by Derrida—as well as Derrida's own frequent discoveries of impossibility, unreachability, and unrepresentability—may be useful to some of us in our individual quests for private perfection. When we take up our public responsibilities, however, the infinite and the unrepresentable are merely nuisances. Thinking of our responsibilities in these terms is as much of a stumbling-block to effective political organization as is the sense of sin. (1998a, 97)

In the above passages, there are several points worth considering. First, Rorty rarely mentions Levinasian ethics without countering it with his own definition and understanding of the term. This suggests that Rorty wants to show why Levinas's conception is not properly what *should* be meant by "ethics." Although given to exaggeration and almost inflammatory comments about the uselessness of Levinasian discourse, Rorty acts as if he had a useful alternative ready to hand. It is precisely Rorty's description of his own ethics that I want to interrogate. Perhaps Rorty's exaggerated claims about Levinas serve as a straw man against which he is able to distinguish his own formulation (of course, given Rorty's suspicion regarding the utility of argument, it is doubtful that such a worry would trouble him).[23]

Second, Rorty's difficulty with Levinas is primarily linguistic, but for ethical reasons. As we have seen, the strength of Rorty's position lies in its apparent willingness to get its hands dirty in the business of real-life situations. What the above passages demonstrate is Rorty's claim that Levinas (and Derrida in his Levinasian

God and the Other

moments) transforms the messiness and visceral unease of ethical decision into esoteric dramatizations that are detached from the question of whether to make this or that choice—choices that might each be legitimate given different situations. If philosophy is to do ethics, it must be able to speak the language of the individuals in the midst of ethical dilemmas—a language that, for Rorty, is simply incompatible with Levinasian ethics, Derridean deconstruction, and the general trajectory of new phenomenology.

As something of a helpful analogy, consider the case of William Wordsworth and Samuel Taylor Coleridge. In his preface to the second edition of the *Lyrical Ballads,* Wordsworth maintains that poetry should be a presentation of "the real language of men in a state of vivid sensation" (Wordsworth 2000, 239). Coleridge takes issue with Wordsworth's claim to speak this "real language," in chapter 17 of his *Biographia Literaria*. Therein, Coleridge rightly asserts that there is a world of difference between the language used in "Mr. Wordsworth's homeliest composition" and the language of "a common peasant" (Coleridge 2000, 484). Even though Wordsworth displayed a noble ambition to capture the everyday life of the common person, he overlooked that common people do not go around speaking in verse and deploying a vocabulary that Wordsworth gained through a life of reading. Just as Wordsworth claimed to speak in "the real language of men," Rorty claims to speak in "familiar, banal terms." But, I contend, we should not be too quick to grant Rorty's account of his own language game. As Richard Bernstein asks: "How are we to descend from Rorty's lofty rhetoric to . . . effective liberal reforms?" (2003, 135). Hence, Coleridge's critique of Wordsworth might be as aptly aligned with an internal critique of Rorty, as with Rorty's critique of Levinasian abstraction.

Third, and most powerful, we should notice the seeming motivation behind Rorty's resistance to the apparent uselessness of Levinasian ethics. On this point it serves us well to take our time, for it is here that the Rortian critique presses most forcefully. One should abandon a Levinasian position, Rorty contends, due to its irrelevance to everyday commonalities and the banality of human interaction. Ethics is a matter of urging people toward ever-expanding "solidarity," guided by nothing other than the sheer ability to identify with other people as being "like us" (see the beginning of Rorty 1998b).[24] Long speeches about a primordial "substitution" for an absolute alterity and demands to give the "bread from one's mouth" do not go very far toward eliminating starvation. Discussions of "the face" do not provide immediate impetus for doing something about the "hungry eyes" of a homeless child. Crucially, whether they are successful or not, Rorty's comments against Levinas are strikingly given *in the name of the other person.* His insistence on moving *past* Levinas is so that we move *toward* a more promising future for us and our neighbors.

By locating his definition of "ethics" with such a stringent view toward the wellbeing of the other person, a type of consequentialism after the fact develops in Rorty's thought. "Moral progress," he claims, is possible[25] but only when such "progress," Rorty will say in a later essay, is defined as "becoming like ourselves at our best (people who are not racist, not aggressive, not intolerant, etc., etc.)" (Rorty 1998c, 5). For Rorty, ethics must call us to a specific type of action, the type that serves to eliminate cruelty and suffering. It is this that he finds a Levinasian ethics is just unable to do. Although Levinas may prove very interesting as a critic of Heidegger and develop a language that speaks "otherwise" than the language of ontology, Rorty's general position is that the Levinasian ethical vocabulary is simply an "obsolete terminology" that we should "sluff off" (1998c, 6).[26]

The significance of this line of argumentation lies in its charge of what might best be called *formalism*.[27] Rorty's critique of Levinas is similar to Hegel's charge that Kant developed an ethical structure that was ultimately of limited assistance in resolving concrete, and decidedly historical, ethical dilemmas (Hegel 1967, 90). Indeed, Rorty seems to argue, just as Kant's "categorical imperative" sounded remarkably but met with crippling difficulties in the messy business of real (i.e., political) life, so the formal structure of Levinas's "face to face relation" ultimately proves worthless when one attempts to fill it with determinate (i.e., practical) content. Subsequently, Rorty finds Levinas's complex articulation and provocative discussion of "the meaning of the ethical" (see EI, 90) to be unhelpful for individuals who face everyday, or even extraordinary, ethical decisions.

I have argued that taking Rorty's criticism seriously is important if one is committed to putting the Other first, even if that requires contesting and rethinking one's allegiance to Levinas. However, it would of course be wrong to conclude that simply because Rorty's criticism is serious it must be correct; and similarly, Rorty's criticism may in fact be so demanding that it puts in question Rorty's own formulation of ethics.

At his best, Rorty is a thinker who stands alongside Levinas regarding the concern for the suffering of the other; at his worst, Rorty is dismissive of and indifferent to thinkers who do not agree with his "pragmatic" leanings. That he would try to alleviate Levinas's suffering were he to encounter him hungry in the streets is important, but this is tempered by Rorty's unwillingness to, according to his own criteria, "increase his imaginative powers" by seeking to engage Levinas deeply. Rorty's inability to philosophically prohibit totalitarianism is displayed by his own thinking often sliding into what Heidegger would call a "total worldview" (see Heidegger 1999, §14). It is difficult not to conclude that Rorty's thought amounts to a lengthy attempt to achieve agreement on the basis of nothing but rhetorical flair. Hence, it seems that his thinking is problematically resistant to pluralism in that it always operates only from where "we liberals" stand, and does not make enough room for substantive disagreement and the demand for justification occurring in light of that disagreement.[28]

The danger of this possible slide toward intolerance may explain why Derrida is so insistent on hospitality being the key term for ethics. The invitation, "come, come, yes come" (viens, viens, oui viens) that we get in the pages of Derrida and Levinas can be itself read as an invitation to Rortians (among others) for sustained engagement (see esp. Derrida 1999). Rorty closes off this engagement rather than fostering it. Rorty's own interpretation of the language of hospitality is very telling: "To say that God wills us to welcome the stranger within our gates is to say that hospitality is one of the virtues upon which *our* community most prides itself" (1999, 85). Whereas Derrida and Levinas seek to give an account of how it is that hospitality to the Other can signify as an imperative without recourse to the language of traditional speculative metaphysics and classical foundationalism, Rorty's account takes the guise of merely describing how "we" already act. Asking a question regarding *why* it is that our community should pride itself in this way is one that demonstrates the ultimate problems that attend Rorty's own conception of "social hope."[29]

Rorty's "enlarged vision" is one that I can agree with in many practical details, but Rorty emphasizes that his perspective is correct because it is "our" idea, instead of recognizing it as worth pursuing due to its content's being better or truer than the alternatives. This is why Rorty is opposed to "radical, revolutionary" politics, and instead chooses to align himself so often with what we might term the status quo of historical Western liberal democracies. Rorty does not propose his political vision because it is good, but because it is what "we liberals" find to be definitive of "our" identity. Ultimately I must abandon Rorty's position in favor of what he takes to be the all-too-religious theory found in Levinas. Although I grant that his self-admittedly "ethnocentric" vantage point is consistent with Rorty's denial of a split between ethics and politics—i.e., between obligation and hermeneutics— it amounts to a good reason to look further than his own position, if what we are seeking is a politics that is not simply less exclusive according to *our* perspective, but actively more just, even to the point of being radically challenged *in our* perspective (which, I will argue, is what the constitutive relation to God and the Other necessitates).

Conclusions and Further Coincidences

Following from the above reflections, it might seem as if I have argued that we should abandon Rorty in the same way that he claims we should abandon Levinas. Nothing could be further from the truth. I want to enlarge the conversation to include all these positions as important interlocutors in contemporary ethical and political debates. This is why I find that Levinasian philosophy provides a more inclusive model for discussion than does Rorty's. In order to be consistent, a Levinasian must constantly invite others into dialogue, and this is what I hope to have done in this chapter. However, it may be that there is no common ground for Levinas and Rorty to get a conversation started. In such a case, it might be simply prudent to count one side of the argument as defeated and move on to figuring out the details of how to proceed according to the more plausible position. Yet, let me suggest that this is not the case with Levinas and Rorty for two important reasons. First, as I mentioned above, Rorty's critique of Levinas is made in an extremely Levinasian fashion. They are both committed to attending to the call of the Other, though they understand this "call" in very different ways. Second, when submitted to a closer investigation, they both offer strikingly similar visions for the future of practical, and decidedly democratic, politics. It would seem, then, that although they are at odds on the issue of "first philosophy," they are at least speaking the same language when it comes to both the motive for critical engagement with the current political situation, and also the goal of such critique.

In the following chapters of part 1, I will bring Levinas together with Kierkegaard and demonstrate that the key to a sustainable notion of political critique offered in the name of justice is a particular notion of subjectivity defined by what I term an *ontology of constitutive responsibility*. The key to this account is the way in which the relation to God and the relation to the Other are kept in tension with each other. When we constantly keep the question open as to whether religion is prior to ethics or ethics is prior to religion, I will suggest, we illuminate important paths that become promising ways forward for both philosophy of religion and political theory.

What we will see over the course of this book is that Levinas and Kierkegaard in particular, and new phenomenology in general, offer an account of human subjectivity and sociality that is worthy of our assent precisely because it is one according to which all inhabitants of the earth are part of the same ethico-political community. Instead of a classical notion of a universal human nature, say, what this strain of Continental philosophy provides is a notion of ontology in which we are constitutively responsible to and for the Other (which yields important results for both human and non-human members of the ethico-political community, as we will see in chapter 12). In opposition to Rorty, I contend that *we should not be worried about being politically radical, but we should be worried about being philosophically reactionary*. The ontology of constitutive responsibility that animates much of the Continental philosophy of religion is something that provides a real possibility for the former while articulating ways of avoiding the latter. The "theological turn" of

French phenomenology offers reasons for being intentional about why one would choose particular ways of moving forward in ethics, politics, and religion, while also offering reasons for why one would choose to reject others. Such reasons require going beyond one's own perspective, and hence beyond Rorty, even if one continues to take him quite seriously.

PART 1

A Question of Priority— Levinas and Kierkegaard

One of the defining characteristics of new phenomenology is the affirmation of some sort of relation to alterity as a central component of human subjectivity. While this general structure is fairly clear, it is far from obvious how we should understand the specifics of such a relation. Is the relation to the "Other" essentially a relation to God? To the other person? To a nondescript otherness in general? A careful analysis will demonstrate that none of the thinkers associated with the "theological turn" of French phenomenology are reductive on this front; that is, they all have multiple layers and dimensions of otherness that are operative in their accounts of subjectivity, obligation, transcendence, and sociality. This is why the title of this book is not God *or* the Other, but God *and* the Other: each is always already implicated in the other.

That said, it is important to ask not only *who* the Other is, but also *how* one ought to conceive of the priority internal to the relation to these various dimensions or conceptions of alterity. Often, however, this "how" cannot be radically separated from its "who." Especially when considering the ethico-political efficacy of new phenomenology, for example, it is important to consider whether the relation to God is prior to the relation to the other person (as it would seem to be in various ways for Jean-Luc Marion, Michel Henry, and Jean-Louis Chrétien), or whether the relation to the other person is prior to the relation to God (as it would seem to be for Emmanuel Levinas and Jacques Derrida). If the former is the case, then it would appear that ethics and politics require theological foundations; if the latter is the case, it would seem that religion is always only a secondary consideration. Either way, the consequences for moral philosophy, political theory, and public policy are profound.

In order to work through this question of priority and set the stage for considering the practical upshots of new phenomenology in the rest of the book, part 1 brings together two thinkers who seem to starkly differ, at least on first glace, in their conceptions of this all-important question of priority. The work of Levinas is the best place to go for an argument for the priority of the relation to the other person. However, for a thinker who advocates the priority of the relation to God, I will turn to someone not directly associated with French phenomenology but who figures centrally in the intellectual tradition that it appropriates: Søren Kierkegaard. Over the course of the next four chapters, then, I will work through the apparent distance between Kierkegaard and Levinas in order to argue that despite their different priorities and emphases, they are in accord when it comes to their basic account of human subjectivity as constitutively responsible.

In light of Kierkegaard and Levinas, my suggestion is that we should not understand the question of priority (God *or* the Other) as a decision between mutually exclusive options, but instead as something that should serve to maintain a productive tension in the lives of individuals in community. It is this *ontology of constitutive responsibility,* as I will call it, which I find to be the core insight that serves to unify the various thinkers associated with new phenomenology. And furthermore, I believe that it is this ontology that provides resources for those who work in Continental ethics and philosophy of religion, and who draw on Levinas and Kierkegaard, to respond to Rorty's charge of political uselessness. As I will argue, this ontology, and the *recursive hermeneutic* project it inaugurates, allows for political critique to operate in the name of an ever-increasing justice.

TWO

Hearing Divine Commands and Responding to the Call of the Other: A Reading of Kierkegaard's *Fear and Trembling*

In *Reason and Belief,* Brand Blanshard asks the following startling question about Søren Kierkegaard's *Fear and Trembling:* "What are we to say of a rhapsody (in forty thousand words) in praise of pure and holy murder, of a defense of the humanly immoral on the ground that it is religious duty?" (1975, 236). Blanshard's question goes far beyond Rorty's concern that religion is politically useless by highlighting the moral problem with attempting to "teleologically suspend" ethics in the name of a "higher," specifically *religious,* obligation. Emmanuel Levinas echoes this concern. In *Proper Names,* Levinas praises Kierkegaard for "rehabilitat[ing] subjectivity" such that it escapes the totalizing tendencies found in the systematic thought of Hegel (PN, 76). However, Kierkegaard does so at too high a cost for Levinas: "in protesting against the absorption of subjectivity by Hegel's universality, [Kierkegaard] bequeathed to the history of philosophy an exhibitionistic, immodest subjectivity" (PN, 76). This immodesty is described by Levinas as a *"tensing on oneself"* (*tension sur soi*) that constitutes the subjectivity of the subject as "an impatience that the outer world (of people and things) . . . cannot satisfy" (PN, 67). Although Levinas applauds Kierkegaard's insistence that interiority is non-integratable into the language of totalization, he is suspicious that this ultimately yields a rejection of ethics rather than its radicalization. This leads him to the second of the two main points of "disturbance" that he finds in Kierkegaard. Namely, he says: "[i]t is Kierkegaard's violence that shocks me" (PN, 76).

Levinas claims that violence emerges in Kierkegaard "at the exact moment when Kierkegaard 'transcends ethics'" (PN, 76). Levinas recognizes that since ethics is for Kierkegaard the "universal" and operates with "rules that are valid for all," it is understandable that he would want to formulate a conception of subjectivity that transcends this eradication of singularity through universal thematization. However, Levinas is quick to add, "it is not at all certain that ethics is where [Kierkegaard] sees it" (PN, 76). Offering his own contrasting understanding, Levinas claims that "ethics [is] a consciousness of a responsibility toward others . . . [that]

far from losing you in generality, singularizes you, poses you as a unique individual, as *I*" (PN, 76).

Crucially, Levinas's critique of Kierkegaard is actually quite close to Rorty's critique of Levinas. That is, Levinas is worried that Kierkegaard's account of religious obligation (or more precisely, the suspension of ethics in the name of such obligation) ends up missing the very others about whom we should be concerned. The difference between Rorty's worry about Levinas and Levinas's worry about Kierkegaard, however, is that Rorty only took Levinas to be ethico-politically "useless," whereas Levinas considers Kierkegaard to be outright "violent." Nonetheless, what does seem clear is that Rorty would align Kierkegaard with Derrida regarding the project of self-creation, rather than with Dewey or Rawls regarding the project of human solidarity.[1] As such, according to Rorty, Kierkegaard is in the same boat as Derrida and Levinas regarding practical, political inefficacy.[2]

Rorty, Levinas, and Blanshard are not alone in their ethical frustration with Kierkegaard.[3] Charges ranging from moral nihilism and selfishness to irrationalism and sloppy thinking have been leveled at Kierkegaard's complex authorship. Such readings illuminate two key problems that are widespread in Kierkegaardian literature in general, and material on *Fear and Trembling* in particular: (1) the assumption that Kierkegaardian ethics are static (even if they are subsequently rejected in favor of faith), and (2) the supposition that when Kierkegaard champions irrational fideism as the alternative to ethics, he actually undercuts the possibility of choice in the first place. We might call the first the *problem of definition* and the second the *problem of rationality*.

Most critics have understood *Fear and Trembling* as follows: the duty to God trumps all ethical duties. As Ronald M. Green claims, Kierkegaard "represent[s] the divine command at its most antirational and antimoral" (1988, 84). The problem of definition and the problem of rationality come together as being directed at the same thing: Kierkegaard's supposed individualism. This individualism is a challenge for ethics because, as Silentio says: "Faith is namely this paradox that the single individual is higher than the universal" (FT, 55; see also 69, 82). In this case, the relation between Abraham and God is "higher" than the relation between Abraham and Isaac. If this is all there is to the story, then Levinas is right to complain. On this front, it seems that Abraham's religious individuality is so important that it excuses (indeed, requires) the death of Isaac if God commands it. Even the most ardent defender of divine election *should* be deeply worried about such a suggestion.

Similarly, individualism is a challenge for thought in that rationality is classically defined by the twin components of necessity and universality. These are exactly what Silentio contests when he asserts that "faith is the paradox that interiority is higher than exteriority" (FT, 62). Moreover, rationality is essentially communal: logic is by definition shared. A private logic would fall prey to the same sort of critique that Wittgenstein levels on the idea of a private language. When Silentio claims that the "ethical as such is the universal; as the universal it is in turn the disclosed," and then proceeds to say that the "single individual, qualified as immediate, sensate, and psychical, is the hidden," he seems to be rejecting rational ethics in favor of irrational faith (FT, 82).

Although there is much in Kierkegaard's authorship to support such readings,[4] in this chapter I will argue that we do not need to go to texts such as *Works of Love* and *Practice in Christianity* in order to combat critiques of "Kierkegaardian ethics." Rather, by considering the role of Isaac in *Fear and Trembling* we can read the drama as not being a story about the subordination of ethics to religion, but about the rejection of a *particular* understanding of ethics that would claim for itself *superiority over* religion. By focusing on Abraham's relation to God, most interpreters overlook Silentio's constant concern for Isaac, and thereby miss the ethical undercurrent that defines "faith" throughout the book. In his singularity, Isaac is the very condition for Abraham's ordeal, and without him there would be no ethical problem in the first place. Far from eliminating ethics, as Levinas takes Kierkegaard to do, Kierkegaard radically rethinks ethics in a way that is neither the "social morality" (*Sittlichkeit*) of Hegel nor the rationalistic universality (*Moralität*) of Kant, but is closely akin to what we find in the thought of Levinas himself.[5] Contrary to Ronald M. Green's assertion that *Fear and Trembling* "is *not* about ethics" (1993b), I will argue that *Fear and Trembling is* about ethics inasmuch as it redefines what "ethics" means and, thereby, offers the reader a story about *responsible subjectivity.*[6] The ethical, or as I will suggest, ethico-religious conception that is advocated by Kierkegaard in *Fear and Trembling* is most properly understood as a bi-directional responsibility to God and the Other.[7] Hence, Abraham's ordeal is not due to the conflict between a non-religious duty and a duty to God, but reflects a tension that is internal to the life of faith itself. Importantly, this reconsideration of religion and ethics in *Fear and Trembling* sets the stage for realizing that the question of priority regarding the relation to God and the relation to the other person is not something that should be decided as a simple either/or. In this and in the next chapter, I will focus on "the binding of Isaac" (*Akedah*) as what might be considered the event *par excellence* for working through the way in which these two relations jointly constitute the ethico-religious encounter that inaugurates subjectivity.

Getting Our Terminology Right: Responding to the Problem of Definition

In order to see the stakes of the crucial relationship between the particularity and singularity of Abraham and Isaac in *Fear and Trembling,* it is important to initially get clear on exactly what the surface conception of ethics displayed within the text is. So in this section I will (1) argue that, on the surface, *Fear and Trembling* primarily understands ethics according to a Hegelian definition, and (2) challenge the idea that Kierkegaardian ethics should be understood as directly mapping onto the "ethical" in particular pseudonymous works. Taken together, these claims open the space for subsequently arguing that Abraham's and Isaac's singularity cannot be reduced to their individual social roles.

Unfortunately, most readers of Kierkegaard take the conception of ethics that is presented in *Fear and Trembling,* and also in the second volume of *Either/Or,* to be equivalent to Kierkegaard's view of ethics as such. However, Kierkegaard had no *static* conception of ethics. Rather, his view of ethics is context-dependent; Kierkegaard is always responding to whatever or whoever he is in conversation with. In *Fear and Trembling,* Kierkegaard's conversation partner is Hegel (or at least, the appropriation of Hegelian speculative thought by many of his Danish contemporaries).[8] This becomes clear in the first pages of the preface:

> I throw myself down in deepest submission before every systematic ransacker: "This is not the system; it has not the least thing to do with the system. I invoke everything good for the system and for the Danish shareholders in this omnibus, for it will hardly become a tower. I wish them all, each and every one, success and good fortune." (FT, 8)

The explicit pronouncement, "This is not the system," indicates that Silentio is aware of the supposition of most of his readers that philosophy should be done in the manner of systematic speculation. The problem with such speculative thought is that it amounts to an overly economic approach to the realm of ideas: "Everything can be had at such a bargain price that it becomes a question whether there is finally anyone who will make a bid" (FT, 5). By making doubt a springboard from which all philosophers must propel themselves, thought is cheapened, since it is available to anyone with the right sort of education. Silentio diagnoses the current philosophical climate of his time as one in which people say: "Yes, well I am glad to have doubted on last Wednesday because now I am done with that and ready to go beyond mere faith and arrive at knowledge." The problem with such a perspective is that faith has become a tool for problem-solving rather than a "task for a whole lifetime," as it was for the Greeks (FT, 7). Faith must not be a *thing* that we have, but rather a *struggle* that defines our existence.

In an attempt to contest the trends of modern philosophy, Silentio speaks into his philosophical milieu by rejecting any claim to a philosophical pedigree: "The present author is by no means a philosopher. He has not understood the system, whether there is one, whether it is completed; it is already enough for this weak head to ponder what a prodigious head everyone must have these days when everyone has such a prodigious idea" (FT, 7). His frustration with the lack of direction in a time when everyone claims to be clearly directed is a frustration that will continue to underlie the body of the book. That this is all a not-so-subtle critique of Hegel should be obvious: Hegel is perhaps the grandest example of a systematic thinker, and Hegel understood his own thought to be a lengthy exposition of the rationality of his Lutheran faith. Why this matters is that faith becomes for Hegel, as for the Danish philosophical scene of Kierkegaard's day, a mere step along the path to knowledge. Faith is the very air that one breathes in nineteenth-century Europe rather than being that toward which one constantly strives. Similar to Jacob's refusal to let the Lord leave without first blessing him (see Genesis 32), the preface to *Fear and Trembling* announces Silentio's commitment to critiquing systematic thought in order to once more open the space for authentic faith. The idea of going further than faith resounds in his ears as being as nonsensical as attempting to go further than excellence: if there is such a thing as excellence, it will always be that horizon toward which we move, rather than a mere moment along the path toward some further horizon.

One could object that although this demonstrates that Silentio understood his writing to be an engagement with Hegelian philosophy, it does not say anything about his understanding of ethics. This would be correct if the book stopped with its preface. However, at the beginning of each of the three *problemata*, we find Silentio explicitly invoking Hegel in his three attempts to define ethics:

Problema I

> The ethical as such is the universal, and as the universal it applies to everyone, which from another angle means that it applies at all times. It rests immanent in itself, has nothing outside itself that is its τέλος but is itself the τέλος for everything outside itself, and when the ethical has absorbed this into itself, it goes not further. . . . If this is the case, then Hegel is right in "The Good and Conscience," where he qualifies man only as the individual and considers this qualification as a "moral form of evil," which must be annulled [*ophævet*] in the teleology of the moral in such a way that the single individual who remains in that stage either sins or is immersed in spiritual trial. (FT, 54)

Problema II

> The ethical is the universal, and as such it is also the divine. Thus it is proper to say that every duty is essentially duty to God, but if no more can be said than this, then it is also said that I actually have no duty to God. . . . Now if this train of thought is sound, if there is nothing incommensurable in a human life, and if the incommensurable that is

present is there only by an accident from which nothing results insofar as existence is viewed from the idea, then Hegel was right. (FT, 68)

Problema III

The ethical as such is the universal; as the universal it is in turn the disclosed. The single individual, qualified as immediate, sensate, and psychical, is the hidden. . . . The Hegelian philosophy assumes no justified hiddenness, no justified incommensurability. (FT, 82)

In all of these passages the ethical (*det Ethiske*) is linked to the universal (*det Almene*); the "single individual" (*den Enkelte*), to the contrary, is opposed to the universal in both form and content. This should come as no great shock since ethics as the universal is precisely the notion of ethics that is prominent in the second volume of *Either/Or*. The ethics prescribed by Judge William and presupposed by Silentio are primarily ethics understood as Hegelian *Sittlichkeit*, rather than Kantian *Moralität*.[9] Judge William does not urge the other man, "A," with whom he is in conversation, to submit himself to the logic of the categorical imperative, but to the laws and customs of the society in which he lives.[10] As Merold Westphal writes:

Judge William is an Aristotelian, for whom right reason is to be defined in terms of the man of practical wisdom rather than the reverse, and a Hegelian, for whom ethics is always a matter of *Sittlichkeit*, the laws, customs, practices, and institutions of a people. The right and the good are to be found, not abstractly in a rational principle but concretely within one's social order, which is, for each individual, the essential mediator of the absolute and the eternal. (1996, 24)

With this estimation, Anthony Rudd is in agreement:

Judge William does not argue that "A" should adopt rationally universalizable maxims, but insists, rather, that he commit himself to social roles and personal relationships. It is this sort of commitment that is central to ethics as Kierkegaard understands it, and as Judge William advocates it. (1993, 72)

The key to the surface understanding of ethics in *Fear and Trembling* is its identification with social roles and cultural positions. Abraham, *the father*, is expected to love Isaac, *the son*. Abraham, *the husband*, is expected to not keep silent to Sara, *the wife*.[11]

Although Silentio's account of faith primarily challenges ethics understood as *Sittlichkeit*, it is just as much a critique of ethics understood as *Moralität*.[12] Yet there are scholars who find Kierkegaard to be more closely linked to Kantian ethics than to the Hegelian version. Consider the following claim by Lenn Goodman: "When Kierkegaard stands to defend the irrefragable demands of faith against the hubris of morality, it is Kant's morality of a universal moral law that he addresses" (1996, 27). In response to various critics, Goodman concludes that Kierkegaard's "target is not Regina in the guise of Isaac but Kant in the guise of Abraham" (1996, 25). Additionally, Edward Mooney suggests deep ties between Kantian and Kierkegaardian ethics (1991, 106–108); Richard Cohen finds Kierkegaard's distinction between the general and the existent to "remain within the orbit of a Kantian reading" (2003, 22); and John Glenn announces that Kierkegaard's "basic ethical ideas . . . amount to a fundamentally Kantian ethics" (1974, 121–28). In stark contrast, however, George Stack goes so far as to argue for the "inapplicability of Kantian ethics for an understanding of Kierkegaard's existential, or subjective ethics" (1977, xiv). What are we to say to this interpretive disparity regarding *Fear and Trembling*?[13] I have already aligned myself with those who read the ethics of Judge William and Silentio to be Hegelian rather than Kantian, but it is important to state why this is the case.[14]

The commentators who have read *Fear and Trembling* in a Kantian way are not without some textual support. As C. Stephen Evans notes, it is "true that the ethical is sometimes described in the book in Kantian language" (2004, 66). Expanding a Kantian reading beyond this particular text, Evans also points out that in other works, "notably *Upbuilding Discourses in Various Spirits* and *Concluding Unscientific Postscript,* various ethical claims associated with Kant are defended" (2004, 66). Nevertheless, such a Kantian reading is misguided, I contend, due to the Kantian stress on rational agency rather than an appreciation of the specific historicity of moral obligation. As we will see, the ethical account challenged by Silentio resists such a rationalization of ethical obligation and instead locates moral duty relative to one's social context.[15]

For all of the personalities through which Kierkegaard writes, there is at least one thing on which they all concur: the inescapability of individual context and socio-historical situation. The person for whom ethics is a question is always an *existing person* rather than a merely *logical possibility*. Therefore, ethics is never simply a matter of speculative thought; ethics is a matter of personal life. There is an intimacy in all ethical intrigue. So, when a person submits to ethics, she submits to a particular understanding and historical manifestation of it. Abstraction is fine in theory but, as Hume pointed out, extremely difficult in daily life. This point is echoed in Kierkegaard's work when Johannes Climacus says of speculative approaches to existence that they require such an "inhuman way of walking that I dare not recommend it" (CUP, 193). The reason that marriage is such a focal point of ethical life in Kierkegaard's early authorship, for example, is because it is the highest expression of submission to social normativity: marriage is the historically located ethical institution *par excellence.*

Ethics must be lived as socio-historically embedded, but one must submit to such an ethical order irrespective of one's particular society (see Mason 1988). This is how the universality of ethics can continue to press. Kant would be just as hostile as Hegel to the idea of the "individual being higher than the universal." The difference is not a matter of *what* one is standing against, but *how* one stands: for Kant, standing against the universal is to stand against reason itself; for Hegel, it is to refuse to be part of the sociality that defines the individual. In both cases, the problem with radical singularity is that it seems to contest the very condition of subjectivity: for Kant, there is no person who is immune to the demands of practical reason; for Hegel, as earlier for Aristotle and later for Sartre, there is no person who is beyond the reach of social obligation. With this in mind, we can understand Rudd's proclamation that "Abraham is as much a scandal to Kantian *Moralität* as to Hegelian *Sittlichkeit*" (1993, 145). Although there is good reason to contest the Kantian reading of *Fear and Trembling,* the point is the same—ethics is identified with the universal in either case, and both a Kantian and a Hegelian reading seem to require that Abraham be condemned as a murderer.[16]

Here we encounter the *problem of definition:* just because some of Kierkegaard's texts present ethics as *Sittlichkeit* (cf. *Either/Or, Fear and Trembling,* and *Stage's Along Life's Way*), this in no way means that Kierkegaard intends that ethics *should be* understood this way. Notice that in all of the passages from the opening of the *problemata* quoted earlier, Silentio transitions from the connection with Hegel by way of a weighty "if." This simple word casts the shadow of conditionality on all the paragraphs that precede it. *If* ethics is understood in this way, then Hegel is right. *If* ethics is nothing other than *Sittlichkeit,* then Abraham is indeed nothing but a murderer. *If* ethics is really just universal normativity, then there is no justification for the "single individual." As Louis Mackey rightly notes: "Everything that is said about the ethical in this section of the book [that is, in the three *problemata*] is qualified by the 'if'" (1986, 54).[17] But strangely, this "if" rarely gets noticed. If it were, there would be far less temptation to think that ethics as defined by Silentio in these moments actually reflects Silentio's own conception. Moreover, even if we assume that Silentio does understand ethics this way (and if only as a foil for his notion of religion), we run into trouble attempting to attribute this understanding to Kierkegaard.

We should read these *problemata* as saying the following: if we understand ethics as does Hegel, then there is no room for singularity, which is itself an ethical problem. For this reason, ethics, for both Silentio and Kierkegaard, must be more than *Sittlichkeit* in order to allow for the possibility of singularity. Thus, Kierkegaard contests the very ethicality of *Sittlichkeit* through the conditionality with which Silentio offers his definitions. This illuminates the error that appears so frequently in the literature when "Kierkegaardian ethics" is defined as the sort of ethics that is advocated by Judge William and conditionally deployed by Silentio.[18]

Rethinking Divine Command Theory: Responding to the Problem of Rationality

If the ethics that gets suspended in *Fear and Trembling* is not the ethics of Silentio or Kierkegaard, but merely the problematic conception advocated by Hegel, then it is likely that readings of the text which see it as being primarily about the supremacy of religion *over* ethics are misguided. Nevertheless, the most common reading of the text puts forth an understanding of Silentio as an advocate of some sort of divine command theory that renders all other formulations of ethical theory secondary and derivative. On this reading, the "teleological suspension of the ethical" is nothing more than a teleological suspension of social morality in favor of the duty to follow the ethical imperatives that come from the mouth of God. Whether or not a divine command interpretation of *Fear and Trembling* is plausible depends on exactly what notion of divine command theory one deploys.

C. Stephen Evans notes that although divine command theory has often been perceived to be in some opposition to what he terms "human nature theory" (2004, 11–12), certain Christian thinkers have demonstrated how such theories are quite compatible with each other. According to Evans, human nature theory was originally developed by Aristotle, who articulated "the classical account of morality in which it is linked to the actualization of certain potential qualities in human nature" (2004, 10). Eventually, Evans claims, traditional Christian appropriations of Aristotle (as in Aquinas, for example) have stressed the notion of human nature as a product of God's creative act. As such, "human nature theories by no means ignore the divine will" (2004, 11). Despite the plausibility of reading Christian human nature theories as being a variety of divine command ethics, Evans argues that such accounts face problems at the level of how to make sense of God's freedom. So, "at least according to one prominent school of interpretation" of Aquinas, divine commands "seem to follow for the most part directly from the character of the human nature God has created" (2004, 12). In response, Evans provides what he takes to be a "stronger" account which understands "divine moral obligations [to be] rooted in a free act of the divine will, an act that is not directly entailed by a judgment of the divine intellect as to what is good in light of human nature" (2004, 12).

Evans's model of divine command ethics is one that attempts to bridge the gap between human nature and divine command by taking quite seriously the "relational character of human life" (2004, 12). Drawing on the work of Robert

Adams (1999), Evans points out that since social relationships are "partly constituted by systems of obligation" (2004, 13), the very nature of human social existence is something that should cause us to recognize that God's plan for individual human flourishing requires living in community. Although there exist obligations inherent to sociality as such, Evans contends that the importance of divine command lies in its giving a particular obligation certain *moral* qualities such as being "objective," "overriding," and "universal" (2004, 299). In this way, divine command theory is teleologically directed toward bringing about a fulfilled human existence, which only occurs amid relationships to others. However, given that the Christian God is a personal God, then for Evans it is sensible to conclude that one's moral responsibility is to cultivate a particular sort of social relationship with God and others.

Evans claims that this basic perspective is true for Silentio as well as for Kierkegaard (2004, 21). Becoming yourself and achieving a relationship with God," Evans writes, "are not two distinct and therefore potentially rival tasks, but the same task characterized in different ways. The self that I must strive to become is a self that is constituted by a God-relationship" (2004, 21–22). Evans's distinction between his model of divine command theory and that displayed by much of the Christian intellectual tradition is that his view recognizes that "God does not create generic human beings, and he does not command us to become generic human beings" (2004, 23). Hence, the divinely commanded, yet existential, task is "to learn to stand before God *as an individual*" (2004, 23, original emphasis). It is here that the link with Kierkegaard is quite clear:

> On my reading of Kierkegaard, the self is fundamentally relational; it is not possible for a human being to be a completely autonomous, independent self, since the self is grounded in relations to something that is an "other." Rather, the idea is that each human being is different from all others, and among the differences that define each of us are the differences in the relations we have with others. (2004, 23)

Evans's argument for the compatibility of human nature theories and divine command theories is significant because when the two are taken as being at odds, then one of two things follows for the theist: either an explicit divine command like that found in Genesis 22 is straightforwardly impossible, given that God has already said all that was required by creating human nature, or such a command becomes relevant only in situations when the everyday conception of morality hits tough cases. Divine command only enters the discussion in cases like Abraham's, when it seems as if there is no other way to understand the act but as *unethical*. That is, God needs to speak when we would, under any other circumstance, act contrary to such a command precisely because of our nature. However, even if one follows Evans's suggestion and understands Christian human nature theory to be a version of divine command theory, it is not clear that these problems are avoided, though they might be minimized to some extent. This becomes clear in the final chapter of *Kierkegaard's Ethic of Love* when Evans considers whether it would be possible for God to command Abraham to kill Isaac. Evans's response is that it is possible for us to believe that God commanded Abraham to act in this way while also believing that God could not reasonably issue such a command *today*. Evans allows for one's not being morally blameworthy for believing that God commanded human sacrifice today only if God causally determines one's belief structure to that effect (2004, 308). "Unless God miraculously determines my thought processes," Evans writes, "I will steadfastly disbelieve any alleged vision or voice that delivers such a command, and disbelieve any other person who claims to have received such a message from God" (2004, 310).

Although I agree with Evans's analysis of the relational dimension of Kierkegaardian thought and appreciate his attempt to provide a plausible defense of a robust divine command theory, I am hesitant to endorse it as the best hermeneutic lens through which to read *Fear and Trembling*. In general, my resistance to Evans's proposal is not because I take it to be false, but because I take it to be a problematic strategy when one is attempting to engage Continental philosophy, as I am trying to do in this work. Specifically, Evans's dependence on the notion of an essentialist human nature is something that is simply a nonstarter for much of Continental philosophy. Furthermore, in order to get this notion of human nature off the ground, Evans decides entirely in favor of the God-relation being prior to relations to the other person (which I will suggest is problematic). And finally, the discourse of divine command theory (in its various forms), I believe, downplays the hermeneutical obstacles that accompany the contextual, historical, embodied existence of beings-in-a-world. That said, what seems quite promising about Evans's account is that, due to its focus on the relational dimension of human existence, it does give greater attention to the social contexts in which moral obligations arise and function than do more traditional versions of divine command theory.

That said, it seems entirely plausible to me that one could contest the general postmodern resistance to "divine command" and "human nature" by reconstructing such ideas in uncharacteristic ways. Divine command theory could be understood not as an order to act in a specific way, but as a structural call to responsibility as constitutive for subjectivity. That this call is essentially *religious* need not detract from its *ethical* status, and indeed, it might even intensify it. If divine command theory were reinterpreted in such a (deconstructive) way and if "human nature" were merely used to indicate something like the structure of an inaugural event of subjectivity (e.g., the ethical or ethico-religious encounter), then it is quite plausible to speak of a postmodern or deconstructive divine command theory that might, indeed, come quite close to what is offered by Evans. But again, the strategic difficulties of such a move seem to make it unadvisable, at least for the time being.[19]

Moving from the general to the specific, I contend that appealing to divine command theory in order to interpret *Fear and Trembling* really amounts to the following two-pronged claim: (1) the point of *Fear and Trembling* is to explain a limit-case for ethical behavior, and (2) the appeal to religion is actually an appeal to a religious understanding of ethics itself. The first is clear in Evans's suggestion that the "parallel with Abraham lies in the possibility of a conflict with prevailing moral standards, even though the prevailing moral standards of our culture are quite different from those of Abraham" (2004, 312); the second is clear in his claim that *Fear and Trembling* demonstrates that "obedience to God may require the individual to oppose conventional moral views, and even suffer as a consequence of this non-conformity" (2004, 314).

There is certainly something to be said for both of these components of a divine command option. On the one hand, it would be difficult to deny that Silentio is concerned with this limit-case: a book on the binding of Isaac that is *not* concerned with Abraham's peculiar ordeal would be quite a text. And on the other hand, no one could successfully maintain that whatever conception of ethics Silentio actually advocates is entirely detached from religion.

Divine command readings also face a twofold challenge from within Silentio's text. First, if Silentio's point is that the good is defined as God's will, then there seems to be no "teleological suspension of the ethical," at all: we simply replace one theory of ethics with another one. Silentio repeatedly protests being able to reformulate Abraham's actions according to another, albeit higher, conception of the ethical. Indeed, Silentio even questions whether something like divine command theory might be operative when he wonders if "this story contains any higher expression for the ethical that can ethically explain [Abraham's] behavior, [and] can ethically justify his suspending the ethical obligation to the son, but without moving beyond the teleology of the ethical" (FT, 59). After considering several cases where such an *ethical* suspension of ethics would occur—namely, cases involving a tragic hero such as Agamemnon, Jephthah, or Brutus—Silentio concludes that "Abraham's situation is different. By his act he transgressed the ethical altogether and had a higher τέλος outside it, in relation to which he suspended it" (FT, 59). The ethical theories displayed by the tragic hero and the divine command theorist are structurally identical (even if the specifics are different). For the tragic hero, the duties to one's family and friends are trumped by the duties to the state or society as a whole. Similarly, according to divine command theory, the duties to one's family are to be (or can be, at least) trumped if the will of God demands it. In both cases, the situation is the same: a higher expression of the ethical overrides its ordinary conception. In neither do we actually move beyond the "teleology of the ethical."[20]

Second, if (at least classical) divine command theory is rejected and Silentio's prognosis is correct—namely, that Abraham had a "higher *telos*" that was "outside" of ethics—then it appears that saving the passionate interiority of faith comes at too great a cost. That is, Kierkegaard's conception of faith as irreducible to any type of social morality is itself a claim that carries normative qualities. However, this normativity contains elements of universality, which is exactly what Kierkegaard rejects as operative in religious faith. Hence, a difficult problem emerges: in order to radicalize faith, Kierkegaard places it outside the realm in which such a radicalization could occur. It seems that by saving the legitimacy of the move beyond ethics to religion, Kierkegaard inevitably moves toward irrationalism. Blanshard drives this point home when, in a discussion of Kierkegaard's fideism, he comments:

> To adopt Kierkegaard's new sense [of Christian faith], peculiar to himself and inconsistently held, which reduces truth to a passionate commitment of feeling and will, would not save Christianity; on the contrary, it would largely destroy it. For it implies that there are no common truths for Christians to accept, no common principles by which their lives may be guided, indeed no common Deity for them to contemplate and worship. (1969, 120)

In the same vein, Alasdair MacIntyre says of *Either/Or* that

> The doctrine of *Enten-Eller* is plainly to the effect that the principles which depict the ethical way of life are to be adopted for no reason, but for a choice that lies beyond reasons, just because it is the choice of what is to count for us as a reason. Yet the ethical is to have authority over us. But how can that which we adopt for no reason have any authority over us? (1984, 42)

Blanshard and MacIntyre both argue, albeit indirectly, that the account Silentio gives of Abraham's relation to God is not defined according to rational standards but still seems to depend upon such standards in order to function as an argument.[21]

The problem with *Fear and Trembling* is that by giving an account of "ethics" that redeems the relevance of moral theory, we contradict the text—and yet staying true to the text and the apparent irrationality it advocates would be intellectually (and also morally) irresponsible. We could express this more pointedly by saying: those who try to help Silentio overcome the charge of ethical treason do so at the cost of missing his point; while those who get his point do so at the cost of being implicit in that treason. For this reason, Blanshard writes, the "Kierkegaardian 'knight of faith,' in electing the 'absurd' is divesting himself of the shackles of all insights. But to do that," he continues, "is not to be a saint, but a moral nihilist" (1969, 118). On this reading, Kierkegaard offers a conception of faith that is dangerously vacuous according to any ethical standards we could use to judge it.

Whereas Blanshard and MacIntyre claim to have demonstrated that Kierkegaard is philosophically and morally disastrous, due to the senselessness of claiming that religion has triumphed over ethics (or the ethical over the aesthetic) and simultaneously denying any standard according to which this change could be evaluated, Francis Schaeffer and R. M. Green find the main problem with Kierkegaard's irrationality to be its devastating influence on subsequent thought. Claiming that Kierkegaard inaugurates an "existential methodology," Schaeffer warns:

> One must understand that from the advent of Kierkegaardianism onward there has been a widespread concept of the dichotomy between reason and non-reason, with no interchange between them. The *lower story* area of reason is totally isolated from the optimistic area of non-reason. The line which divides reason from non-reason is as impassable as a concrete wall thousands of feet thick, reinforced with barbed wire charged with 10,000 volts of electricity. There is no interchange, no osmosis between the two parts. So modern man now lives in such a total dichotomy, wherein reason leads to despair. "Downstairs" in the area of humanistic reason, man is a machine, man is meaningless. There are no values. And "upstairs" optimism about meaning and values is totally separated from reason. Reason has no place here at all; here reason is an outcast. (1976, 174)[22]

Similarly, Green writes: "Kierkegaard's surface argument amounts to a powerful nonrational and nonmoral reading of the biblical episode. It is this uncompromising, antirational interpretation of Genesis 22 that has shaped our modern approach to the biblical text itself" (1988, 86).

Now I grant that it has been decades since these charges were first published, but in more recent literature similar ones continue to appear. Consider, for example, the fact that Alasdair MacIntyre's irrationalist reading of Kierkegaard in *After Virtue* (1984, 39–45) continues to be so influential that in 2001 a collection of essays was devoted to engaging *Kierkegaard After MacIntyre* (Davenport and Rudd 2001). We would do well to ask, then, is this potentially devastating charge of irrationality correct?

C. Stephen Evans (1981 and 1993) argues that Kierkegaard only advocates an *existential* irrationality, rather than a *logical* irrationality.[23] With Evans, I also want to suggest that Kierkegaard's fideism cannot be reduced to the belief in a logical contradiction.[24] A paradox (*det Paradox*) does not necessarily entail a contradiction (*den Modsigelse*). When Johannes Climacus claims that the paradox is the fact that "the eternal truth has come into existence in time," he indicates the way personal existence ruptures the rational categories in which speculative thought dwells (CUP, 209). This claim is not a logical contradiction of the form (A & ~A). Rather, it is a *paradox* because it is only approachable from *within* existence. What is logically impossible is never the case; the paradox, however, is existentially impossible and yet it happened *in time*. Existence is the medium in which all thought must occur, but it is also the space in which the adequacy of thought is contested. Hence: "Existence itself is a system—for God, but it cannot be a system for any existing [*existerende*] spirit" (CUP, 118). Explaining the paradox according to rational categories might indeed be impossible, but not because it involves affirming contradictions.

The difference between a paradox and a contradiction can be helpfully illuminated by considering the difference between the first-person and third-person perspectives. The only way to explain the paradox "would then be to comprehend ever more deeply what a paradox is and that the paradox is the paradox" (CUP, 220). Such comprehension is not reducible to a rational account, because it is the story of one's lived relation to the paradox rather than a detached elucidation of it.[25] Nowhere does Kierkegaard actually ask the reader to believe a logical contradiction in order to have faith. Rather, he encourages her toward passionate appropriation, purity of relation, and depth of commitment—even to the point of suffering and death. When Silentio concludes that the move from ethics to religion is "by virtue of the absurd," he does not mean that it is contrary to the rules of logic, but simply that it contests the adequacy of rationality to lived experience. It should be noted that for Kierkegaard this is not to say that somehow faith is unique in its requirement of a "leap." Indeed, Kierkegaard never uses the exact phrase "leap of faith" which is so often attributed to him. Evans explains that the leap is "simply the category of decision, a concept that metaphorically emphasizes the decisiveness human existence demands" (1983, 46). Hence, he continues: "The transition from each sphere to the next demands a leap" (1983, 46). The leap is not always a religious leap of faith, rather it is more like a *Gestalt* shift, as Jamie Ferreira suggests (1998, 216). The only way to move from one lived *Gestalt* to another is to radically shift between conceptual schemes. Of course there are more or less circumspect movements—i.e., certainly there is evidence for the validity of a given transition; for instance, recognizing that ironic self-deception might count as evidence for moving from the aesthetic to the ethical, while realizing what Anthony Rudd calls the "limits of the ethical" might drive someone toward the religious—

but in no way do such evidences offer anything like a *guarantee*.[26] Still, just because such leaps must be made without guarantee does not mean that they are irrational.

The charge of irrationalism ultimately amounts to a claim about the inability of Kierkegaard to be instructive for ethical or religious life because he is unable to provide the type of certainty that we desire. Consequently, critiquing Kierkegaard on these grounds actually says more about the perspective of the critic, I believe, than it does about Kierkegaard. One further aspect deserves mention, however. In addition to his "logical" point about Kierkegaard's cutting his feet out from underneath himself, Blanshard also claims that Kierkegaard's "ethics are curiously egoistic" (1975, 225). Perhaps the real problem with Kierkegaard is not his irrationality, but rather Kierkegaard's selfish preoccupation with his own frustrated existence. Blanshard is not alone in this insinuation. H. J. Paton writes:

> If ever a person was self-centered it was Kierkegaard: he hardly ever thinks of anyone but himself. Self-centeredness is the very antithesis of religion; and if the paradox of faith is—as he says—a willingness "to do the terrible and to do it for its own sake" (as well as for God's sake), then the less of this kind of faith we have the better. (1955, 121)

Richard Cohen more recently remarks that *Fear and Trembling* stands in a "long tradition of philosophical hubris"; for Kierkegaard's argument to be coherent, he must *"usurp* the place of God" (2003, 29).

In the next section, I will argue that by rereading *Fear and Trembling* with an eye toward the role of Isaac, Kierkegaard emerges not as a self-absorbed egoist, but as someone whose concern for the relation to other persons is inscribed in his unyielding passion for God.

What about Isaac?

Understanding the role of Isaac in *Fear and Trembling* amounts to understanding his relation to Abraham and Abraham's relation to him—that is, understanding them both in their particularity *and* their singularity. Up to this point, the terms "singularity" and "particularity" have been deployed in intentional ways, but without a sufficient explanation of the difference between them. *Particularity* indicates the actuality of a person's socio-historic location or his or her status as an instantiation of a universal (namely, an example of "humanness" or some similar conception). Particularity is what identifies a person as distinct from all other people, and yet as interchangeable with those others; it amounts to a collection of identity markers (race, religion, class, gender, etc.). Even understood as a merely statistical unit of numerical distinctiveness, particularity is located in the sphere of historical actuality. Since at least Locke, most of the political philosophy focused on liberty and individualism is concerned with a conception of particularity as I have articulated it above. The individual liberties of persons must be protected for no other reason than the distinctness of every person as a particular instantiation of what it means to be human. Rousseau's opening lines of the *Confessions* capture this modern conception well:

> Myself alone! I know the feelings of my heart, and I know men. I am not made like any of those I have seen; I venture to believe that I am not made like any of those who are in existence. If I am not better, at least I am different. (1999, 429)

Notice that for Rousseau, the distinction to which he points is simply that he is "different" from all other people. This difference, however, is something that he realizes after comparing himself to all others he has seen. Hence, he continues to assert the idea that the difference of his individuality is comparative: I am different from all others in that I am able to consider myself as distinct from those to whom I compare myself. Now, I admit that Rousseau's conception goes much deeper than a mere claim about his looking different or having been raised differently, but instead illuminates a uniqueness that might seem to suggest something more than the historical determinateness that characterizes particularity. However, I find that Rousseau's description here ultimately amounts to a merely numerical claim: I am different in being distinct from all others. This is not, however, *yet* a normative assertion that it is "better" to be "different." Rather, it simply indicates that if *quality* does not allow for subjective affirmation, at least *quantity* does.

For Kierkegaard, the notion of particularity is primarily understood in a Hegelian way. According to Hegel's logic, there are three moments of the Concept: universal (*Allgemeine*), particular (*Besondere*), and singular (*Einzelne*). Particularity (*Besondereheit, Partikularität*) is what stands over and against the universal by being an instantiation of it. Consider the following passage from the *Encyclopædia Logic*:

> To say, "This plant is curative," implies that it is not merely this single plant that is curative, but that some or many plants are, and this gives us the *particular* [partikulär] judgment ("Some plants are curative," "Some men are inventive," etc.). By virtue of this "particularity" [*Partikularität*] the immediately single instance loses its independence and becomes interconnected with something else. As *this* man, a man is no longer merely this single man; he now stands beside other men instead, and is one of the crowd. But precisely for this reason, he also be-

longs to his universal and consequently he is elevated. The particular [*partikulär*] judgment is just as much positive as negative. (Hegel 1991, 252; "Addition" to §175)

Notice that in this passage particularity is essentially related to universality in that the particular is itself overcome by "belonging" to the universal as a constitutive negation.

Although Hegel will use the term "singularity" (*Einzelnheit*) to refer to a distinct moment of the Concept and will differentiate it from particularity, both terms fall under the domain that I am labeling "particularity" here. The distinction for Hegel is really one of consciousness. Singularity is the isolated object (although it need not necessarily have material existence) *as* isolated; particularity is the object in relation to Universality insofar as it is an instance of the universal. Hegel encapsulates this tripartite relation as follows:

> Man thinks and is something universal, but he thinks only insofar as the universal is [present] *for* him. The animal is also *in-itself* something universal, but the universal as such is not [present] *for* it; instead only the singular is ever [there] for it. The animal sees something singular, for instance, its food, a man, etc. But all these are only something singular for it. In the same way our sense experience always has to do only with something singular (*this* pain, *this* pleasant taste, etc.). Nature does not bring the *nous* to consciousness for itself; only man reduplicates himself in such a way that he is the universal that is [present] *for* the universal. This is the case for the first time when man knows himself to be an "I." When I say "I," I mean myself as this singular, quite determinate person. But when I say "I," I do not in fact express anything particular about myself. Anyone else is also "I," and although in calling myself "I," I certainly mean me, this single [person], what I say is still something completely universal. (1991, 57; "Addition 1" to §24)

What should be taken from this passage is the way in which particularity and singularity are both related to universality for Hegel. Singularity is almost a deficient mode of particularity in that it alone is available for animals, for whom universality is never present. As such, singularity is a matter of mere distinctness, while particularity requires the universal *as* universal even *in* its distinctness. But absent from Hegel's conception of particularity as well as his conception of singularity is anything like a resistance to totalization and incorporation. For Kierkegaard, such resistance is precisely what constitutes the *singularity* of the self, and his development of this idea is a direct criticism of the false closure that he finds to be characteristic of Hegelian philosophy. As Marie Thulstrup writes, "Kierkegaard's interest in 'the single individual' can be traced quite early in his notes and writings, but its appearance is particularly notable in his criticism of Hegelianism" (1988, 9).

Referring to the seeming grandeur of Hegel's system, in which everything is included and in which everything is given a positive account, Climacus says that "all of this [positivity] fails to express the state of the knowing subject in existence; hence it pertains to a fictive objective subject, and to mistake oneself for such a subject is to be fooled and to remain fooled" (CUP, 81). The problem with Hegel's system, Climacus argues repeatedly, is that it focuses on the self as a concept rather than the self as an existing reality in the world. I contend that *singularity* should be understood as opposed to Hegel's understanding of the self as a mere instance of a universal. This notion of singularity is more appropriately found when Kierkegaard develops the notion of "the single individual" (*den/hiin Enkelte*). Referred to as "my reader" in the prefaces of *Eighteen Upbuilding Discourses,* this "single individual" is radically non-integratable, absolutely un-assimilable, and represents un-assailable interiority (EUD, 5, 107, 179, 231, 295).[27] The singularity of the self is both constitutive of selfhood and also an achievable status for the self. In the first place singularity is what Anti-Climacus depends upon when he describes the self who has "rooted out" despair: "in relating itself to itself and in willing to be itself, the self rests transparently in the power that established it" (SUD, 41). Moreover, it is the self who stands "before God" not in Christian commitment, but in simply being created. The idea here is that as constitutive of selfhood, singularity is the uniqueness of each and every person who stands before God as before their creator, and who is defined by the possibility of *choosing* to stand before God as their Lord. Singularity is what simultaneously lies *beneath* particularity and *transcends* it—namely, the uniqueness of God's call to Abraham and the irreplaceability of Abraham's response.

In his important book *Kierkegaard's Concept of Existence,* Gregor Malantschuk persuasively contends that for Kierkegaard, the single individual far outstrips the idea of mere individuality.[28] As such, Malantschuk focuses on singularity as an existential possibility. For Kierkegaard—as for Levinas and, arguably, for Heidegger—singularity is a normative claim. Distinguishing oneself from the crowd is not merely about being different, as it is in Rousseau's *Confessions.* Rather it is about viewing the crowd as exhibiting a deficient mode of being. Ultimately linked to Christianity, the single individual is the person for whom selfhood is not a result of their own power, but about relinquishing all claims to power. This is the difference between aesthetic and religious subjectivity. The aesthete chooses herself, as does the religious person—but the aesthete chooses to be herself as a mode of *self-actualization.* The religious person chooses to be herself as a moment of *self-dispossession*—the self is achieved by giving oneself over to God. It is here that

I find that Evans's (2004) account of the social relation of the self to God is quite productive regardless of whether one pursues his specific moves relative to divine command theory.

When it comes to the differentiation between particularity and singularity, Kierkegaard's critique of Hegel is mirrored by Levinas's critique of Heidegger. Levinas recognized that whereas Kierkegaard understood singularity to be the non-incorporability of the self, he found it to be located in the other person: "It is not I who resist the system, as Kierkegaard thought; it is the other" (TI, 40). Despite this difference of location, the notion of singularity, and thus of real alterity, is common to Levinas and Kierkegaard. It is with this in mind that I propose that *Fear and Trembling* be read in such a way as to focus on the "other" that so often gets overlooked, and to Levinas's mind, cast aside—namely, Isaac. Kierkegaard does not privilege Abraham's singularity over that of Isaac, but instead keeps the singularity of both in play at all times.

The distinction between particularity and singularity is important because what Kierkegaard chastises the ethical for occluding is this singularity in the name of a respect for individuals. For Hegel, the ethical status of an individual is due to her occupying specific social and familial roles within a social and historical context. Silentio expresses this nicely, saying: "In ethical terms, Abraham's relation to Isaac is quite simply this: the father shall love the son more than himself" (FT, 57). According to Hegelian ethics, the distinctness of Abraham *as Abraham* is displaced in favor of Abraham *as father*. Similarly, Isaac is not singularized in his being Isaac, but simply by filling the role of the son in the social network. Ethics demands this movement toward individuality, realized as the occupation of social roles. "The single individual," Silentio writes, ". . . is the individual who has his τέλος in the universal, and it is his ethical task continually to express himself in this, to annul his singularity in order to become the universal" (FT, 54). Given these brief descriptions, we might say that particularity is a fundamentally *political* concept while singularity is an *ethico-religious* one.

Importantly, although singularity can be occluded in favor of particularity/individuality,[29] particularity cannot be eradicated in the name of singularity. The whole point of singularity is that there is something about the self that is uniquely irreducible to the totality of a person's political relations. This uniqueness is precisely what shines through in the particularity of the individual's historical situation. David Stern finds this particularity to be strangely lacking in the story of the binding of Isaac (the *Akedah*):

> We know, to be sure, that Abraham is the son of Terah, husband of Sarah, father of Isaac, and has been promised that he will become the father of a great people; but Abraham's response [to the call of God]

invokes none of this. He does nothing to establish his identity as the person addressed. Nor can he know who speaks to him, or whether he should do what he is bidden to do. Nonetheless, he responds, but only with "Here I am." (2003, 36)

That Abraham's particularity is not voiced in his response to God does not mean that his singularity is also lacking. Rather, Stern claims, it is his "responsiveness to singularity that only [he] in [his] singularity can muster" (2003, 37). Although Abraham's singularity cannot be reduced to his particular situation, his singularity is only accessible *through* his particularity—that is, only as existing in society and history is Abraham's distinctness before God a possibility. In other words, as Stern also indicates, *we do know* Abraham's identity and, although Abraham does not directly invoke it, this identity cannot be dislocated from his response to God at the critical moment on top of Mount Moriah. Silentio realizes this as well, and throughout *Fear and Trembling* there are points that speak to the particularity of Abraham, which in almost every case also speak to the particularity of Isaac.

In the four exordiums, Silentio highlights the particularity of Abraham and Isaac in such a way that they emerge as singular and unique selves-in-relation. In the first, he writes that Abraham "left the young servants behind and, *taking Isaac's hand,* went up the mountain alone"; and after a brief pause to bless Isaac, "Abraham *lifted the boy up* and walked on, *holding his hand*" (FT, 10; emphasis added). Recognizing the primarily Hegelian conception of ethics deployed in *Fear and Trembling* is crucial for understanding the significance of the fact that, within these midrashic embellishments, Silentio offers the reader an insight *not* into the relation of the roles of father and son, but into the relation of one singular self who loves another singular self. Silentio's description of the tenderness of Abraham's relation to Isaac and the trust with which Isaac receives Abraham's affection transcends the ethical expression of the duty that a father has to his son and instead gestures to the depths of this specific relation between singular persons who are defined by their responsibility to each other, *not out of social obligation, but out of love.* This continues in Exordium II, where Sarah is introduced into this relation of love: Abraham *"embraced* Sarah, the bride of his old age, and Sarah *kissed* Isaac, who took away her disgrace, Isaac her pride, her hope, for all the generations to come" (FT, 12; emphasis added). This sentiment is repeated almost verbatim in Exordium III. In both, we are privy to the intimacy between these persons and not the universality of their duties to one another. The claim that *Fear and Trembling* disregards the particularity of Isaac is also contested in the final exordium. There, Silentio writes almost as though from Isaac's point of view: "Isaac saw that Abraham's left hand was clenched in despair, that a shudder went through his whole body—but Abraham drew the knife" (FT, 14). Here we do not merely find a depiction of a son seeing a father's trembling; we see Isaac himself looking at Abraham—Isaac sees *his* father in despair.

Frequently, Silentio speaks of Abraham's age. We have just seen the reference to Sarah as "the bride of his old age," and he later writes that "Abraham became old" (FT, 18). Later still, in a description of Abraham at the moment of decision—that is, in the moment of crisis—he presents him as "the old man with his solitary hope" (FT, 22). This is relevant to a discussion of the role of Isaac, because by realizing Silentio's concern with the particularity of Abraham, we are able to see his joint concern with the particularity of Isaac. Isaac was the young child of this old man. Isaac is the instantiation of God's promise, just as he is the manifestation of Abraham's relation to God. But he is also the young man who had to deal with his older half-brother Ishmael. He has grown up under the weight of the responsibility of providing the seed of the future generations God has promised: the pressure to fulfill Sarah's pride and Abraham's hope defines him. Silentio's text undermines its own Hegelian conception of the ethical duty between Abraham and Isaac by complicating this universal duty with an insistence on the particularity of the persons involved. By focusing on their *particularity*, he highlights their *singularity* and not only their socio-historic location. Thus, a tension develops between the textual performativity and the philosophical argument that can be stated as follows: ethics in *Fear and Trembling* is equated with the universality of one's individual role in normative social conditions, but the discussion itself presents the characters in a way that contests this conception of ethics. There are two possible ways to understand this situation: (1) as an implicit dramatic strategy designed to undergird the explicit argument regarding the singularity of religious faith; or (2) as an explicit argument for understanding ethics in a radically different way than what is presented as *the ethical* in the text.

If we see these two options as mutually exclusive, then there is no clear manner of deciding which interpretation is correct without running into difficulties on both fronts. If we accept option (1), then Levinas's claim about ethical violence remains unaddressed. Specifically, Levinas admits that Kierkegaard radicalizes the notion of *religious* subjectivity, but worries that in so doing he has lost any idea of *ethical* subjectivity. Alternatively, if we advocate option (2), then there is a danger of doing what all of *Fear and Trembling* is fundamentally against—namely, reducing religion to ethics. With these difficulties in mind, let me propose that the best way forward is by realizing that option (2) is already amenable with option (1). In *Fear and Trembling* we find a notion of ethics that already resists the totalization that is necessarily involved in the universal ethics which Silentio so radically opposes. This alternative understanding of ethics can be accessed by considering the status of Isaac as always already troubling the isolated relation of Abraham and

God. In this way, Levinas's reading of Kierkegaard misses the point: where Levinas has Kierkegaard locate ethics is actually where Silentio has Kant and Hegel locate it. Accordingly, Levinas's critique of Kierkegaard can indirectly help us understand Silentio's critique of ethical theory as traditionally defined (at least within the framework of German Idealism).

There are a couple of reasons for understanding Isaac as the very condition for Abraham's ordeal.[30] First, Silentio speaks of a "new interiority" that cannot be eradicated from the life of the knight of faith. He writes:

> In the ethical view of life it is the task of the single individual to strip himself of the qualification of interiority and to express this in something external. . . . the paradox of faith is that there is an interiority that is incommensurable with exteriority, an interiority that is not identical, please note, with the first but is a new interiority. (FT, 69)

The presentation of two levels of interiority mirrors Kierkegaard's account of the two types of immediacy. The first level of interiority/immediacy is located in the aesthetic stage of life and is identified as a certain kind of egoism which, like faith, resists the universality of ethics. However, this first level is full of deception and irony. The aesthete is the individual who does not realize that his interiority is actually only a negativity before the positive demands of ethics. In contrast, the second level of interiority/immediacy is found in the religious sphere and is defined by a suspension of the ethical demand, not in the name of egoism, but in the name of God.

The relation to God constitutes the individual as singularly irreplaceable. No one can sacrifice Isaac *for* Abraham. No other person could fill the "role" that Abraham plays in the drama because there is no role to be identified; only Abraham is commanded and this command is constitutive of his subjectivity. Repeatedly Silentio drives this point home when he talks about Abraham's silence, his madness, and his incommunicability. Silentio cannot understand Abraham because Abraham does not understand himself. Abraham's relation to God is one that is immediately interior in such a way as to isolate Abraham in his responsibility. As Silentio says, "the knight of faith" is the person "who in the loneliness of the universe never hears another human voice but walks alone with his dreadful responsibility" (FT, 80). Whereas the demand of ethics is always a demand for everyone in every situation, the demand of faith can never be convertible to such a shared conception. "Partnership in these areas," Silentio insists, "is utterly unthinkable" (FT, 71).

What does this religious interiority have to do with a rethinking of the ethical? Notice that when Abraham suspends the ethical in favor of the religious, he stands before God as before the Absolute Good. There is not a suspension of the Good in the name of God, but instead, a suspension of a rationalistic conception of ethics in the name of a deep gratitude for God's gift of responsibility. It is here, I believe, that the notion of divine command theory begins to emerge as a plausible interpretive frame, but is also robustly contested as problematic. That Abraham stands in an "absolute relation to the Absolute" means that he recognizes God as the condition for the Good and not the Good as the actuality of God. However, this implies that there is a conception of the Good present in the text that is not identifiable with the Good of universal normativity. Goodness must be understood as constitutive of *who I am* (the constitutive obligation to God and/or the other person) rather than as a mere possibility for my existential activity (that I can affirm this or that activity as "right"). It should go without saying that these can never be held in radical separation from each other. As I will argue in various ways throughout this book, to understand oneself as constitutively obligated demands that we affirm certain sorts of actions and institutions while contesting others. Critique does not end in light of responsibility, but instead originates there. Similarly, ethico-epistemological certainty is not achieved within the relation to God and the Other, but is perpetually challenged in the name of a humble hospitality to the Other, which is itself offered "in the name of God."[31]

The "new interiority" described by Silentio should be read as the realization of the unavoidability of the singular responsibility before God as this conception of the Good. We must be careful here not to allow God to slide into the position of being nothing but an "invisible vanishing point, an impotent thought," which would occur if "his power is only in the ethical, which fills all of existence" (FT, 68). If the ethical expands to be coterminous with God, God ceases to be the personal God of Abraham's encounter and becomes simply the name we give to the source of ethics. How can a conception of the Good be maintained without such a problematic reduction? The key is in the person of Isaac.

Isaac is the one who troubles the immediacy of Abraham's relation to God. Isaac lays claim to Abraham in Abraham's singularity, and Abraham's particularity is intrinsically tied up with Isaac's. This relationship, however, is not reducible to the relation between a father and a son, but is always pierced by the singularity of Isaac as the fulfillment of God's promise to Abraham, and Abraham as the one whose faith opened a future for Isaac. Just as Abraham's relation to God is not identical with his relation to the universality of ethics, Abraham's relation to Isaac is not identical with his duty as a father—but instead, it is his duty as "Abraham" as distinct from "Abram" (Genesis 17: 1–8). Abraham and Isaac are both singularly identified by God's call. Hence, Abraham's duty to Isaac is always already involved in his duty to God and neither of these demands is universalizable in the way *Sittlichkeit* and *Moralität* frame ethical duties.

The second point is that there is a responsibility to Isaac that is *not* suspended by Abraham's relation to God, but is instantiated and continually deepened because of it. There is an ethical excess, we might say, that causes the religious relation itself to tremble when it stands in isolation from what I will term the *ethico-religious*. Silentio makes this explicit in the following passage:

> The absolute duty can lead to do what ethics would forbid, but it can never lead the knight of faith to stop loving. Abraham demonstrates this. In the moment he is about to sacrifice Isaac, the ethical expression for what he is doing is: he hates Isaac. But if he actually hates Isaac, he can rest assured that God does not demand this of him, for Cain and Abraham are not identical. He must love Isaac with his whole soul. Since God claims Isaac, he must, if possible, love him even more, and only then can he sacrifice him, for it is indeed this love for Isaac that makes his act a sacrifice by its paradoxical contrast to his love for God. (FT, 74)

Abraham's love for Isaac is itself not suspended. Only the specific normative codes that would normally have sway over this love are overcome. I propose that this passage is the key moment of the entire text.[32] Here we are told that Abraham's love for God and his love for Isaac are never isolated from one another; rather, it is the *tension between their claims* upon Abraham that constitutes the drama of his *responsibility to both*. The life of faith deepens the love for the other person rather than suspending it because of the love for God. This is the distinction between Abraham and Cain as well as between Abraham and all others who would commit murder while claiming to hear from God. As Silentio says: "It is only by faith that one achieves any resemblance to Abraham, not by murder" (FT, 31).

This realization allows us to differentiate between Abraham and others who propagate violence in the name of a particular sort of religious fundamentalism.[33] Abraham's love for Isaac is the very condition for the possibility of Abraham offering a sacrifice, rather than simply committing murder.[34] Devotion to the other person is required by the relation to God. In order to flesh this point out a bit, I want to offer one way in which to understand Silentio's claim such that Abraham cannot be viewed as the father of monotheistic violence (or as someone like David Berkowitz, the "Son of Sam" who killed after claiming to hear a divine voice). As claimed above, the sacrifice of Isaac requires the deepest love possible. Only by loving Isaac is Abraham able to offer him up to death; love underlies Abraham's relation to Isaac, and as such allows for the trial to be trying. For violent fundamentalists, hatred of difference takes primacy and there can be no trial apart from self-sacrifice, which, as Silentio points out, is ethically easy (and aesthetically beautiful) when compared to sacrificing someone else. Again the distinction between Abraham and Cain is instructive: to sacrifice, we must offer our best—that which we *love wholeheartedly.*

But Abraham's devotion is never publicly understandable because it signifies only within the space of his singular relation to God, which is always in tension with and inseparable from his singular responsibility to Isaac. This is not the competition between religion and ethics that Silentio describes explicitly in the text; the ethico-religious tension that I am highlighting here is *internal* to the relation to God.[35] Hence, what we learn from Silentio's presentation of Abraham is that *the relationship to God heightens the responsibility to love the other person while the relationship to the other person makes the relationship to God tremble in its paradoxicality.*

The Logic of Gift and Gratitude

Abraham's love for Isaac is the condition for the possibility of his sacrifice: *devotion to the other person is the condition for the possibility of obeying God.* This is why Silentio cannot understand Abraham. If love for the other person were simply reducible to one's social duty, then there would be no occasion for faith. Problematically, however, if this love cannot be suspended, Abraham's actions make no sense because he is killing his son *whom he loves more than himself.* This is why Abraham cannot become a tragic hero. His actions are not understandable according to some *higher* expression of the teleology of the ethical, as when Agamemnon sacrifices Iphigenia for the sake of his fleet. Instead, his actions are never fully understandable because they signify only within the space of his singular relation to God, which is always in tension with and inseparable from his responsibility to Isaac. This is not the competition between religion and ethics that Silentio describes explicitly in the text—that is, a teleological suspension is not really a competition— but instead, as Merold Westphal (1995a) successfully argues, an *Aufhebung.* The ethico-religious tension is *internal* to the relation to God; or to go in the other direction, but no less validly, it is internal to the relation to the other person. God always stands between me and the Other in such a way as to constantly contest the potential isolation of a couple, and the Other stands between me and God in such a way as to contest any retreat to quietism—and to forbid any violent fundamentalism. Again, Westphal is helpful here: *"When the Other does not get in the way of my seeing God, God will end up getting in the way of my hearing the Other. That is what the teleological suspension of the religious is all about"* (1995a, 158).

Separating ethics from religion (or the other person from God) assumes that there could be one without the other. It is uncontroversial to say that, for Kierkegaard, God stands between me and the other person, but Isaac's singularity illuminates the way in which the other person also stands between me and God. This is not to say that the other person stands in such a way as to be able to understand my relation to God: Abraham had to walk his lonely road by himself. However, his isolation was essentially in the midst of a social setting. The knight of faith does not stop existing in order to believe, but continues to exist while struggling to believe. Hence, the lonely path is the very gift of God's grace, and is precisely a result of an obligation to others that cannot be jointly borne. This is the fruit of a rethinking of ethics at the hands of Kierkegaard (and under the name of Silentio). By emphasizing this bi-directionality, I do not mean to insinuate that there is no priority for Kierkegaard in the question of God or the Other, but simply that the question of priority should never be a matter of mutual exclusion or final decision. This is a tension that is productive not only for subjective existence, but also for ethical relationship, religious community, and political life. Although I agree with Westphal's assessment that the "import of this difference deserves the most careful attention" (1995a, 159), with him, I want to ask the following question:

> Is it not possible that the voice of the visible human face and the voice of the invisible God are in agreement? Is that not exactly what we should expect if, as the Genesis story found in both Jewish and Christian Bibles tells us, the Other is created in the image of God? Indeed, would it not be the deepest grace of all if in our violent world we could learn to hear the harmony of Kierkegaard and Levinas's hope for the widow, the orphan, and the refugee in the commandment *"You shall not commit murder"*? (1995a, 159)

It is only from within a relation to God that Abraham *receives* Isaac as the child of his, and Sarah's, old age. Isaac is far more clearly and literally than most children, a *gift* from God. Consequently, Abraham's duty to Isaac cannot be detached from his duty to God. Caring for Isaac is what God has called Abraham to do. Abraham's willingness to sacrifice Isaac is not an expression of violence, as Levinas might suppose, but is instead an expression of Abraham's recognition of his inability to possess what has been given to him by grace: *ethics itself is a divine gift!* Abraham's belief that he will get Isaac back "by virtue of the absurd" is something that operates according to the aporetic *logic of the paradox*—or we might say, following Derrida, according to the *logic of the gift*.[36] Isaac is given to Abraham as an expression of God's love for Abraham; that God demands Isaac back is a reminder of Abraham's lack of self-sufficiency. Ethics as described by Kant and Hegel is self-sufficient in that the limits of ethics are the limits of rationality and social respectability, respectively. Alternatively, Kierkegaard's supposed irrationality is a reminder (*pace* Wittgenstein) that the limits of rationality are *not* identical with the limits of our world—passion, desire, love, and responsibility to God are all moments that rupture an enclosed system. Similarly, Abraham's reception of the responsibility for Isaac is not primarily an expression of his rationality and his social position, but instead of his insufficiency before the God who knows how to give good gifts (Matthew 7: 11; James 1: 17). In this way, *Fear and Trembling* offers an understanding of *constitutive responsibility* that is best understood as being *ethico-religious* rather than merely another, although higher, form of ethics as such.

Conclusion: Divine Orders, Ethico-Religious Openness, and the Singular Ordeal

I want to conclude by considering a possible objection to my argument in the preceding: by focusing on the role of Isaac as the condition and engine of Abraham's ordeal, haven't I eliminated the real weight of the ordeal itself? That is, by suggesting that *Fear and Trembling* is meant as an illustration of the constitutive obligation to alterity that defines subjectivity, perhaps I have made everything too *palatable*? Am I guilty of omitting from the story precisely what Silentio claims has been left out in the comforting and comfortable reflections so often shared in living rooms and pulpits—namely, the *anxiety* (FT, 28)? I do not believe so and, indeed, my intention is to take seriously why the story ought to "render sleepless" all those who contemplate it (FT, 28). If my interpretation of the text is correct, then, along with rethinking ethics, *Fear and Trembling* provides an occasion for rethinking the ordeal itself. Such a rethinking does not eliminate Abraham's anxiety, but merely repositions its locus.

Classically, Abraham's anxiety is viewed as a product of the conflict *between* religion and morality. As just one example of such an interpretation, consider Gene Outka's description of the central question of the text: "*can* or *must* religious duty conflict with moral duty?" (1973, 205). In reply, Outka quickly comments that "Kierkegaard opts for the stronger contention: collision must occur" (1973, 205).[37] It is only if we grant the reality of two duties that are at odds with each other that we arrive at the necessity of such a collision. Hence, Outka rightly goes on to suggest that such a strong conclusion depends upon the fact that Abraham knew with certainty (1) that it was God who commanded him, and (2) the specific content of the command itself. In order to highlight Abraham's privileged relationship to God's command, Outka draws a series of parallels between Kierkegaard and Aquinas.[38] In resonance with Aquinas's notion of "inward inspiration," Outka concludes, "Kierkegaard is confident that God permits Abraham to know with the requisite certainty, despite the corrosive effects of sin, so as to make the trial a test of fidelity" (1973, 249). Thus, on Outka's account, it would appear that Kierkegaard accepts Aquinas's claim that "being admonished in a prophetic vision, [Abraham] prepared to sacrifice his only-begotten son, which he nowise would have done had he not been most certain of the Divine revelation" (Aquinas 1947, 1894; q. 171, art. 5). If so, then what emerges is a fairly straightforward account of the way in which the "absolute" duty to God does, in fact, trump all other "relative" duties.

However, does such a move really maintain Abraham's anxiety, or instead, simply eliminate it in the name of an internal, and thereby objectively unquestionable, religious certainty? If Abraham really had certainty in this way,[39] then we would be right to wonder why he had any agony about sacrificing Isaac in the first place. Given Abraham's history with God, we should assume that Abraham affirmed God's wisdom and love above all else; when this affirmation is coupled with the certainty of the command, then it seems that all anxiety evaporates. In the face of a *certain* command from an absolutely *loving* God, agony is removed from decision; only devotion and obedience are legitimate. As such, hesitation would seem to be nothing but an expression of a failure of faith and not a demonstration of it. So it appears that such an account will not serve, if our intent is to maintain the agony with which Silentio describes Abraham's ordeal.[40]

On my interpretation, Abraham's ordeal is not simply maintained as unique to his own experience; it is an inescapable component of faith itself. Abraham's confidence in God cannot be adequately translated into the certainty that might accompany an ordinary epistemic claim; the relation to God requires a rethinking of what "knowledge" could mean internal to the life of faith. The anxiety continues, because though Abraham stands in relation to God, he also stands in this relation—so Westphal reminds us—*as a human* (2004, 206). Abraham might be the knight of faith, but he is still inescapably human. It is only because of such a paradoxical identity that faith could be the "task" for Abraham's "whole lifetime" (FT, 7). But, as such, the anxiety of never having finished his task constantly looms. When Silentio writes that Abraham "*knew* it was God the Almighty who was testing him; he *knew* it was the hardest sacrifice that could be demanded of him; but he *knew* also that no sacrifice is too severe when God demands it—and he drew the knife" (1983, 22; emphasis added), we should not read this as a statement that illuminates conflicting knowledge claims, but instead as a statement inviting us to rethink what religious "knowing" entails.[41]

Insight into such a rethinking is offered on the last page of *Fear and Trembling*. There Silentio draws an analogy between the life of faith and the life of love: rather than the lover coming to a "standstill" in love, he states that "I have my whole life in it" (FT, 123). Like love, faith is that in which we have our whole lives. Faith is not, therefore, a simple addition to one's set of beliefs, but instead the very relation that defines one's subjectivity. Just like the relation to the beloved, the relation to God requires constant diligence and devotion. This devotion can never, as Dietrich Bonhoeffer says, be "cheap" (1959).[42] Faith, like love, is always *costly*. *The ordeal is not properly the struggle to understand how God could demand the death of one's*

son, but instead the weight of how to appropriate the constitutive bi-directional responsi-
bility to God and the other person that defines the life of faith itself.

The cost demanded by such a life can never be paid in full ahead of time, but must be constantly paid at every moment. To be faithful, one must love God *and* the Other (whether human or not). Thus, it is precisely because the relation to the Other is never separable from the relation to God, but is actually inscribed within it, that Abraham must constantly struggle with how to understand responsibility as a singular human self in a shared world. In comparison with what one finds in Kierkegaard's account of ethico-religious life, Hegelian *Sittlichkeit* removes the essential ambiguity and Kantian *Moralität* removes the crucial anxiety. Due to the singularity of Abraham's selfhood, Abraham's love for Isaac received as a gift from God, and the paradox of Abraham's faith, Kierkegaard uses his exemplary story as a way of working out the structures of relationality that constitute the ethico-religious stakes of subjectivity.

THREE

Bi-directional Relationality: Levinasian Readings of the *Akedah* and the (Dynamic) Ethical in Kierkegaard

In the previous chapter, I argued that equating ethics and universality is absolutely correct as a characterization of ethics as understood by Judge William in the second volume of *Either/Or*, or Silentio's presentation of Hegelian *Sittlichkeit* in *Fear and Trembling,* but as a claim about "Kierkegaardian ethics" it fails to hit the mark. *Fear and Trembling* presents a complex account of ethics that requires us to think of the relation to the other person as a reception of a gift from God. I have claimed that this revised interpretation is in line with certain Levinasian tenets—despite the fact that Levinas is a staunch critic of *Fear and Trembling* as "violent," because it apparently advocates a relation to God that "transcends ethics." Having provided an outline of the possible points of intersection between Kierkegaard and Levinas, it is important that we now do a bit more work on filling out the content of this engagement. I will continue to focus on the event that I take to highlight the most striking divergence in their perspectives on ethics and religion, while still providing an occasion for understanding the essential harmony of their notions of subjectivity—namely, the binding of Isaac (*Akedah*).

If one accepts a Levinasian understanding of ethics as a consciousness of our constitutive responsibility toward other people, then the Kierkegaardian (or more properly, Silentian) interpretation of the *Akedah* may still stand in need of revision precisely because of the priority it gives to the God-relation over the Other-relation. Even if Levinas is wrong to miss the dynamism of the ethical in Kierkegaard, he still may be right to contest the interpretive account of Genesis 22 found in *Fear and Trembling*. His critique may be misguided relative to Kierkegaard's philosophy, but quite profound in relation to the interpretation of the Genesis account itself and the way in which interpretations of that event may evidence divergent understandings of the relationship between ethics and religion. In a move from critique to a positive alternative, Levinas offers his own interpretation of the story that stands in contrast to Silentio's. Levinas's interpretation is distinctively Jewish in its focus on the divine responsibility to other people as an expression of God's law, over against the more Christian interpretation that emphasizes the interiority of *private* faith in a personal God.[1] In an attempt to further consider the question of priority with which part 1 of the book is concerned, in this chapter I will consider Levinas's own interpretation of the *Akedah*, look at what I take to be other interpretations of it that are in line with the Levinasian trajectory (namely, those offered by Jacques Derrida and Jeffrey Stolle), and then return to Kierkegaard's complex account of ethics in order to argue that we would do well not to quickly decide between Kierkegaard and Levinas on the priority of ethics over religion (or vice versa).

By maintaining the tension between the relational polarities that constitute human subjectivity—God *and* the Other—I will argue that Levinas and Kierkegaard open productive spaces for making sense of the general trajectory of new phenomenology for revisioning human social life as well as contemporary philosophy of religion and political philosophy (claims that will be developed in later chapters). But this tension is only possible if we see the resonances between their positions, while keeping the points of disparity clearly in view. I am not advocating anything like a *Kierkegaardian* Levinas or a *Levinasian* Kierkegaard. My claim is that when we really see Kierkegaard *as* Kierkegaard and Levinas *as* Levinas, we will begin to view them as moving forward together while constantly challenging each other on the best way toward the singularizing goal of faithfulness to God and justice for the Other.

Levinas and the *Akedah*

Since much of Levinas's disagreement with Kierkegaard regarding the *Akedah* results, I believe, from a difference in their religious traditions, it is important to note that there is no such thing as "the" Christian reading of this event as recounted in Genesis 22—there are only Christian *readings*.[2] The same holds true for Judaism.[3] After surveying several lines of interpretation surrounding the *Akedah* in Jewish thought, Louis Jacobs concludes: "In this and similar matters of biblical interpretation there is no such thing as an 'official' Jewish viewpoint and it is extremely doubtful whether the whole concept of 'normative Judaism' is more than a myth" (1981, 8). To demonstrate the legitimacy of Jacobs's point, consider Jerome Gellman's extremely informative analysis of Hasidic readings of the *Akedah*, where he claims that even though the Hasidim generally did not focus upon Abraham's inwardness with an eye toward his personal suffering and struggle in the way that Kierkegaard does, there remain significant resonances between the different approaches. "Despite this general divergence on inwardness between Kierkegaard and the early Hasidim," Gellman writes, "there were at least two Hasidic masters whose thought, respectively, reverberates with the existential depth of Kierkegaard's writing on the *akedah*. These are Rabbi Nachman of Breslav, Ukraine, and Rabbi Mordecai Joseph Leiner of Izbica, Poland" (2003, 7). Similarly, Jacobs points out that the omission of Abraham's inner struggle is not uniform in the Jewish tradition. He notes that the Talmud (Sanhedrin 89b) actually has a Midrashic exposition of the *Akedah* that highlights the personal turmoil of Abraham (1981, 5). Jacobs then goes on to demonstrate the resonances between the Kierkegaardian interpretation and those offered by such important Jewish thinkers as Maimonides and Soloveitchick (1981, 5–7). All of this stands in startling opposition to R. M. Green's supposition that "within the Jewish sources, there is not a hint of Kierkegaard's interpretation" (1988, 102).[4] However, given Levinas's own rather monolithic reading of Kierkegaard, I believe that he would have agreed with Green's assessment that "Kierkegaard's rendition of Genesis 22 differs markedly from that found in the Jewish sources," and additionally that "his interpretation from a Jewish point of view is 'ethically and religiously impossible'" (1988, 86).

With this in mind, I will quote at length Levinas's own reading of the *Akedah* because it will bear heavily on what follows:

> In his evocation of Abraham, [Kierkegaard] describes the encounter with God at the point where subjectivity rises to the level of the religious, that is to say, above ethics. But one could think the opposite: Abraham's attentiveness to the voice that led him back to the ethical order, in forbidding him to perform a human sacrifice, is the highest point in the drama. That he obeyed the first voice is astonishing: that he had sufficient distance with respect to that obedience to hear the second voice—that is the essential. Moreover, why does Kierkegaard never speak of the dialogue in which Abraham intercedes for Sodom and Gomorrah on behalf of the just who may be present there? Here, in Abraham, the precondition of any possible triumph of life over death is formulated. Death is powerless over the finite life that receives a meaning from an infinite responsibility for the other, from a diacony constituting the subjectivity of the subject, which is totally a tension toward the other. It is here, in ethics, that there is an appeal to the uniqueness of the subject, and a bestowal of meaning to life, despite death. (PN, 77)[5]

There are two crucial aspects of this Levinasian reading.[6] First, ethics becomes the condition for singularity, rather than the eradication of it; and second, responsibility to God is equated with / reducible to the responsibility for the other person. Both of these points are encapsulated when Levinas transfers "the highest point in the drama" from the moment when Abraham lifts the knife above Isaac, effectively having sacrificed him in his heart, to the moment when Abraham hears and responds to the voice of God forbidding him to sacrifice his son. The first voice—the command to sacrifice—is now challenged as perhaps being only a delusion; the distinctiveness of the voice of God comes as a call *to* ethics rather than a call *to transcend* the primary ethical imperative. This interpretation can be found elsewhere in Jewish scholarship. For example, Lenn Goodman claims that "it is here, with the knife poised in the air, as the painters and sculptors of the event have understood, not when Abraham stretches out his hand to take the knife, that the crisis comes" (1996, 21). According to Goodman, the crisis Abraham faces is whether or not to respond to the *true* voice of God—namely, the duty to Isaac. As Mendel of Kosov writes: "None but God can order us to take a life, but an angel suffices to demand that we save one—even if it contravenes a divine command" (Buber 1947–1948, 2: 96; cit. Goodman 1996, 22).

This statement, and the idea it represents, resonates nicely with Levinas's insistence that we "love the Torah more than God."[7] "Loving the Torah more than God," Levinas asserts, "means precisely having access to a personal God against Whom one may rebel—that is to say, for Whom one may die."[8] For Levinas, the relationship to God cannot be separated from the relationship to the other person: to love God is to love the engagement with others that occurs in study; to love Torah is, then, also to love the dialogical exchange between those who love it. The love for God is present only in this community and enacted by its intersubjective practices. As evidenced in Elie Wiesel's work, a critique of God is only possible from within a relationship with God.[9] Likewise, Job's wife could only encourage Job to "curse God and die" *because of* Job's faith. What Levinas's reading of the *Akedah* presents is a way of understanding the story that is devoid of the existentialist turmoil of a person having to decide between the duty to God and the duty to the other person. These two duties, on Levinas's re-telling, are inseparable because they are, in actuality, the very same duty.[10]

For Levinas, the angel supplies all the rationale that is required for contesting God according to God's own revelatory instruction, because the angel represents the fact that a relation to God is only possible as mediated by human discourse. If there were direct access, then the very idea of God needing a messenger would be redundant, if not ridiculous. The "absolute relation to the Absolute," which Silentio (and also Anti-Climacus) describes in such detail, would be for Levinas nothing other than a singular relation to each and every other person. As Levinas will repeatedly indicate, God comes to mind (*vient à l'idée*) only in the exposure to the face of the other. Consider the following claim from *Otherwise Than Being*:

> God is not involved as an alleged interlocutor: the reciprocal relationship binds me to the other man in the trace of transcendence, in illeity. The passing of God, of whom I can speak only by reference to this aid or this grace, is precisely the reverting of the incomparable subject into a member of society. (OTB, 158)

Here we see that, for Levinas, the relation to God is never simply a relation between oneself and God. Rather, the relation to God occurs precisely at the moment when I *take up my relation to others*. According to Levinas, faith in God is more properly understood as an embrace of one's sociality. By giving priority to ethics over religion—or at least seeing ethics as the only space in which religion would make any sense—Levinas eliminates any possibility of seeing God directly (i.e., without mediation). God is always derivative for Levinas, or perhaps a better way of saying this is that God has always already left. I am too late to see God; like Moses, I only see the back or shadow or trace of God. Thus God is, as Levinas writes, "transcendent to the point of absence."[11] This inability to see God is relevant to the Genesis 22 account because according to one possible translation of the Hebrew text, when Isaac asks Abraham about the lamb, Abraham responds by saying: "God will see to [*yir'eh*] the lamb for himself, my son." Additionally, the name Abraham gives to the place of sacrifice can be read as "The Mount Where the Lord Reveals Himself" (Goodman 1996, 22). When read in light of the Levinasian interpretation of the *Akedah*, God is seen in the revelation that Isaac *should not* be sacrificed—a command that must be understood in the context of an epoch when human sacrifice was not entirely uncommon.[12] On a Levinasian interpretation of the *Akedah,* a glimpse of an otherwise unseen God is made possible in the ethical relation to other people.

Other Levinasian Readings

There are several contemporary thinkers who deeply depend upon Levinas for their own readings of the *Akedah*. For the sake of brevity, I will consider only those of Jeffrey Stolle and Jacques Derrida.

Drawing upon Levinas, Stolle offers a reading of the *Akedah* in which "the voice that stops Avraham just before he kills Yitzhak, is no one other than Yitzhak qua face of the Other" (2001, 132). Stolle's contention is that when Abraham is commanded to sacrifice Isaac he undergoes not merely a moral test, but a test "which compels Avraham beyond all moral homelands" (2001, 133). This reading is compatible with Levinas and Kierkegaard, in that they agree when it comes to the idea that ethics is not primarily a matter of codified social morality. It is unfortunate that Levinas was unable to see this tie with Kierkegaard. Levinas's reaction to the "teleological suspension of the ethical" is one that runs counter to his own insistence that the an-archic relation to the other can never be circumscribed by normative codification (which is, for him, the domain of the political). Ethics is what stands as a critique of all political institutionality. We would be warranted, however, in asking why Levinas seems so convinced of Abraham's moral certainty when the majority of his authorship is devoted to contesting anything like a *guarantee* when it comes to obligation. What Stolle rightly demonstrates is that when it comes to the idea of going beyond such guarantees, Levinas and Kierkegaard are in the same uncharted territory and must proceed without the assistance of a definitive map. However, Stolle does find a divergence between the two when it comes to the idea of directionality. They both leave the homeland of moral certainty behind, but the countries into which they are headed are quite different:

> According to Levinas, Avraham's movement out from his moral homeland is indeed a movement toward a new individuality, but not the movement Kierkegaard thinks it is. It is not a movement away from others but toward them; individuality is ethics, ethics qua responsibility to the concrete Other immediately encountered. . . . Here is a different conclusion than the one Kierkegaard draws, even if one not entirely at odds with it. Kierkegaard was right; Avraham transcended the moral order. He went further. But there is reason to believe he went further toward ethical responsibility for the concrete Other. (2001, 140–41)

What I want to highlight is Stolle's passing remark regarding the fact that the Levinasian conclusion he advocates is one that Kierkegaard might not be "entirely at odds with." This is crucial. Even though Stolle argues for a Levinasian interpretation instead of a Kierkegaardian one, he leaves open the possibility that these interpretations might not be *so* disparate after all.

One of the most influential re-readings of *Fear and Trembling* in the past century is surely that of Jacques Derrida in *The Gift of Death*. Derrida's take on the text by "Kierkegaard–de Silentio" is unique due to its tripartite focus on *singularity, responsibility,* and the *sacrifice* implicit in political life (1995, 58). The first two components of Derrida's reading are not unusual, but when read in conjunction with the last, his understanding of them is radically different than one might expect. With respect to singularity, Derrida's focus is on the irrevocable and non-substitutable position that Abraham occupies in relation to God's command.[13] No one can decide for Abraham; his simple phrase, "here I am," makes this clear. As Levinas was fond of remarking, the "here I am" (*me voici*) is the response to alterity that singularizes oneself into a subject—that is, a *sub-jectum,* one who is under the weight of responsibility:

> "Here I am" as a witness of the Infinite, but a witness that does not thematize what it bears witness of, and whose truth is not the truth of representation, is not evidence. There is witness, a unique structure, an exception to the rule of being, irreducible to representation, only of the Infinite. (OTB, 146)[14]

Levinas's words make clear that singularity is unavailable for thematization. It is literally un-translatable. Derrida makes much of this, as it concerns Abraham's silence. The secret that Abraham keeps is not simply a secret because Abraham is good at zipping his lips. Abraham remains silent not because of something *he knows*, but because of something *he is*.[15] *The secret is his very subjectivity.* "He is sworn to secrecy," Derrida notes, "because he is in secret" (1995, 59). Everything about this sentence depends on where one puts the emphasis. Because *he* is in secret: what matters is Abraham as Abraham; as unique, as distinct from all the others, as a singularity. Because he *is* in secret: Abraham is defined by the secret that he keeps; his very subjectivity is the secret; he does not posses a secret, he *is* one— to himself, to Isaac, to Sara, to his servant Eliezer, and to anyone else who might ask him to justify himself. Because he is *in secret:* where Abraham's singularity lies is in secret; he is unique inasmuch as he does not know what his uniqueness entails; he is open to the command but does not understand it. *Because* he is in secret: justification is only available as a pointer to God; Abraham's response is always required but never finished; he is justified inasmuch as he is continually laid bare without recourse to justification: "Here I am" is the response that says everything and nothing—what else could one say when God calls?

For Derrida, there emerges a "contract" that is "both paradoxical and terrifying" which serves to "bind infinite responsibility to silence and secrecy" (1995, 60). Why should responsibility be paradoxical and terrifying? Why would there be "fear and trembling" at the word of God if God's word is what defines me in the first place? For Derrida, the answer has to do with the very structure of discourse. To be responsible to the command, I cannot speak—and yet responsibility is always a *responsibility to* others inasmuch as I must justify myself before them.[16] If I were alone before God, then silence would be a silly idea. Abraham's silence only takes on significance because he is surrounded by the others to whom he "ought" to speak. In my very responsibility, "I don't account for my actions . . . I answer for nothing and to no one . . . I make no response to others or before others. It is both a scandal and a paradox" (Derrida 1995, 60). What should be scandal-free (for it is the place of resolving and accounting for scandal) if not responsibility? Yet, Derrida finds the genius of Kierkegaard's account to be that responsibility itself becomes scandalous. Responsibility is best understood as an *aporia:*

> Responsibility . . . demands on the one hand an accounting, a general answering-for-oneself with respect to the general and before the generality, hence the idea of substitution, and, on the other hand, uniqueness, absolute singularity, hence nonsubstitution, nonrepetition, silence, and secrecy. (1995, 61)

This *aporia* is what Silentio illuminates when he remarks that Abraham's temptation is "the ethical itself" (FT, 60). As either *Sittlichkeit* or *Moralität,* ethics is generality as such. To translate one's responsibility into the general is to negate the secrecy of the command as well as one's own subjectivity. Paradoxically, however, it is precisely such a translation that responsibility seems to demand if it is to indeed be ethical. It is at this point that Derrida makes the most important move of his argument, and with it casts the "spiritual trial" (*Anfægtelse*) of *Fear and Trembling* in an entirely new light. Namely, he sees the *aporia* of responsibility as not being isolated to Abraham's case, but rather as the very structure of responsibility. Derrida reads the *Akedah* not as a consideration of an ethical limit-case, but as a description of ethics as a *political* possibility.

Here he depends heavily upon Levinas's notion of the "third" (*le tiers*). Developed with most precision at the end of *Otherwise Than Being,* Levinas uses the idea of the third to account for how infinite responsibility for the Other can extend over multiple others. That is to say, it is Levinas's attempt to explain the existential reality of intersubjective plurality—or, the relationship between ethics (the constitutive exposure to alterity that singularizes the subject as infinitely responsible) and politics (the domain of institutionalization, of implementation, of codification, and of calculation). Expressed in the phrase *"tout autre est tout autre,"* Derrida takes the Levinasian question to be: "Whom to give to?" On this point, Derrida finds Levinas and Kierkegaard to be in one accord.

According to Derrida, both Kierkegaard and Levinas recognize that political decision necessarily requires ethical sacrifice. To fulfill my responsibility to one person is to fail to fulfill it to another. As Derrida paradoxically notes:

> I must come to hate what I love, in the same moment, at the instant
> of granting death. I must hate and betray my own . . . not insofar as I
> hate them, that would be too easy, but insofar as I love them. I must
> hate them insofar as I love them. (1995, 64)

He gives this theoretical proposition existential bite when he notes that by devoting his time to doing philosophy, he is "sacrificing and betraying at every moment all my other obligations: my obligations . . . to my fellows who are dying of starvation or sickness" (1995, 69).[17] Derrida's conclusion is that Silentio's account of the *Akedah* sets the relation between responsibility and sacrifice in stark relief. I do not need to stand atop Mount Moriah lifting my knife above my son to get the point: at every moment in every situation, I make calculated decisions about how I will live and what I will do with my time. At every moment I am infinitely obligated to each and every other person, but at every moment I am unable to tend to this obligation. In order to be ethical, I must betray ethics and do so without *ultimate* justification. The upshot of the Derridean reading of the *Akedah* is that there is no final certainty. It is here that the main difference emerges between my own rethinking of what might be termed "divine command theory" (though I have expressed my significant reservations regarding such a description) and the account offered by C. Stephen Evans. As I noted in the previous chapter, for Evans the "parallel with Abraham lies in the possibility of a conflict with prevailing moral standards" (2004, 312). On my reading of Kierkegaard, drawing on Derrida and Levinas, the parallel with Abraham lies in his ordeal that illuminates the structural reality concerning the *inherent risk* of translating obligation into action, rather than a mere historical possibility of defying cultural norms.

I must act. Only *I* can decide for me, and no one can relieve me of this necessity. No one else can eliminate or even obviate my singularity.

I *must* act. The necessity of decision is always present and pressing. It is what makes me a self in the first place. As Climacus was fond of saying, existence itself is the moment of decision—"Here I am," before God *and* every other.

I must *act*. My decision is always a political reality. I cannot delay my action, for to do so is simply to continue to be complicit in the world's suffering.

I must act. I must go up to Mount Moriah, and in so doing, I respond to God's call (religion) as an obligation of love for the Other (ethics) in such a way that sacrifice is inevitable (politics). Here we can begin to see the potential relevance for politics that emerges from a specifically Kierkegaardian/Levinasian conception of subjectivity as constituted in the relation to the Other (God in Kierkegaard's case, the other person in Levinas's).

In chapter 5, I will provide a more extended consideration of this conception of subjectivity as the very condition for a just notion of political criticism. Before moving on, however, I want to first articulate some further ways—as adumbrated by Stolle and Derrida—in which Levinas and Kierkegaard are "not entirely at odds" regarding the text of Genesis 22. Building on chapter 2, we can begin to see that Kierkegaard's reading is not so far from the Levinasian alternative above (although there are important differences). Given the centrality of Isaac to Abraham's ordeal, in the next section I will suggest how Levinas's understanding of ethics does not run counter to Kierkegaard's, but rather is in agreement regarding the necessity of going beyond ethics in the name of a constitutive responsibility for the Other that defines a singular ethico-religious subjectivity.

Levinasian Resonances in *Fear and Trembling*

The majority of the classical critiques of *Fear and Trembling* that were considered in the previous chapter stem from the belief that Kierkegaard places the religious sphere *above* the ethical sphere. However, as I have suggested, all that gets transcended by the religious sphere is ethics as a socially recognizable normativity and not as an ontological exposure to the other person that is simultaneously made possible by the relation to God (and yet troubles that very relation). It is important that one not cover over the deep differences between Levinas and Kierkegaard regarding the priority of ethics (the other person) and religion (God): they are certainly at odds in their articulation of which one underlies, grounds, makes possible, opens, establishes, or situates the other. Kierkegaard's account finds the Other in the face of God, as it were, while Levinas finds God in the face of the Other. Nonetheless, I want to suggest that by appreciating the differences between their respective accounts of the *Akedah,* we are able to see the crucial need to keep the question of priority open.[18] God and the Other are co-implicated in the matter of the binding of Isaac. Reading Kierkegaard and Levinas together allows for a constant critical reorientation if one is tempted to forget God in the name of the Other, or to allow the Other to eliminate the need for a relation to God.

Though there are significant dissonant strands in their readings of Genesis 22 that result from their respective religious traditions and philosophical accounts of the sources of obligation, I want to quickly demonstrate how the ethico-religious conception that Kierkegaard advocates in contrast to (Hegelian or Kantian) conceptions of ethics as a universal "teleology of the ethical" is itself illuminated by understanding it in a Levinasian way. As we have already seen, Levinas understands ethics to be a constitutive exposure to the other that yields an unavoidable responsibility, and it is this responsibility that defines my subjectivity as singular. Levinas articulates the basic premise of his philosophy in an interview with Philippe Nemo, saying:

> I speak of responsibility as the essential, primary and fundamental
> structure of subjectivity. For I describe subjectivity in ethical terms.
> Ethics, here, does not supplement a preceding existential base; the
> very node of the subjective is knotted in ethics understood as respon-
> sibility. (EI, 95)

There are four important points of resonance between what I have described as the "ethico-religious" in Kierkegaard's and Levinas's description of "ethics" here. First, the ethical, for Levinas, is neither a matter of universality nor of rationality. The exposure to the other person is what opens the space in which thought and discourse occur. Thus, any specific codification of ethical imperatives is always too late to capture the meaning of ethics as this relation. Levinas argues that because Western philosophy begins with the question of being, all attempts to express the ethical relation in philosophical language run up against the problem of expression. His methodological answer is to integrate Jewish wisdom into revisited Greek philosophical structures. Silentio also recognizes this problem of expression:

For if the ethical—that is, social morality—is the highest and if there is in a person no residual incommensurability in some way such that this incommensurability is not evil . . . then no categories are needed other than what Greek philosophy had or what can be deduced from them by consistent thought. (FT, 55)

Although Kierkegaard and Levinas use language from different religious traditions (i.e., Christianity and Judaism), the same attempt to access the *relationality* that underlies all "Greek" (i.e., ontological) categories is present in both. "Together," Merold Westphal claims, "Kierkegaard and Levinas raise the question whether prominent forms of the postmodern challenge to the Enlightenment project are simply variations of the same theme of excluding radical alterity so as to make philosophy (human reason in its reflective mode) the final arbiter of truth" (1995b, 273). With the critique of Enlightenment rationality there also comes a critique of universally normative ethics. In other words, the relation to alterity stands for both thinkers as a constant critical reminder that any rationalist claim to have captured ethics as such in this or that set of codified laws faces insurmountable obstacles.

The second point of similarity is that the ethico-religious relation cannot be totalized in either Kierkegaard or Levinas. The key here is that for Levinas, as for Kierkegaard, a theory that "adequately explained" this relation would be self-defeating because it would redirect one's attention from where it should rightly be focused. Thus, both authors resort to what could be called a hyperbolic performativity in their writing. I have suggested that, for Kierkegaard, this is made manifest in the way his texts articulate a conception of the ethico-religious that is distinct from any ethics that could be adequately theorized in philosophical speculation. To make this point even stronger, Kierkegaard's repeated use of what he calls "indirect communication" allows the reader to see that what he is trying to express calls for a textured presentation that requires personal investment rather than merely intellectual assent. Though Kierkegaard certainly does not eliminate the need for clear and rigorous argument, he does realize that sometimes more than arguments are needed for personal (i.e., existential) transformation. This is what I take Silentio to be conveying when he remarks, "Abraham cannot speak, because he cannot say that which would explain everything" (FT, 115).

It is my contention that Kierkegaard also "cannot say that which would explain everything" because what he is trying to explain is the relation to God that makes explanation possible—and it is this same explanatory relation (though conceived slightly differently), I believe, that Levinas terms *ethics*. It would seem that religion for Kierkegaard and ethics for Levinas may be alternate expressions for the same notion of *subjectivity as relationally*—and for both of them, thereby *responsibly*—*constituted*. That there are important differences between their conceptions is sure, but in order to even get at these discrepancies properly, we would do well to first take stock of the resonances.

Third, drawing on the final section of chapter 2, we should notice that Levinas also understands ethics as a gift. Of course, the source of the gift is, for Levinas, understood as the other person and not God as such, but interestingly, Levinas does view God as the giver of justice: "'Thanks to God' I am another for the others" (OTB, 158). Again, and this can't be stressed enough, the relation to God is intimately intertwined with the relation to the Other. Levinas goes as far as claiming that since "[c]onsciousness is born as the presence of a third party," we can conclude that: "The act of consciousness would thus be political simultaneousness, but also in reference to God, to a God always subject to repudiation and in permanent danger of turning into a protector of all the egoisms" (OTB, 160–61). It would seem that Levinas is suggesting that God is the very condition of consciousness—or at least political consciousness (although I would contend that there is no difference in this regard for Levinas). Hence, ethics understood as *Sittlichkeit*—i.e., as the space in which political adjudication is possible—could be considered, on a Levinasian model, to be a "divine gift" in a very similar way as I have argued that it should be understood for Kierkegaard.

Fourth and finally, although differing on how to conceive of the Other, Levinas and Kierkegaard also agree on the passivity with which one receives the call to responsibility. For Levinas, the self is understood as being a self only as a response to the call of the Other (read: other person); for Kierkegaard, the self is understood as being a self only as a response to the Other (read: God). That both of these responses *can be* occluded in the realm of everyday existence is certain; but that they *should not be* is also something about which we can be confident. With this *should*, there also comes responsibility and obligation, which in turn give rise to the domain in which ethics *can emerge as Sittlichkeit*. Social morality is only a possibility because humans are the sorts of beings *for whom* existence is, as Climacus writes, the moment of decision. With this assessment, I believe that Levinas would be in complete agreement: existence is defined by the question of whether or not one will politically take up her singular ethico-religious responsibility.

So, Why Kierkegaard in the First Place?

At this point, one could argue that the consequence of my argument thus far is not a renewed engagement between Kierkegaard and Levinas regarding the question of the priority of God or the Other, but simply a reason for ignoring Kierkegaard in favor of Levinas. Surely, a critic might point out that if Kierkegaard's project resonates with Levinas's in the way I have suggested, then the fact that Levinas is able to speak about ethics as the constitutive relation to otherness (and only subsequently make reference to God, whereas Kierkegaard requires God from the beginning) should stand as a reason to abandon Kierkegaard and turn to Levinas alone. Such a turn, this critic might say, could be motivated at least for the sake of simplicity—but also out of good, enlightened (perhaps read: atheistic) taste. Although I am sympathetic to the spirit of this critique, I find it to be misguided in a couple of regards. First, despite the fact that Levinas's thought cannot be adequately interpreted without some incorporation of God (e.g., as the condition of justice), there are some who might advocate an attempt to "read out" discussions of God from his otherwise extremely helpful and original contribution to moral philosophy. "If only Levinas had never mentioned God, everything would have been so much simpler," they might suggest.[19]

Such a view requires *either* that we understand Levinas's own discussions of religion and usage of the term "God" to represent nothing more than his unwillingness to let go of his ethno-historical heritage (which is intimately tied to a religious tradition), *or* that we view religion as functioning for Levinas in a similar way as it does in the thought of Richard Rorty: namely, as nothing more than a certain kind of social hope. Neither of these possibilities is ethically innocuous. In the first case, religion is read out of Levinas at the cost of accusing him of self-absorption—for someone devoted to the status of others, the constant privileging of his own tradition and Jewish heritage would be quite problematic. In the second case, religion is maintained, but at the cost of reducing it to a role that is potentially patronizing to many religious believers (I will return to this possibility in chapter 7)—including those of Levinas's own religious tradition. I am neither suggesting that it is inappropriate to celebrate one's own heritage, nor am I claiming that religion does not yield hope for society. But I am suggesting that by ignoring the religious aspects of Levinas's thought, we actually ignore his personal ethical import—in revising him in this way, we run the risk of either making him selfish or making him patronizing.

Drawing on the similar sorts of critiques leveled against Kierkegaard (that he is irrational, egoistic, etc.), we can now understand that such objections only gain traction when one ignores the "ethical" dimension that is internal to the life of faith and the religious aspect that is inherent in ethics. Accordingly, both thinkers face difficulties in this way *only if* we finally decide in favor of the relation to God over the relation to the other person, or vice versa. On my view, each relation is most effectively conceived in conversation with, engagement with, critique of, expectation of, and invitation to the other relation. Neither can stand in isolation, but already implicates the other—this is the crux of the *ethico-religious* as opposed to the *simply ethical* or *simply religious*.

Rather than being an unnecessarily theological distraction, Kierkegaard has much to offer readers of Levinas. Kierkegaard helps us come to grips with Levinas's own religiosity—while conversely, Levinas helps us understand the intrinsic dynamism of Kierkegaardian ethics by continuously warning us against falling into the trap in which Levinas's own reading of Kierkegaard gets caught. The difference between the two thinkers on this front is that whereas Kierkegaard foregrounds the relation between religion and philosophy, Levinas constantly claims that religion should be kept in the background of ethics considered as "first philosophy." It is not unimportant that while Kierkegaard claimed in *Point of View for My Work as an Author* that his entire authorship (aesthetic and religious) was directed at what it means to "become a Christian," Levinas repeatedly insists that his Talmudic writings are to be kept separate from his philosophical writings (indeed, as he is fond of reminding us, he used different publishers for them).

The decisive privilege Levinas gives to ethics forces religion into an ancillary role; hence he is potentially unable, or unwilling, to see the deep ethicality of religion itself. In contrast, Kierkegaard's particular way of privileging religion (when understood in relation to the *ethico-religious* as I have discussed it) does not relegate ethics to a secondary position, but instead recognizes the essential religiousness of obligation. Kierkegaard understands ethics to be a gift from God not in the sense of classical divine command theory, for which justification would be seemingly assured, but instead in an attempt to demonstrate the inescapability, and yet tenuousness, of responsibility at every moment. *I embrace my responsibility as an expression of gratitude; I express my faith by embracing my responsibility.*

A Thought before Concluding: The Plurality of Kierkegaardian Ethics

Earlier, I showed why most interpreters of Kierkegaard are mistaken to assume that ethics was a static conception that is definable as the general, the universal, or the socially acceptable. It has been my contention that such readings do not adequately take account of the dynamism with which ethics is treated in Kierkegaard's thought. In this chapter, we have observed how this dynamism can be recognized and brought into conversation with Levinasian interpretations of the *Akedah* in order to facilitate a bi-directional relationality between one's responsibility to God and the Other. This intersection perpetually maintains a space of critical engagement with our actions insofar as it never allows us to decide finally in favor of God *or* the Other, but instead encourages an awareness of subjectivity as constituted by a constant tension of responsibility to God *and* the Other. Before concluding this chapter, I want to briefly articulate what I take to be the (at least) three versions of ethics that appear in Kierkegaard in the hope that, when coupled with my re-reading of *Fear and Trembling,* this will help dispel widespread rumors of Kierkegaard's worldlessness, indifference, and violence. Since the following considerations are meant to be preliminary and intended as a supplement to the discussion in chapter 2, they will not be fully worked out here, and are not meant to be. Rather, I offer the following as a provisional context in which to understand the way *Fear and Trembling* fits into Kierkegaard's authorship as a whole. No doubt there is much work yet to be done if we are to adequately re-think Kierkegaardian ethics in light of its proper dynamism; this is meant to be a step in that direction, not a final dash to the finish line.

In *The Concept of Anxiety,* Vigilius Haufniensis distinguishes between "first ethics" and "new ethics" (CA, 20ff.). First ethics, he claims, "was shipwrecked on the sinfulness of the single individual," and hence, "fell into an even greater and ethically more enigmatic difficulty, since the sin of the individual expanded into the sin of the whole race" (CA, 20). In response, the new ethics "presupposes dogmatics, and by means of hereditary sin it explains the sin of the single individual, while at the same time it sets ideality as a task, not by a movement from above and downward but from below and upward" (CA, 20). Dualistic expressions of Kierkegaardian ethics are beginning to be more commonplace. Nearly forty years ago, Gene Outka (1972) deeply marked the Kierkegaardian landscape when he read Kierkegaard's authorship through the understanding of God as love. Moreover, the last decade has seen increased interest in Kierkegaard's later, specifically Christian works and a deeper engagement with what Philip L. Quinn unabashedly terms "Kierkegaard's Christian Ethics" (1998). For example, C. Stephen Evans (2004), M. Jamie Ferreira (2001), and Amy Laura Hall (2002) have all written books that focus on ethics as presented in *Works of Love.*

Although this shift of interest is promising for Kierkegaard scholarship, what I find to be a dark cloud in an otherwise blue sky is the way in which most thinkers continue to take Haufniensis's distinction to be the end of the matter. Recent scholarship seems to have concluded that if Kierkegaard's ethics are not monolithic, they are dual: the ethics of Judge William as distinct from those of Kierkegaard himself (if not Anti-Climacus).[20] I find that this dualistic conception, although a drastic improvement on the static reading that was offered by many in the last century, overlooks two main things: (1) Johannes Climacus's notion of "ethical subjectivity," and (2) the distinction between the Levinasian conception that I have located in *Fear and Trembling* and (although still resonant with Levinas) the specifically "Christian" conception displayed in several texts of the late 1840s. For this reason, I suggest that there are actually (at least) three notions of ethics at work in Kierkegaard:

A. Ethics as Ethical Subjectivity
B. Ethics as Universal Normativity
C. Ethics as Love

And the last sense of ethics can be helpfully split into two forms:

C1. Constitutive relationality
C2. Christian imitation

I will consider each of these in turn and then offer a few words on how the re-reading of *Fear and Trembling* and the re-thinking of Kierkegaardian ethics go a long way toward helping us re-conceive Kierkegaard's political relevance when read in concert with new phenomenology. Upon seeing Kierkegaard anew in this way, I believe that Continental philosophy of religion after the "theological turn" might, by extension, begin to be viewed as not ethico-politically detached, but as a discourse that investigates the possibility of political life for bi-directionally responsible selves.

Ethics A—Ethics as Ethical Subjectivity

Earlier, I suggested that to understand which conception of ethics Kierkegaard is deploying in a given text, it is important to bear in mind his stated or tacit philosophical interlocutor. When it comes to responsible or, as he terms it, "ethical subjectivity," Kierkegaard—here as Climacus—is critically engaging Hegel's conception of subjectivity as an abstraction from life as it is singularly lived. In the *Concluding Unscientific Postscript,* Climacus differentiates between "actual subjectivity" and "ethical subjectivity" but then shows that such a distinction is possible only in theory. Indeed, one's existence is the only space in which one can be theoretically engaged. As Climacus points out, "the only actuality there is for an existing person [is] his own ethical actuality" (CUP, 316). Ethical actuality is understood as an infinite concern for one's own existence, not in a Spinozistic sense, but rather as taking interest in oneself and one's life. Climacus draws our attention to the way in which Hegelian speculative philosophy assumes the posture of a spectator rather than a participant: whereas life is the *object* of Hegel's philosophy, it is the medium *in which* philosophy is possible for Climacus. Hence: "The ethical grips the single individual and requires of him that he abstain from all observing, especially of the world and humankind, because the ethical as the internal cannot be observed by anyone standing outside" (CUP, 320). Ethical subjectivity is the term for one's own investment in one's own existence. This investment is only possible *from within.*[21] Similar to Schleiermacher's comments on the interiority of religious communities, Climacus urges us to stop trying to observe subjectivity from outside and begin living it with the passion of someone who is intimately invested in the task of "becoming a self."

We would do well to consider Climacus's account of ethical subjectivity alongside Heidegger's conception of authenticity (*Eigentlichkeit*). For Heidegger, at least in *Being and Time*, Dasein actualizes itself by taking itself up as its ownmost project. As an expression of care and concern, Dasein breaks with the quotidian thinking of "the They" (*das Man*) by investing itself in its own existence—in its own mortal singularity, if you will. Although Heidegger understands Dasein as always already "being-in-the-world," some scholars have claimed that for Kierkegaard, ethical subjectivity results in a "loss of the world" such that the individual is only concerned with herself to the exclusion of being concerned about others (cf. Mackey 1986, esp. chap. 6). Although I take this to be a genuine worry, Climacus's contention is that when one takes up oneself as an ethical actuality, the world itself becomes a possibility in such a way that the ethical actuality of others should be taken into consideration alongside one's concern for oneself (CUP, 341–42). Of course, there is no way to have the first-person perspective on someone else's ethical subjectivity, and for this reason, the threat of acosmism is always around the corner, as it were, but for Climacus ethical subjectivity is always in relation to ethical intersubjectivity and cannot be rigidly separated from it (see Søltoft 2000).

Ethics B—Ethics as Universal Normativity

Not much is required here. I have already given a lengthy consideration to this form of ethics in the last chapter. Whereas Ethics A is engaged with Hegel's account of abstract subjectivity, Ethics B is engaged with Hegel's account of *Sittlichkeit* (and possibility Kant's notion of practical reason as well). Interestingly, while Ethics A represents a contestation of Hegel, Ethics B represents a summation of him. The reason for this is easily understood in the light of my arguments in the present chapter: if Kierkegaard is trying to overcome ethics as social morality and universal normative codes, then what better way to do so than to give as rigorous an account as possible and then undermine it from within? This is exactly what I have argued he does, through Silentio, in *Fear and Trembling*. The most developed accounts of Ethics B appear in the second volume of *Either/Or*, as a foil in *Fear and Trembling*, and also in *Stages on Life's Way*.

Ethics C—Ethics as Love

A complete account of Ethics C would require writing another book, but what follows will have to suffice for the purposes of this one: Ethics C represents the later, specifically religious work of Kierkegaard from around 1846 on. Appearing in such works as *Works of Love, Practice in Christianity, For Self-Examination,* and *The Gospel of Sufferings,* Ethics C is defined as obedience to the love commandment: "You Shall Love Your Neighbor As Yourself." Understood in this way, Ethics C is antithetical to egoistic self-love and instead, given its specifically religious orientation, inserts God as the middle term between oneself and one's neighbor. Proper love (love without recourse to egoism) is only possible through loving God. Expressed as the inverse of Levinas's notion that loving God is only possible through loving the neighbor, Kierkegaard insists that only by loving God is neighbor-love possible. Therefore, Ethics C is *intrinsically* religious: love is "commanded" by God, and only as such is love emptied of selfish desires.[22] We serve our neighbor because of our love for God and not so that we might receive something in return. What is distinctive about Ethics C is that it displays a positivity that is lacking in Ethics A and B. Ethics C treats not love in the abstract, but *works* of love. What Climacus said of subjectivity regarding the impossibility of abstractly existing, Kierkegaard now says about abstractly loving: only through concrete action is the love commandment obeyed (here is the link, again, between the ethico-religious and politics). Speculation has no real place in Ethics C; only justice serves here. As Anthony Rudd remarks: "A reading of *Works of Love* is enough to refute the claim that [Kierkegaard's] ethic is 'asocial'" (1993, 123). All of these characteristics can be observed in the prayer that opens *Works of Love:*

> How could one speak properly about love if you were forgotten, you God of love, source of all love in heaven and on earth; you who spared nothing but in love gave everything; you who are love, so that one who loves is what he is only by being in you! How could one speak properly about love if you were forgotten, you who revealed what love is, you our Savior and Redeemer, who gave yourself in order to save all. How could one speak properly of love if you were forgotten, you Spirit of Love, who take nothing of your own but remind us of that love-sacrifice, remind the believer to love as he is loved and his neighbor as himself? O Eternal Love, you who are everywhere present and never without witness where you are called upon, be not without witness in what will be said here about love or about works of love. There are indeed only some works that human language specifically and narrowly calls works of love, but in heaven no work can be pleasing unless it is a work of love: sincere in self-renunciation, a need in love itself, and for that very reason without any claim of meritoriousness! (WL, 3–4)

There are four main points that I want to highlight regarding this prayer:

1) Notice that, for Kierkegaard, theocentric otherness is the "source" of love in the social relation. Because of God's love, there is the possibility of intersubjective love. Unless God sacrificed for humanity, humanity would be unable to love without reinscribing the relation to others as an extension of self-love.

2) Following from this is the connection between love and sacrifice.[23] There is no way of conceiving God's love for humanity without grasping the sacrificial relationship to humanity— "For God gave His only begotten Son" (John 3: 16). Love is the gift of transcendence to immanence such that it transforms the horizon of immanent relations by introducing the consciousness of sin as failure in relation to God's kenotic expression of grace (there will be substantially more on this in chapter 8).

3) The gift of God is neither a "thing" nor an "object" of any kind: it is the gift of the God-relation itself. God gives Godself and in doing so God gives the other person. In the biblical instruction regarding the imitation of Christ, we find the meaning of love as a giving of oneself—to borrow from Levinas, we must "substitute" for the Other, give ourselves *for her.* Thus, love is a gift to the Other of our own self-renunciation. However, this self-renunciation is the "source" of a genuine relation between oneself and the Other. For Kierkegaard, this should be read in light of Philippians 1: 21: "To live is Christ, and to die is gain." For Kierkegaard, Christ's death is a necessary moment in the actualization of Christ's redemptive resurrection (which, in turn, makes possible *true* life for all who would enter a relation with God). Without sacrifice there is no love; without sacrificial death there is no life. According to Ethics C, unless one loves God one cannot love the Other. Of course, the question that remains, especially for a Levinasian, is whether one can love God without loving the Other.

4) However—and this is perhaps the most salient aspect of Ethics C—love contains no reciprocity! I do not give and then require a gift in return. God does not give so that we will give back. God gives *out of love* and thereby establishes the possibility of our giving to God and other persons *in a similar fashion.* As Kierkegaard makes clear, when an action is impelled by "love itself," it does not in any way seek "compensation." Could we say that God is the condition of an economy of exchange *without* reci-

procity? Isn't the divine sacrifice exactly a gift that demands it be "paid forward"—namely, toward the Other? In Ethics C, we live toward the other person in love because of an understanding of God's having "first loved us" (1 John 4: 19).

There is one further point to be made regarding Ethics C. I have already indicated the way in which Ethics C is intrinsically religious, but although this has specifically Christian overtones for Kierkegaard, it does not require such Christian specifics for us (well, at least not initially). That is, the love commandment can be read as inscribed in the nature of existence—as is the case for Levinas and Derrida. In this way, let me suggest that Ethics C should actually be sub-divided into Ethics C1 and Ethics C2. Ethics C1 is best understood as the kind of ethico-religious understanding that stands in contrast to the notion of Ethics B in *Fear and Trembling*. Although that text does present the tension between ethics and religion as perpetual, it does not require affirming a particular Christian creed or adhering to a sanctioned, orthodox doctrine. All that is required is an awareness of the constitutive obligation to alterity that is inaugurated by and through the relation to God. Ethics C2, on the other hand, is determinately Christian and not only includes creedal and doctrinal commitments, but is defined in relation to a transcendent God as the source of love, and more specifically to the person of Christ as an incarnational exemplar. Ethics C2 is best understood as *imitatio Christi*. Here is where *Practice in Christianity* and *For Self-Examination* become relevant as not only religious but ethical, and, I believe, political texts.

My distinction between Ethics C1 and Ethics C2 is heavily dependent on Merold Westphal's notion of "Religiousness C," which he claims should be added to Climacus's distinction between "Religiousness A and B." Ethics C2 should be read as the ethical counterpart to Religiousness C, which Westphal defines as follows:

> For Religiousness C Christ is not merely the Paradox to be believed but the Pattern to be imitated. . . . For Religiousness C it is not the bare facticity of the life of Jesus that is most important. Rather, the specific content of that life as a threat to the established order is what matters. By challenging the hierarchical structure of that order Jesus guarantees the opposition of the powers that be. (1992a, 116–17)

Here we see Westphal's contention that Religiousness C is intrinsically linked to political critique (which, in the context of Kierkegaard's nineteenth-century Denmark, can be rightly understood to be primarily a critique of the established Protestant church). When Westphal speaks of the political import of Religiousness C, he focuses on the way in which Kierkegaard directed his last religious writings toward an open "attack on Christendom." While I am in complete agreement with

Westphal on this point, I want to slightly alter his focus such that Ethics C would be directed at far more than the established churches—all that remains of the old Christendom, especially represented for Kierkegaard by the teachings of Jakob Mynster and Hans Martenson—and toward *all established political institutions*. In comparison to Ethics A and B, which were both responses to Hegelian thought, both forms of Ethics C challenge the instantiation of political conceptions as *finished and complete*. Religiousness C is able to critique Christendom because, as guided by the imitation of Christ, the church should never be finished, but always moving closer to Christ's example of how to live. However, what it means to live as Christ is often linked to what it means to suffer and, as we will see in the cases of Dietrich Bonhoeffer and the Ten Boom sisters in chapter 13, to die for the truth of Christ. Ethics C2 is the ethico-political complement to this radical faith. It demonstrates that not only the life of faith, but the life of service, when undertaken faithfully, requires some sort of sacrifice.

Both Religiousness C in Westphal and Ethics C2 here are guided by the life of Christ, but the former is focused on how to be a witness to the church, while the latter is focused on how to be a witness to society. And importantly, when considered in Kierkegaard's cultural context, these forms of witness were not as disparate as they might be taken to be now. It should be noted that it may turn out that the positive conception of ethics offered by Ethics C1 and C2 might turn out to yield the same sort of life—that is, someone who attempts to live according to C1 will live in a very similar manner, I believe, as someone who attempts to live according to C2, if both are taken as ideal cases. However, as Kierkegaard's whole corpus was intended to illustrate, life is *not* ideal and the messiness of human existence is never eradicated (nor should we want it to be). This is why I find Ethics C2 to be of great importance not only for Kierkegaardian scholarship, but for moral philosophy and political theory. Seeking to imitate Christ as the prototype and paradigm of human existence, Ethics C2 is potentially instructive in a way that Ethics C1 is not.

Though I have reservations about considering Christ as an ethico-political exemplar (see chapters 8 and 13), Christ can offer to ethics a historical embodiment of holiness in practice, rather than merely a contribution to theoretical speculation about the Good. Now, in no way does this indicate that Ethics C2 can itself easily be translated into a codified and stable moral code. Rather, Christ's life offers an example of how to live according to the principles of humility and invitation that characterize God's love for the world. This does not mean that we wear bracelets embossed with "WWJD" and conceive of the Bible as a manual to be consulted when we just can't figure out how to act.[24] It may turn out that we find the specifics lacking when we look to the life of Christ in order to figure out whether to do this or that. Ethics C2 may still lack the foundational guarantee that we desire for our ethical lives, but what it does offer that C1 does not is the possibility that when we walk the lonely road of ethics, we do not have to walk it completely alone. Ultimately, I find C1 and C2 to be manifestations of the same ethico-religious understanding of constitutively responsible subjectivity, but along with Kierkegaard, I want to continue to call our attention to the example set by Christ as a paradigm of taking up one's constitutive obligation to God and others.

Despite the fact that there are implications yet to be worked through, given these various conceptions of the ethical in Kierkegaard, what should be clear is that a static or even dualistic conception simply will not do. If we are to see the relevance of a Kierkegaardian-Levinasian perspective for contemporary political life, and thus adequately respond to the Rortian critique that such approaches are "gawky, awkward, and unenlightening"—and, to be honest, of no use in the "real" world—then appreciating the dynamism of Kierkegaardian ethics is crucial.

Conclusion: Anticipating Ethico-political Futures

Allow me to conclude with some remarks that anticipate issues I will consider later in the book, by outlining a few ways in which the reading of *Fear and Trembling* I have put forward is relevant for contemporary moral philosophy and political theory. The crucial relationship between Levinas and Kierkegaard is that they advocate a sustained critique of those theories of ethics that cover over the initial relatedness to alterity. Any ethics that starts with an autonomous subject rather than a subjectivity that is always already engaged is itself reducible to a kind of unethical egoism. For Levinas and Kierkegaard, subjectivity amounts to a constitutive relation to alterity (i.e., responsibility is the condition for freedom, and not vice versa). The consequence of their resonance on this point is that both thinkers offer a vision for ethico-political theory that centers on a rigorous conception of criticism in the name of singularity. Since the ethico-religious relation that they describe cannot be totalized, no specific political formulation could encapsulate it. Thus, the result is a constant process of revision that never allows any particular instantiation or codification to rest assured in its universality.

The singular is always the excess that makes claims to universality tremble in their finitude. However, it is an open question whether the ethico-religious relation is able to do any positive work on its own. It appears to be clearly *proscriptive*, but it is not so clear whether it is *prescriptive*. This is especially the case for Levinas, who will express the first word of the Other to be, simply, "Don't kill me." This proscriptivity might find a prescriptive counterpart in Kierkegaard's proposal of the centrality of the love commandment. However, though Kierkegaard will understand the positive moment of the ethico-religious relation to be inaugurated by the command "You shall love your neighbor as yourself," nowhere in *Works of Love* (or elsewhere) does he give a codification of what one should do in particular situations. Rather, he dialectically spirals in the complexity of the command itself as corrosive to any account of subjectivity that does not recognize responsibility to God *and* the Other as constitutive of selfhood. As David Stern writes: "God is both the figure and the name of the absolute, singular other to whom I am obligated to respond; but every decision to respond involves a sacrifice of Isaac, and of all others" (2003, 40). The tripartite structure of relationality (Self, Other, God) is more than a simple explication of a troubling scriptural story. Rather, Genesis 22, when interpreted by Levinas *and* by Silentio, describes the conditions for the possibility of authentic subjectivity—a subjectivity poured out to the other person in the name of God, and constantly moving toward God by loving the Other in her singularity. In the next chapter we will further explore this notion of subjectivity by seeing how Kierkegaard's notion of "transparency" and Levinas's conception of "exposure" can be read as different articulations of the same ethico-religious ontological trajectory.

FOUR

An Ontology of Constitutive Responsibility: Kierkegaardian "Transparency" and Levinasian "Exposure"

The Ontological Stakes of Politics

In *Rethinking Democracy*, Carol Gould claims that "every social and political theory presupposes, whether explicitly or tacitly, an ontology, that is, a conception of the nature of the entities and relations that constitute social life" (1988, 91). In this passage, Gould rightly recognizes that the stakes of politics are ontological. To assume, as so many do in the wake of quite particular readings of such thinkers as Žižek (2006), Agamben (2005), and Hardt and Negri (2000), that the political goes all the way down, as it were, is to miss the profoundly ethical, or ethico-religious, dimensions of the political itself. As I suggested regarding Rorty in chapter 1, when the political is all-encompassing and is then plausibly understood as a network of sheer power play, it becomes impossible to make sense of what *better* or *worse* play could mean except as another dimension of power itself. I contend that if the "religious" gestures of new phenomenology are going to be of use in political philosophy, then it is due to the way in which such gestures allow for an ontological narrative that is more robust than those which currently underlie competing accounts of sociality.[1]

In agreement with Gould's comment, then, I find that the accounts of ethics in Levinas and Kierkegaard are not politically irrelevant because they involve discussions dealing with a constitutive relation to alterity, as Rorty might contend, but instead that they are dramatically relevant to the political precisely due to them. Levinas and Kierkegaard should jointly be read as not only providing a theory of normativity (viz., I ought to do and not to do certain things because of my relationship to God/Other, etc.), but more importantly as offering an ontology (viz., an account of selfhood itself as fundamentally responsible). This *ontology of constitutive responsibility*, as I will refer to it, is not a traditional ontology—where a priority is given to freedom over responsibility, and self-presence defines the ego—but is instead the narrative of subjectivity that stands behind (or within) the idea of "ethics as first philosophy."[2] For Levinas and Kierkegaard, ethical and political relationships are not to be primarily considered according to a particular notion of *what we value*, but instead as a matter of *who we are* such that valuation is even a possibility in the first place.

In the two preceding chapters, I argued that Kierkegaard does not hold to a static conception of ethics, but instead advocates a dynamic notion of responsibility and obligation that is shaped by the particular sphere of human existence in which an individual finds herself. I suggested that *Fear and Trembling* presents an ethico-religious vision of constitutive obligation to the other person such that an essential responsibility defines the very subjectivity of the self. In this chapter, building on my reading of *Fear and Trembling*, I will consider Kierkegaard's notion of "transparency" as it is developed by Anti-Climacus in *The Sickness Unto Death* and argue that this notion is strikingly similar to the idea of "exposure" that runs throughout Levinas's authorship. These specific ideas, I will argue, highlight the way in which both thinkers offer an ontology of constitutive responsibility as the backbone, or perhaps, the very *condition,* of any political critique offered in the name of justice. In what follows, I will work through these respective notions in Kierkegaard and Levinas, and in the next chapter I will show how the ontology that underlies them serves to inaugurate the political project of *recursive hermeneutics.*

Kierkegaardian Transparency

The opening paragraph of *The Sickness Unto Death* is perhaps one of the most challenging in all of Western philosophy.[3] Within this short passage, Anti-Climacus does all of the following: defines what it is to be a "human being," defines what it is to be "spirit," articulates the essential relationality of subjectivity, and concludes by undercutting everything he has just said by claiming that none of it succeeds in answering the question of how a human being is a self.

> A human being is spirit. But what is spirit? Spirit is the self. But what is the self? The self is a relation that relates itself to itself or is the relation's relating itself to itself in the relation; the self is not the relation but is the relation's relating itself to itself. A human being is a synthesis of the infinite and the finite, of the temporal and the eternal, of freedom and necessity, in short a synthesis. A synthesis is a relation between two. Considered in this way, a human being is still not a self. (SUD, 13)

The tone of this passage is essentially Hegelian. Anti-Climacus uses the language of synthesis, which is reminiscent of Hegel's dialectical logic, and speaks of a relation that relates itself to itself, which, for Hegel, would be a way of expressing the self-actualization of *Geist.* However, in the last sentence, there emerges a slight divergence from the Hegelian formulation when Anti-Climacus claims that a "relation between two" is inadequate to bring about the actual selfhood of a human being in the proper way: this should be read as a critique of the fundamentally Hegelian method of definition through negation. To put this in the language of Hegel's logic, Anti-Climacus suggests that the *in-itself* and the *for-itself* are never, of themselves, adequate to establish the *in-and-for-itself*. The synthesis between thesis and antithesis is, for Anti-Climacus, best understood as a repetition of the original polarity.

To get beyond this repetition of negativity, Anti-Climacus goes on to announce that what is required is a "third" aspect of the relation that defines selfhood:

> In the relation between two, the relation is the third as a negative unity, and the two relate to the relation and in the relation to the relation; thus under the qualification of the psychical the relation between the psychical and the physical is a relation. If, however, the relation relates itself to itself, this relation is the positive third, and this is the self. (SUD, 13)

Here we see that the emergence of a "positive third" is required for breaking the cycle of immanence and totalization—for these are simply two sides of the same Hegelian coin. Importantly, however, such an accounting of the self as is offered by Anti-Climacus does not seem to describe the relation that is constitutive of self-hood as anything other than a relation *to* oneself. That is, it would appear that such an understanding serves to contest the reading of *Fear and Trembling* that I put forward earlier, inasmuch as this definition seems to exclude any relation to alterity by reducing it to a mere aspect of the existing self and not the inaugural relation that defines self. Surely, if this is what Anti-Climacus is suggesting, then Levinas was right to conclude in *Proper Names* that, for Kierkegaard, the self is best understood as a "tensing on oneself" (*tension sur soi*).[4] Where is the Other in such a self-related relationship? Isn't this just an extreme form of subjectivity as self-centering and ontology as egoism?

If Anti-Climacus were to conclude his comments here, then the charge of self-centeredness would perhaps be warranted. However, he continues on to announce that "such a relation that relates itself to itself, a self, must either have established itself or have been established by another" (SUD, 13). This is the first mention of otherness in the Anti-Climacian ontological narrative of self-constitution; but it is certainly not the last. Indeed, Anti-Climacus proceeds to essentially link this question of establishment to the question of a constitutive relation to alterity. "If the relation that relates itself to itself has been established by another," he writes, "then the relation is indeed the third, but this relation, the third, is yet again a relation and relates itself to that which established the entire relation" (SUD, 13). With this complicated claim, Anti-Climacus contests any conception of self-presence as the definitive trait of subjectivity. Moreover, he challenges the Hegelian notion that there could be some sort of *telos* to such a constitutive relationality. The self is fundamentally traumatic unto itself; it is unable to secure itself within itself because the self is ruptured by a relation beyond itself. Or, as Anti-Climacus will conclude: "The human self is such a derived, established relation, a relation that relates itself to itself and in relating itself to itself relates itself to another" (SUD, 13–14).

This last sentence expresses the constitutive relation to alterity that also characterizes Johannes de Silentio's notion of subjectivity in *Fear and Trembling*. There is no interiority that is essentially closed off in such a way as to allow a self to be shut up in itself. In the deepest recesses of subjective interiority, we find, as Levinas would say, that we are already disturbed by the Other. Up to this point in *The Sickness Unto Death,* this disturbance is not in any way *ethical,* however. The self that is in a relation to itself such that it is related always already to another, is not said to be *responsible* for/to that other, but merely in a relationship with it (or him, or her—which pronoun to use is very much an open question). Although we will shortly see how this relation is in fact rightly thought of as ethico-religious, what matters here is that the ontological narrative being offered is one that contests any notion of ontology as primarily about a self-enclosed and self-sufficient subject. Interiority is not, for Anti-Climacus or Silentio or Kierkegaard, a protected inviolable space that reflects the essential freedom of the subject. Rather, it is best understood as traumatic, as ruptured, as inalterably opened to alterity. But wouldn't an "open interiority" be simply a contradiction? Such a contradiction would arise only if we conceive of the self as originally situated *unto itself* rather than *unto the Other.* Following Anti-Climacus, we can see that by denying the isolated status of the Cartesian *cogito,* the transcendental status of the Kantian self, the absolutism of the Fichtean ego, and the freedom and supposed neutrality of the liberal subject described by Locke, Rousseau, and even Rawls, we do not necessarily move beyond the sphere of ontology, but merely contest that such a sphere need be egoistic (and onto-theo-logical). Yet what if ontology were *already* ethically invested? Wouldn't this allow for ethics to be *prima philosophia,* and yet still communicable as a story about subjectivity?

Anti-Climacus moves toward the ethical, or ethico-religious, component of such a radicalized ontology by differentiating between the three forms of despair that are intrinsic to human existence. The first, "not willing to be oneself," is possible, he says, without the "positive third" that emerges with heterogeneous establishment (SUD, 14). This form of despair is rooted in an ironic, or more precisely, comic relation of oneself to oneself. To "will to do away with oneself" is described by Anti-Climacus as being a form of "weakness" (*Svaghed*) (SUD, 49ff.). The self must view itself with a certain sort of fantasy or illusion in order to suppress the ironic fact that it is only by having a self that such willing to do away with oneself is a possibility. In essence, such willing forgets the relation that defines it. The self who wills not to be a self is a self that lacks all interiority: it is solely defined by the physical rather than what Anti-Climacus terms the spiritual. Defined by an exteriority that lacks all relation to interiority instead of a relationship to exteriority that marks the very establishment of interiority, *weakness* is characteristic of this type of despair because it is always an expression of "immediacy." The self has deluded itself into believing that it is identical to its sensible manifestations. "The man of immediacy" Anti-Climacus proclaims, "does not know himself, he quite literally identifies himself only by the clothes he wears, he identifies having a self by externalities," which is always "infinitely comical" for those he encounters (SUD, 53). Anti-Climacus illustrates this nicely with the following parable:

> There is a story about a peasant who went barefooted to town with enough money to buy himself a pair of stockings and shoes and to get drunk, and in trying to find his way home in his drunken state, he fell asleep in the middle of the road. A carriage came along, and the driver shouted to him to move or he would drive over his legs. The drunken peasant woke up, looked at his legs and, not recognizing them because of the shoes and stockings, said: "Go ahead, they are not my legs." (SUD, 53)

Here we see that not willing to be oneself leads to tragic, or perhaps darkly comic, outcomes. This form of despair does not require that the self is established by another. Rather, the self has its being entirely within the domain of self-immediacy and, thereby, perpetually undermines itself as the self continues to forget that only by being a self is there a self to deny.

The second form of despair, "willing to be oneself," requires the self's being established by another because it presupposes that, in itself, the self is not identical to itself. This conception of despair is "the expression for the inability of the self to arrive at or to be in equilibrium and rest by itself, but only, in relating itself to itself, by relating itself to that which has established the entire relation" (SUD, 14). I can only will to be myself if I originally am not myself in some way. To borrow from Heidegger, we might say here that authenticity is only a possibility because of a pre-original "thrownness" (*Geworfenheit*) that defines the self as the sort of being for whom authenticity is a possibility. I am a stranger to myself and only as such can I will to get to know myself better.

Whereas the first form of despair was an expression of *weakness*, this second form is an expression of *defiance (Trods)* (SUD, 67ff.). Defiance characterizes this despair because unlike the immediacy of willing not to be oneself—which amounts to a retreat from its own condition—willing to be oneself recognizes the heteronomous relation that defines it, and then disavows that relation. This self is not trapped in immediacy and finitude, but instead despairs "through the aid of the eternal." Eternity is now incorporated into the constitutive synthesis of selfhood, and thus grants the spirituality of the self. So "in a certain sense it is very close to the truth," Anti-Climacus admits (SUD, 67). Yet, he continues, "it is [also] infinitely far away" (SUD, 67). Simultaneously near and far, the self who wills to be itself makes the mistake of thinking that action is what is required for gaining oneself. Although the self displays courage, "it is unwilling to begin with losing itself but wills to be itself" (SUD, 67). Instead of admitting that trauma defines subjectivity, the self who wills to be itself enacts a revolution against the very Other that established it. In the first form of despair, the rejection of otherness is due to a somewhat passive occlusion; in the second, it is a product of active resistance. Just as with the first type, Anti-Climacus offers a parable that crystallizes this distinction. "Figuratively speaking," he says regarding the second type of despair, it is

> as if an error slipped into an author's writing and the error became conscious of itself as an error—perhaps it actually was not a mistake but in a much higher sense an essential part of the whole production—and now this error wants to mutiny against the author, out of hatred toward him, forbidding him to correct it and in maniacal defiance saying to him: No, I refuse to be erased; I will stand as a witness against you, a witness that you are a second-rate author. (SUD, 74)

With the third type of despair we arrive at the possibility of understanding the ontology articulated by Anti-Climacus as an expression of the call to responsibility. The third form of despair is, in a word, *sin* (SUD, 77ff.). Anti-Climacus goes on to say that sin is *"before God, or with the conception of God, in despair not to will to be oneself, or in despair to will to be oneself."* Thus, he continues, "sin is intensified weakness or intensified defiance: sin is the intensification of despair" (SUD, 77). In an intimately Lutheran stance, this definition of sin depends upon the status of the self as "before God" (*for Gud*). *Before God* can be read in several ways. It can mean in the light of God, as in the statement, "I am acting in the light of God's commandments." This understanding would primarily reflect a certain kind of conscience and acting out of a certain kind of recognition. So, thinking *in the light of* Heidegger would be to think in his wake and with a degree of indebtedness to him for having opened the space in which one continues thinking. Additionally, *before God* can refer to the directionality of our actions and thoughts such that we *stand before by moving toward*. On this interpretation, we might say that our existence is defined by the horizonality of God's presence. Moreover, we could say that *before God* is meant to convey a call that defines our existence. I stand *before God* to the extent that I relate to my existence in a specific sort of way. Further, it could indicate more than just a way of taking up one's existence, and extend to the condition for existence in the first place. On this account, standing *before God* is a universal structure that gives content to the idea that I did not establish the relation that defines me as a self. In this sense, it is fundamentally a recognition of dependence.

I find that all of these possible interpretations of "before God" are in play in Anti-Climacus's use of the phrase. At various times, Anti-Climacus will say that God is the "criterion" (*Maalestok*) against which everything is measured, the "goal" (*Maal*) toward which we ethically strive, and also that "the greater conception of God, the more self there is; the more self, the greater the conception of God" (SUD, 79–80). One's conception of God is intrinsically connected to the conception one has of oneself. And this is why standing before God intensifies despair: we move beyond the idea that despair is a claim about our own status by realizing that our own status is never adequately our own. The relation to God is what transforms the self from being "merely human" to being "the theological self" (SUD, 79). The human self in both of its forms essentially tries to gain itself by itself. The theological self realizes that the only way to take up one's life is to realize that it is not one's own. To will not to be oneself or to will to be oneself while standing before God would be to sin against the very power that established the self in the first place. However, to evacuate the stability of one's own subjectivity and yet will to be oneself or will not to be oneself is really to stand before God and fail to respond to the demand that such a position requires. To stand before God, and this is the crucial point, is to *respond* to God's call. What would such a response look like? As we already learned from Silentio's consideration of Abraham, the answer is *faith*.

"The opposite to being in despair," Anti-Climacus concludes, "is to have faith" (SUD, 49). What is faith? "Faith is: that the self in being itself and in willing to be itself rests transparently [*gjennemsigtigt grunder*] in God" (SUD, 82). And again: "The formula that describes the state of the self when despair is completely rooted out is this: in relating itself to itself and in willing to be itself, the self rests transparently in the power that established it" (*Dette er nemlig Formelen, som beskriver Selvets Tilstand, naar Fortvivlelsen ganske er udryddet: i at forholde sig til sig selv, og i at ville være sig selv grunder Selvet gjennemsigtigt i den Magt, som satte det*) (SUD, 14).[5] Here the term which I find to be crucial for understanding Kierkegaard's ontology in its ethical overtone, "transparency" (*gjennemsigtighed*), is deployed and enters our discussion. Notice that there is a play in the original of the passage I have just cited. The Danish term used for "rests" is *grunder*, which can also mean "to found or establish." The term used for "establish" is *satte*, which is another form of *sætte*, and means "to set, to put, or to place." We can thus read this passage as follows: "the self is *established/grounded* transparently in the power that set it up." On both of these readings, the *resting* of the self is very much tied to the *founding* of the self as such. When read this way, it becomes untenable to view the self's "willing to be itself" as *only* being a conscious activity. And I say "only" here intentionally: for Kierkegaard all of human existence is, as Johannes Climacus will say, "the moment of decision." It would be wrong to simply *equate* "transparency" in Kierkegaard to "exposure" in Levinas, because for Kierkegaard the notion of transparency is both the *condition* of selfhood and also an *achievement* by a self who makes the movement of faith.[6] That such a decision constantly confronts every individual presupposes that when it is considered ontologically (as opposed to existentially or even politically), standing transparently is not really a *willing*—as is the case for all the forms of despair—but instead is a *letting-go*. We rest transparently when we grasp the futility of trying to avoid or overcome the relationship to alterity that is constitutive of subjectivity. Here it seems that we have run into the same problem with which we started. Doesn't my use of the term "grasp" betray the link between subjectivity and consciousness? Wouldn't this still articulate ontology in terms of comprehension? Don't I *understand, conceive, know* that I stand before God? Such an interpretation is unsustainable when we realize that resting transparently before the power that established the self is precisely the definition of *faith* and not some sort of ordinary *knowledge* (which we already saw to be an important distinction for maintaining the struggle that is central to Abraham's "ordeal").

If there is one theme that runs throughout Kierkegaard's authorship it is the idea that faith is not to be defined in terms of knowledge. Rather, as Johannes Climacus repeatedly notes, faith is essentially a risk. To stand in faith is not to have an objective knowledge about an object, but to subjectively define oneself in relation to that which could only be held subjectively (i.e., with passion). Faith is not simply "weak knowledge," but rather operates according to an entirely different criterion than does knowledge. Proof does not remain any longer a lingering possibility to be sought—as if we only had to find enough evidence to convert faith into knowledge! Faith is fundamentally a positioning of oneself on a different basis than the certainty of knowledge and strong foundational accounts of rationality. Instead, it is a being grounded on the paradox—which is not to be confused with the shifting sands Jesus warns of in the Sermon on the Mount (see Matthew 7). This paradox is precisely the existence of the eternal in time. The interesting point here is that the faith relation is thus a relation to the very synthesis that defines the self as a spirit. We can now see that the "power" that established the self as a "relation that relates itself to itself," is also "spirit" and a "self" in that it is also a synthesis of the infinite and the finite as actualized in the person of Christ. With the idea of resting transparently, Anti-Climacus has brought us from an ontological claim about what it means to be a self, to an ethico-religious claim about the fact that there is no selfhood outside of a relation to God, and back again to a claim about the essentially ethico-religious aspect of all ontology. It is in the light of this progression that we can understand what Anti-Climacus means when he writes that having a self is "eternity's claim" upon us (SUD, 21). Selfhood is defined as an infinite task. And yet, this task is not something to be completed through my active labor, but through my passive release. Only by losing myself can I find myself. Only through letting go of the attempt to establish myself by myself, am I established as a self *before God*.

Standing before God has a dual status: it is both the *task* and the *goal* of selfhood. Only by being constituted by another (by alterity) can I be someone for whom faith is a possibility; only by having faith can I be someone for whom selfhood is actualized. Crucially, the task is never finished and the goal never reached, as long as there is the supposition that it is up to me. Standing "before God" is both the condition and fulfillment of subjectivity.

What, then, *is* transparency? And *to whom* am I transparent? There are three possibilities here: (1) I am transparent to myself, (2) I am transparent to the Other (in this case, God), or (3) both 1 and 2. I want to suggest that the third option is the most accurate interpretation of the notion in Kierkegaard. When I am transparent to myself it means that I am not troubled by irony, as is the aesthete. I literally have sight-through (*sigte/gennem*) myself, such that I am able to see the lack of any space that is closed off within me where I stand alone *unto* myself. I am denuded and exposed. I stand without pretense because I do not return to myself, but always go toward the Other who established me. This Other is also the one *to whom* I am transparent. The Other sees through me in such a way as to hold me in its gaze. There is no possibility of avoidance. There is no chance of escape. I am held fast by this power in that there is nowhere I can hide *within* myself—I am transparent. Attempting to hide from the very condition of our visibility is similar to Adam and Eve, when they "realized they were naked" and then tried to hide from God among the trees of the garden (Genesis 3: 7–9 (NIV)). Simply put, such an attempt is futile. Anti-Climacus's account suggests that we respond, rather, as did Peter when Jesus asked him if he wanted to leave Jesus' company. Peter simply replies: "Lord, to whom shall we go? You have the words of eternal life" (John 6: 68 (NIV)). The point is this: transparency is the term that captures the idea that the self never recurs as a totality unto itself. What it means to be a self is to be constitutively related to the Other from whom I cannot leave—and even if I could, where would I go? Only in relation to God is selfhood a possibility, and only then am I able to overcome despair. Anti-Climacus summarizes this aptly:

> Every human existence that is not conscious of itself as spirit or conscious of itself before God as spirit, every human existence that does not rest transparently in God but vaguely rests in and merges in some abstract universality (state, nation, etc.) or, in the dark about his self,

regards his capacities merely as powers to produce without becoming deeply aware of their source, regards his self, if it is to have intrinsic meaning, as an indefinable something—every such existence, whatever it achieves, be it most amazing, whatever it explains, be it the whole of existence, however intensively it enjoys life esthetically—every such existence is nevertheless despair. (SUD, 46)[7]

Earlier I claimed that this ontology is rightly considered "ethical" or, better, "ethico-religious." We can now see how this is the case for Kierkegaard. Anti-Climacus announces that

the person sitting in a showcase is not as embarrassed as every human being is in his transparency before God. This is the relationship of conscience. The arrangement is such that through the conscience the report promptly follows each guilt, and the guilty one himself must write it. (SUD, 124)

Transparency is presented here as intimately related to conscience and guilt: to stand transparently is to stand as one who is guilty. And thus, to stand transparently before God is to stand as before a judge. This is a claim that runs throughout Kierkegaard's authorship (in both the pseudonymous and signed works). For example, at the conclusion of the second volume of *Either/Or*, Judge William recounts a letter from a Jutland priest titled "The Edifying in the Thought that Against God We Are Always in the Wrong," and a year later, in 1844, Kierkegaard published an *Upbuilding Discourse* titled "To Need God Is a Human Being's Highest Perfection." In both of these texts we find it expressed that guilt is not something that reflects poor historical decisions which can be discharged through just actions. Guilt is something that defines human reality: to exist is to stand accused without recourse.

Does this mean that we should throw up our hands in frustration and turn away in quietist resignation? Absolutely not. Guilt need not produce inaction, but should spurn us to act in the light of the fact that no matter what we do, we will not have done enough, said enough, cared enough, or loved enough to finally justify ourselves before God. Here is where my reading of *Fear and Trembling* becomes relevant: the ethico-religious is not primarily about *something that I do*, but about a *responsibility that defines who I am*. In my relation to God, I am ordered to other people. The word of God that constitutes human subjectivity is: "Love your neighbor as yourself." I stand guilty before God as always under accusation for not having adequately fulfilled this command. The key is to realize that it cannot be fulfilled through *my* powers and *my* efforts. Only by "resting transparently" can

I genuinely take up the command to love. As I have argued in previous chapters, the highest conception of ethics (what I termed C2) in Kierkegaard is best understood as *a gift*, and the appropriate response is always *gratitude for our obligation itself.* This is why the thought that I am always in the wrong before God is *edifying;* this is why I am *upbuilt* by the thought that I am made perfect only by evacuating myself of egoistic suppositions. Simply put, *transparency is a mode of ethico-religious response* to the call that constitutes the self in its singularity. The power that establishes me is also that which is called the *source* of ethics in *Works of Love* (WL, 8ff.). For Kierkegaard, to relate to God is, at least in part, to be responsible to God for the other person. Hence, merely terming this ontological conception "religious" would miss the key tension that defines and animates the life of faith. Ontology is always a story about constitutive responsibility and as such we arrive at an ethico-religious conception of the self as fundamentally exposed and obligated to both God and the Other.[8]

Having worked through Kierkegaard's notion of ontology as found primarily in the conception of "transparency" in the work of Anti-Climacus, I will now turn to Levinas's idea of "exposure" in order to demonstrate the resonance between these ideas. As I hope will become clear, although Levinas and Kierkegaard disagree on the priority that exists in the self's relation to God and the Other, they share a conception of ontology as essentially ruptured by the encounter with alterity—an encounter that inaugurates responsibility. This shared vision of bi-directional relationality that occurs in the tension between the relation to God and the relation to the Other yields productive results for ethics, politics, and religion.

Levinasian Exposure

There is a certain amount of risk involved in saying that what Levinas's philosophy offers us is an *ontology,* albeit a qualified one. I understand that this might strike some as a foolish claim, on the order of saying that Hobbes was a democrat, Nietzsche a Christian, or Heidegger a metaphysician. We could say that Levinas's entire mature philosophy is a negative response to his own 1951 question: "Is ontology fundamental?" Am I now trying to affirm that which all of Levinas's work tried to show was anathema—namely, that ontology *is* fundamental? I do not believe so. When Levinas speaks of ontology he has a very specific conception in mind. Ontology, Levinas claims, is characterized by "comprehension and signification grasped within a horizon."[9] It is "the comprehension, the embracing of Being" (TI, 47) and, as first philosophy, it is a "philosophy of power" (TI, 46). Ontology "subordinate[s] every relation with existence to the relation with Being," and thus "affirms the primacy of freedom over ethics" (TI, 45). Ontology is identified with the sphere of the "Same" and is not only linked to "Totality" (TI, section I.A), but described as a "totalizing discourse."[10] The ontological domain of the same is recognized by its "essential self-sufficiency . . . its identification in ipseity, its egoism" (TI, 44). Philosophy as ontology, Levinas concludes, "is an egology" (TI, 44). And to make just one further reference, in 1976 Levinas gives a lecture titled "The Ethical Relation as a Departure from Ontology," and speaks of the "presence to self" that defines ontology as being precisely what ethics seeks to contest (GDT, 181).

Given that Levinas's philosophy is so reasonably characterized as a challenge to ontology, why would I choose to recast his thought as ontological? Understanding "ontology" in the way Levinas does reflects and illuminates much of the Western tradition. However, Levinas himself tries to rehabilitate the term "metaphysics" (*métaphysique*) as not being necessarily linked to onto-theological speculations from an extramundane, *sub specie aeternitatis* position. Rethinking "metaphysics" as an insatiable desire for the infinite, Levinas demonstrates that the danger is not found in the term itself, but in the conceptual framework into which it is deployed. He rethinks metaphysics "ethically," and offers what Edith Wyschogrod and Adriaan Peperzak will both call an "ethical metaphysics."[11] Similarly, "ontology" is, for Levinas, problematic because of its essential connection with power, freedom, totalization, violence, ipseity, self-identification, and comprehension. Within this notion of ontology there can be no room for alterity without reinscribing it in the egoism that defines the very horizon of thought. But need this be the case for ontology as such?

I want to suggest that in order to see the political relevance of Levinasian ethics we need to offer a rethinking of "ontology" that is analogous to Levinas's rethinking of "metaphysics." A word of warning is in order, however. Just as Levinas does not mean to suggest that what "metaphysics" has meant in the tradition is what he means by it now, so we would be mistaken to think that the sort of "ontology" I attribute to Levinas and Kierkegaard is what was meant by the term in the seventeenth century or since. Exactly the opposite is the case. The very reason that I find Levinas and Kierkegaard to be such promising interlocutors with critics like Rorty is that they offer a distinct and vital understanding of the self, the other, ethics—and ontology. Crucially, however, the ontology I am attributing to Levinas *is not ontology* on the order of a Platonism,[12] Cartesianism, Kantianism, or Hegelianism.

Moreover, if we understand ontology to be a story about being—and primarily, about the being of the self—then according to this minimal criterion, narratives concerned with subjectivity are by definition *ontological*. Reading a large amount of the literature on Levinas would lead one to conclude that Levinas's primary concern is with the Other. However, if we consider the opening pages of his two major works, we see a very different concern shape his thought. In the preface to *Totality and Infinity*, Levinas situates the entire text around the question of subjectivity: "This book then does present itself as a defense of subjectivity, but it will apprehend the subjectivity not at the level of its purely egoist protestation against totality, not in its anguish before death, but as founded in the idea of infinity" (TI, 26). Contesting what he takes to be the "immodest subjectivity" of Kierkegaard and the supposed existentialism found in Heidegger, Levinas sees himself as striking out on new ground (see Simmons 2008). Importantly, I have argued that Kierkegaard does not offer such an egoistic account, but is actually closely aligned with Levinas. Regardless, we might assume that Levinas's devotion to subjectivity is merely a momentary lapse in judgment and is due to the "ontological terminology" that he later admits having deployed throughout *Totality and Infinity* (PM, 171). However, in *Otherwise Than Being*, the text in which Levinas supposedly moved beyond such ontological terminology, we find him saying in his opening note:

> To see in subjectivity an exception putting out of order the conjunction of essence, entities and the "difference"; to catch sight, in the substantiality of the subject, in the hard core of the "unique" in me, in my unparalleled identity, of a substitution for the other; to conceive of this abnegation prior to the will as a merciless exposure to the trauma of transcendence by way of a susception more, and differently, passive than receptivity, passion and finitude; to derive praxis and knowledge in the world from the nonassumable susceptibility— these are the propositions of this book which names the *beyond essence*. (OTB, xlvii–xlviii)

There are several points that are worth considering here. First, just as with *Totality and Infinity*, Levinas identifies the main issue of the book to be a revisiting of subjectivity. Where are we to look to catch a glimpse of the "beyond essence"? In subjectivity. Subjectivity is the locus of the "exception" that contests the priority of ontology. Does this mean that subjectivity offers a challenge to ontology? Yes. As was the case in his earlier work, Levinas does not see subjectivity as necessarily linked to ontology, because he continuously seeks a way to conceive the self as irreducible to the power-relation of comprehensive thematization and structural totality. This does not mean that he goes beyond ontology, however; only that he recasts how we are to understand it. In 1976, he speaks of ethical subjectivity as opposed to ontological subjectivity. This problematic distinction could be addressed in a variety of ways, but the crucial difference for us here, the point at which everything is constantly at stake, is that the ontological subjectivity that Levinas contests is a closed system, whereas the ethical subjectivity that he favors is non-systematizable due to its constitutive openness to the beyond-being. *Transcendence-in-immanence:* with such a formulation there could be no account that is not, at least to some degree, reductive due to the very surpassing fullness of the "real" (which should not be taken as just another name for Being).

The second point follows on the heels of the first. Namely, it is only within the sphere of ontology that the ethical relation can be confronted as a rupture to the supposed security and stability of self-identity. For the relation to be present to consciousness, I am already violating the status of the relation as beyond-being. To use Levinas's own terminology, only within the said (*le dit*) does the saying (*le dire*) appear—but this does not mean that the said is "prior" to the saying. The very appearance of the saying, which actually is a *non*-appearance—a mere trace that haunts the adequacy of the said—requires the said for it to signify in its very absence.[13] Finally, Levinas suggests that it is this new ethical conception of subjectivity as susceptible—as exposed to the Other—that allows for the "derivation" of both "praxis and knowledge," or we might say, of politics and philosophy.

What Levinas offers us, as did Kierkegaard before him, is *not* best thought of as a non-ontological relation to the Other, but as fundamentally *an ontology of constitutive responsibility.* Levinas's is a story about the self which is never for-itself by-itself, and thus never free of the demand to concern itself with and for the Other. It is *ontology* because it is still an account of selfhood; it is about *constitutive responsibility* because the Other always contests the ipseity of the self. It is about *constitutive responsibility* inasmuch as freedom is only a possibility from within that responsibility; it is *ontology* inasmuch as I *am* in my responsibility. It provides a narrative of *constitutive responsibility* because immanence is always ruptured by transcendence; it is *ontological* because the rupture is only present as a "trace." It is *ontology* because comprehension is required, even though it remains inadequate; it is about *constitutive responsibility* because the Other to whom I am responsible always "overflows" comprehension.[14]

Whereas *transparency* was the key term for Kierkegaard's notion of subjectivity, *exposure* is for Levinas's. An important difference between these conceptions is that while transparency is solely a characteristic of the self and does not, at least initially, apply to God, the role of the Other in exposure is more ambiguous.[15] Sometimes Levinas speaks as if the Other stands exposed before me:

> Face, before any particular expression and beneath all expression that— already countenance given to self—hides the nakedness of the face. Face that is not unveiling but pure denudation of defenseless exposure. Exposure as such, extreme exposure to the precariousness of

the stranger. Nakedness of pure exposure that is not simply emphasis of the known, of the unveiled in truth: exposure that is expression, a first language, call and assignation.[16]

At other times, I seem to stand exposed before the Other:

> Vulnerability, exposure to outrage, to wounding, passivity more passive than all patience, passivity of the accusative form, trauma of accusation suffered by a hostage to the point of persecution, implicating the identity of the hostage who substitutes himself for the others: all this is the self, a defecting or defeat of the ego's identity. And this, pushed to the limit, is sensibility, sensibility as the subjectivity of the subject. It is a substitution for another, one in the place of another, expiation. (OTB, 14)

I propose that we should *not* try to eliminate this ambiguity, but instead recognize it as a tension that ceaselessly troubles the relation itself. The ethico-religious quality of the relation rests in precisely this tension: the Other is both the destitute one (the needy other person) *and* the one who commands me (the absolute authority).[17]

Just as the self for Kierkegaard always stood "before God," Levinas fundamentally conceives of the self as "before the Other." The emphasis should be on the *before*. Admittedly without sufficient etymological warrant, I want to offer the following idiomatic presentation of this term: *be-for(e)*. When written this way, it expresses the weight of the Levinasian/Kierkegaardian conception:

> *Be*-for(e): I literally *am* in front of the Other, in the sense of having my being there
>
> Be-*for*(e): I am only a self in my responsibility *for* the Other, in the sense of being obligated-for
>
> Be-for(*e*): My selfhood is established as a responsibility for the Other because I am also responsible in the sense of moving toward the Other—walking into the *fore*-ground

Unlike what we might term the *ontology of relation* described by Hegel, in which A is constituted in-and-through ~A, for Kierkegaard and Levinas, the position in which we stand is a "non-space" (*non-lieu*) and, thus, not primarily a logical relation but an ethico-religious one.[18] "The whole" of *Totality and Infinity*, Levinas announces,

> aims to show a relation with the other not only cutting across the logic of contradiction, where the other of A is the non-A, the nega-

tion of A, but also across dialectical logic, where the same dialectically participates in and is reconciled with the other in the Unity of the system. (TI, 150)

So, on the one hand, the ontology of constitutive responsibility is not a mere ontology *of* the self. To be before God/Other is to be without a place to stand, while standing under accusation. There is no self prior to this relation who then subsequently encounters the Other. Rather, as Levinas will write, there is a "priority of [the] orientation over the terms that are placed in it" (TI, 215).

On the other hand, neither is it an ontology *of* the Other. The Other is not best conceived as an *object* that exists as such. The Other is only "there," Levinas claims, as approached in conversation (TI, 71).[19] However, the Other is also the very condition for such an approach. It is this simultaneity between condition and consequent that causes Levinas to say that the "invoked is not what I comprehend: *he is not under a category*" (TI, 69; original emphasis). To put this in Kantian language, we might say that the relation to the Other is an intuition before all concepts, such that it is this very intuition that makes conceptually determined intuition possible: it is an intuition before the ability to intuit. It is pre-intuitive *and yet* I am confronted. Confrontation is a being-struck-by that establishes and simultaneously interrupts. Interestingly resonating with Kierkegaard's claim in *Works of Love* that the category of the "neighbor" is only possible because of the relation to God, Levinas will say that "the neighbor is not a phenomenon."[20] Neither the Other nor the self is reducible to an object within the horizon of phenomenological intelligibility; in both *Totality and Infinity* and *Otherwise Than Being* Levinas will remark that the Other cannot relate to the self as members of the same "genus":

> The alterity of the Other does not depend on any quality that would distinguish him from me, for a distinction of this nature would precisely imply between us that community of genus which already nullifies alterity. (TI, 194)

> The ego is an incomparable unicity; it is outside of the community of genus and form, and does not find any rest in itself either, unquiet, not coinciding with itself. (OTB, 8)

Such passages convey the paradoxicality of the constitutive relationship to alterity. It is *para-doxical* because it could never form part of a common belief or opinion. However, *doxa* does not stand here in opposition to *episteme,* as it does in Plato (see *The Republic,* 477c–480a). Just as in Kierkegaard, belief *or* knowledge is a false dichotomy; these are not our only options. They are both on this side of (too late for, yet only possible because of) the encounter with the Other.[21] Belief and knowledge require at least a certain kind of universality and objectivity; both of which are only possible after the fact of the ethico-religious encounter. I can believe that, believe in, know that, or know how, only inasmuch as that to which I relate can be understood under a general form. For Levinas, knowledge is only available as a "theme." Thematization, however, is what constantly eludes me because it always requires a spectatorial relationship—a third-person perspective. Such an objective stance is never available in the ethical relationship: "The relation proceeding from me to the other cannot be included within a network of relations visible to a third party" (TI, 121).[22] There is only a first-person perspective in the ethico-religious relation.[23] Just as Abraham was singularized in his relation to God, Levinas suggests that I am singularized by my relation to the other person. Lacking a comparative genus, there can be no position outside the ethico-religious encounter from which to view it, and thus: "Speech and its logical work . . . unfold not in *knowledge* of the interlocutor, but in his *proximity*."[24]

Proximity is Levinas's term for the relation to the Other that is not merely an epiphany of some *thing*.[25] It is his attempt to offer a different structure of engagement than that offered by Husserl's noetico-noematic structure. *Consciousness-of* is not primary in relation to the Other, which would make of the Other a thing that is first observed and encountered by a self-sufficient being immediate unto itself. Proximity is "beyond intentionality" because it does not sublate language to thought.[26] Language, here, is not to be understood as a verbal utterance within the framework of signification, but the very signification itself of the relation to the Other. "An approach [to the Other] is not the thematization of any relationship," Levinas suggests; "it is this very relationship."[27] Building upon this conception, Levinas will differentiate between "community" and "sociality." As he says in a 1990 interview:

> The other, the loved one, the loved one as loved, is unique to the world. This is beyond the individual, beyond the shared belonging to the genus. In this relation of the unique to the unique there appears, before the purely formal community of the genus, the original sociality.[28]

Again, we see Levinas remark that there is no genus under which the Other could be placed. There is not original separation *and then* sociality. There is "the original sociality" which is not a relation between particular instances of a general category, but is always the singular relation of "the unique to the unique" (which we might hear in some harmony with the Kierkegaardian notion of the "absolute relation to the absolute"). What Fabio Ciaramelli will say of Levinas could also be said (albeit in a more religious tenor) of Kierkegaard: "For Levinas, my own ineradicable ethical responsibility becomes the only valid *principium individuationis*" (1991, 83).

The ontological subject that Levinas rightly contests is defined by power. We have seen how the subjectivity that emerges in both Levinas and Kierkegaard is one that is defined by a *lack* of power—to the very point of destitution (*je ne peux pouvoir*) (TI, 39).[29] Similarly, the original freedom that characterized the self is now eradicated and only emerges as a possibility within obligation. Anti-Climacus does not find true freedom to lie in the supposed liberty of the aesthete, but in the life lived on the other side of despair. Beginning in the early 1950s, Levinas also offers a challenge to the idea that true freedom is found in whimsical willing. In the 1953 essay, "Freedom and Command," he flips the table on classical moral and political philosophy by claiming that only as commanded—as established *by* a command (consider here Kierkegaard's discussion of the centrality of divine command in *Works of Love*)—could there be freedom that is not reducible to the violence of egoism. Transparency and exposure should be read as openings to freedom rather than moments of limitation (consider Paul's account of freedom and submission in Romans 6). Simply put, the ontology that is required for freedom to precede responsibility is an ontology of original violence, because it conceives of individuals as in a state of essential war of all against all.[30] The political promise of the ontology offered by Levinas and Kierkegaard is that, from the start, it contests this picture.

FIVE

Levinasian Subjectivity and Political Critique

In this chapter I hope to demonstrate how the ontology of constitutive responsibility makes an ethically minded political critique possible by inaugurating the task of recursive hermeneutics. But in order to set up this discussion, I will briefly consider the crucial transition in Levinas's understanding of subjectivity that occurs between *Totality and Infinity* and *Otherwise Than Being*.

Levinasian Subjectivity I: *Totality and Infinity*

As we have seen, Levinas does not begin with an isolated self who then enters the social relation, but instead conceives of subjectivity as always already fundamentally social. However, *Totality and Infinity* is something of a conflicted text on this point. Therein, Levinas begins by talking about the "separation" which is required for there to be any real notion of alterity. Only as separated—or as he will sometimes say, as "atheist"—is there the possibility of the sort of desire that characterizes the metaphysical relation. Drawing upon Plato's understanding of the philosopher as the one who perpetually desires the good, Levinas will offer a narrative that seems to start with an original separation that articulates the encounter with the Other as a subsequent interruption of the already established self. Hence, it would appear that there was already an "ontological" relation (of the self to itself) prior to ethics, which is the very sort of situation that Levinas describes at the opening of the text as being "violent."

In the early pages of *Totality and Infinity*, Levinas speaks about the "I" (*moi*) as having its individuation in the act of "identifying itself, in recovering its identity throughout all that happens to it." He calls this the "primal identity" (*l'identité par excellence*), and refers to this process of self-identification as its "original work" (*l'œuvre originelle de l'identification*) (TI, 37). The self is initially "at home with [it] self" (*chez soi*) and defined by its ability "to do" (*faire*) what it will: it is free (TI, 38). *Je-suis est je-peux.* It is as a free, powerful, and self-sufficient subjectivity that I encounter the other. This self is said to "*enter into* relationship with an other" (TI, 38; emphasis added), such that the "Stranger" comes along and "disturbs the being at home with oneself" (TI, 39). This Other "call[s] into question . . . my spontaneity" (TI, 43). All of this indicates that there is initially a spontaneous self who is at home with itself prior to the inauguration of ethical responsibility.

If this is indeed the story that Levinas wants to tell, it confronts several significant problems.[1] Most importantly, it is unable to adequately displace traditional ontology as first philosophy, and this makes ethics at best a secondary relation. Due to this secondary status, it becomes incredibly difficult to see how Levinas can give the ethical relation the weight he indicates that it has. That is, if I am originally situated and standing in my "place in the sun" only to be subsequently contested by the Other, it seems that the call to responsibility could always fall on deaf ears. Hence, the problem of the moral monster (i.e., someone who finds absolutely no moral obligation to lay claim to him or her) becomes truly acute for the formulations of *Totality and Infinity*. The significance of the ontology of constitutive responsibility is that there is no possibility of original deafness (though one could always decide *after the fact* to ignore this obligation), because there are no ears, as it were, until *formed by* the call from the Other in the first place.[2] Additionally, Levinas runs into difficulty regarding his notion of the "desire" for the infinite. On the one hand, if it is only by meeting the Other that such a desire is established, then we run back into the problem of how to explain the necessity of a certain kind of response to this encounter. On the other hand, if the desire is what precedes the encounter as anticipation precedes a big event in one's life, then the source of such desire is problematic. This leads Levinas to speak about the necessity of understanding the self as "created" (TI, 104–105, 293–94).[3] As created, the self is posited as separate, but not entirely independent. Only as *created* is "atheism" (i.e., radical separation) a real possibility.[4]

It is not only the argumentative and philosophical difficulties raised above that trouble Levinas's 1961 account. Within *Totality and Infinity* itself, there is much to contest the ontological story with which Levinas begins. As demonstrated in the previous chapter, it is Levinas's writings throughout the 1950s and early 1960s that serve to challenge the primacy of classical ontology. In "Is Ontology Fundamental?" (1951), "Freedom and Command" (1953), "The Ego and Totality" (1954), "Philosophy and the Idea of Infinity" (1957), *Totality and Infinity* (1961), and "Transcendence and Height" (1962), we find the relation to the Other not only to *challenge* the pre-established self, but also to serve actually to *inaugurate* subjectivity. He will speak of the "originality of the encounter with a face," which offers a "command prior to institutions."[5] When Levinas claims that "the condition that is necessary for there to be thought is a conscience," he suggests that accusation opens reflection.[6] Rather than the same being contested after its establishment, Levinas will speak of the "more in the less" as definitive of human subjectivity.[7] Remembering also that it is in *Totality and Infinity* that Levinas contends that ethics is an orientation that *precedes* the terms in the relationship, we are left in a bit of a quandary.

Rather than ignore this ambiguity, Levinas attempts to address it head-on, which, unfortunately, frequently causes him to offer rather unhelpful formulations. One metaphor offered in *Totality and Infinity* that I find to be especially difficult to understand involves the notion of a door. "In the separated being," Levinas writes, "the door to the outside must hence be at the same time open and closed" (TI, 148). A cryptic comment such as this does not provide much assistance in the task of interpreting an already complicated narrative. Does Levinas simply mean that totality can never be separated from infinity? This would be in line with the idea that comprehension is always required and yet never adequate. And certainly, Levinas never places totality and infinity in an exclusive disjunction. However, this particular metaphor, which Levinas apparently believes is able to do a significant amount of work, just serves to exacerbate the problem. To say that the front door is both open and closed is to suggest that there is some amount of confusion in either the question that would anticipate such an answer, or in the status of the object being described. Are we talking about one door, or two? Perhaps the screen door is open and the main door is shut? Maybe vice versa? Could it be that the door is just open *slightly,* but is *mostly* closed?

I want to suggest that the problems faced by Levinas's metaphor are due to the ambiguity that haunts his writings from this period. On the one hand, we need a self that is open and closed because Levinas seems to think that only as separated could there be the possibility of "absolute alterity" and not just "relative alterity." And yet, on the other hand, it is only by understanding the self as constitutively open that the above problems can be adequately addressed. What results from this ambiguity is an overall ontological narrative that is not far removed from Kantianism. If Levinas is to mount a successful critique of what he takes to be the essential egoism of the liberal self, something must change about this story. Fueled largely, I believe, by Derrida's 1964 essay "Violence and Metaphysics," we can see this change beginning to appear in 1965, in Levinas's "Enigma and Phenomenon." Then, by 1968's "Substitution," Levinas has eliminated the ontological/ethical ambiguity in favor of a full-fledged account of subjectivity as always already having responded to the call of the Other. Pushing this conception to its linguistic and conceptual breaking point in *Otherwise Than Being,* published in 1974, he no longer speaks about being simultaneously open and closed but instead of nakedness, destitution, passivity, traumatic rupture, and even uses the language of hostage and sacrifice. The self is no longer initially at-home with itself, but instead is a self "despite-itself" (*malgré soi*). One finds oneself originally "torn up from oneself in the core of one's unity." "This absolute noncoinciding, this diachrony of the instant," Levinas continues, "signifies in the form of one-penetrated-by-the-other."

"I" am essentially, without recourse to any isolated essence, "a nudity more naked than all destitution" (OTB, 49).

Levinasian Subjectivity II: *Otherwise Than Being*

Since I have already outlined much of Levinas's later conception of the self in discussing his notion of exposure in chapter 4, I will not repeat myself here, but instead offer an analysis of Robert Bernasconi's essay "To What Question is 'Substitution' the Answer?" in which he aptly considers the role of subjectivity in the transition between *Totality and Infinity* and *Otherwise Than Being*. Bernasconi begins by saying that "the initial hypothesis to be examined is that Levinas introduces the concept of substitution to address the question of what the subject must be like for ethics to be possible" (2002, 234–35). The idea here is that substitution is the account of subjectivity as "for the other" such that sacrifice would be possible as a concrete reality in history. Noting that this idea of substitution is described by Levinas as the condition of possibility for "pity, compassion, pardon, and proximity,"[8] Bernasconi says that this is purely a descriptive rather than a normative claim. "Levinas is not preaching," Bernasconi insists, and then goes on to conclude that "he is not saying that one *should* sacrifice oneself. He merely wants to account for its possibility" (2002, 235). This question of description as opposed to normative admonition is not something which Bernasconi adequately returns to in the essay, but he does indicate that if normativity is to be understood in Levinas, then it must be a matter of maintaining a tension between the transcendental and empirical elements in his thought (and our ethical lives).

Bernasconi contends that Levinas's account of subjectivity is in contest with three "rival accounts" (2002, 235). Let's glance at each before moving to a positive articulation of the Levinasian alternative. The first is identified as a form of egoism and is primarily associated with Thomas Hobbes. On Hobbes's model, the self is a situated, individualized, and embattled body defined by self-concern; Levinas will refer to this as a theory of "original war."[9] The warlike component is presupposed because if the self is defined by an original egoism, then there is no way to move from obsession with oneself to an obsession by the Other. Accordingly, there would be no transition from egoism to generosity and, hence, no way that this presupposed original war could give way to actual peace except by extension or redirection of everyone's fundamental commitment to oneself. And this is, mediated by a sovereign power, precisely Hobbes's hope for civil peace: the concern for the other person is a late, calculative modulation of the concern for oneself. But such a peace and such a secondary concern for others could never be, for Levinas, properly considered *ethical*.

The second account identifies the human subject as "concerned for its own existence" and is associated with the thought of Heidegger. The difference between this and the first account is one of degree rather than kind. The Hobbesian subject shares with the Heideggerian subject a primary concern for self, but whereas Hobbes locates this in an original "war of all against all," Heidegger investigates it as a matter of existential anxiety and commitment to one's projects. Both accounts make use of a particular notion of *conatus* (decidedly reminiscent of Spinoza's use of the term), but they provide differing conceptions of the directionality of the ego. For Hobbes, one's self-concern constantly coils back upon itself, while for Heidegger it constantly passes over into one's situation, one's future, and one's death. The third conception that Levinas rejects is "the hypothesis that the condition of the possibility of sacrifice lies in freedom" (Bernasconi 2002, 236). This is primarily associated with Sartre, who stridently claims that human being is defined by the condition of being "condemned to be free" (Sartre 1985; see also 1956).

Bernasconi goes to great lengths to convey the way in which Levinas's whole consideration of substitution is an attempt at "tak[ing] responsibility out of the realm of consciousness" (2002, 236). Levinas takes peace to be more originary than war, concern for the death of the other person to be more primary than a concern about my own, and obligation to be prior to freedom. At stake in all of these priority-shifts is the notion of subjectivity no longer being seen as a self-constitution that happens to be troubled by the Other, but rather as a self that is constituted by such a troubling. In order to provide such a notion of responsible subjectivity, Levinas moves from the self as an *arche* to the self as *an-archically engaged*. Subjectivity is, thus, not a matter of consciousness, but of an exposure to the other person that awakens the self to consciousness. There is not first a waking subject who then falls asleep only to be awakened by the Other, but instead there is only a self at the moment of waking up. Importantly, this metaphor of sleep and waking conveys the idea that waking up is itself a response to that which disturbs peaceful sleep. This is how the response can "precede" consciousness, responsibility can be understood otherwise than on the basis of freedom, and the self can be engaged without yet being within the domain of ontology. Accordingly, Bernasconi describes the relation between the self and the other as now being a "bond rather than a form of separation, as it was in *Totality and Infinity*" (2002, 240).

Hence, "the initial task that Levinas sets himself in 'Substitution' is to provide an account of subjectivity that runs counter to that offered by those representatives of the Western philosophical tradition according to which the primary relation to beings takes place in knowledge" (2002, 237–38). Immediately, however, Levinas is confronted with the problem of how to represent that which would contest representation. This was just as problematic in *Totality and Infinity*—namely, how to represent the face. The difficulty of speaking about that which would contest speech is not overlooked by Bernasconi. Indeed, he recognizes that "Substitution" is an essay that "self-consciously resists any attempt to reduce it to a thematic analysis" (2002, 238). The reason for this is the theory of language that Levinas deploys.

By developing the distinction between "the said and the saying," which in many ways is reminiscent of Silentio's discussion of Abraham's silence, Levinas provides an account that makes it impossible to *say* what you really mean, because the meaning is precisely not a *statement,* but a *relation* prior to language (though only considered therein). Without sliding into a Wittgensteinian analysis of language games, Levinas attempts to torture language in such a way as to let its seams show, as it were. Where language starts to pull apart from itself, there is the glimpse (dare we say "trace") of what could not be contained within language. If we agree with Levinas that *Totality and Infinity* was still too ontological, we can see why in a discussion of subjectivity that a new account of language is offered as a central component. It is this account of subjectivity and language that Levinas offers after 1965 which stands in harmony with the reading of Kierkegaard that I have already described.

Having considered the way in which both Levinas and Kierkegaard advocate an ontology of constitutive responsibility, I will now argue that this ontology provides a sustainable basis for articulating a notion of political critique offered in the name of justice.

Constitutive Responsibility as Condition for Political Critique

In "The Ego and Totality," Levinas lays out what he considers to be the conditions for criticism:

> One can inaugurate the work of criticism only if one can begin with a fixed point. The fixed point cannot be some incontestable truth, a "certain" statement that would always be subject to psychoanalysis; it can only be the absolute status of an interlocutor, a being, and not of a truth about beings. An interlocutor is not affirmed like a truth, but believed. This faith or trust does not designate here a second source of cognition, but is presupposed by every theoretical statement. Faith is not the knowledge of a truth open to doubt or capable of being certain; it is something outside of these modalities, it is the face to face encounter with a hard and substantial interlocutor, who is the origin of himself, already dominating the forces which constitute him and sway him, a you, arising inevitably, solid and noumenal, behind the man known in that bit of absolutely decent skin which is the face, which closes over the nocturnal chaos and opens upon what it can take up and for which it can answer.[10]

Levinas speaks of a "fixed point" as the basis upon which critique is possible. This is fundamentally against the grain of Richard Rorty's thinking. This fixed point may indeed be *fragile*, but it is not, and can never be, *ironic*. Levinas is careful to delimit what such a fixed point cannot be: it can be neither an "incontestable truth" nor a "'certain' statement" available for psychoanalytic probing.[11] What is highlighted in both of these prohibitions is the inapplicability of ordinary knowledge claims to obtain regarding the fixed point as if it were another object in a room next to the file cabinet and lamp. In a very Kierkegaardian turn of phrase, Levinas announces that "an interlocutor is not to be affirmed like a truth, but believed." Does this mean that the belief is not itself true? Or perhaps he simply means to suggest that the fixed point is never "provable," and so cannot ascend to the heights of knowledge? Levinas attempts to challenge both of these interpretations by saying that "faith" is not simply a weak claim about an object that confronts our intellect; rather, it is "presupposed by every theoretical statement." I understand Levinas to mean that there is an investiture that defines the self prior to the ability to distinguish between theory and practice. This investiture is the encounter with the Other to whom, and for whom, I am responsible prior to my freedom. Accordingly, *ethico-religious exposure is an inaugural event:*

> The idea of infinity (which is not a representation of infinity) sustains activity itself. Theoretical thought, knowledge, and critique, to which activity has been opposed, have the same foundation. The idea of infinity, which is not in its turn a representation of infinity, is the common source of activity and theory. (TI, 27)

In an attempt to offer commentary on the notion that ethics precedes the split between theory and practice, Adriaan Peperzak offers the following important observation:

> Levinas does not say (as some interpreters attribute to him) that metaphysics ought to be based on ethics, as if moral philosophy as such, in distinction from ontology or a non-normative metaphysics, were the basic discipline of philosophy on which the others should be built. First philosophy must show that "is" and "ought," the theoretical and the practical, are not originally distinguishable, and thus that "the Good" is another name for the very source. (1997, 207)

Peperzak's comment crucially suggests that the relation to the Other is not itself properly an object for thought, but the very "source" from which thought would proffer as a thought, distinct from practical activity. *Theoria* and *praxis* are not original contraries; they spring from the same fountainhead, which is the exposure to alterity. Hence, the fixed point that Levinas mentions is neither metaphysics as set off from moral philosophy, nor epistemology as set off from ontology. Rather, it is prior to such distinctions. So when Peperzak says that "'the Good' is another name for the very source" of the "is" no less than the "ought," he is noting that, for Levinas, there is no distinction between ethics and ontology properly speaking, but that they only separate as disciplines due to the original moment of exposure. Exposure establishes and yet explodes; it ruptures and simultaneously constitutes.

The Other is thus "the origin of himself," καθ αὑτό. I am not confronted within a horizon of intelligibility. Rather, the confrontation is what allows for all horizonality. The Other "does not affect us in terms of a concept. He is a being and counts as such."[12] Levinas can say, therefore, that the ethical relation is "otherwise than being": since the relation does not properly occur in time but in the *lapse* that troubles the chronological progression of time itself, claiming that it is temporally prior to theory is nonsensical. The very distinction between logic and lived existence is too late as a characterization of the relation to the Other.

So, are we to conclude that there is a certain unsurpassable negativity in this relation? Does the "fixed point" operate as the vanishing point of intelligibility? Does saying that the relation to the Other constitutes the condition for criticism really mean that criticism is always elusive? These questions are not easily answered, but while recognizing their complexity, we could answer them in the affirmative only at great cost. What must be remembered is that Levinas never says the Other is incomprehensible; only that the Other "overflows comprehension." Inadequacy need not suggest impossibility. Walking the fine line between quietism and apophaticism on the one hand, and reduction and violence on the other hand, is the task that Levinas demands of us as not only philosophers, but as human beings.[13]

The importance of this ontology is that it keeps alive the tension between the necessity of comprehension and the inadequacy of all attempts to comprehend. The ontology of constitutive responsibility is not equivalent to the ethico-religious relation. Rather, this ontology is the said that always accompanies the saying while serving to unsay itself, and this is why it is so crucial for the political efficacy of the inaugural encounter. Although ethico-religious exposure is actually what Levinas intends to reference with the idea of a "fixed point," it is only as offered in a theoretical presentation that this "fixed point" can be operative in the political arena. *We do not only put our "faith" or "trust" in the Other, but also in the story we tell about who we are in relation to the Other.*[14] Admitting this is a key step in articulating the political significance for thinkers who otherwise appear to be so abstract and so detached from existential reality that the only political result they could provoke would be a monastic withdrawal from society. I contend that the "fixed point" is best understood as this traumatic story of the origination of subjectivity. Without the notion of the alternative ontology articulated here, Levinas's entire philosophy falls prey to the Derridean critique that absolute alterity would be absolutely non-encounterable. Levinas's transition from the "ontological" language of *Totality and Infinity* to the language that speaks "beyond essence" in *Otherwise Than Being* is not really a shift from ontology to something else, but a transition from a problematic story about a self-enclosed, separate, atheist self to a narrative of constitutive rupture, exposure, and investiture. The former is unavailable for self-critique because it affirms itself as finished; the latter is only possible along with the seed of its own contestation.

When I say that an ontology of constitutive responsibility is crucial for political criticism, I mean that without a conception of the self that is always already responsible for the Other, a politics that is laid open to contestation seems to re-inscribe this contestation back into a form of self-interest. It would be difficult to see how politics could never be more than a battle between interests without any rationale for why one contention is *better* than another. Marginalization may indeed always be a consequence of political life, but in Levinas and Kierkegaard, marginalization is able to be seen as *violent* rather than simply as *unfortunate*.

This point can be illustrated by considering Rorty's oft-repeated claim that liberals are defined by the feeling that "cruelty is the worst thing we can do" (1989, xv). Whether or not this statement is true is certainly something that should concern us—for certainly, it is possible that Rortian liberals are wrong. Yet due to the Rortian conflation of truth and utility, this is a question that Rorty would find to be irrelevant except as a concern for the consequences of one's beliefs. The truth of this statement lies not in the relation between cruelty and goodness, but in the effect that this belief has on the future of one's political projects. For Rorty, being a liberal is a *good* thing to be *not* because it is somehow logically justified, but because it is the best way to bring about the liberal utopian future that he envisions. Notice, though, that Rorty's liberalism stands in conflict with other of his philosophical commitments. That we *should* not be cruel means nothing other than *we* don't like cruelty, so *you* shouldn't either. Obligation becomes another term for personal (or collective) desire. I contend that unless obligation constitutes the self, rather than being a particular possibility for the already constituted (free) self, then there is no way to normatively differentiate between the desires of a sadist and those of an altruist—according to Rorty's account, they seem to suggest only individuals operating according to a different notion of the "we" to which they belong. If responsibility follows from freedom rather than, as Levinas contends, responsibility preceding freedom, responsibility itself becomes indistinguishable from self-concern.

According to the ontology of constitutive responsibility, no action or set of actions could ever be adequate to discharge the obligation of each to every other. If there were such an action (cf. Kant), sets of character traits or habits (cf. Aristotle), or ways of life (cf. Socrates), then there could potentially be an end to the quest for justice; justice could, at least logically, be achieved. Politics might continue, but it would be the politics of angels—if we can conceive such a thing—rather than of flawed human beings. Yet here we should pay attention to Susan Wolf's contention that the notion of moral perfection or moral saintliness "does not constitute a model of personal well-being toward which it would be particularly rational or good or desirable for a human being to strive" (1982, 419). The ontology of constitutive responsibility begins in the very failings of finite humans and demonstrates how these failings are not merely limitations, but opportunities for service. It is only as finite, embodied, contextual, and limited, that history is not for us necessarily a "slaughter-bench," as Hegel purported, but the very time in which justice can be sought.

My claim that an ontology of constitutive responsibility, or at least something quite similar, is required for a sustainable notion of political criticism depends on two interrelated points. First, *politics cannot go all the way down.* If it does, then there would be no way of differentiating between a just politics and an unjust politics because the very distinction would itself be merely another political gesture. This is a fundamental contestation of the Rortian supposition that the only normativity we require is spawned from within our political lives. My resistance to this can be framed in a Kantian way: normativity may *come from* within politics, but it does not *have its origin* there. For Kierkegaard and Levinas, the political sphere is defined by the task of bringing about justice, and this requires that we give some sort of account of how this task is not itself *only* politically motivated. An ontology of constitutive responsibility animates our political life such that justice is definitive and criticism is demanded. Unless we presuppose such a notion, bringing about self-interested goals through force, or conversely, withdrawing from society altogether, would both be potentially "legitimate" options for political life (so long as "we" view them as acceptable). Yet there would seem to be, then, no sense of "legitimacy" that does not re-entrench a variety of egoism.

Second, *the ontology of constitutive responsibility does not allow for the Pascalian task of weighing and considering alternatives from outside of one's existential situation.* There is no non-political position in which one could stand in order to critique politics. But within our political existence—and this is the weight of construing politics as always already ethical—we are more than merely political beings. Politics does not go all the way down, and yet one's political situatedness is inescapable. An exhaustive reading of politics would, I believe, represent the height of ontological reductionism. We must not replace the traditional supposition that we can transcend our social embeddedness to obtain a God's-eye view, say, with the claim that we are nothing other than our embeddedness. The former is problematic because it eliminates transcendence by thinking it on the basis of immanence; the latter is problematic because it refuses to think transcendence at all. Both are ontologically reductive, and, as such, fundamentally arrogant. Strangely, both require that the human occupy the absolute position of God—the difference is that this is done theistically in the former and atheistically in the latter. The Levinasian-Kierkegaardian alternative proposed in a variety of ways by new phenomenology never allows for immanence to be thought outside of a relation to transcendence, and yet it never allows for this transcendence to tempt us with an escape from the specific, particular, historical world in which we live.[15]

Accordingly, the ontology of constitutive responsibility provides important spaces for thinking about political criticism when it demands that no political institution could ever be sufficiently just. By engaging in constant critique, however, I can ethically *be* political. Roger Burggraeve expresses this thought nicely when he says that the "charity of 'one-for-the-Other' is never completely fulfilled by public justice or any socio-political system. This is why there is always a need for better justice and greater peace, indeed sometimes even a new justice and a new peace— *ad infinitum*" (2002, 150). It is this *ad infinitum* that I want to call *recursive hermeneutics:*

> *Recursive:* always *re*-occurring, occurring ever again . . . and then again
> *Hermeneutics:* ethics demands everything of me, but politics demands that I interpret this demand according to socio-historic situations
> *Recursive hermeneutics:* the task of justice is always infinitely expansive and at every moment demands action (which itself requires further interpretation) here and now

Rehabilitating Transcendental Language

Frequent references to the "conditions for the possibility of . . ." will suggest to some that I am advocating a reading of Levinas and Kierkegaard that aligns them with the transcendental method. Let me address this directly by saying that this is indeed what I am claiming—with a few minor modifications, of course. The transcendental method, as performed so thoroughly by Kant, is the process of moving from specific experiential data to the logical conditions for experience as such to be possible. This procedure has fallen into disrepute because it has led to such notions as the "transcendental unity of apperception," the "absolute ego," and "pure consciousness" (as well as philosophical and theological arrogance, which in turn can lead to political violence). Under the impact of Nietzsche's genealogies, Heidegger's articulations of being-in-the-world, and Wittgenstein's discussion of the contingency of language games, such transcendental accounts are no longer deemed viable in much of contemporary Continental philosophy.[16]

But must a particular method yield predetermined results? Is there something metaphysically laden in the transcendental method that weds it to some sort of idealism? Those who answer these questions in the affirmative would seem to do so for the following reason: discussions of logical conditions of possibility continue to give a priority to logic (thereby privileging theory over praxis), and thus such notions depend on an Enlightenment conception of rationality that has rightly fallen from grace. Additionally, they might continue, the transcendental method is foundationally logocentric because it equates being with thought, such that pure reason becomes the tool by which knowledge is absolutely secured. Although I am sympathetic to the concerns displayed in this objection, I am not convinced by the objection itself. Simply put, the transcendental method is not necessarily linked to the Kantian metaphysics in which it was first given shape. To understand Levinas's notion of the "fixed point" that is the condition for critique, we need to view his philosophy as a sustained consideration of what must be the case for responsibility to be a *lived reality*.[17] When Levinas begins his preface to *Totality and Infinity* with the question of "whether we are not duped by morality" (TI, 21), he sets the scope for all that follows (not just in that text, but in his entire subsequent authorship). Levinas's fundamental concern is with locating what it is that would make morality *not* something we are duped by: he is investigating what would be required for morality to be an actuality in the lives of human beings. We can hear the transcendental echoes in this question when we rephrase it as: what are the conditions for the possibility of morality as an existential reality?

We do not have to wait long for an answer to this question. A mere three pages later, Levinas writes:

> Without substituting eschatology for philosophy, without philosophically "demonstrating" eschatological "truths," *we can proceed from the experience of totality back to a situation* where totality breaks up, a situation that *conditions* the totality itself. Such a situation is the gleam of exteriority or of transcendence in the face of the Other. (TI, 24; emphasis added)

The first reference to the face in *Totality and Infinity* is made in a sentence describing the methodology of the text itself. We arrive at an account of the face—that is, at an account of the traumatic situation that lies at the heart of ontological sameness—only by beginning in lived experience and *working backward* (*remonter*) to the conditions that underlie that experience. Levinas is not shy about this connection: "The way we are describing to work back and remain this side of objective certitude," he quickly adds, "resembles what has come to be called the transcendental method (in which the technical procedures of transcendental idealism need not necessarily be comprised)" (TI, 25). Notice that Levinas affirms what I have suggested above—namely, the transcendental method does not need to presuppose or reinforce Kantian metaphysics. I propose that this is why Levinas says his method "resembles" rather than "is" the transcendental method: he maintains the crucial structure of working backward without the content of an Absolute Ego that has so often been said to underlie it.

The transcendental method that I ascribe to Levinas breaks with the specifics of Kant's usage in several important ways. The condition that Levinas continues to argue for is not properly understood as an *a priori* logical condition. He offers, instead, what I will term a *quasi-logical existential condition*. I grant that this formulation may appear to explain the complex by appealing to the obscure, but with a couple of clarifications, I believe that this can be lucidly expressed. For Levinas, there are difficulties with too rigidly deploying the idea of "logical" conditionality regarding the ethical relation. Basically, the idea is that Levinas is attempting to represent that for which representation is always too late. It is similar to the idea of trying to *see* light: light would be that on the basis of which we could see anything, but not properly a visual object itself.[18] Similarly, claiming that the exposure to alterity, or the idea of infinity, or the face of the Other, is a straightforwardly *logical* condition of something can invite one to forget that the very distinctions between knowledge/opinion and theory/practice are products of trusting that such a relation obtains and, as such, cannot be deployed as having any original status of themselves (which would be required for the very notion of logical condition to make sense). This is why I have chosen to term these conditions quasi-logical *and yet* existential. This rehabilitated transcendental language is not primarily concerned about conditions *as such,* but about conditions *as situated* relative to one's lived existence.

My account here can be clarified by drawing on Paul Ricœur, another thinker who is closely associated with new phenomenology (albeit from a more hermeneutical direction than Levinas). His notion of "post-Hegelian Kantianism," an expression he borrows from Eric Weil and then develops in *The Conflict of Interpretations* and *Hermeneutics and the Human Sciences,* offers, I believe, a model of situated conditionality that is closely related to what I am putting forward here. In an essay titled "Appropriation," Ricœur distinguishes between the "*self*" which emerges from the understanding of the text" and the "*ego* which claims to precede this understanding" (1981, 193; original emphasis). Making sense of the relationship between the self and the ego would require "a long explanation in order to situate hermeneutic philosophy in relation to the reflective Kantian tradition on the one hand, and the speculative Hegelian tradition on the other" (1981, 193). Rather than favoring one over the other, hermeneutics "must place itself at equal distance from both traditions, accepting as much from one tradition as from the other but opposing each with equal force" (1981, 193). As he explains:

> By its concern to secure the link between understanding meaning and self-understanding, hermeneutic philosophy is a continuation of reflective philosophy. But the critique of the illusions of the subject and the permanent recourse to the great detour of signs distances it decisively from the primacy of the *cogito*. Above all, the subordination of the theme of appropriation to that of manifestation turns more towards a hermeneutics of the *I am* than a hermeneutics of the *I think*. (1981, 193)

Because of the hermeneutic concern for conditionality, Ricœur's distance from Kant's reflective philosophy is not absolute. Nonetheless, Ricœur makes clear that the hermeneutic emphasis on embodied, existential encounters with texts (and the historico-cultural frames in which these texts are always implicated) requires a resistance to the epistemologico-metaphysical framework according to which reflective philosophy operates. In order to avoid the conclusion that this distance from Kant amounts to a thoroughgoing embrace of Hegel, he continues:

> It may be thought that what distances hermeneutic philosophy from reflective philosophy brings it nearer to speculative philosophy. That is largely true. Thus Gadamer can say that his hermeneutics revives Hegel insofar as it breaks with Schleiermacher. Fundamentally, the concept of manifestation of a world, around which all other hermeneutical concepts are organized, is closer to the idea of the "self-presentation" (*Selbstdarstellung*) of the true, following the preface to *The Phenomenology of Mind*, than to the Husserlian idea of constitution. But the permanent return of this self-presentation to the event of speech in which, *ultimately*, interpretation is accomplished signifies that philosophy mourns the loss of absolute knowledge. It is because absolute knowledge is impossible that the conflict of interpretations is insurmountable and inescapable. (1981, 193)

To the extent that Hegel rightly maintains the centrality of history (or existential horizonality, in general) in his philosophy (which was largely lacking in Kant), Ricœur is willing to see in him a resource for hermeneutics. However, despite this improvement on reflective philosophy, speculative philosophy maintains the idealist presumptions to "absolute knowledge," which is incompatible with the hermeneutic gesture. "Between absolute knowledge and hermeneutics," Ricœur claims, "it is necessary to choose" (1981, 193). For Ricœur, it is by reading Kant *after* Hegel (while still being critical of Hegel) that we are able to see that hermeneutics requires attention to the conditions of possibility for experience, and to the historical situations in which such conditions could be themselves appropriated *as* experiential. "We are," Ricœur notes, "as radically post-Hegelian as we are post-Kantian" (1974, 412). The problem with Kant is the absolutism of reason as located in relation to the transcendental ego; the problem with Hegel is the absolutism of history as finished. For Ricœur, it is by reading them in conversation that we see the problems of each when taken in isolation. In light of Hegel, Kant becomes, for Ricœur, not someone to move past, but to rethink and productively appropriate.

One issue on which Ricœur finds Kant to be particularly helpful is what he terms the "philosophical appropriation of freedom in the light of hope" (1974, 411). Ricœur's discussion of hope, which draws heavily on Jürgen Moltmann's rethinking of Christian theology in an eschatological tone, demonstrates an openness to starting from a "kerygmatic core of hope and freedom" in order to then "search out a philosophical approximation" of such notions (1974, 411; see also Moltmann 1967). Here one finds Ricœur engaged in what could rightly be called the philosophical project of inquiring into the possibility of religious phenomena, and further, in a specifically hermeneutic investigation into how hope and freedom can function as such in human experience and discourse.

In granting this legitimacy of philosophical inquiry regarding the conditions for particular religious phenomena, Ricœur appeals to Kant and, more specifically, to a rehabilitated transcendental language:

> The Kantian concept of the transcendental illusion, applied to the religious object par excellence, is one of inexhaustible philosophical fecundity; it grounds critique that is radically different from that of Feuerbach or Nietzsche. It is because there is a legitimate thought of the unconditioned that the transcendental illusion is possible; this latter does not proceed from the projection of the human into the divine but, on the contrary, from the filling-in of the thought of the unconditioned according to the mode of the empirical object. That is why Kant can say: it is not experience that limits reason but reason that limits the claim of sensibility to extend our empirical, phenomenal, spatio-temporal knowledge to the noumenal order. (1974, 415)

Similar to my notion of quasi-logical existential conditions, Ricœur avoids both reflective dogmatism and speculative certainty while yet allowing for openness to the very sorts of "religious" concerns that animate new phenomenology. A central aspect shared by Ricœur's post-Hegelian Kantianism and the search for quasi-logical existential conditions is the attempt to maintain the legitimacy (and perhaps necessity) of *philosophically* considering what might be termed and often dismissed as "theological" issues. In a statement that should cause us to think of

Jean-Luc Marion's "saturated phenomena," Levinas's "idea of Infinity," Derrida's "democracy to come," Kierkegaard's "faith," and Michel Henry's notion of "Truth," Ricœur claims:

> Hope, in its springing forth, is "aporetic," not by reason of lack of meaning but by excess of meaning. Resurrection surprises by being in excess in comparison to the reality forsaken by God.
>
> But if this novelty did not make us think, then hope, like faith, would be a cry, a flash without a sequel; there would be no eschatology, no doctrine of last things, if the novelty of the new were not made explicit by an indefinite repetition of signs, were not verified in the "seriousness" of an interpretation which incessantly separates hope from utopia. (1974, 415)

My use of the phrase *quasi-logical existential conditions of possibility* is meant to indicate the way in which we arrive at the account of the ontology of constitutive responsibility by rigorously investigating what is presupposed by existence. Yet such a gesture is not without difficulties. Namely, it might seem that such transcendental language depends upon a foundationalism that is at odds with Levinas's own thought. Adriaan Peperzak nicely articulates the basic difficulties of attributing a foundational status to the face, while recognizing that this is precisely what it seems like we must do:[19]

> If we could use the word 'foundation' without immediately becoming conscious of its inadequacy with regard to the "*pre*-original" or "an-archic" character of Levinas's main concepts, we could maintain that his philosophy is a philosophical "foundation" of ethics, or a "fundamental" ethics, not so very unlike Kant's *Critique of Practical Reason*. (1997, 222)

How are we to bring the an-archic status of Levinasian ethics together with the seeming need to affirm ethics as foundational? Perhaps we might propose something like an *an-archic foundation* as a way of making sense of the Levinasian perspective. Yet, could such a distortion even be thought? Although I will return to the possibility of a deconstructive foundationalism in chapter 11, here I simply want to suggest that we must entertain something along these lines in order to see the role that the transcendental method plays in Levinas's philosophy (and as I will argue in chapters 10 and 11, eventually to allow for the possibility of a deconstructive notion of justification within political discourse). Anticipating the arguments of part 2, we might suggest that another way to access this offense to thought is by viewing Levinas as offering a *phenomenology of transcendence*.[20] But the trouble with the latter formulation is that phenomenology seems to be by definition about that which *appears*—that is, with phenomena. But, as we have seen, Levinas explicitly resists describing the Other as a phenomenon.

We must remember that Levinas describes the metaphysical desire at the beginning of *Totality and Infinity* as a desire for the *invisible*. The *aporia* that would be intrinsic to a phenomenology of the invisible is also what separates Levinas's formulations from those of Kant. It is true that for Kant, the "forms of sensation" are not properly sensible and that the "categories of the understanding" are never properly objects of intuition, but in no way are these conditions to be understood as being obstacles for that which they make possible. The transcendental method for Levinas constantly arrives at that "situation" or "relation" which contests the adequacy of any method which forgets the paradox that lies at the heart of all philosophical methodologies once ethics is recognized "as first philosophy." Hence, an *an-archic foundation* and a *phenomenology of transcendence* can be understood to be markers for the aporetic structure of rationality itself.[21] Levinas continues to remind us of this when he keeps pushing beyond mere "conditionality" to the "uncondition" of experience. Levinas speaks of the "movement of a being back to what precedes its condition," and suggests that philosophy "penetrate[s] beneath its own condition" (TI, 84, 85). All of this is reminiscent of Climacus's statement in the *Concluding Unscientific Postscript* that it "cannot be expressed more inwardly that subjectivity is truth than when subjectivity is at first untruth, and yet subjectivity is truth" (CUP, 213). Truth is inadequate to the interiority that it is supposed to express; when read in this way, truth itself is initially untruth. This paradoxical gesture can be found not only in Climacus, but throughout the authorships of Kierkegaard, Levinas, and Derrida. For all of these thinkers, the *condition* of possibility is also its *uncondition,* or as Derrida says, the conditions of *possibility* are also the conditions of *im-possibility.* On this front, Christopher Norris rightly points out that Derrida broaches "something like a Kantian transcendental deduction, an argument to demonstrate ('perversely' enough) that *a priori* notions of logical truth are *a priori* ruled out of court by rigorous reflection on the powers and limits of textual critique" (1987, 183).[22]

Having now worked through why the 'quasi' must precede 'logical' (as a certain form of contestation that is coordinate with a recognition), we can now more directly consider the role being played by the term 'existential'. Robert Bernasconi insists on a "tension" in the relation between the transcendental and empirical aspects of Levinas's thought. Noting that Levinas will say things like, "It is only this hostage's unconditition that makes pardon, pity, or compassion possible,"[23] Bernasconi cautions us against too quickly concluding that Levinas simply decides in favor of the transcendental over the concrete, that is, favors the formal structures of ethics more than the deformalized concretization of ethical life. He interprets

Levinas so as to have these poles constantly directing attention toward one another, as it were. Bernasconi contends that, for Levinas, "if one asks how sacrifice or giving is possible, one will ultimately be led behind consciousness and knowing to the one-for-the-other of substitution, but his thought remains directed toward the concrete, which is where the encounter takes place" (2002, 248). Working backward is never a one-way street. It is the encounter with other people every day that leads me to ask the philosophical question about the status of morality, but it is such a question that constantly re-entrenches me in the concrete situation itself.[24] Giving voice to this multi-directionality, while running strangely counter to what I consider his own fairly stilted vision of the transcendental method, Theo de Boer writes: "Ontology without metaphysics is blind; metaphysics without ontology is void" (1986, 110).

Conclusion: Faithfulness to God and Justice for the Other

Doing moral and political philosophy always runs the risk of being another form of violence if it does not constantly let itself be troubled by the very face that inaugurated its speculations. In this way, an ontology of constitutive responsibility functions as a *quasi-logical existential* condition of possibility for political critique, because the relation to the Other is not simply a proposition to be *believed,* but a life to be *lived.* If such an account of ontology is false, and the ontology that underlies Rortian liberalism or Foucaultian webs of power or the neo-Marxism of Hardt and Negri, say, is true, then the possibility of living the ethical life as anything other than a particular manifestation of egoistic and chauvinistic existence becomes difficult to maintain.[25] Without recognizing ethico-religious exposure as constitutive of subjectivity, these other models conceive of the Other as "counting" according to one's own standards (whether selfishly articulated or not), instead of "counting as such."[26] As Roger Burggraeve has argued, only by starting from a self-as-exposed-to-the-other is there the possibility of conceiving of a new basis for justice, human rights, and a lasting political peace (2002, chaps. 2 and 3).

Here I want to return to Rorty and sketch the potential sites of congruence and dissimilarity between his political goals and those that the ontology of constitutive responsibility might anticipate. In order to do this, I will conclude this chapter by bringing Rorty's idea of a "liberal utopia" into conversation with Levinasian ethics and the Derridean idea of a "democracy to come."

Rorty characterizes the concerns of liberalism as revolving around the seminal question, "[a]re you suffering?" (1989, 198). Drawing on Wilfrid Sellars's idea of "we-intentions" and Judith Shklar's definition of a liberal as someone for whom "cruelty is the worst thing they do," Rorty offers an account of a "liberal utopia" toward which we should strive (1989, 74). He outlines his liberal utopia as follows:

In my utopia, human solidarity would be seen not as a fact to be recognized by clearing away "prejudice" or burrowing down to previously hidden depths but, rather, as a goal to be achieved. It is to be
achieved not by inquiry but by imagination, the imaginative ability
to see strange people as fellow sufferers. Solidarity is not discovered
by reflection but created. It is created by increasing our sensitivity to
the particular details of the pain and humiliation of other, unfamiliar
sorts of people. Such increased sensitivity makes it more difficult to
marginalize people different from ourselves by thinking. . . . This process of coming to see other human beings as "one of us" rather than as
"them" is a matter of detailed description of what unfamiliar people
are like and of redescription of what we ourselves are like. . . . More
important, [culture] would regard the realization of utopias, and the
envisaging of still further utopias, as an endless, proliferating realization of Freedom, rather than a convergence towards an already existing Truth. (1989, 74)

While it is clear that Rorty continues to resist all ontological sources, religious
foundations, and metaphysical language in his articulation of the political, we
should not be too quick to dismiss his account as still displaying a certain Levinasian quality when it comes to the commitment to seek justice for those who have
been the victims of historical injustice. Indeed, Simon Critchley notes that "there
is room to ask how far apart Rorty and Levinas really are from each other" (1996,
33). For example, Critchley takes Rorty's proposal for how we as a community of
sufferers are to go about "achieving" such a "utopia," and this proposal raises the
same difficulties and offers the same challenges as Levinas's impossible demand on
politics. Critchley continues in this vein by asking: "Are not Rorty's definition of
liberalism and Levinas's definition of ethics essentially doing the same work, that
is, attempting to locate a source for moral and political obligation in a sentient dis-
position towards the other's suffering?" (1996, 33).

Although he would no doubt cringe at my phrasing, I find that when charita-
bly interpreted, a case could be made that Rorty also sees the need to rethink politics in light of the violent history of institutional blindness to the singularity of
the Other. Don't Levinas and Rorty both "agree that cruelty is the worst thing that
there is," Critchley wonders, "and that, furthermore, this is the only social bond
that we need" (1996, 33)? On Critchley's interpretation, by paying too much attention to the idea of "ethics" in Levinas and why it does not express his understanding of it, Rorty misses the eventual productive convergence of his own thought
with Levinas's political goals.

While I agree with Critchley regarding the importance of seeing possible lines of intersection between Levinas and Rorty, I find his account of their unity to be quite overstated. My discussion of the ontology of constitutive responsibility should allow us to see that there is much more to Levinas's theory of human inter-subjectivity and political interaction than a mere agreement not to be cruel. This resistance to cruelty, I would argue, is not merely a contingent social arrangement (though it certainly involves such an arrangement), but instead reflects something deeper that is constitutive of what is involved in the very possibility of social re-lationships. Even though there might be points on which Levinas would agree with Locke, Rousseau, and Rawls regarding the historical ways in which humans come together around shared interests, Levinasian sociality should not be con-fused with traditional social contract theory. It may be that the only practical norm that is required to get a certain vision of politics going is such a shared repulsion to cruelty, but motivated by the concern to eliminate the suffering of concrete oth-ers, Levinas argues that the responsibility to engage in such an activity is based in a constitutive relation to the very otherness of the Other. Critchley's formulation, although helpful for seeing lines of constructive engagement, deceptively over-states the agreement between Levinas and Rorty in this regard.

Moreover, Rorty and Levinas might initially seem quite close to each other in their resistance to "totalization." Both are explicitly committed to the rejection of any *meta*-narrative that would describe a final and non-revisable way of going about achieving a political goal. It would appear that political visions, for both Rorty and Levinas, resist completion in any future (understood here as a possible present). Indeed, they both announce that the real hope is precisely the continued revisability of any political structure. For Levinas, this would be the political up-shot of the "eschatological vision" inaugurated by the ethical relation; for Rorty, this would be the political result of being an "ironist" who opposes "final vocab-ularies." But despite this seeming convergence here, we need to pay attention to Rorty's ambivalence regarding the achievability of the liberal utopia. Ultimately, this ambivalence exposes a flaw in his formulation that is absent in the Levinasian account.

For example, in *Achieving Our Country*, Rorty indicates that this utopia could be plausibly instantiated: "But the country of one's dreams must be a country one can imagine being constructed, over the course of time, by human hands" (1998a, 102). It is difficult to make sense of how it is that Rorty's earlier claim that "the envisaging of still further utopias, [is] an endless, proliferating realization of Freedom" (1989, 189) could be reconciled with the construction of the utopia "over the course of time, by human hands." Now, one might attempt to defend Rorty by suggesting that the only thing he has described as "endless" is the continual "envisaging" of utopias and not the task of achieving the particular utopian vision that we currently hold. However, structural difficulties abound. Even if one grants that there is no political vision that is irrevisable in light of future developments and experiences, there is also no reason to conclude that one's vision *must* be continually revised. The difficulty that Rorty faces is that he is caught between two desires without the conceptual resources to respond adequately to them. On the one hand there is his pragmatic desire to only work toward those things that one can reasonably be expected to achieve. On the other hand there are his ironic tendencies that cause him to resist all theoretical finality.

It is here that the rather odd notion of the "liberal ironist" (it is odd given that ironists and liberals are set against each other as respectively concerned with the private and public) that I considered in chapter 1 demands reconsideration. If irony is a private matter regarding how one understands one's own existence and moral universe and, conversely, liberal hope is about how one understands one's political engagements and social expectations, then it is at least plausible that Rorty could overcome the tension between desires, here, by simply saying that the task of "envisioning" is "endless" because it is ironic while the task of "constructing" is achievable by "human hands" because it is a matter of actualizing a shared social hope. Accordingly, it would not be the public act of *bringing about* the utopia that is perpetually reconsidered, but the private venture of reflecting on what one would take the utopia to entail relative to what one considers to be the goals of one's existence. In this way, one would be a "liberal ironist" to the degree that one continually operates in both spheres, while continuing to respect the important distinction between them.

Were Rorty to deploy such a strategy, however, he would not eliminate the problems but simply relocate them. He would still have to explain how it is that one could keep the domains so separate (and as we have seen, he eventually comes around to admitting that they certainly overlap and mutually influence each other). Further, Rorty does not appear to allow for revisability in relation to one's liberalism as such. That is, the commitment that cruelty is the worst thing one can do is not something that Rorty seems ready to abandon if his particular social context were altered. Ironically, such an unwillingness, though out of step with his overall philosophical position, would be something to take quite seriously. What the ontology of constitutive responsibility makes clear is that there are some things— the ethico-religious relation to God and the Other—about which one should not be ironic. Now, it is likely that Rorty's response would be that his only point is that one's commitments are products of one's context and not of theological or philosophical foundations. Yet such a claim continues to stand in conflict with at least the structural possibility that one could bring about a liberal utopia that would, in the context of its own establishment, be understood as irrevisable, and thus, finally established. In the end, it looks like Rorty can only maintain his neo-Pragmatist commitment to ironic revisability by abandoning his neo-Pragmatist understanding of the liberal utopia.

In contrast, we can begin to really appreciate the significance of the tension that the paradoxical relationship between the ethico-religious (the infinity of obligation to God and the Other) and the political (the necessity of adjudication in light of conflicting obligations) necessarily maintains. As Diane Perpich writes: "Justice is just only as long as it recognizes its own constitutive incompleteness" (1998, 69). Yet this incompleteness is not now owing to the expanding imagination of human beings, but to the inaugural encounter with the Other articulated by Kierkegaardian transparency and Levinasian exposure. Although Kierkegaard, Levinas, and Rorty all appear to be in willing agreement regarding the incompleteness of justice, Kierkegaard and Levinas have a theoretical apparatus that can accommodate its truth while Rorty does not.

If Rorty wants to maintain his liberal commitment while also affirming constitutive revisability, then he would do well to consider the way in which the ontology of constitutive responsibility operates in such harmony with Derrida's idea of "a democracy to come" (*une démocratie à venir*).[27] In his more explicitly ethico-political writings such as *The Politics of Friendship, Specters of Marx*, and *Rogues*, Derrida offers a vision of politics as constitutively open-ended (see also Derrida 2000; 2002). No political structure or institution could ever account for each person in her or his radical singularity, and thus marginalization and violence are unavoidable in the domain of the political. As we saw earlier, in *The Gift of Death* he effectively argues that to fulfill my obligation to one person is to fail to fulfill it to another, and so on. Hence, the only ethically minded political system would be one that recognizes its incompleteness and continues to try to hear the voice that the religious traditions of Levinas and Kierkegaard refer to as "the widow, the orphan, and the stranger." Democracy is, then, always *yet to come*. It is only actualized in the promise of its actualization. The ethico-religious relation that demands this constant critique is also what issues this unrealizable promise toward which, in a very Levinasian-Kierkegaardian way, we continue to strive.

If the democracy to come were merely *another* or *different* democracy that human effort could achieve, then it would be structurally possible to adequately address the responsibility to every Other internal to such a system. At that moment, though, totalization comes dangerously close to totalitarianism because the relation to the Other is reduced to a finitely achievable task internal to a particular social arrangement. Responsibility would be finished internal to the demands of a state rather than continuing to make demands on any possible state. This slide to totalization (and even totalitarianism) is what Rorty's account is unable to close off as a possibility. In contrast to Rorty's claim about imagining the utopia's being achieved through "human hands," Derrida asserts that

> when I speak of democracy to come, this does not mean that tomorrow democracy will be realized, and it does not refer to a future democracy, rather it means that there is an engagement with regard to democracy which consists in recognizing the irreducibility of the promise when, in the messianic moment, "it can come." (1996, 83)

Despite the apparent similarities with Rorty's dream of an "endless, proliferating realization of Freedom," Derrida's notion is compatible with the "messianic" possibility announced by the "it can come" while Rorty's is not. Kierkegaard, Levinas, Derrida, and Rorty (as well as other new phenomenologists such as Marion, Henry, Lacoste, and Chrétien) can all be read as "envisioning" a quite similar, and perhaps even specifically democratic, political future. Now, I grant that the 'democratic' moniker is less *explicitly* apt for Kierkegaard, but when democracy is understood as the political structure that allows for constant self-critique, I would argue that it is applicable nonetheless. Because of the way that the ontology of constitutive responsibility operates to constantly bring the ethico-religious to bear on the political (and vice versa), for Kierkegaard, Levinas, and Derrida, among others, this future is "absolute" in its distance from where we find ourselves. For Rorty, it is never "absolute" in this way, but merely a long way off given the realities of contemporary existence. The im-possible (and we might even say "religious") status of the to-come is what makes it so important in new phenomenology, but also what makes it so unhelpful according to Rorty. In this way, Rebecca Comay (1987) has argued that Rorty's thought lacks what we might term the "deconstructive" openness to futurity so important for a continual commitment to justice (see also Simmons and Perpich 2005). Thus, with Comay, I want to suggest that Rorty should be viewed as an advocate of the status quo rather than of the to-come. If I am right about the importance of the ontology of constitutive responsibility for political critique, then what Rorty found to be "gawky, awkward, and unenlightening" might prove to be the very thing that Rorty requires for his own democratic vision to be coherent.[28]

In conclusion, it may be that, after a genuine engagement, Rorty's position and the position I have defended here will need to be substantially revised in light of one another. However, the basic strength of the Kierkegaardian-Levinasian-Derridean model is that it recognizes that exclusion may indeed be politically necessary, but contends that such exclusion can never be finally ethically, or ethico-religiously, justified. Keeping the distinction between the ethico-religious and politics open maintains this tension between necessity and justification because of the necessity of recursive hermeneutics.

Once it is made clear that Rorty shares with Levinas a deep concern for the future of "human solidarity," my hope is that those who find themselves working in Rorty's wake will be able to extend the invitation of "come, come" to Levinas and those working in the context of recent French philosophy. This, I want to suggest, is a much richer picture of "social hope" than can be found in Rorty's own authorship. And of course, as I have repeatedly argued, that this is lacking in Rorty should give us pause before we take him to be simply offering a neo-Pragmatist version of Kierkegaardian faith, Levinasian ethics, or Derridean deconstruction. Ironically, it is the strength of Rorty's critique and simultaneously the weakness of his alternative that assert the need to open a space for what promises to be a rich dialogue not only between various thinkers, but various philosophical traditions (e.g., see Haverkamp 1995).

By reading Kierkegaard and Levinas in conversation around issues of supreme importance, we are able to realize the importance of maintaining the tension between the relation to God and to the Other and the value that such an ethico-religious-ontological conception might have for political philosophy. A conversation between these figures—who were separated by time, faith, and circumstance—is a crucial backdrop for considering the recent developments in French phenomenology (often termed the "theological turn") and the potential contributions that such developments can make to mainstream philosophical debates and to contemporary social existence. In the next part of the book, I will consider the emergence and central commitments of "new phenomenology" in light of the ontology of constitutive responsibility that has been developed in Kierkegaard and Levinas, and then in part 3, I will bring the new phenomenology to bear on particular issues in ethics, politics, epistemology, and religion.

PART 2

Obligation and Transcendence in New Phenomenology

Up to this point I have been focusing almost exclusively on the way in which Søren Kierkegaard and Emmanuel Levinas, when taken together, are able to respond effectively to the critique offered by Richard Rorty regarding the political uselessness of the "religious" dimensions of Continental ethics and philosophy of religion. However, throughout the first five chapters I have frequently made reference to "new phenomenology" as the general trajectory in which I locate Levinas, and of which I understand Kierkegaard to be a forerunner. I will now transition to a more sustained consideration of new phenomenology in order to show how the "theological turn" of recent French philosophy stands as a resource for mainstream debates in contemporary ethics, politics, epistemology, and religion, which will be addressed in part 3.

Often dismissed by Continental thinkers as being too "theological" and by non-Continental thinkers as simply being unnecessarily opaque, new phenomenology is rarely considered, or even recognized, as presenting a coherent philosophical trajectory. Along with such descriptions as "the theological turn of French phenomenology," "Continental philosophy of religion," "religion without religion," and so on, references to "new phenomenology" are most often deployed as a loose way of referring to those French thinkers in the second half of the twentieth century who were working in the wake of Husserl (or more specifically, Heidegger) and who frequently used God-talk in their writing. Accordingly, even though books abound on the various thinkers affiliated with new phenomenology (Derrida, Henry, Levinas, Marion, etc.), it is fairly difficult to find considerations of new phenomenology as such. It is because of this general disregard for new phenomenology as expressing a unified philosophical perspective (while still displaying significant diversity among its proponents) that I chose to devote so much time to articulating the ontology of constitutive responsibility in part 1. It is the notion of subjectivity as established in an ethico-religious encounter with God and the Other that, I believe, functions as the underlying gesture of new phenomenology. The basic claim of part 2, then, is that new phenomenology is a single movement consisting of diverse threads, rather than a vague group of thinkers who all happen to be French and tend to speak about God.

My argument over the next three chapters will unfold as follows. First, I will provide a basic introduction to new phenomenology and situate it in the context of Husserlian phenomenology and Heideggerian thought. Second, I will argue that the "theological turn" is not a turn away from philosophy to theology, but a deepening of the phenomenological impulse originally articulated by Husserl. And third, I will show how the specifically "religious" (though still thoroughly philosophical) language found in new phenomenology—and in particular, the notion of *kenosis*—opens spaces for thinking productively about democratic politics.

SIX

Mapping Twists and "Turns": An Introduction to the Current Debate and Suggestions for Moving Forward

"Wasn't God Already Excluded?"

In response to Richard Rorty, I have argued that the decidedly "religious" themes and vocabulary of Kierkegaard and Levinas are socially relevant and politically useful. However, if we move from an engagement between contemporary phenomenology and neo-Pragmatism to a consideration of new phenomenology in the context of the phenomenological tradition itself, new problems seem to arise concerning such "religious" gestures. Considering the fact that Edmund Husserl explicitly excludes God from his phenomenology and that Martin Heidegger claimed by the mid-1920s that atheism is a methodological requirement for real philosophical inquiry, it might seem odd that God-talk is becoming prominent in contemporary phenomenology. Who would have thought that one of the most important French philosophers of the early twenty-first century—namely, Jean-Luc Marion—would on occasion write explicitly as a *Christian*? Indeed, many contemporary French philosophers are not simply talking about God as a philosophical problematic, but *actually believe in God*. Inaugurated by such post-Heideggerian French thinkers as Levinas, who published *Totality and Infinity* in 1961, and Michel Henry, who published *The Essence of Manifestation* in 1963, and continued by Jean-Luc Marion, Jean-Yves Lacoste, Jean-Louis Chrétien, and Jacques Derrida[1]—and gaining traction in the work of many philosophers currently working in America, for instance, Merold Westphal, John Caputo, Jeffrey Bloechl, and Hent de Vries—the "theological turn in French phenomenology" has been touted by some as a crucial step toward being able to think transcendence, alterity, and obligation in a postmodern context.[2]

Yet such God-talk faces a couple of basic challenges. On the one hand, there are those who see it as not really being a discourse about "God" at all. In light of Derrida's account of "religion without religion" and "messianism without a messiah," one does not need to look very far in post-Heideggerian philosophy for reason to wonder whether all this talk of "God" deserves to be called *religious*.[3] For some, Slavoj Žižek's desire for something more substantive than the watery stuff that passes as discourse on the "Postmodern God" might stand as a shared longing.[4] On the other hand, some critics such as Dominique Janicaud (1991; 2000) contend that contemporary phenomenology is perhaps legitimately religious, but this comes at the cost of no longer being phenomenological.

In the light of these lines of opposition, and depending upon the alternative ethico-religious ontology of constitutive responsibility, in this chapter I will give an overview of the recent seeming turn to religion in the phenomenological tradition.[5] First, I will lay out the stakes that surround contemporary phenomenological God-talk by offering a brief discussion of the Husserl-Heidegger heritage concerning philosophical considerations of God, and then raise Janicaud's major criticisms of the "theological turn." Then, in light of the ontology of constitutive responsibility, I will outline the main themes and arguments of those affiliated with this turn by articulating five unifying issues on which their thought tends to converge. Finally, as a way of anticipating part 3, I will conclude by suggesting several ways in which this philosophical trajectory is relevant to contemporary analytic philosophy of religion and other debates in mainstream philosophy.[6]

An *Excluded* God: Husserl, Heidegger, and Janicaud

In order to understand why the "theological turn" in phenomenology is plausibly considered as no longer representing *phenomenology,* it is important to go back to the original accounts of phenomenology in the work of Husserl and, subsequently, Heidegger. For Husserl, phenomenology is best understood as a presuppositionless inquiry into the structures of consciousness that accord with the very appearing of that which appears. Depending on such notions as "intentional consciousness" (the idea that consciousness is always a consciousness *of* something) and phenomenological "reduction" (bracketing from phenomenology everything that remains transcendent to the stream of intentional consciousness—e.g., questions regarding the existence of the external world), Husserl attempts to make phenomenology stand as the condition for all other science.[7]

Committed to the "principle of all principles," Husserl says that phenomenology is guided by the idea that intuition is self-legitimating (see 1982, §24). Intuition—which for Husserl is a rather commonplace notion of looking at something or observing something for oneself (see Russell 2006, chap. 5)—does not mediate between reason and an object, say, but instead is immediately receptive of the self-givenness of phenomena. This is the basis of the phenomenological maxim: "To the things themselves!" The principle of sufficient reason is not required in addition to what we directly intuit; and moreover, all intuition occurs only against a "horizon" that serves as the limiting condition of all phenomenality. This horizon gets worked out in various ways by Husserl, but for our purposes we can summarize the point by considering two articulations of it.[8] First, there is what might be called a *spatio-temporal horizon*. This can be demonstrated by the fact that when I perceive an object, I only perceive it from one "adumbrated" perspective. I only intuit a chair or a book, for example, from one specific position relative to it. Nonetheless, Husserl notes, all the other possible perspectives are co-presented with the intuition of the object itself. Second, there is in Husserl's later work what can be understood as a *horizon of situated meaning*. Developed primarily in *The Crisis of European Sciences and Transcendental Phenomenology*, this notion is described as the "lifeworld" (*Lebenswelt*) (see Husserl 1970). The lifeworld functions as a space of interpretation such that what appears is always already situated against a background of, as Matheson Russell writes, "complex social, political and religious forms of intersubjectivity" (2006, 194).[9] Accordingly, the "world" is not simply a collection of discrete objects, but the very space in which things are perceived as valuable, useful, hated, irrelevant, etc.

The upshot of this brief synopsis of Husserlian phenomenology is that we see that two things are essential: (A) phenomenology is limited to that which is immanent to the "sphere of consciousness" and attempts to describe those structures that comprise the "essence of *any consciousness whatever*" (Husserl 1982, §33, 65); and (B) all phenomena appear in the context of a horizon. If there is no horizon, then there is no appearance; and if no appearance, then no phenomenological inquiry.

Instantly, we can see why the idea of God is problematic for phenomenology. According to (A) above, the *existence* of the world is bracketed from phenomenology because of its transcendency to the sphere of consciousness. Accordingly, although possessing a transcendency other than that of the world, God is also appropriately bracketed (see Husserl 1982, §58). As if to remove all ambiguity, Husserl titles section 58 of *Ideas I*, "The Transcendency, God, Excluded." Additionally, in order for God to legitimately appear *as* God, God would seem to have to be "given" (or "appear") outside of all horizons and, as such, violate the requirement of (B). As *religious*, religious phenomena would have to operate according to their own standards in order to resist reduction to merely psychological, historical, cultural, or economic explanation.[10] The problem is that such a criterion seems unintelligible for phenomenological analysis because it would be radically particular (or better, singular) and not available as an essential structure of "any consciousness whatever." In light of Abraham's silence, we might say, religious experience looks as if it resists universalizability in the way that phenomenology requires in order for it to be the "rigorous science" that Husserl demands. Within the philosophical constraints that Husserl prescribes, a "religious phenomenon" would amount, as Marion suggests, "to an impossible phenomenon, or at least it [would] mar[k] the limit starting from which the phenomenon is in general no longer possible" (2000, 176).

While it is true that Heidegger takes a more expansive stance on the potential areas of phenomenological research by presenting what could be viewed as a *phenomenology of the excluded,* he too argues for an exclusion of God. His reasons for this are threefold. First, philosophy and theology are distinguished by their respective orientations. As he claims in his essay "Phenomenology and Theology" (1927/28, cited as Heidegger 2002a), the relationship between philosophy and theology is not a problem of the relationship between two worldviews, but "a question about the *relationship of two sciences*" (2002a, 50). Heidegger thus separates the *ontic* or "positive sciences," which are "sciences of beings," from philosophy which is an *ontological* science, that is, "*the* science of being" (2002a, 50). "Our thesis, then," Heidegger announces, "is that *theology is a positive science, and as such, therefore, is absolutely different from philosophy*" (2002a, 50). Theology, then, investigates not historicity as an ontological determination, but instead the historical phenomenon of "Christianness."

Second, theism does not allow for the radical questioning that characterizes the Heideggerian project. In the introduction to *Being and Time,* Heidegger defines questioning as a "seeking" (1996, §2, 3). In order to restore the meaning of the question of Being, fundamental ontology must be a seeking into the very nature of seeking itself. Yet if we start from a position of theism, then our seeking begins by already having found what it searches for: namely, God. Theism eliminates fundamental questioning because it claims to already possess the answers to that questioning. For this reason, Heidegger insists that philosophy must be a-theistic. By this he means that philosophy must be about the business of really following inquiry wherever it leads.

And finally, in order for God to be an object for inquiry and religious experience to remain adequately "religious," they must be thought otherwise than in the traditional philosophical—i.e., metaphysical—categories in which they have been hitherto articulated. This is Heidegger's later, quite famous critique of "onto-theology," which he described as follows:

> The original matter of thinking presents itself as the first cause, the *causa prima* that corresponds to the reason-giving path back to the *ultima ratio,* the final accounting. The Being of beings is represented fundamentally, in the sense of the ground, only as *causa sui.* This is the metaphysical concept of God. Metaphysics must think in the direction of the deity because the matter of thinking is Being. (2002b, 70)

For Heidegger, this philosophical appropriation of God is something to be over-come not just because it misunderstands the ontological difference (viz., that Be-ing is not *a* being), but also because it also misconceives God. *Causa sui* is "the right name for the god of philosophy," Heidegger comments, but the problem is that "man can neither pray nor sacrifice to this god. Before the *causa sui*, man can neither fall to his knees in awe nor can he play music and dance before this god" (2002b, 74). Heidegger, thus, advocates a "god-less thinking which must abandon the god of philosophy" (2002b, 75).

Although he excludes the transcendency of God from proper phenomeno-logical inquiry, Heidegger also, whether intentionally or not, opens the door for a radial re-thinking of how God might signify in human discourse and lived expe-rience. He wonders whether the particular version of godlessness he describes is "perhaps closer to the divine God." That is, "god-less thinking is [perhaps] more open to [God] than onto-theo-logic would like to admit" (2002b, 75). Despite advo-cating this a-theistic mode of thinking, Heidegger leaves room for a way forward that would *possibly* allow for divine encounters. Not explicitly developing where this way forward might lead, Heidegger offers it as something of an invitation to those who come after him: "No one can know whether and when and where and how this step of thinking will develop into a proper . . . path and way and road-building" (2002b, 75).

In his 1973 seminar in Zähringen, Heidegger again refers to this "path" that phenomenology offers to those who would attempt to follow:

> In philosophy, there are only paths; in the sciences, on the contrary, there are only methods, that is, modes of procedure. This understood, phenomenology is a path that leads away to come before . . . and it lets that before which it is led show itself. This phenomenology is a phenomenology of the inapparent. (2003, 80)

This "phenomenology of the inapparent" is precisely what Dominique Janicaud (1991; 2000) resists.[11] In the move toward a phenomenological openness to that which does not appear (at least not in a straightforward manner), Janicaud finds a dangerous temptation to leave the fundamental commitments of the phenome-nological method and veer into religious dogmatism—a far cry from the rigorous science of Husserl, to be sure. Without Heidegger's turn from the a-theism of fun-damental ontology to the possibility of a phenomenology of the inapparent, Jani-caud contends, "there would be no theological turn" (2000, 31).

Summarizing Janicaud's position, Bernard Prusak writes, "put dramatically, Janicaud inverts the scenario of Plato's *Apology:* he indicts Lévinas et al. for corrupt-ing the future of French philosophy by introducing into phenomenology a god—

the biblical God—who does not belong there" (2000, 4). For Janicaud, as an investigation into that which appears, phenomenology cannot concern itself with the inapparent. Although anticipated by Heidegger, the decisive moment in this turn away from the neutral method of Husserl, Janicaud suggests, occurs in the work of Levinas. Occupied primarily with the ethical relationship to the Other, Levinas's philosophy is a long demonstration of what a phenomenology of the inapparent might look like. Levinas claims that this ethico-religious "idea of the infinite" that is placed in us by the Other is not simply a qualitative or quantitative conception of the unlimited, but first and foremost a demand by the Other that inaugurates the very subjectivity of the subject. In the preceding chapters, it is this (pre)original demand (described by Levinas as "exposure" and by Kierkegaard as "transparency") that I suggested serves to establish an ontology of constitutive responsibility. However, as we saw in chapter 3, this ethico-religious encounter is best conceived as a bi-directional relationality according to which the self stands before God *and* the Other. On my reading of Levinas and Kierkegaard, God signifies in the relation to the Other, while this relation to the Other is precisely a gift from God. Paradoxically, our relation to the most desirable (God, the Infinite) necessarily directs us to the least desirable (the needy other person). The self is, thus, constituted in the response to God's demand that I be Other-directed. However, it is immediately clear that this entire account requires that we somehow apply phenomenological description to that which can't properly be "experienced" (viz., the constitutive relation to alterity) and does not "appear" as such (viz., the "command" of God and/ or the "call" of the Other). We can now clearly see the phenomenological problem that confronts what I consider to be the essential characteristic of new phenomenology: it would seem that at the very place where the ontology of constitutive responsibility goes beyond traditional ontology, it also goes beyond phenomenological consideration.[12]

Referring to Levinas's notion of the "idea of infinity," Janicaud asserts that "between the unconditional affirmation of Transcendence and the patient interrogation of the visible, the incompatibility cries out; we must choose" (2000, 26). Although Levinas claims to be following the original "inspiration" of phenomenology, Janicaud considers his thought to "suppose[e] a nonphenomenological . . . metaphysico-theological montage, prior to philosophical writing." Rather than being presented with a rational decision on the basis of good (i.e., phenomenological) evidence, "the dice are loaded and choices made; faith rises majestically in the background" (2000, 27). Not only is Levinas unphenomenological, on this account he is a bad philosopher who is prone to question-begging and sophistry. It is important that we understand that Janicaud's critique, here, does not only apply to Levinas in particular, but more appropriately to the basic gesture of an ethico-religious encounter and bi-directional relationality. In this way, we should consider

Janicaud's frustration to be directed toward new phenomenology as a coherent (non-phenomenological) trajectory, and not merely toward the claims of a specific thinker.

Refusing to let phenomenology be intimidated by this "faith," Janicaud insists that once we leave the domain of that which appears, we have left phenomenology.[13] There were good reasons that Husserl, and even Heidegger, excluded the transcendency of God and, as far as Janicaud is concerned, we ought to consider the matter to be settled. What takes the name of "phenomenology" after Levinas is simply non-phenomenological.[14] While some have suggested that Husserl is more open to the possibility of God than Janicaud's rather restrictive reading allows (a claim I will consider in chapter 7),[15] I will forego this question in order to offer an account of exactly what such a discourse involves, as developed in the work of new phenomenology.

A *Possible* God: New Phenomenology

The most prominent application of phenomenology to questions of religion occurred in the "phenomenology of religion" articulated by such thinkers as Rudolf Otto, Mircea Eliade, and Gerardus van der Leeuw. These thinkers followed Schleiermacher's idea that if we want to understand religion, we need to understand the lived realities of religious believers in their actual practices. Bracketing normative questions such as the truth or falsity of religious beliefs, phenomenology of religion was guided by the question: what is religion as lived? This strain of phenomenological God-talk, or better, "sacred"-talk, has lost its prominence in contemporary philosophical debates. Jeffrey Kosky suggests two reasons for this decline: (1) it did not adequately defend itself against the charge of being disguised theology, but was better suited to spiritual seekers than to rigorous scholarship, and (2) it lacked the critical relationship to its own discourse that is required in order for it to argue for its own legitimacy (2000, 111–12).

What primarily distinguishes "new" or "radical" phenomenology, with which Janicaud is so frustrated, from these classic figures in the phenomenology of religion is the way in which new phenomenology takes as its very starting point the critical question of its possibility *as a phenomenological project*. Importantly, this question is self-consciously considered according to a Husserlian framework. While sharing concerns regarding religious phenomena with the phenomenologists of religion mentioned above, such issues are now raised within the context of a serious engagement with the very possibility of extending a Husserlian account of phenomenology to matters ostensibly "excluded" from it.

New phenomenology tends to resist extremely precise definition. Consisting of thinkers who are Jewish, Protestant, Catholic, and at least one who claimed to "rightly pass for an atheist,"[16] this loose confederation also boasts scholars of modern philosophy, psychoanalysis, ancient philosophy, and Thomism. While widely divergent, their philosophies tend to share (to varying degrees) the following five characteristics: (1) an insistence that what they are doing is philosophy and not theology, (2) a connection between God and the Other, (3) a specifically kenotic understanding of God, (4) a stress on the immediacy of religious experience and the difficulty of expression, and (5) a post-foundationalist epistemology of trust.[17] I consider all of these to be importantly related to the underlying ontology of constitutive responsibility that functions in new phenomenology.

Philosophy, not Theology

While Hent de Vries affirms with Janicaud that there has been a religious turn in phenomenology, he is markedly at odds with him regarding the way this turn should be understood. For Janicaud, as we have seen, this "turn" is a veering away from phenomenology (and even philosophy) and toward theological orthodoxy. Alternatively, de Vries argues that the turn should best be understood as an attempt at finding a new resource to aid phenomenological study. This new resource is, in fact, the very old theological archive located specifically (though not necessarily) in the Jewish and Christian traditions. For de Vries, dipping into this vast literature for alternative descriptions and vocabulary is not a movement toward positive religion, but a heuristic device that allows philosophical inquiry to recognize its own critical limits and continual hermeneutic struggle (1999, 2).[18]

Let's consider just a few examples of this philosophical, rather than theological, directive. In the philosophies of Derrida, Levinas, Marion, and Henry, the "religious" is raised more as a *possibility* for thought than as an *actuality* to be affirmed (even though some of them *personally* profess religious commitments). More importantly, they all rely on solidly phenomenological criteria to guide their inquiries; appeals to the authority of religious traditions and sacred texts are strictly prohibited. This is the upshot of the self-critical relation to its discourse that is displayed by new phenomenology and was lacking in the classic "phenomenology of religion." As Marion writes, "the question concerning the possibility of the [religious] phenomenon implies the question of the phenomenon of possibility" (2000, 177). Accordingly, new phenomenology as a whole invites a rethinking of transcendental methodology in the same way that Kierkegaard and Levinas did in chapter 5. By considering, on the one hand, the conditions for religious phenomena, while on the other hand taking seriously the need to rigorously think through the im-possibility of such conditions, new phenomenology requires that philosophy wrestle with what I earlier termed *quasi-logical existential conditionality*. Such a project is undertaken in new phenomenology relative to the following questions: are phenomena philosophically accessible *as* "religious," and if so, would this accessibility allow such phenomena to remain properly religious in the ways that matter? To put this question in a more Janicaudian tenor, we might ask: if a horizonless appearance is impossible, then why is it still under phenomenological consideration? Disagreement abounds regarding how such questions should get worked out—Derrida and Marion, for instance, have very different responses—yet all agree that the answers must be achieved through arguments concerning phenomenality and not disputes over religious doctrines (see Caputo and Scanlon, 1999).

As an example of this procedure, Levinas repeatedly deploys his own Jewish tradition, but he makes very clear that he does not do so as appeals to their authority as *religious*. Indeed, if they are to be authoritative, it is because they accord with what the inquiry into lived existence has already affirmed. They are, however, significantly *illuminative*. Like Levinas, who throughout his career authored a series of "Talmudic Lectures," which he carefully distinguished from his philosophical authorship, Marion makes very clear when he is writing as a philosopher (e.g., Marion 2002a; 1998) and when he allows himself to speak from his own Christian tradition (e.g., Marion 1991). Similarly, when Henry provides an extended consideration of Jesus' statement, "I am the truth," he does so as an interrogation of what it could mean for this statement to be meaningful and true, rather than as an affirmation of its truth. That is, his investigation never claims that it *is* true, but only that certain things would be required for it to be a *possibility* (Henry 2003). The same could be said of Chrétien's robust discussions of prayer, hope, memory, and touch (see Chrétien 2004; 2002).

In all of these cases, the crucial issue is one of coming to grips with the basic questions of appearance, existence, consciousness, and expression—solidly philosophical notions, to be sure. Despite leaving room open for philosophical arguments in favor of theological truths, new phenomenology is actually in agreement with Janicaud that "phenomenology and theology make two" (Janicaud 2000, 99–103). If anything, a commitment to tarrying on the supposed barriers between these discourses makes it likely that new phenomenologists are all the more sensitive to worries of inappropriate crossings (and concerned about articulating the conditions under which such moves would be inappropriate). It is in this regard that I take the importance of bi-directional relationality to signify. By maintaining the tension between the relation to God and the relation to the Other—i.e., by not settling the question of priority—the relation between philosophy and theology will remain something that does not demand finished articulation, but is able to function as a dynamic engagement between discourses. This relation should continue to be thought and rethought as new issues and questions occur in the lives of individuals who are committed to philosophical rigor while seeking to be faithful to God and working for justice for the Other.

The Trace of God in the Face of the Other

This second characteristic theme of new phenomenology is directly related to the ontology of constitutive responsibility. What I take to be the most prominent strand running through new phenomenology arises from the question of how phenomenology is able to account for radical otherness (alterity) without, again, needing to decide the question of priority. Part of the problem with Husserl and Heidegger, suggests Levinas, is the fact that the horizon in which everything presents itself is always egoistic. That is, they all fall into an ontological discourse that fails to respect the primacy of the ethico-religious. In particular, Levinas reads Husserl's "Fifth Cartesian Meditation" as suggesting that the other person should be primarily thought of as an alter-ego (another being like me). Further, Levinas claims that Heidegger's early notion of "mineness" serves to eliminate all possibilities of really encountering an other *as* Other. The obstacles that one faces when attempting to articulate a phenomenology of the inapparent harks back to Marion's contention that the religious phenomenon would have to be an "impossible phenomenon": in signifying according to phenomenological criteria, it would no longer be properly religious, but alternately, if it remains properly religious (i.e., properly Other) then it is unavailable for description in phenomenological terms. When confronted with this "disastrous alternative," as Marion terms it, we are forced to confront the limits of our discourse, our conceptualities, and our world. How then can alterity, as such, signify at all?

Though the new phenomenologists all work out answers to this question in different ways, what tends to unite them is an affirmation of the connection between God's self-showing and the relation of the self to the other person. That is, they all in one form or another affirm the ontology of constitutive responsibility. For Levinas, as we have seen, the trace of God only appears in the face of the Other. God appears as the *command* to love my neighbor. In other words, I am not first in a relationship with God and *then* a recipient the divine ethical imperative. Rather, the intersubjective ethical relation is what constitutes me as a self and only as such can I subsequently recognize God as the source of this relation.

Expressing the basic insight of bi-directional relationality, for Levinas this divine encounter occurs in the space of political life. In order to love God I must care for my neighbor, because there is no space where I meet God except in a life lived in service to "the widow, the orphan, and the stranger." Derrida (1994; see also Caputo 1997b) extends this line of thought when he describes a "messianism without a messiah." The idea here is that the time spent awaiting the messiah should not be understood according to the categories of a determinate religion, but as an expectation of justice. Messianism is, thus, not primarily a theological doctrine, but another name for the structure of the "to-come" (à venir). And yet Derrida appropriates decidedly religious vocabulary in order to tap into the model of expectation that historical messianisms have successfully articulated. The way that Judaism and Christianity, for example, have conceived of faith as structurally defined by such notions as the promise, the gift, and the eschaton becomes a resource for philosophical considerations of how we should live today relative to the not yet—for example, in Heidegger's account of "being-toward-death" or Ricœur's attempt to think "freedom in light of hope" (as considered in chap. 5). For Derrida this religious faith is expressed as a political commitment to constantly work, as Levinas would say, for an "ever increasing justice." This is a goal that is never actualizable, but instead is perpetually expected in the "democracy to come." As we saw earlier in contradistinction to Rorty's "liberal utopia," this democracy is not a specific political system to be instantiated, but an ideal that continuously contests our existing institutions and practices as failing to be *sufficiently* just. This political project is, on Derrida's model, ethico-religiously invested. God's infinity is glimpsed through the infinity of the responsibility for each and every other person; as Derrida has it in *The Gift of Death*, "tout autre est tout autre." Building upon this idea, new phenomenology rethinks temporality as essentially eschatologically oriented, and the *eschaton* can be loosely understood as the coming kingdom of God. For Levinas and Derrida, God's "coming" is not necessarily affirmed as a religious thesis but as a political expectation lived out here and now (see Simmons and Kerr 2009).

Though not as explicitly, Marion, Henry, Lacoste, and Chrétien also stress this political dimension of new phenomenology. For Marion (esp. 2002b), God is the absolutely self-given pure gift of love. This gift is not presented with the expectation of payback (i.e., according to an economic logic), but is an-economic. It is pure givenness (*donation*) without return. Henry (2003) claims that according to Christianity all humans exist in the condition of being "sons" of God according to the "truth of life." This status requires a radical rupture of the power-relations that obtain according to the objectifying tendencies which constitute the "truth of the world." In pure Life, all beings are constituted in their relation to God / Life as such and not according to their socio-economic, gendered, raced, and sexed identities. This is not to say that these identity markers are not radically important, but merely that in relation to God, our relations to others are bathed in the light of other-service and not self-interest. Similarly, Lacoste (2004) proposes a "kenotic treatment of the question of man" in which the self is established precisely in its being dispossessed *of itself.* This dispossession is a fundamental challenge to all egoism and arrogance. Overcoming these self-interested dispositions is hard work, and Lacoste contends that our task is to live toward the "kingdom of heaven" in which the relation of self, God, and others is able to come into absolute harmony (2004, chap. 9). Extending this idea, Chrétien (2004) argues that at stake in hearing God's voice is the very idea of hearing the "call of the Other" in the first place. Reminiscent of the Levinasian articulation, for Chrétien, responding to this call is the fundamental act that constitutes subjectivity. The world is the space in which we hear and respond to this voice. In all of these various ways, the new phenomenologists are committed to the ontology of constitutive responsibility and the way in which the self is defined by a relation to God *and* the Other.

Kenosis

On any measure, new phenomenology talks quite a bit about God. But what sort of God is talked about? It is clearly not the God of onto-theology described by Heidegger. The onto-theological or metaphysical God is a God of power, self-sufficiency, and distance. In stark contrast, the God of new phenomenology is a God of love, service, humility, and proximity. In short, for new phenomenology, God is *a kenotic God*.[19]

Because I will return to this idea in detail in chapter 8, for now I want to roughly describe *kenosis* as the idea of God's being in a self-emptying relation to the world. This kenotic God looks at me in the face of the Other (Levinas), gives Godself as pure love (Marion), humbly hopes for my works of love and justice (Derrida), constitutes me as a "son" (Henry), serves as the condition for lived hope (Ricœur), calls to me in the voice and touch of the Other (Chrétien), and disrupts the egoism of the self (Lacoste). Rather than focusing on God's omnipotence and omniscience, new phenomenology begins its discourse on God by focusing on the reality and fragility of the human situation, and hence, its God-talk stresses what could be considered the invitational "weakness" of God, as Caputo would say (Caputo 2006).[20]

Of crucial importance to a kenotic articulation of God and humanity is the way in which it opens up a radical ethics of humility, invitation, and gratitude. This is not without importance for the political stakes of new phenomenology. When the relation to God is understood as inaugurating an invitation to a life of service, this explodes all presumptions of egoistic (and often, as in Rorty's case, ethnocentric) isolation, whether in our discursive practices or our political policies. The most specific way that this kenotic conception of God gets translated into interpersonal relations is in the expression of *hospitality*. Hospitality is a salient theme in Derrida's late works (e.g., 1999; 2000; 2002) and extends back through the phenomenological tradition to Heidegger's rather cryptic deployment of the Heraclitus fragment in the *Letter on Humanism*. There, Heraclitus responds to strangers who have requested to see the great philosopher in action by inviting them into his house and claiming that it is there that the "gods come to presence" (Heidegger 1993, 257). If God is to "appear," it will likely be in the space where we open ourselves up to the call, *and critique,* of the Other.

Religious Experience and the Difficulty of Expression

As we have seen, according to the Husserlian "principle of all principles" all intuition must be given against a horizon. Yet, the religious phenomenon seems to resist such horizonality. Can religious experience be described phenomenologically while still allowing its religiosity to remain? For new phenomenology, there is room for debate on this issue. Some, like Derrida, suggest that all phenomena must be given according to horizons, for this is the very condition of givenness, and so religious phenomena are constitutively im-possible; but as we have seen, this does not prevent a consideration of them in their very im-possibility. Marion (see 1998; 2002a) disagrees, and contends for a pure givenness without recourse to horizon. This is what he terms the "fourth reduction" of phenomenology: everything is bracketed except the actual givenness of the given itself. What results is a "saturated" phenomenon (Marion 2000), that is, the religious phenomenon is meaningful beyond the bounds of intelligibility. Simply put, divine revelation, if such a thing exists, would have to be received as expressing more than can be articulated within the limits of human discourse and conceptualization. Both Derrida and Marion agree that regardless of their possibility or im-possibility, religious phenomena present problems for expression (see Caputo and Scanlon 1999). This same problematic can be seen in Henry's notion of "Life" (how do we speak about that which does not allow for objectification?) and Lacoste's notion of "Liturgy" (how do we conceive of that which is the condition for conceptualization in the first place?).

In the more determinate analyses found in Chrétien's (2000) phenomenology of prayer and Ricœur's (2000) consideration of scripture, the problem of expression is confronted in detailed descriptions of concrete experience. In these texts, we find a heightened sensitivity to the necessity of considering the phenomena as they confront us in lived existence. And yet, as Ricœur notes, we are unsure of how to assess the status of the *"immediacy* that could be claimed by the dispositions and feelings allied with the call-and-response structure in a religious order" (2000, 129). Here he is distinguishing between the question/answer structure and that of the call/response structure. Religious discourse operates according to the latter in its recognition of Christ's words being imperatives and religious life being one of obedience. It is easy to give a historical or third personal account of religious discourse, but how do we account for its being *immediately* intuited as such? Chrétien (2000) asks a similar question when, after describing prayer as the "wounded word" that breaks our status as self-sufficient egos, he wonders what serves as the condition for its being received at all.

In all the preceding themes, we have seen the self-critical relation of new phenomenology to its accounts of phenomenality. Implicated in the description of religious experience is the question of the possibility of this experience itself. With
that said, we can also see one more way in which new phenomenology tends to
converge on a thematic: it resists strong foundational justification and infallibilist
affirmations. New phenomenology is a phenomenology of "questions and question marks," as Nietzsche might say. Even so, in anticipation of chapter 11, let me
suggest that we can find a potential thread for developing what might be called a
deconstructive theory of justification by considering Derrida's claim that "there
is no society without faith, without trust in the other" (Caputo 1997a, 23). Some
of the most prominent conceptions of new phenomenology—Levinas's "Other,"
Ricœur's "hope," Derrida's "justice," Henry's "Life," Chrétien's "call," Lacoste's
"Liturgy," and Marion's "gift"—are all offered as matters of trust and not claims of
certainty (as with Abraham's relation to God's command, I want to leave open the
question of whether the term "knowledge" is applicable here). This does not mean
that we fall back into blind fideism, however. Instead, new phenomenology provides strong arguments and gives considered reasons to, like the author of Psalms
34 encourages us, "taste and see" for ourselves. Phenomenology has always been
about first-personal engagement; and new phenomenology is no different. Its diverse accounts are all conjoined in the commitment to offering accounts of that
which itself requires, perhaps demands, a singular self-investment. As Levinas will
often say, echoing Kierkegaard, we cannot achieve absolute guarantees that these
phenomenological and existential possibilities actually obtain, but while still being philosophically rigorous (and perhaps even because of this rigor), we can *trust*
that the relation to God *and* the Other is a "fine risk" (OTB, 167).

God as *Invitation:* New Conversations across Old Lines

There is no shortage of accounts of the marked divide between Continental
philosophy of religion and what occurs in "traditional" or "classical" philosophy
of religion, either in its historical forms originating in the Middle Ages or in contemporary Anglo-American analytic manifestations. As John Caputo writes, "the
talk about God and religion in contemporary continental philosophy bears almost
no resemblance to what passes for traditional 'philosophy of religion'" (2002, 2).
Philip Goodchild concurs when he claims that the "problems, tasks, concepts, reasoning, and cultural location" of Continental philosophy of religion "are markedly different from [the] identity" of Anglo-American philosophy of religion (2002,
1–2). While there are certainly dangers in too quickly covering over the differences
between these philosophical traditions, I want to point out that there are also sub-

stantial problems with too rigidly keeping them apart. Unfortunately, many on both sides of the aisle have simply rejected the discourse of the other side: Continental philosophy of religion is often dismissed as lacking seriousness, while analytic philosophy of religion is often depicted as existentially irrelevant. In other words, when viewed from the outside (and perhaps even sometimes from the inside), phenomenological complexity can be interpreted as masking philosophical and theological vacuity, while analytical rigor can be seen as a cover for philosophical and theological arrogance. This situation has made it extremely difficult for proponents of either approach to hear the insights and challenges of the other.

Having described the importance of humility and invitation in accounts of a kenotic God, there is good reason to believe that by attending to possible lines of contact between these perspectives would better prepare us to receive the call of the Other—even when that call comes from a "rival" philosophical tradition. To this end, and in order to set up part 3, I want to offer a few brief points of overlap (certainly not an exhaustive list by any means) where I think there is much work to be done in bringing the themes of new phenomenology into conversation with the debates of contemporary analytic philosophy of religion.

First, the phenomenological focus on the connection between religion and justice stands as a much-needed interlocutor in current debates surrounding religion in the public square (see chapter 10)—which is as relevant (if not more relevant) to contemporary political philosophy as it is to the philosophy of religion. Possible areas in which this connection might be pursued include: whether political justification should be understood primarily as an epistemological task or an ethical task; how to understand the stakes of leaving aspects of one's subjectivity out of public discourse; and whether liberalism and/or democracy emerge as viable political visions.

Because I will go into more depth on the matter in chapter 10, I will here just provide one quick example of how new phenomenology might be a resource for such debates by considering the role of religion in the public square. Especially since (and largely because of) John Rawls, questions regarding the status of religion in the public square have primarily been addressed in terms of the norms and expectations of reason-giving. As is well known, Rawls's "political liberalism" insisted that all "comprehensive doctrines" be excluded as justificatory accounts in the public square.[21] According to this framework, justificatory accounts that cannot be accepted by all rational persons—and thus, appeals to revealed texts or specific religious traditions—are illegitimate as political reasons.

It has been frequently suggested that basic Rawlsian framework has serious problems. For example, Nicholas Wolterstorff argues quite convincingly that public reason is not really "neutral" with respect to comprehensive doctrines; rather, it privileges those who are not religious (see Audi and Wolterstorff 1997).[22] Indeed, religious persons are asked to leave decisive aspects of their own identity out of the public square, which in turn assumes that religion can be marginalized in its impact on a person's commitments and social vision. In order to fully participate in public discourse, religious individuals have to abandon (or at least suspend the influence of) some of their most deeply held convictions. Such a defense of the necessity of marginalizing certain beliefs, many claim, is tantamount to an outright exclusion of religious persons from the political square—a place which is supposed to ensure "justice as fairness," and maintain equal opportunity for all.

While there are crucial epistemological stakes regarding the above political debate, new phenomenology encourages an ethico-religious rethinking, and reframing, of the issue. Rather than cast the public role of religion as a question about what epistemic standard is going to be publicly recognized, these thinkers offer resources for considering the matter as a task of how to be constantly open to the speech of the other person. Those with differing comprehensive doctrines are not to be viewed as impediments to social discourse, but instead as opportunities for hearing criticism of one's own position. Justification is, then, not first and foremost about *fixing a criterion* but about *listening to difference.* When viewed this way, we are able to pay better attention to the ways in which religion is always already politically situated and "the political" is a name for the existential situation of being constitutively responsible to multiple other people.

Bringing Levinas's claim that "responsibility precedes freedom" to bear on the idea of a neutral "public reason"—which, whether intentionally or not, often leads to marginalization in the name of stability—might open new spaces for how to understand the politics of difference in a democratic context.[23] Here we find important questions about how to "hear" the speech of the other and incorporate this speech into a national identity. Along with scholars of feminism, critical race theory, queer theory, postcolonial and multicultural politics, new phenomenology helps us realize that if we assume that certain citizens should leave decisive aspects of their identities out of public life *tout court,* then we problematically fall back into a liberal version of the very problem of exclusion and injustice that Rawls attempted to overcome with the ideas of the "original position" and the "veil of ignorance."

This thematic of political difference is also relevant to the phenomenological difficulties with speaking about God and receiving God's "speech" to us. Here Marion, Ricœur, and Chrétien stand as important contributors to issues raised by Wolterstorff's work on "divine discourse" (see Wolterstorff 1995).[24] Perhaps, as new phenomenology tends to suggest, questions of political expression, religious experience, and ethical responsibility are most productively considered together. The links that contemporary French philosophy has drawn between the gift, ethical responsibility, social justice, and religious transcendence have the potential to redirect the ways in which these debates in political philosophy and philosophy of religion are considered.

Further, as I will discuss in chapter 11, the post-foundationalist epistemology of trust articulated by recent French thought has not been adequately explored in its connection with both contemporary advocates of "modest foundationalism" and also the account of trust advocated by proponents of "Reformed epistemology," for example. Alvin Plantinga's idea that belief in God is a "properly basic belief" which can serve as the justificatory basis for other beliefs without itself being justified relative to something else (see 1998, chap. 5), provides important possibilities for understanding the role of justice in Derrida, the ethical relation in Levinas, the gift in Marion, or the Truth of Life in Henry. All of these figures, in various ways of course, require the affirmation of particular assertions without contending that these assertions are strongly foundational or inferentially derived from other beliefs. In new phenomenology and, I believe, on certain readings of Reformed epistemology, trust and hope are championed rather than final knowledge, certainty, and epistemic guarantees. On this front, Plantinga's suggestion of proper basicality and Wolterstorff's conception of "control beliefs" are important counterparts to ideas in new phenomenology that serve as the inspiration for continued philosophical thought and social life.[25]

Moreover, although a bit more wide-ranging, Keith Lehrer's (1997) nonreligious notion of an epistemology of trust regarding the idea of a relationship to oneself (I must trust myself as a reliable truth-seeker), and occasionally suggested by Annette Baier (1995) and even Richard Rorty (1999) in regard to social relations (interpersonal, political relationships depend upon a confidence that others will respect the agreements we have made with each other), would make for productive conversation partners with the Continental idea that justification is about an existential investment rather than a logical necessity.

In the same vein, the critique of the adequacy of language, propositional form, and intellectual comprehension relative to the actual content of the "saturated" religious phenomena should be considered in non-Continental debates regarding the limits of reason in religious belief. Old disputes over the role of arguments for the existence of God, and disagreements about whether a priori arguments suffice (as in Anselm) or a posteriori evidence must be considered (as in Aquinas), could be reinvigorated by Marion's and Derrida's work on God's relationship to experiential and conceptual horizons. On this front, issues of philosophical skepticism and contemporary philosophy of language are also implicated. For example, are certain language games (Marion's as opposed to Swinburne's, say) better able to countenance religious phenomena while still remaining philosophically viable?

And does the move from conditions of possibility (e.g., Aquinas, Kant) to conditions of im-possibility (e.g., Levinas, Derrida) actually suggest a reason for skepticism when it comes to religious truth-claims?[26]

And finally, as implicitly suggested above, historical debates surrounding figures like Augustine and Aquinas, who have both in various ways have been inspirational resources for much of the very recent in new phenomenology, would likely be enriched by, and be an enriching influence upon, the new phenomenological considerations of such religious expressions as testimony, worship, and praise. Given the postmodern commitment to the historical contextualization of all truth-claims and the humility of perspective that results, scholarly work being done in the history of Christian thought continues to redefine the ways in which we find ourselves as inheritors of this tradition—whether religiously in Marion, or epochally in Heidegger, or ideologically and culturally in Gianni Vattimo. And furthermore, as more work is done on comparative philosophy and religious pluralism, the potential for new spaces of discourse to open up within the hitherto primarily Jewish and Christian orientation of Continental philosophy of religion also significantly increases.

Having offered these few suggestions for how Continental philosophy of religion can be productively brought into conversation with more mainstream philosophical debates, I do not want to give the impression that these areas have not received any serious attention to date. In almost all of the above areas, there are individuals pursuing similar lines of inquiry as those I have touched on.[27] While wanting to celebrate the work of those scholars, we should also realize that such research often faces a difficult reception: it is often too Continental for analytic philosophers, or the reverse. As someone who attempts to work at an intersection, I am convinced that by carrying the conversation across lines that appear to be forbidding, philosophers of religion can make substantial movements toward not only thinking the radical invitation of God as an invitation to engage one another, but toward accepting the invitation in our professional activities.

Conclusion: Envisioning New Possibilities

Many commentators have suggested that contemporary philosophy of religion is facing new opportunities. In this chapter I have argued that such opportunities invite conversation across traditional lines of philosophical opposition. Taking seriously the bi-directional responsibility inaugurated by the ethico-religious encounter offers promising avenues for Continental thought to be involved and engaged in such a conversation. In the next chapter, I will give fuller consideration to the distinction between phenomenology and theology and suggest one particular way of understanding this relationship that is especially productive.

SEVEN

Reconstructive Separatism:
On Phenomenology and Theology

Having now outlined the basic characteristics that I take to unify new phenomenology as a philosophical trajectory, I want to further explore the relationship between phenomenology and theology occurring in the work of these predominantly French thinkers. In the previous chapter, I suggested that the distinction between these communities of discourse is taken quite seriously by new phenomenologists, but in a way that maintains an important dynamism rather than a final separation. Perhaps no one has been so robust in advocating an absolute split between phenomenology and theology as Dominique Janicaud. Though I have briefly discussed Janicaud's frustration with the "theological turn," there is quite a bit more to be done detailing exactly how and why his critique continues to stand as something with which new phenomenologists would do well to contend. So here I not only want to lay out Janicaud's position in more detail but to offer a more thorough defense of the decidedly philosophical and phenomenological work of those affiliated with the "turn" in French phenomenology.

In what follows, I will consider Janicaud by way of an engagement with a collection of essays published in 2005 under the title *God in France* (Jonkers and Welton 2005; see also Simmons 2005). The nine essays in *God in France* are all agreed that, despite Janicaud's influential contention, there has not been a properly "theological turn" in French phenomenology. Instead, in various ways, the authors suggest that new phenomenology does not represent a theological or religious influx into a formerly philosophical discussion, but rather brings phenomenology to bear on issues of central importance to the philosophy of religion. This shift of emphasis may indeed push phenomenology beyond the limits that were laid out by Husserl in *Logical Investigations* and *Ideas I,* but the work done by Marion, Henry, Levinas, Derrida, Lacoste, Chrétien, and others on this front, is still correctly regarded as *phenomenology.*

Although I agree with the general contention of *God in France* regarding the legitimately phenomenological enterprise of new phenomenology, it would be quite naive to suggest that that volume has decided the question of the relationship between phenomenology and theology. In *God in France,* contesting Janicaud's reading of recent French philosophy does not result in the suggestion of a theo-phenomenology or phenomeno-theology, but rather an affirmation of Janicaud's deeper position that "phenomenology and theology make two" (Janicaud 2000, 99ff.). *God in France* does not, I contend, open a new space for thinking the relationship between phenomenology and theology, but merely offers a new reading of phenomenology itself as more hospitable to God-talk. While the authors recognize that this will have implications for theology, they all stop short of articulating what these implications are and how we might begin to envision a conversation across boundaries that continue to be all too rigid, though still quite necessary. It is because *God in France* resists Janicaud's reading of new phenomenology *and* falls prey to a temptation to establish too solid a divide between phenomenology and theology that I have chosen to focus on it here.

In this chapter, then, I aim to more deeply engage and critique Janicaud's reading of new phenomenology and to propose what I take to be an account of the relationship between phenomenology and theology that is both functional and flexible. I will first recount the way in which *God in France* contests Janicaud's estimation of the "theological turn," and rightly contends for the philosophical/phenomenological viability of new phenomenology. Then I will show that even if one affirms this conclusion, which I do, it can serve to problematically reinforce the strict division between phenomenology and theology announced by Janicaud rather than to rethink it. Namely, while Janicaud's *separatist* strategy occludes the historical situatedness of reason and the contextuality of all human thought, the strategy of *God in France* comes close to merely *reconstructing* theology on phenomenological grounds, which tends toward replacing the particularity of specific religions with the abstraction of what we might term the "postmodern religious." Accordingly, in response to what I consider to be the inadequacies of both strategies, I will advocate a notion of *reconstructive separatism* that maintains the distinctiveness of each discourse while avoiding the dangers of worldlessness and abstraction that accompanies the latter strategy. And in conclusion, I will briefly outline the way in which such a reconstructive separatism could open the space for a postmodern apologetic enterprise, which I take to be crucial if new phenomenology is not to be viewed as incompatible with determinate religious traditions.

Phenomenologists after All?

As I see it, Janicaud's position contains three major interrelated assertions: (1) phenomenology must be about appearances; (2) staying true to Husserl's "principle of all principles" (Husserl 1983, §24) requires phenomenology to be only about immanence; and (3) ultimately, then, as Husserl notes, any discussion of "absolute" and "transcendent" being must "remain excluded from the new field of research which is to be provided" by phenomenology (Husserl 1983, §58). Janicaud asserts:

Between the unconditional affirmation of Transcendence and the patient interrogation of the visible, the incompatibility cries out; we must choose. But are we going to do so with the head or with the heart—arbitrarily or not? The task, insofar as it remains philosophical and phenomenological, is to follow the sole guide that does not buy itself off with fine words: interrogation of method. (2000, 26)

Differentiating between Merleau-Ponty's method of "intertwining" and Levinas's of "aplomb," Janicaud concludes that the method that emerges as truly phenomenological is Merleau-Ponty's, which he takes to be neutral with respect to questions about transcendence. Phenomenology, on Janicaud's reading, is essentially agnostic (if not atheistic), and only as such can it continue to be properly philosophical as opposed to theological. The distinction between the two is clearly articulated during Janicaud's engagement with Levinas. According to Janicaud, the non-phenomenology of Levinas

supposes a metaphysico-theological montage, prior to philosophical writing. The dice are loaded and choices made; faith rises majestically in the background. The reader, confronted by the blade of the absolute, finds him- or herself in the position of a catechumen who has no other choice than to penetrate the holy words and lofty dogmas. . . . All is acquired and imposed from the outset, and this all is no little thing: nothing less than the God of the biblical tradition. Strict treason of the reduction that handed over the transcendental I to its nudity, here theology is restored with its parade of capital letters. But this theology, which dispenses with giving itself the least title, installs itself at the most intimate dwelling of consciousness, as if that were as natural as could be. Must philosophy let itself be thus intimidated? Is this not but incantation, initiation? (2000, 27)

Although perhaps reminiscent of John Rawls's idea that public reason should be void of "comprehensive doctrines" (2005, 134–35) and Richard Rorty's encouragement of the privatization of religious belief (1999), Janicaud's concern is not primarily with public accessibility and political efficacy, but with presuppositionlessness. Janicaud considers presuppositionlessness to be the hallmark of philosophy as opposed to theology. Echoing Heidegger's call for a "god-less" thinking, Janicaud claims that it is only by beginning from an agnostic perspective, as it were, that philosophy can continue to strive to be a "rigorous science" and not merely a mystifying expression of one's prior commitments. Importantly, however, we must realize that his question of the theological intimidation of philosophy is not innocuous: it is a positive assertion regarding the status of philosophy as neutral both methodologically and, far more problematically, in regard to content. Notice that, for Janicaud, the phenomenological method is not simply about *how* to proceed in philosophical investigation; it is also about *what* is available for investigation in the first place.

The basic problem with Janicaud's contention is that to delimit the domain of phenomenological inquiry from the outset is to subvert the supposed neutrality of the phenomenological method itself. To say that phenomenology is a method of studying that which appears in its very way of appearing, and to describe it as a movement "to the things themselves," is not to determine how appearance itself does function, but instead should be understood as a stance of openness and receptivity to all possible modes in which appearance might function. For just a few examples of how the authors of *God in France* challenge Janicaud's narrow account of phenomenology, consider the following: Guido Vanheeswijck says that, following René Girard, phenomenology should include a consideration of the very possibility of appearance itself (Vanheeswijck 2005); Johan Goud interprets Levinas as contending that phenomenology should investigate the way in which alterity "appears" (or doesn't appear) as a trace (Goud 2005, 99); Ruud Welten says of Henry that Life is the very conditionality of appearance and is coordinate with all that appears (Welten 2005a); and Welton further proposes, regarding Marion, that unless we interrogate the possibility of "givenness" (*donation*) then we are starting our inquiry too late (Welten 2005b). On the interpretations offered by all of these authors, Husserl's phenomenology cannot and should not be restricted in the way that Janicaud's interpretation of it seems to require. *God in France* successfully demonstrates that the apparent and the inapparent might not be as radically separable as Janicaud's reading would require.

Of course, to be fair to Janicaud, it is important to note that he does consider Merleau-Ponty's discussions of the "invisible" to be phenomenologically viable since they avoid any reference to transcendence and instead refer everything back to the domain of the immanent experiential world. Hence it might be more accurate to say that the "invisible" is alright as long as it remains of this world, and thus definitively *not* referred to as "God." So, we could assume that Janicaud might allow for the "appearance" of the back side of an angel's wing, say, if we could get a glimpse of the front side. On this account, the inapparent is not denied a phenomenological status as such, but is restricted to the inapparent that *could become apparent* given a different location. But this restriction simply begs the question of what criterion Janicaud uses in his decision to localize and limit the notion of "appearance" in this way. The point here is that the burden of proof is on Janicaud's shoulders as to exactly how certain new phenomenological examples are inappropriate extensions of the phenomenological method. Because of this, I take *God in*

France to successfully demonstrate that, without straying too far afield from Husserl's own thought, God-talk can be viewed as a properly phenomenological possibility. Of course, this in no way means that God *should be* the topic of conversation, but simply that if we are to be true to phenomenology we cannot reject the *potential legitimacy* of such a conversation without first attempting to have it.

Yet doesn't this discussion itself confirm the reality of a "theological turn" within phenomenology? That is, doesn't this demonstrate the way in which phenomenology has taken a decisive move toward the biblical God, say, as the proper name for the transcendence that underlies and accompanies phenomena? Undoubtedly, there is some reason to believe that this is the case. Levinas does not simply refer to the Hölderlinian-Heideggerian "gods" but to the God of Abraham, Isaac, and Jacob; he does not produce "quasi-religious writings" but *Talmudic Writings.* Similarly, although Marion uses examples from aesthetics to illuminate his notion of the "saturated phenomenon" (viz., Kant's sublime), he also goes as far as to suggest that the example *par excellence* is the Incarnation (see Marion 2000). And further, in *God Without Being,* Marion does not merely talk about the possibility of various iconic rituals, but speaks of the importance of the Eucharist (in a specifically Catholic conception).[1] This liturgical framework can also be found in Lacoste's discussions of presenting oneself before God (2005) and in Chrétien's focus on the phenomena of prayer and hope (2000; 2002; 2004). Further examples could no doubt be offered in support of the idea of a "theological turn," but according to Peter Jonkers, what should not be sidestepped is the question of the way in which these thinkers *relate* to the examples that they offer.

In contrast to Janicaud, Jonkers contends that the texts I have referred to are not engaged in an *apologetic* but a *heuristic* enterprise. Their authors "consider the way in which the Bible and Christian mystics speak about God as showing a sensitivity to a radical mystery, which, time and again, eludes notice of traditional metaphysics in spite or just because of its thinking force" (Jonkers 2005, 7). It is this sentiment that causes me to wonder whether, precisely in his rejection of the "theological turn," Jonkers is actually quite close to de Vries's account of the "turn to religion." Even though de Vries is often coupled with Janicaud on this topic, it is important to note that, unlike Janicaud, he goes to great lengths to demonstrate the way in which contemporary French philosophy has merely tapped into an *archive* that it would do well not to foreswear (de Vries 1999; 2002; 2005). For Janicaud, the turn to theology represents an abandonment of the neutrality and universality that should characterize philosophical discourse, as opposed to the partiality and particularity of positive theologies. De Vries, in contrast, stringently argues that "the turn to religion . . . must not be understood as a turn to theology in the conventional or confessional sense of the word" (1999, xi). Claiming that

Janicaud's position "badly needs correction," de Vries contends that the turn to religion has not been a turn away from philosophy, but instead calls us to reexamine how we understand the relationship between philosophy and religion in the first place. As such, de Vries contends that the Continental interest in theology does not positively advocate the doctrinal positions and creedal commitments of a particular faith, but is merely a helpful resource for how to think after, or beyond, metaphysics. As such, he and Jonkers offer similar accounts of the solidly heuristic aspect of such an appropriation.

Accordingly, despite its significant contribution to the debate surrounding whether there has been a "theological turn" in French thought, God in France tacitly concedes to Janicaud the assumption that phenomenology is no longer phenomenological if it is *theo*-logical. Whereas Janicaud was quite comfortable labeling the new phenomenologists as no longer being philosophers, the authors of God in France display an underlying ease when they label them philosophers— and not theologians. Even though I affirm the conclusions of God in France on this point, I want to challenge the ease with which such conclusions are reached. Accordingly, we should be quite attentive when Ruud Welten suggests that although Michel Henry's discussion of Life and transcendence might draw on Christianity, "Henry is not a theologian or a mystic" (2005a, 125). And similarly, in his essay on Marion, Welten claims that both Henry and Marion "approach theology phenomenologically, not dogmatically" (2005b, 197): Marion resists simply doing theology because he does not "show us God; he just makes sure there is room for God to show *Himself*!" (2005b, 206). Similarly, although Johan Goud challenges the "one-sided moral and non-religious interpretations" of Levinas, and even goes so far as to say that Levinas's "philosophical thought hinges on philosophical theology" (2005, 99), he still insists that Levinas does not "discuss God in theological terms" (2005, 98). "In short," Goud concludes, "Levinas' thought must be read, valued and perhaps criticized as a philosophy" (2005, 112).

Even though I agree with the claim that new phenomenology does distinguish between phenomenology and theology (indeed, in the previous chapter I suggested that this was one of the five main gestures of new phenomenology itself), must it be the case that phenomenology can't be theologically concerned *precisely as phenomenology*? The ethico-religious encounter described in the ontology of constitutive responsibility seems to stand as a challenge to a strict dichotomy here. Accordingly, in contemporary Continental philosophy of religion, the question of how to conceive of the relationship between phenomenology and theology continues to press. In the next section I will offer three possible ways of answering this question—separatism, reconstruction, and reconstructive separatism[2]—and argue that the third offers the most promising way forward in this important debate.

At What Cost? Rethinking the Relationship with Theology

The Strategy of Separatism and the Question of Neutrality

The first way in which theology and phenomenology can be driven apart is according to a separatist strategy in which philosophy is posited as neutral in both method and content. This is the strategy put forth in Janicaud's distinction between Merleau-Ponty and Levinas. According to Janicaud, Merleau-Ponty's work remains "passionately" phenomenological "in that it seeks to think phenomenality intimately, the better to inhabit it." Thus, Merleau-Ponty "excludes nothing, but opens our regard to the depth of the world" (Janicaud 2000, 27). As we saw above, this characterization stands in stark contrast to the "loaded dice" that Janicaud accuses Levinas of throwing on the table of philosophical discourse.

This strategy is *separatist* in that it intends to place theology over and against phenomenology due to (1) theology's object of inquiry being inapparent and its subsequently being termed "God" (or another name that does the same work: Life, Liturgy, Other, etc.), (2) theology's point of departure being the presupposition of a particular tradition or discourse (the dice are not simply loaded with "gods" but with the biblical God), and (3) the non-scientific dogmatism of theology (there is no possibility of a "rigorous science" because we have placed ourselves in a domain of irrational faith).

Janicaud's overriding worry is that contemporary French phenomenologists are simply postmodern versions of traditional presuppositionalists.[3] That is, they affirm specifically religious presuppositions while postmodernly contesting the absolute status of religious doctrines. For Janicaud, it is as if they have done philosophically what our parents do in preparation for an Easter egg hunt: hide in the morning what we are to find in the afternoon. Janicaud might claim that the ontology of constitutive responsibility is thus really something that begins by affirming that with which it hopes to conclude: wanting to make sure that God stays relevant to philosophy, Kierkegaard, for example, constructs a notion of selfhood that requires God as an essential component. Simply put, Janicaud's charge here is that new phenomenology is problematically question-begging.

Yet as I have argued, instead of offering an innocuous method of neutrality, Janicaud no less problematically places out of bounds at the beginning that which he *does not want* to find later in the day. It is important to realize that presuppositionalism can take both positive and negative forms. The problem with the "neutral" and "presuppositionless" approach to phenomenology in particular and philosophy in general is that it necessarily retains the modern worldless subject that it was meant to overcome. It is one thing to say that we must already be *in-a-world* in order to take account of the way in which things present themselves to consciousness, but it is quite another to say that this embeddedness itself serves as a neutral starting point. The first claim is a descriptive recognition of the way in which the subject/object dualism so present in philosophy following Descartes has been overcome in favor of the realization that consciousness is always a *consciousness-of*. The second claim goes beyond this recognition and actually sets up a particular notion of being-in-the-world as the *only* legitimate origin for philosophical investigation.

It is highly problematic to assume a particular definition of what a "rigorous science" is and then claim that this definition is offered from a neutral position regarding the objects of investigation at issue. Moreover, to predetermine what "appearance" means and how it can be made manifest is already to delimit certain methodological aspects that will remain untouched by the phenomenological reduction. All of the aspects that differentiate theology from phenomenology according to separatism require a decidedly non-neutral origin and assume certain presuppositions. This might all be fine, but if so, how are we to continue to reject theology for doing precisely what phenomenology does in order to differentiate itself from theology?

The Strategy of Reconstruction and the Question of Positive Content

While separatism tries to isolate theology from phenomenology according to certain criteria, the reconstructivist strategy does not differentiate between theology and phenomenology by declaring God-talk beyond the pale or by presupposing a narrow definition of "appearance." Rather, it distinguishes between radical phenomenological talk of the "transcendent," "givenness," and "absolute alterity" on the one hand, and theological speech within a particular religious tradition on the other. If separatism eliminates the quasi-religious aspect from phenomenology, reconstructivism re-conceives God as no longer residing within decidedly theological boundaries. What results is not a phenomenological inquiry into Christianity, Judaism, or Islam, but a postmodern conception of transcendence that, although it makes reference to specific religious traditions, lacks any strong connection to the content of a determinate religion. That is to say, it is related to a tradition without being a part of it.

Rico Sneller's essay on Derrida nicely articulates the key move of reconstructivism. "I think that Derrida aims at *renewing* traditional God talk (within the philosophical-religious traditions)," Sneller comments, "and not, as for example Sartre did, at abandoning it as if it were something obsolete" (2005, 163). This *renewed* discourse is not properly about "God" as a revealed, confessed, and worshipped Lord, but about "God" as a linguistic, existential, and performative phenomenon. For Derrida, "'God' means: relation, interplay, interaction-between-inside-and-out-side, or even *correlation*" (Sneller 2005, 154).[4] Even for the decidedly

Catholic Marion (and we might say for the Jewish Levinas as well), the topic of conversation is "no longer God, but the non-ontological way in which God appears" (Welten 2005b, 195). Despite the fact that Rorty's opposition to Levinas was largely due to the "religious" dimensions of Levinas's thought, in light of the above statements, we might say that Rorty was wrong to see such religious aspects as present in the first place. That is, perhaps all the God-talk in new phenomenology is *strategic* rather than *substantive*.

In light of such a possibility, I think that the appropriate questions to ask in response to this reconstructed "God" are actually found in *God in France:* "does God feel at home in France?" (Jonkers 2005, 38), and "[do] men and women [feel] at ease with this 'French' God?" (Schrijvers 2005, 225). In both of these passages, I take "France" and "French" not to refer to a particular nationality, but as a general philosophical gesture toward a postmodern or deconstructive notion of religious belief and existence. Regarding the first question, then, it is not unproblematic to reconstruct the biblical God into a deconstructive "God" or "gods." Although it maintains the distinctiveness of phenomenology while allowing for a more theological orientation, reconstructivism does so at the cost of detaching transcendence from the particular historical (and religious) narratives in which transcendence has often been honored and confessed. If separatism leads to a modern conception of the detached subject by forgetting socio-historical embeddedness, reconstructivism affirms this *personal* historicity while failing to adequately engage the *interpersonal* particularity and specificity of determinate religious traditions (rites, scriptures, creeds, confessions, etc.).

I do not mean to suggest that in order to remain true to particular religious traditions we must maintain the onto-theological frameworks and metaphysical schemes in which they have commonly been articulated. Rather than falling back into onto-theology, new phenomenology offers a sustained attempt to think philosophically about the inaugural ethico-religious encounter. While the importance of such a project cannot be overstated, such an attempt *need not* entail a rejection of creedal or doctrinal components of the Jewish or Christian religions (or any other religious tradition). All that is required is a rejection of the way in which such doctrines and creeds are appropriated and held as self-evident, certain, and infallible. As I have described it, and as we saw in the extended consideration of Kierkegaard and Levinas in part 1, the ontology of constitutive responsibility offers at least one way of understanding religious existence as a commitment to God's love as constitutive of human reality and expressed in the relation to the neighbor, instead of understanding it as a metaphysical conception of God's Being. Affirming such a conception is, I believe, possible while still positioning oneself internal to determinate faith traditions and the specificity of belief and behavior of those traditions.

Regarding the second question about the comfort of religious believers with this "French God" (again read "generally postmodern or deconstructive approach to religion"), I want to suggest that the potential danger of reconstruction is that it can end up patronizing committed religious believers.[5] Rather than opening a new space for Christianity, Judaism, or Islam (or any religion for that matter) in a postmodern context, it can leave them behind in the name of a nondescript (and, I would argue, potentially vacuous) relation with a similarly opaque conception of alterity. Only by taking particular religious narratives seriously can we *re-source* the theological archive by being *invested* in it, rather than merely appropriate it for our own (intrinsically) political purposes.[6] While the first is a method defined by hospitality, the second comes dangerously close to being a sheer power play under the guise of openness.

Now, I want to make clear that I am not saying postmodern reconstructivism *is* patronizing. I am merely raising the awareness of the dangers that accompany *all* reconstructivist strategies. This danger is an ethical one, and it should continue to press upon all postmodern philosophy of religion. This concern about patronizing religious believers is really a concern that reconstruction can become merely a variant of separatism; the ontology of constitutive responsibility offers crucial resources for addressing this concern. Due to its affirmation of the reality of responsibility as the very locus of subjectivity, new phenomenologists, in general, recognize the ethico-political stakes that accompany all discourse. New phenomenology attempts to rethink how to take religious belief seriously after the death of metaphysics, and thereby it allows for a renewed engagement with not only religious *belief*, but also with religious *believers* in a postmodern context.

Reconstructive Separatism and the Question of Authority

Rather than the restrictive, negative dogmatism of separatism and the potentially patronizing emptiness of reconstruction, I want to suggest a third way of understanding the relationship of phenomenology to theology. I term this strategy "reconstructive separatism" because it maintains the valuable aspects of each of the other options while rejecting the worldlessness of the first and the problematic relationality of the second. On this view, phenomenology and theology are still distinguishable from each other (we might say "separated"), but only because of the variant sources of authority to which they appeal—and not because of the particular content of one or the other. Phenomenology should be distinguished from theology not because it is "neutral" as opposed to being biased, but according to the particular biases that shape its discourse as historically developed and currently presented. Theology, I propose, begins with the authority of divine revelation, canonical texts, and/or ecclesial frameworks; phenomenology begins with the openness to investigate appearance in whatever form, or lack of form, appearance takes.

This strategy maintains the decidedly philosophical character of phenomenological inquiry by resisting a move from dialogical openness to creedal faith. Hence, it is *separatist* inasmuch as it says that phenomenology must not appeal to any authority other than its own method. Yet this does not result in the worldless modern subject. Rather, this strategy begins from the recognition of the deep situatedness of rationality itself—and therefore, of the phenomenological method. This method admits that there is no "neutral" reason: reason is always internal to the play of human discourse. Hence, reconstructive separatism does not say that phenomenology differs from theology because of phenomenology's rationality and theology's credulity. To do so would be to assume that reason could be a criterion outside of the specificities of the particular language games in which it operates. However, reconstructive separatism does differentiate between the reason that is *internal* to a revelational context and the reason that starts by trying to discover the *possibility* of revelation. The key here is not that phenomenology is presuppositionless while theology is presuppositionalist, it is merely that the content of their presuppositions is differently conceived.

While this approach does admit of a bias at the heart of phenomenology, this is not as troubling as it might initially seem when we remember that new phenomenology (in distinction from the phenomenology of religion) is committed to a critical engagement with its own authoritative source. Moreover, as I have already claimed regarding quasi-logical existential conditions in chapter 5 and will suggest concerning deconstructive foundationalism in chapter 11, new phenomenology can operate according to a foundational model of justification without viciously question-begging (as Janicaud would contend).

Although theology might indeed appropriate phenomenological methodology in order to investigate particular aspects of its own reality—prayer, worship, forgiveness, the Eucharist, etc.—it should do so while still affirming the authority of its sacred texts and ecclesial structures. Alternatively, phenomenology is neither *prima facie* nor *finally* cut off from theological concerns. Instead, if the investigation into phenomena (whether apparent or inapparent) leads toward the insights of a particular religious tradition, then that movement should be recognized as perfectly valid according to Socrates' instruction that the "lover of inquiry must follow his beloved wherever it may lead" (Plato 1997, *Euthyphro* 14c). Due to the inherent contextuality of reason, "the beloved" may indeed lead toward a God who is "otherwise than Being," but this is not to say that it will necessarily evacuate the specificities of determinate religion in doing so. To be *reconstructive* on this model is not to say that religious discourse is allowed *if* it has been reconceived according to phenomenological norms. Reconstructive separatism maintains the possibility of a postmodern *Christianity*, a postmodern *Judaism,* or a postmodern *Islam,* rather than merely some "religion without religion." Granted, these postmodern versions may not be acceptable to many Christians, Jews, and Muslims, but this is not necessarily because the postmodern alternative is really *new,* but likely because it is *newly presented.* However, sometimes old wine does need new wineskins.

Conclusion: Opening the Space for a Postmodern Apologetics

The value of the reconstructed separatism that I have outlined is that it opens the space for more than a merely heuristic relation between phenomenology and theology. *It leaves room for the possibility of a postmodern apologetics*—an apologetics on the far side of a deconstruction of onto-theology. By postmodern apologetics, I do not necessarily refer to traditional issues such as arguments for the existence of God, responses to the problem of evil, articulations of divine attributes, etc. Instead, I take this notion to simply be the idea that one can give rational defenses of determinate religious belief and practice (which may or may not include traditional matters as mentioned above). Such defenses need not, and I would even say will not, entail finality, certainty, and universality. Yet, postmodern apologetics might allow one to give arguments for why the biblical God is already "not contaminated by Being," as Levinas would say. As another example, I take Kierkegaard's "attack" on Christendom to be an apologetic gesture in the name of what he considered to be authentic Christianity. Further, Henry's account of the importance of the "Truth of Life" as distinct from the "Truth of the World," might stand as an argument for Christianity insofar as it admits of such a distinction. Though such moves may not necessarily be apologetic, to close off from the outset the possibility that they could be would be narrow-mindedly atheistic rather than scientifically agnostic.

This does not mean that we should do phenomenology in order to convince our interlocutors of religious truth. It does mean, however, that we should remain *as open* to the possibility that our inquiry may point toward the truth of a religious tradition, as we are that it may lead away from such a tradition. Postmodern apologetics is only oxymoronic if we assume that apologetics can only operate on the basis of neutral reason and natural theology.[7] Such a notion of apologetics would, indeed, seem to stand or fall with the fate of onto-theology. But just as overcoming onto-theology does not entail the overcoming of God, though it will certainly render some accounts of god implausible, so overcoming onto-theology does not mean overcoming apologetics as such, though certain forms of apologetics will become nonstarters. What the ethico-religious account of the ontology of constitutive responsibility offers is an invitation to move beyond both the interpretations of God that ignore human existence and the defenses of religious faith that seek to operate outside history. Contemporary Continental philosophy of religion, especially in the phenomenological and deconstructive veins, should continue to be willing to do more than simply argue *against* onto-theology. There must also be a concern for plausibly offering robust arguments *in favor of* a non-onto-theological Christianity, or Judaism, or Islam, etc.[8] Such a positive project need not reduce phenomenology to theology or philosophy to religion, but should keep the relationship between them dynamic and flexible. To keep these communities of discourse distinct is not to keep them radically separate; it merely serves to keep open a lived conversation between different perspectives. Maintaining such a conversation is valuable not only for increasing rigor in theological thinking, but also for the expansion of philosophical horizons. Adriaan Peperzak suggests that a "post-postmodern renaissance of Christian spirituality in philosophy is necessary" (1999, 129). I think that it is necessary in order that our phenomenology not become near-sighted and our theology not become stagnant.

By taking seriously the real differences between phenomenology and theology while leaving open the space for seeing their potential subsequent interplay (the situatedness of reason always already involves a certain amount of faith), we do not simply challenge Janicaud, but recognize him as a critical interlocutor in the project of postmodern philosophy of religion. In the next chapter I will argue that in addition to the philosophical reasons I have offered for allowing God-talk (or at least not *prima facie* rejecting it), there are substantial political reasons for Continental philosophy continuing to appropriate a specific sort of God-talk, namely, that of *kenosis.*

EIGHT

Is Continental Philosophy Just Catholicism for Atheists? Critique and *Kenosis*

After hearing talks by, and even studying with, a number of prominent Continental philosophers, a former colleague of mine came to the conclusion that "Continental philosophy is just Catholicism for atheists." Although he intended the comment to be derogatory and dismissive, I find it to be a description that, upon reflection, calls for a deeper engagement with a tradition that appears to be at odds with itself.[1] My colleague is not alone in his worry about a Continental slide from philosophy to theology. In the last two chapters, we have considered more prominent examples of thinkers who have expressed such a concern—de Vries and Janicaud. Although he will offer a more charitable reading of new phenomenology than Janicaud, de Vries still asks, "why is religion a relevant philosophical or theoretical topic at all?" (1999, xiii). According to de Vries, "By renegotiating the limits and aporias of the ethical and the political in light of the religious and the theological, we can rearticulate the terms and oppositions in which the most pressing and practical present-day cultural debates are phrased" (1999, xii). De Vries makes clear that the stakes of contemporary Continental discussions of God are both *philosophical* and also, perhaps even more importantly, *political*.

In line with de Vries, in this chapter I will build upon my claims in the last two chapters regarding the specifically phenomenological deepening of new phenomenology by offering a defense of a particular sort of God-talk that I proposed in chapter 6 as one of the primary unifying characteristics of the movement: namely, talk of divine *kenosis* or self-emptying. Not only is the ontology of constitutive responsibility something that makes room for a particularly viable model of political critique in general, but when it is enriched by the notion of *kenosis,* we can begin to fill in the ways in which it yields profoundly political, and specifically democratic, consequences.

Crucially, the Continental appropriation of kenotic God-talk is not limited to those primarily working in the phenomenological tradition. Indeed, perhaps the most sustained consideration of *kenosis* in recent Continental discourse is offered by Gianni Vattimo—a thinker who is certainly inspired by Heidegger and Derrida, but more directly working in the wake of Nietzsche and the tradition of philosophical hermeneutics. Nonetheless, by bringing Vattimo together with

Levinas, Heidegger, and Derrida, we can see how they are all committed to a decidedly *kenotic* understanding of God and/or the self. I will suggest that the upshot of this focus on a kenotic expression of love is an argument for a democratic politics committed to the critical task of charity. When considered in light of the bi-directional relationality that is coordinate with the ontology of constitutive responsibility, this democratic reading of charity should be understood as *ethico-religious*.

While my former colleague's claim should be made more modest in order to read, "certain strains within Continental philosophy can be understood as Judaism and/or Christianity for people otherwise disposed to reject religion," I suggest that such a description is not something to worry about, but should, instead, serve to highlight a serious philosophical project and an important political task.[2]

The Political Relevance of *Kenosis*

Somewhat ironically, given my rather constant use of Richard Rorty as the model of someone who opposes "religious" discourse for political reasons, I want to offer his collaborative project with Gianni Vattimo, *The Future of Religion*, as an example of how kenotic God-talk can facilitate productive political discourse. In *The Future of Religion* we see Rorty revise his earlier view of religion as a "conversation stopper" (1999) and affirm that a decidedly Christian perspective can provide helpful ways of envisioning social engagement.[3] Of course, Rorty does not go so far as to urge using religious language, but (at least in a couple later essays) he does see such discourse as potentially politically advantageous. Along with Vattimo, Rorty focuses on the idea of "God as love" and suggests that this notion supports a truly inclusive democratic politics. Being explicit about the relevance of this conception of God, Rorty writes: "I think the hermeneutical or Gadamerian attitude is in the intellectual world what democracy is in the political world. The two can be viewed as alternative appropriations of the Christian message that love is the only law" (Vattimo and Rorty 2005, 74). Two important points are worth noting here. First, in line with my own claim about the way in which the ontology of constitutive responsibility inaugurates a recursive hermeneutic task, Rorty connects the idea of Christian charity with a specifically democratic politics and the project of interpretation. Second, in contrast to my own suggestions about the ontology of constitutive responsibility, Rorty certainly does not consider anything having to do with religion as a "condition" under which hermeneutics or democracy is possible; rather, it is simply a helpful narrative for supporting such activities.[4]

I earlier claimed that it might be the case that Levinasians could learn from Rorty, and here I think we have a situation in which Rorty is on to something worth taking very seriously. Let me suggest that underlying Rorty's (and Vattimo's) willingness to connect the Christian account of love with philosophical hermeneutics and democratic politics is the intrinsically *critical function of charity*. While recognizing this function, Rorty is unwilling to consider such ethico-religious discourse as a condition for political critique—though it is love that allows for truth to be spoken to power without reducing this speech to mere power play. The theological name for understanding "love as the only law" is *kenosis*. In the second chapter of Philippians Paul writes the following, perhaps echoing an early Christian hymn:

> [Christ Jesus] being in the form of God, thought it not robbery to be equal with God. But made himself of no reputation, and took upon him the form of a servant, and was made in the likeness of men. And being found in fashion as a man, he humbled himself, and became obedient unto death, even the death of the cross. (Philippians 2: 6–8, KJV)

Here we see the importance of *kenosis* to Christian faith in particular insofar as it anticipates one of the central themes of Christianity: God *is most fully revealed as God* when God empties Godself in the person of Christ. In this way, Christology should, I believe, be fundamentally understood as a way of relating to God as a loving servant rather than a self-sufficient power (see Oord 2010).

So why is Christology relevant to political discourse? There are two important reasons. I will briefly sketch each and then move on to give examples of how this idea has been appropriated as politically instructive in recent Continental philosophy. On the one hand, *kenosis* contests the idea of the detached, isolated modern subject. If God is not primarily conceived of as a self-enclosed, absolutely immutable being standing over and against the world, and as best defined in terms of power, but as an originary outpouring of love toward the world (this can be read as a statement about Creation, or Christ, or both), then it follows that, as *imago Dei*, the self is plausibly understood as also originarily poured-out to others. This is another way of expressing the bi-directional relationality that accompanies the ontology of constitutive responsibility. On the other hand, the narrative of Christ's kenotic presence in history serves to challenge legality itself as reducible to anything like a legal code. Consider Christ's claim that he did not come to "destroy the law . . . but to fulfill it" (Matthew 5: 17, KJV), alongside Paul's contention that "all the law is fulfilled in one word, even in this: Thou shalt love thy neighbour as thyself" (Galatians 5: 14, KJV).

These comments resonate with the deconstructive claim that legality is simultaneously ruptured and completed by the relation to the Other.[5] No normative code could capture this relation because it is this relation itself that calls for the instantiation of normative codes that recognize the obligation to others. It is for this reason that when he was asked "Who is my neighbor?" Christ did not offer a story about national borders or ethnic boundaries, but instead tells about a "Good Samaritan." When the Good Samaritan offers help to someone who has been passed by all those who "should" have helped due to their communal bonds (viz., the priest and the Levite), he was able to recognize something that stood *behind and beyond* his political allegiances and social bonds: he expresses a recognition of humanity which transcends all historical ties. The Good Samaritan does not see a Jew who is part of the community that excludes him; rather, he sees a "neighbor."

Let me pursue the specifics of this story just a bit further. Importantly, the Samaritans were a people without an identity. They were not Jews, but neither were they identifiable as belonging to a unified Gentile community. They were of mixed descent both biologically and socially. This lack of belonging makes the example all the more relevant to my point here. It is not as simple as an Israeli reaching out to a Palestinian, a Muslim to a Jew, or a Sunni to a Shiite. The point is that it is a *no-one* reaching out to a *someone* and by so doing contesting how it is that we define ourselves. When Jesus claims that the Samaritan was the "neighbor" to the man who had fallen into the hands of the robbers, he is saying that being a neighbor might even go directly against what being a member of society might otherwise dictate.

Further, the priest and the Levite were within the community to which the wounded man belonged. Notice that *he was passed over by his fellow citizens, as it were, and was aided by the outcast.* This is a wonderful demonstration of how the (pre)originary devotion to "the widow, the orphan, and the stranger" is not a reference to social position but existential need. Anyone in need of kindness and mercy falls into this group; and the crucial thing to realize is that we are *all* defined by this need. Here we might say that the story conveys a similar point as that expressed by Derrida in the phrase *"tout autre est tout autre"* (1995, chap. 4). The example of the Good Samaritan is an example to all in how to be a neighbor, and how to understand oneself as never self-sufficiently isolated from others. The ontology of constitutive responsibility entails that existence is always simultaneously singular (I am the only one who can respond to the call I receive) *and yet* social (I find myself always already before the Other to whom I am responsible and other others who also lay claim upon me). As such, we can read this story as demonstrating the way in which we all, as singular and social, occupy the position of the man lying on the side of the road, the priest who passes by or the Samaritan—and, lest we forget, the robbers. Like Kierkegaard's account of the *Akedah,* the story of the Good Samaritan confronts us as a picture of the very structure of political reality in light of the ethico-religious encounter.

One could argue, however, that I have translated this story about a simple expression of generosity that could easily be accounted for according to ordinary ethico-political discourse of interest groups and conversation partners into something much more complicated. As we have seen, according to Rorty, such translations frequently serve to undermine the real political promise of inspiring ethical narratives (he sees the hyperbolic "Levinasian strains" in Derrida as doing this). Yet I want to suggest that, in actuality, it is the tension between the everyday (finite) and the exceptional (infinite) articulated in the ontology of constitutive responsibility that makes this story such a remarkable demonstration of the ethico-political promise of *kenosis*. We should remember that Levinas insists that his philosophy of infinite responsibility is actualized in the simple expression, "After you, sir" (*Après vous monsieur*).

Building on Levinas's notion of infinite responsibility in "The Force of Law," Derrida comments that deconstruction "hyperbolically raises the stakes of exacting justice; it is sensitivity to a sort of essential disproportion that must inscribe excess and inadequation in itself and that strives to denounce not only theoretical limits but also concrete injustices" (1992b, 20). Although Derrida claims that such a hyperbolic gesture actually increases the sensitivity to injustice in both theory and practice, it may be hard to see how this is the case. In the next section, I will offer an argument for how hyperbolic accounts of responsibility as "infinite" might actually prove to be quite politically important.

In Defense of Hyperbole

In chapter 1, we saw that Rorty's frustration with Continental ethics, and in particular, Levinasian ethics, was largely due to its quasi-religious tendencies. "Emphasizing the impossibility of meaning, or of justice," Rorty writes, "is a temptation to Gothicize—to view democratic politics as ineffectual, because unable to cope with preternatural forces" (1998a, 97). Rather than focus on the "infinite demand" of the Other and the "extreme hospitality" of the Good Samaritan, we should come together with our fellow citizens and make common cause around goals which transform our local communities: "It seems pointless hype to dramatize our difficulties in knowing what to do by labeling our goal 'indescribable,' 'unexperiencable,' 'unintelligible,' or 'infinitely distant'" (1996b, 42).

Given Rorty's frustration, it does not seem that speaking of the face of the Other, the democracy to-come, or (as I will do in chapter 13) "saintly" ethico-political exemplars could be of real political use. Recognizing the life of Christ as a demonstration that ethics cannot be conceived as an absolute code which we follow or an algorithm we deploy seems a far cry indeed from helping navigate the claims of conflicting interest groups. This is especially troubling when we consider that the highest form of ethics for Kierkegaard (which I discussed as Ethics C2) is best understood as the encouragement to live in *imitatio Christi*. Regarding the conception of ethics as an imitation of Christ, Edith Wyschogrod comes into a very rare harmony with Rorty when she comments that the "*Imitatio Christi* is an unrealizable imperative because the life of Christ cannot be replicated" (1990,

13). For Wyschogrod, we need to look to "postmodern saints" as exemplars precisely because their lives are those that we could historically emulate. I will return to Wyschogrod's conception at length in chapter 13, but here let me note that, even for Kierkegaard, the imitation of Christ is complicated by the status of his being *God-in-time* and claiming to be "the way, the truth, and the life" (John 14: 6).[6] In such respects, Christ would certainly not be available for imitation by non-divine (human) beings. For such reasons I am inclined to agree with Wyschogrod that Christ (understood as God) is not the best example of a "saint." However, one could argue that what one seeks to imitate about Christ is not his divinity, but his historical expression of a particular way of being human. While this approach would stress the *possibility* of imitating Christ, contra Wyschogrod there is also something to be said for the ethico-political relevance of the *impossibility* of such a task. Desiring ethics to be readily possible (as Rorty seems to do) can easily become a reflection of mere self-concern. Such a desire can quickly reduce to the claim that I want to be able to know what to do, when to do it, how best to go about doing it, and when I have finished doing it. Although it might conceivably be nice to have such knowledge, it would actually undermine the very ethicality of decision itself. "A decision that didn't go through the ordeal of the undecidable would not be a free decision," Derrida remarks; rather, "it would only be the programmable application or unfolding of a calculable process. It might be legal; it would not be just" (1992b, 24).

What Christ's example makes so clear is that what we seek as the answer to ethical decision is never reducible to an act, yet it only has its value in action. Consider the following passage from the book of Matthew:

> Now a man came up to Jesus and asked, "Teacher, what good thing must I do to get eternal life?"
>
> "Why do you ask me about what is good?" Jesus replied. "There is only One who is good. If you want to enter life, obey the commandments."
>
> "Which ones?" the man inquired.
>
> Jesus replied, "Do not murder, do not commit adultery, do not steal, do not give false testimony, honor your father and mother, and love your neighbor as yourself."
>
> "All these I have kept," the young man said. "What do I still lack?"
>
> Jesus answered, "If you want to be perfect, go, sell your possessions and give to the poor, and you will have treasure in heaven. Then come, follow me."
>
> When the young man heard this, he went away sad, because he had great wealth. (Matthew 19: 16–22, NIV)[7]

When the rich young man comes to Christ to ask what he must do to gain eternal life, Christ's response is simple: keep the commandments. The young man's response clearly indicates that he is not aware of the complexity of this apparently easy instruction. He replies that he has kept the commandments. We should read this statement as an attempt to argue with Christ in the following way: "Haven't I done enough? What more is required?"

Christ's next comment exposes that as long as we understand "commandments" to mean a clear-cut guide for right living, we have missed the point. "Sell everything you have and give it to the poor," he says. Are we to read this as simply being one specific example of the "commandments" that the young man was initially told to keep? No. This statement, I contend, is intentionally hyperbolic. Sure, the young man could have had an estate auction and fed and clothed some of the poor for a while, but as long as he viewed this action as simply a particular action in which he could engage, rather than as the way in which he should entirely reorient his life (i.e., ethics is presented again as about who I am rather than merely what I do), he would miss the real "commandment" of Christ. One might ask here, what could be simpler to do than follow someone? However, as Dietrich Bonhoeffer points out, to follow Christ is to follow him to the cross (Bonhoeffer 1959). There can be no half-measures. This is neither Sunday-only religion nor Rortian bourgeois liberalism (whether it be postmodern or not).

In *An Interpretation of Christian Ethics,* Reinhold Niebuhr questions whether an "impossible ethical ideal" can have any political relevance. His answer is extremely helpful for understanding the efficacy of the hyperbole that pervades Continental ethics and deconstructive political theory. Niebuhr writes:

> In Christian theology, at its best, the revelation of Christ, the God-man, is a revelation of the paradoxical relation of the eternal to history, which it is the genius of mythical-prophetic religion to emphasize. Christ is thus the revelation of the very impossible possibility which the Sermon on the Mount elaborates in ethical terms. If Christian orthodoxy sometimes tends to resolve this paradox by the picture of a Christ who has been stripped of all qualities which relate him to man and history, Christian liberalism resolves it by reducing Christ to a figure of heroic love who reveals the full possibilities of human nature to us. In either case, the total human situation which the mythos of the Christ and the Cross illumines, is obscured. (1963, 73)

Although Niebuhr deploys a theological rhetoric that might make most Continental philosophers uncomfortable, his point is nonetheless extremely appropriate. We can read him to be saying that if the paradox of the ethical demand made on political life is eliminated, then we do not adequately take stock of our existential condition. That is, if we strip away the hyperbolic quality of the demand that constitutes subjectivity, then we fall back into a problematic ontological story that so often underlies egoistic individualism. The essential relatedness to God and the Other articulated by the ontology of constitutive responsibility does not make an appeal to objective moral standards, but instead allows for the realization that all moral standards can themselves become immoral when they end the recursive hermeneutic task in favor of final judgment. This is an ontology that resists all triumphalism. The mythos of the Christ and the Cross illuminate the possibility of what Levinas will call "charity after justice" (PM, 175). When Christ pleads, "Forgive them Father, for they know not what they do," he performs the hyperbolic infinity of responsibility. Niebuhr goes on to note: "Every appeal to moral standards . . . degenerates into a moral justification of the self against the enemy. Parties to a dispute inevitably make themselves judges over it and thus fall into the sin of pretending to be God" (1963, 77).

Far from resulting in quietistic resignation, the extreme rhetoric of Levinas and Derrida, among others, serves to remind us of the essential situation of humanity, which Merold Westphal aptly describes as the inability to look over God's shoulder.[8] In politics, hyperbole can function as a stimulus to embrace humility while engaging in the critical enterprise. In order that egoism not re-entrench itself in our daily practice, we must avoid the temptation to feel that we have fulfilled our obligation to the Other by being critical of our political structures. That is, we must continually realize that our task continues without end (and in this sense, it is appropriately described as "infinite").

Hence, I contend that *kenosis* gives further shape to the general structure of the ontology of constitutive responsibility by providing a conception of both the self as constitutively opened, and also of the Other as the neighbor for whom I am responsible. On both fronts, the political manifestation is *criticism*—of the injustice of political institutions, of the exclusion of the marginalized, of the indifference toward those who suffer. In order to articulate the ways in which this connection between *kenosis* and political critique can be viewed as central to certain strands of Continental philosophy, I will briefly look to Vattimo's nihilistic Christianity, and then to the deconstructive focus on hospitality and the democracy to come. Crucially, these instances demonstrate that *kenosis* is not limited to a specifically Christian framework and serve to illuminate the way in which a particular notion within the theological archive is able to open spaces for continued philosophic discussion and provide impetus for critical political action.

Vattimo's Nihilistic Christianity

Of any figure in Continental philosophy, perhaps Gianni Vattimo has provided the most substantial and incisive analysis of *kenosis* as it concerns post-

Heideggerian thought. Even though he owes as much to hermeneutics as to phenomenology, and though he is Italian rather than French, he should still be read alongside new phenomenology when it comes to the notion of bi-directional relationality (though perhaps not the ontology of constitutive responsibility). The distinction between Vattimo's deployment of this bi-directionality and that found in Levinas, say, is that for Vattimo this relationality is more a matter of interpretive history than of the fundamental structures of ethico-religious subjectivity. Nonetheless, like the new phenomenologists, for Vattimo, postmodernism does not represent an elimination of God, but simply a rejection of certain accounts of theism (and atheism).

If God is conceived primarily in terms of being (and power), and hence remains within an onto-theological framework, then postmodernists would be right to move away from all God-talk. But if we follow Nietzsche and Heidegger in particular, Vattimo suggests, we begin to see the philosophical (and theological) possibilities of a God *after* God, as it were. As Vattimo claims in *After Christianity,* "there are many indications . . . that the death of the moral God has paved the way for the renewal of religious life" (2002, 15). For Vattimo, the God that is "recovered" in the postmodern epoch is not a God of theoretical speculation, but instead is "the God of the Book." He explains the difference as follows:

> The God who is given to us in the Book and who does not "exist" as an objective reality outside of salvation's announcement is always handed over in historically changing forms offered, in the sacred Scriptures and in the living tradition of the Church, to the continuing reinterpretation of the community of believers. (2002, 8)

Since the God that Nietzsche rightly declared "dead" is the metaphysical God, Vattimo contends that the God of the Book is a God best understood as kenotic. As incarnated, emptied, historical, and human, the kenotic God is not representative of classical theistic claims to God's omnipotence, but instead exemplifies what John Caputo (2006) refers to as "the weakness of God." As Vattimo writes:

> The incarnation, that is, God's abasement to the level of humanity, what the New Testament calls God's kenosis, will be interpreted as the sign that the non-violent and non-absolute God of the post-metaphysical epoch has as its distinctive trait the very vocation for weakening of which Heideggerian philosophy speaks. (1999, 39)

The name that Vattimo gives to this general trend that he takes to unite the kenotic dimensions of the New Testament, Nietzsche's notion of nihilism, and Heidegger's philosophical project is "weak ontology." Such an ontology is certainly related to the ontology of constitutive responsibility in that the latter also contests the classical notion of God (and self) as defined by self-sufficiency. However, the difference between these accounts is that Vattimo's weak ontology is best thought of as a name for a historical development and not as a constitutive aspect of subjectivity. Moreover, weak ontology lacks some of the weight that the ontology of constitutive responsibility gives to obligation. These differences become clear in the following passage, in which Vattimo describes how weak ontology could only develop internal to a specific historico-cultural context:

> It is only as the heir of a Judeo-Christian tradition that conceives of the real in terms of creation and the history of salvation that postmodern thought has freed itself from the objectivistic metaphysics of scientism so that it can live up to its experience of cultural pluralism, namely of the historicity and contingency of existing. (2002, 7)

We might say that weak ontology begins with recursive hermeneutics and then develops an ontology out of such a history while the ontology of constitutive responsibility begins with the ethico-religious encounter and then derives the hermeneutic task from it.

Despite the differences between these ontological accounts, Vattimo is quite close to new phenomenology when it comes to his basic contention that Christianity (or Judaism, or Islam, etc.) is a possibility once again because of the way in which Nietzsche and Heidegger have helped us all to come to terms with the death of a particular notion of God—one that is metaphysical, detached, speculative, and primarily articulated in terms of Being.[9] In so doing, they have also reanimated the space in which God can be not just *thought,* but *encountered.* Their approach "emphasizes that the weakening of Being is one possible meaning—if not the absolute meaning—of the Christian message, through the radical reading of incarnation as kenosis. This message speaks of a God who incarnates himself, lowers himself, and confuses all the powers of this world" (Vattimo 2002, 80). The nihilism that results from the death of metaphysics, foundationalism, and strong ontology is not something that stands in opposition to Christianity. Rather, Vattimo contends that this nihilistic view is the outcome of Christianity's own internal movement.

Within this alternative conception of nihilistic Christianity we can begin to understand the significance of the Italian saying for which Vattimo repeatedly expresses his fondness: "Thanks to God, I am an atheist" (2002, 7). Unfolding from his understanding of history, Vattimo contends that rejecting God is only possible in the framework that is already (in)formed by the presence of the historical reception of the Christian articulation of God's self-emptying. "None of us in our western culture—and perhaps not in any culture—begins from zero with the ques-

tion of religious faith," Vattimo claims in *Belief* (1999, 21). Instead, we find ourselves having always already embarked. The history of the weakening of Being is
also the history of *receiving* the kenotic narrative as part of one's own history. And
this does not only call for intellectual assent under the name of "faith," but also
(and perhaps primarily) for a radical commitment to recursive hermeneutics as
being central to how one takes up one's faith. In a very Kierkegaardian way, Vattimo contends that faith is not primarily something we either have or lack but instead a certain kind of task we face. Belief is a project of interpretation, critique,
affirmation, and engagement (Vattimo 1997). However, such a project is always
conducted in the context of one's social situation. As such, Vattimo depends upon
what I have termed bi-directional relationality when he claims that one stands in
relation to God only insofar as one stands with others in a shared history. Before
moving on, I want to make one quick clarification. While affirming the importance of Vattimo's account of belief, I want to note that he potentially goes too far
when it comes to minimizing the role of belief as a "what" in favor of belief as a
"how." While it would certainly be wrong to reduce Christianity to a set of propositional beliefs, it is also wrong to eliminate such beliefs as a crucial part of what
it is to be a Christian (the same would be true for other religions as well). Indeed,
even Vattimo's radical interpretation of nihilistic Christianity requires that one affirm certain things as true as opposed to others. Johannes Climacus understood
that although problems certainly arise when the how is eliminated in favor of the
what, the pendulum can also swing too far in the opposite direction; the goal is to
get both the how and the what right.

Crucial to my argument in this book, we must not miss the political importance of Vattimo's claim that *kenosis* "confuses all the powers of this world." Making clear that this kenotic message is not one of purely otherworldly import, Vattimo proclaims that "the Logos did not humiliate himself just so that we might
understand his teaching, and then go back to the heavens to prepare for us an eternal life that can be reached only in another world" (2002, 53). Instead, Christianity
brings a decidedly *this*-worldly, political message to bear on all apolitical instanti-
ations of what has historically gone under the name "Christianity":

> It is neither absurd, nor perhaps blasphemous, to maintain that the
> truth of Christianity is not the dogmas of the churches but the modern
> system of rights, the humanization of social relations (where it has
> come about), the dissolution of the divine right of all forms of au-
> thority, even the Freudian discovery of the unconscious, which de-
> prives the voice of conscience (which is also the voice of the most
> sanguinary kinds of fanaticism) of its supposed ultimacy, its unques-
> tionable sacrality. (Vattimo 2004, 31–32)

The political upshot of the kenotic import of the weak ontology that Vattimo advocates is in harmony with the democratic tendencies I have located in the recursive hermeneutics that arises from the ontology of constitutive responsibility: "A weak ontology, or better an ontology of the weakening of Being, supplies philosophical reasons for preferring a liberal, tolerant, and democratic society rather than an authoritarian and totalitarian one" (Vattimo 2004, 19)

Hence, we might revise Vattimo's oft-quoted Italian phrase to more specifically reflect his reading of Christianity (resonant with new phenomenology) as follows: Thanks to the centrality of *kenosis* in the cultural history of the West, I/we can affirm the death of an onto-theological God and thereby fully embrace the contingency of historical existence as the space in which I/we undertake the ethico-political (liberal, tolerant, and democratic) relation my/our neighbors. Vattimo's explicit focus on *kenosis* is helpful to filling out one specific way in which new phenomenological God-talk might productively proceed. However, Vattimo's account is enriched by the ontology I have proposed because this provides a more robust account of how responsibility is inscribed in one's very selfhood rather than being a historical contingency of one's cultural narrative.

Although there are important differences between Vattimo and the other thinkers we have been considering, we should view them as fellow travelers. Accordingly, Vattimo, Kierkegaard, and Levinas can be read constructively alongside the argument that Richard Kearney offers in *The God Who May Be*. There, Kearney contends that incarnation should not be limited to a unique historical event that has happened once and for all, but should be expanded to include the very structure of the real such that every act of love—or as Kierkegaard might say, every "work of love"—incarnates God. God's incarnation—God's kenotic nature—is present as poured out every time I pour myself out toward my neighbor. As such, for Kearney, God "neither is nor is not, but may be" (2001, 1) according to how I live in the present and yet toward the *eschaton*. Drawing on Kearney's interpretation, we can see how Vattimo's rather unorthodox Christianity and Levinas's particular take on Judaism, say, need not stand in the way of a distinct appropriation of the idea of an "incarnate" God. By reading these thinkers together, both Judaism and Christianity can be understood such that *God's incarnation is best interpreted as our ethico-political project*.

A Note on Religious Language and Political Violence

Just as we should see the resonances as well as the differences between weak ontology and the ontology of constitutive responsibility, we should also be careful not to confuse *kenosis* as found in Levinas with the same notion found in Vattimo,[10] but instead is better understood as the emptying relation of my self to each and every other with whom I share the world. This difference of religious tradition, however, need not stand in the way of still finding sites of resonance in the various thinkers that can operate across differences in particular vocabularies. For example, in *Levinas and Theology,* Michael Purcell convincingly argues that one of the best ways of understanding Levinasian subjectivity is as "eucharistic" (2006, 142). While such a notion would perhaps be most obviously compatible with the work of Marion, it is odd to think of the Eucharist as a lens through which to view Levinas's Judaism. It might even seem that such a move is an example of how reconstructivism can become patronizing; indeed it could almost seem to amount, on the worst construction, to a forced conversion of Levinas's work. Nonetheless, Purcell overcomes these worries and helpfully describes the "liturgical intentionality" that translates into what he terms a "eucharistic subjectivity": "Its ultimate task is to defeat the power of subjectivity and affirm the primacy of alterity, which signifies by its own power and authority, and yet gives sense to subjectivity by exposing its liturgical nature as for-the-other. This is extreme *kenosis,* or *kenosis in extremis*" (2006, 143). Here we can see that the specific terms of one's religious vocabulary are not really what matters: the goal is to find a way in language (being) to refer to that which always resists adequately being given linguistic expression (the relation to alterity). The recourse to religious language on the part of so many Continental philosophers of religion is due to its ability to express at the very limitations of expression. So, for Purcell, the Eucharist helps convey the "primacy of alterity," which should remind us of the key theme of new phenomenology that we have seen to be expressed in Kierkegaard's account of "transparency," Levinas's notion of "exposure," Henry's account of "Life," Chrétien's notion of the primacy of the "call," Marion's description of the "interlocuted," and Lacoste's account of "liturgical" existence. Underlying all these various notions is an affirmation, whether explicit or not, of *kenosis* as the defining characteristic of both God and the self, which gets expressed as both an ethico-religious constitution and also as a political charge. Purcell brings a number of these threads together when he claims:

> *Kenosis* is a displacement of the self in favour of the other person, a yielding of my place in the sun to make way for the other who has prior claim. Such a kenotic self-displacement is the transfiguring movement of the self from its signification as *"pour-soi"* to its signification as for-the-other-person. (2006, 152)

Purcell's reference here to the passage from Pascal's *Pensées* that Levinas quotes as an epigraph to *Otherwise Than Being* is very telling in regard to the way in which kenotic subjectivity functions as a bi-directional claim about God *and* political life. Levinas quotes Pascal and says: "'That is my place in the sun.' That is how the usurpation of the whole world began" (OTB, vii). And it is difficult *not* to hear this reference to the "usurpation of the whole world" as standing in relation to the dedication of *Otherwise Than Being:* "To the memory of those who were closest among the six million assassinated by the National Socialists, and of the millions on millions of all confessions and all nations, victims of the same hatred of the other man, the same anti-semitism" (OTB, v). We must realize that the *ontological* usurpation of the world is tantamount to *ethico-political violence;* or to put it a bit more poetically, as Jesus once said, a tree will be known by its fruits.

To claim one's own place in the sun—i.e., to locate subjectivity as *pour-soi*—is to refuse to hear the call of the Other. According to the ontology of constitutive responsibility, this call simultaneously establishes the self and contests its self-sufficiency. In order *not* to be complicit in the victimization and hatred of the other person, Levinas advocates a fundamental upsurge of alterity which causes the self to never rest easy in itself, but unceasingly take itself up as a project of caring for others: this is the work that Purcell and Lacoste both term "liturgy." This task is fundamentally political (as Levinas's reference to National Socialism makes clear), yet it is not to be separated from the way we stand in relation to God. The passage that concludes Levinas's "Note" at the beginning of *Otherwise Than Being* regarding the project of "hearing a God not contaminated by Being" must be read alongside the moral and political failure represented by the swastika. As Caputo notes, "the promise of the democracy to come is menaced by the threat of the National Socialism to come" (2006, 5). Kenotic subjectivity and a kenotic God come together in the postmodern task of rethinking the self in light of the transcendence of God and the Other. For new phenomenology, God is not first and foremost a transcendent being (though as Marion admits, God might be *at least* that), but rather God's transcendence *happens* in the life lived for-the-other.

The Deconstructive Focus on Hospitality and the Democracy to Come

Since the mid-1990s, deconstruction has been almost obsessed with the idea of hospitality, along with associated notions such as the promise, the gift, and forgiveness (see Derrida 2001; 2000; 1999; and 1992a; see also Caputo and Scanlon 1999; and Horner 2001). Although drawing on Levinas's writings from the late 1950s onward, the real inaugural event leading to this obsession was the 1947 publication of Martin Heidegger's essay, *Letter on Humanism*. Therein, Heidegger attempts to respond to Jean Beaufret's questions about the absence of any discussion of ethics in Heidegger's thinking. Toward the end of the essay, Heidegger retells the famous story of Heraclitus inviting strangers, who wanted to see him in the midst of thinking, into his house with the words: "Here too the gods come to presence" (*Einai gar kai entautha theous*) (1993, 257). Rather than understanding ethics as a normative code, as a law of practical reason, or as being directed at happiness, Heidegger argues that ethics is really about the Greek *ēthos*, which he translates as "abode." Ethics is a matter of a certain kind of "dwelling" in the world. What the story involving Heraclitus illustrates is the way in which good dwelling amounts to an expression of invitation. We rightly dwell in the world not by protecting ourselves from others (though sometimes such an act is necessary), but when we care for the strangers at the gate.

When coupled with Levinas's claim that ethics occurs in the simple phrase, "After you, sir," Heidegger's rethinking of ethics is not detached from the insights offered by the preceding discussion of *kenosis*. Heidegger also taps into the theological archive when he gives an exposition of what Heraclitus means in saying that the "gods come to presence."[11] Anticipating Levinas's claim that God "comes to mind," Vattimo's "nihilistic" Christianity, and Kearney's re-reading of incarnational theology, Heidegger demonstrates that the best *ēthos* is the one that constantly contests its own adequacy. When Heraclitus invites the strangers into his house he invites them to discourse—that is, rather than having them merely watch him philosophize, he brings them into the conversation itself. By doing so, Heraclitus opens himself up to the possibility of their critique, their chastisement, and their scorn. In contrast to Rorty's later, "ethnocentric" reinforcement of the status quo, Heidegger demonstrates that to open the gates to the stranger is to open up the possibility that the stranger might have a different (and perhaps better) idea of how to operate within those gates. The gods come to presence in the expression of hospitality to the stranger and, lest we think that we have been hospitable enough, the stranger serves to keep us open to the gods' presence. Again, we can see how important it is to maintain the tension between the relation to God and the relation to the Other: when one finally decides in favor of one over the other, the question of priority is settled at the cost of no longer being receptive to the call to responsibility in whatever form it might take.

As we have seen at various points in this book, nowhere is this point more clearly articulated than in the recent work of Derrida. Derrida's most important contribution to this deep and complex discussion is his willingness to give a name to the most ethical political structure—namely, "democracy." Yet what he names is always a democracy that is *not democratic enough*. Resonating with the ideas of a kenotic God and kenotic selves who ever keep open their hermeneutic requirements and ethical responsibilities, Derrida notes that a democracy is legitimate only insofar as it recognizes its constitutive incompleteness. Hence, as I have already suggested, the democracy that we seek must always be a "democracy to come." As Derrida writes: "Democracy is the only system . . . in which, in principle, one has or assumes the right to criticize everything publicly, including the idea of democracy, its concept, its history, and its name" (2005, 87). Importantly,

Derrida repeatedly insists that the "democracy to come" must always signify "here and now"; in other words, we can only await the *eschaton* by working to enact it. Justice *to come* is only possible when we live toward justice *today*.

Derrida reflects on this intersection of hermeneutics, hospitality, and political engagement in his January 1996 seminar entitled "Foreigner Question: Coming from Abroad/ from the Foreigner" (*Question d'étranger: venue de l'étranger*) (Derrida 2000). There, Derrida notes that it is the stranger/foreigner who, "putting the first question," also always "puts me in question" (2000, 3). To be greeted by the stranger at the gate is to be challenged regarding one's personal and civil fortifications. As Derrida so aptly asserts, "the question of hospitality is thus also the question of the question" (2000, 29). This is to say that in the encounter with others, we are met with (at least) two options: "Does hospitality consist in interrogating the new arrival? Does it begin with the question addressed to the newcomer? . . . Or else does hospitality begin with the unquestioning welcome?" (2000, 28–29). Original interrogation or unquestioning welcome? Is the question, "What is your name?" or is the invitation simply, "Yes, yes, come" (*Oui, oui, venir*). These are the options that the Good Samaritan faced and between which he had to decide. Unquestioning welcome is a translation of what Levinas refers to as "substitution," what Heraclitus activated in his response to the people at his door, and the movement reflected in the narrative of God's self-emptying. Yet this is also a political problematic with which we must continuously wrestle: to offer an unconditional "yes" may be to let in a loving neighbor, but it might also be to let in a murderer at the door (as Kant realized).

At the end of the same 1996 seminar, Derrida contrasts his position with Kant's in "On the Supposed Right to Lie for Philanthropic Concerns." Derrida summarizes Kant's position with the thought that it is "better to break with the duty of hospitality rather than break with the absolute duty of veracity" (2000, 72). But, Derrida reminds us, this entire situation presupposes the reality of the law without allowing the law the last word. Invitation, affirmation, welcome—all these are options that condition and are conditioned by the legal framework in which we operate as selves in community. We cannot proceed except at the intersection of affirming an unconditional invitation *within* a system of conditions. In other words, ethics and politics are never separable even though ethics (or the ethico-religious) may maintain some sort of priority—namely, as a quasi-logical existential condition.[12] This situation (i.e., human existence) necessitates that we display constant diligence and accept constant revisability as both singular selves and communal citizens. Simply advocating political and epistemic fallibilism is not enough, since it continues to traffic in the realm of thought rather than recognizing that for thought to be initiated as a kenotic response to the Other, we must recognize *caritas* as the core of *veritas*. Since *caritas* is essentially critical, *democracy* is the name that Derrida gives to the political system that best recognizes this loving-truth—that truth is first and foremost love. Perhaps here we can see why Levinas claims that the love of wisdom (*philo-sophia*) should be understood as "the wisdom of love in the service of love" (see also Burggraeve 2002). This wisdom only occurs within the space of service to love-truth in relation to one's neighbor (who will also most demandingly be in some respects a foreigner/stranger).[13]

In short, I believe that we should recognize and affirm the essential democratic import of *kenosis* that is variously developed in the work of Heidegger, Levinas, Derrida, Purcell, Kearney, Vattimo, and others.[14]

A Critical (Christian) Democracy?

Referring to the death of God, Nietzsche's madman shouts: "This tremendous event is still on its way, wandering; it has not yet reached the ears of men" (Nietzsche 2001, 120). Even if much of twentieth-century Continental philosophy has embraced this news, I have demonstrated that a substantial portion of the same tradition has also attempted to renew the question of what it means to even testify to such an event. Has this "tremendous event" *yet* reached our ears?

In the last chapter, I argued that there are good philosophical reasons for being open to the deployment of "religious" discourse in the decidedly philosophical work of new phenomenology. In this chapter, I have offered what I take to be good political reasons for advocating a specifically kenotic form of God-talk in such philosophical work. If we understand postmodernity as requiring not that we abandon God-talk altogether but merely that we focus such talk on divine *kenosis* rather than a self-sufficient, omnipotent *summum ens*, then we have good reason to view the proclamation of the death of God as being the precursor for *beginning to talk* more appropriately (though probably never adequately) regarding God.

And thus, to the characterization of Continental philosophy as "just Catholicism for atheists" we should reply that Continental philosophy is not "just" anything. Rather, as I have argued, within the numerous strands and trajectories of Continental thought there is a decidedly philosophical, ongoing appropriation of certain religious themes that are deeply relevant to contemporary politics. Importantly, however, this should not be something that worries either Continental philosophers or those who identify as Jewish or Christian. Rather, this development should be seen as a challenge for continuing to rethink God in line with the kenotic message that illuminates the critical function of charity. We have also seen how this critique is best undertaken within a "democracy" as defined by the ethico-political challenge and recursive hermeneutic task to contest any community or institution that forgets its inceptual responsibility to God and the Other. It is in this light that we can return to the passage from Derrida that serves as an epigraph to this book:

More than any other form of democracy, more than social democracy or popular democracy, a Christian democracy should be welcoming to the enemies of democracy; it should turn them the other cheek, offer hospitality, grant freedom of expression and the right to vote to antidemocrats, something in conformity with a certain hyperbolic essence, an essence more autoimmune than ever, of *democracy itself,* if "itself" there ever is, if ever there is a democracy and thus a Christian democracy worthy of its name. (2005, 41)

Constituted as selves by the bi-directional responsibility to God and the Other, we should hear unconditional welcome as God's kenotic message to humanity and, subsequently, it should be our political message to each other—irrespective of whether we are Christians, Jews, Muslims, or rightly pass for atheists.

PART 3

Intersections and Applications

In the first two parts of this book I have made the case that the ontology of constitutive responsibility stands as a resource for contemporary political philosophy. Specifically, I have shown how the ethico-religious account of subjectivity articulated by Kierkegaard and those affiliated with new phenomenology provides for a notion of political critique in the name of justice and offers reasons to advocate a decidedly democratic model of political life. Though I consider these realizations to be absolutely crucial in light of Richard Rorty's dismissal of Continental ethics and philosophy of religion, in order for this book not to fall prey to a tendency I noted in the introduction—namely, that Continental philosophy remains comfortable in the sphere of abstraction and speculative thought rather than showing why particular speculative moves offer a promising way forward in practice—I will now turn to five areas in which I find the ontology of constitutive responsibility to be particularly relevant: these are religion, epistemology, politics, ethics, and what I will term the ethico-political.

I have not chosen these areas at random, but consider them to follow quite nicely from what I outlined in part 2 as the primary unifying characteristics of new phenomenology. In what follows, then, I will first (in chapter 9) return to the question of whether postmodernism is compatible with determinate religious traditions and suggest that it *is* when "religion" is considered through a specifically Kierkegaardian lens. In chapter 10, I will build upon the claim, made in chapter 6, that bi-directional relationality is an asset in rethinking the issue of religion in the public square: this notion allows for a shift from an epistemological to an ethico-religious frame in which to consider the issue. Following this rethinking of the ethico-religious as underlying the epistemological, in chapter 11, I will turn to epistemology and, in light of the discussion of a rehabilitated transcendental language in chapter 5, I will provide an argument for a specifically foundationalist interpretation of how justification operates internal to new phenomenology. Then, in chapter 12, I will turn to the area of environmental ethics and show that the Levinasian distinction between ethics and politics, earlier discussed as being crucial to the possibility of political criticism, is also helpful in the project of constructing a theoretical framework that is able to motivate serious transformation in light of climate change. And finally, in chapter 13, I will outline one possible model—namely, that of ethico-political exemplars—by which we are able to recognize the impossibility of finding clear-cut guides for moral decision, while still offering assistance for living here and now toward a democracy to come.

Intersections and Applications

The Religious: Maintaining the Paradox— Wittgenstein and Kierkegaard on Postmodern Christianity

Throughout this book, I have suggested that new phenomenology opens spaces for rethinking God after the collapse of onto-theology. In chapter 7, however, I claimed that what was needed was not some vacuous notion of the "postmodern religious" or "religion without religion," but a thoroughgoing postmodern approach to determinate religious traditions. In this chapter, I will extend this claim by considering how a postmodern Christianity is possible and offering suggestions as to what such a notion might entail.

Now, the idea of postmodern Christianity might strike some as just being contradictory. How is it possible to invite a philosophy that seemingly claims that all truth is relative, contingent, and historically located, into constructive dialogue with a religion that is often described as grounded on Absolute Truth? For many believers and non-believers alike, the disintegration of classical metaphysics is viewed as being the death-knell of Christianity as well. In his important book, *After Christianity,* Gianni Vattimo contests this idea and suggests that the "death of God" opens the space for a re-birth of Christianity:

> The God I have recovered after liquidating metaphysics and the illusion that one could demonstrate that the real has a certain structure and a determinate foundation is not the God of metaphysical certainties, of the *preambula fidei.* The natural theology expressed by scholastic metaphysics was grounded on the idea that a healthy, natural reason was capable of demonstrating the existence of a supreme Being—cause and *telos* of the world. . . . Instead, the God recovered in the postmetaphysical and postmodern epoch is the God of the Book. . . . [This is] the God who is given to us in the Book and who does not "exist" as an objective reality outside of salvation's announcement, [and which is] always handed over in historically changing forms . . . in the living tradition of the Church, to the continuing reinterpretation of the community of believers. (2002, 8)

In his striking collaboration with Rorty, Vattimo goes even further and suggests that "hermeneutics—expressed in its most radical form in Nietzsche's statement ['there are no facts, only interpretations'] and in Heidegger's ontology—is the development and maturation of the Christian message" (Vattimo and Rorty 2005, 47). In chapter 8, I remarked that this engagement between Rorty and Vattimo is quite promising as a model of how to understand the political value of Christianity. However, let me now say that I also find their collaboration to have unfortunate aspects as well. As we have seen, the promise of *The Future of Religion* lies in the *performative impact* of a positive conversation between a Catholic, postmodern hermeneuticist and an atheist, eclectic neo-Pragmatist who are alike committed to the project of democratic politics and the important way that Christian accounts of charity can help to support such a project. This is definitely an admirable step in setting aside hostilities between philosophical perspectives that often are viewed as at odds with each other. Nevertheless, their collaboration is unfortunate in that it too closely aligns Vattimo's important contribution to envisioning a postmodern Christianity with Rorty's neo-Pragmatist tendency toward *separatism* in his early work (in which he encouraged the privatization of religious belief) and toward *reconstructivism* in his later work (in which he allows religious discourse as long as it really just means a shared vision of social hope). Although Vattimo and Rorty clearly part company at crucial points in their text, the book can lead one to suspect that the flippancy and indifference with which Rorty so often treats religion is endemic to all post-metaphysical appropriations of religious traditions. To draw such a conclusion, however, would be to miss the relevance of Vattimo's retrieval of the "God of the Book" to contemporary debates on how to think God after strong foundationalism and Christianity after onto-theology.

While Vattimo wrestles (like Kierkegaard and new phenomenology) to maintain the tension between theological truth and existential contingency, Rorty's neo-Pragmatist approach to religion, I contend, serves to eliminate all perspectives that are not in line with his rather narrow conception of social progress (see Talisse and Aikin 2005). The worry that postmodernism necessarily leads to such a reductive account of religion is why many choose to draw the battle lines at the idea of postmodernism itself, rather than being willing to recognize the important contributions that thinkers such as Kierkegaard, Vattimo, and the new phenomenologists offer to contemporary philosophy of religion. What all of these philosophers affirm (to some degree), and what Rorty denies, is that Christianity itself is constituted by a tension (or paradox) between the truth of Christ (see esp. Henry 2003) and the socio-historical contingency that serves as the necessary context in which this truth could be held. I take this to be a particular way of understanding bi-directional relationality as historically undertaken; that is, to be a Christian, I contend, is to live out a relation to the kenotic message of Christ amid one's particular social location.

Hence, I will argue that the contingency, contextuality, and singularity that are central to the ontology of constitutive responsibility are not obstacles to participation in determinate religious traditions. Rather, such notions allow for a conception of religious life that makes room for both the paradoxical commitments of some traditional Christian beliefs (the Virgin Birth, an Incarnate God, and the Resurrection, say) and also the actuality of the individual Christian's existence in the world. Along with other pragmatic discussions of religion, Rorty often appropriates Ludwig Wittgenstein's work as a model of how to understand religious belief as a "language game" that is quite distinct from the discourse that should characterize public debate. In light of this appropriation, I will offer a decidedly Kierkegaardian reading of Wittgenstein in order to show that, far from supporting Rorty, Wittgenstein stands as a valuable resource for anyone committed to Christianity *and yet* convinced by the postmodern critique of metaphysics. Lest anyone claim that this turn to Wittgenstein is a distraction from my overall focus in this book, we should remember that Wittgenstein was a careful reader and deep admirer of Kierkegaard (see, for example, Monk 1990), and is also recorded as saying, "you could say of my work that it is 'phenomenology'" (Drury 1984, 116).

I will proceed as follows. First, I will consider the neo-Pragmatist account of religion provided by Rorty and demonstrate how it eliminates all paradox from religious belief—thereby eliminating what I take to be the key aspect of religion itself. Then, I will give a brief outline of the history of the deconstruction of Western ontology / metaphysics and show how the demise of the onto-theological conception of God actually reinvigorates the possibility of a postmodern Christianity. Moving from the general to the specific, I will then contend that the failure of the project of "transcendence" (see Hodges 1990) within Wittgenstein's *Tractatus* actually mirrors the failure of modern Western metaphysics. With these contextual elements in place—Rorty's pragmatic religion, the postmodern critique of metaphysics, and the Wittgensteinian contribution to this critique—I will turn to the idea of *a struggle with paradox* as constitutive of religious life by looking to Kierkegaard as a, perhaps unexpected, guide for interpreting Wittgenstein's own approach to the philosophy of religion.[1]

Richard Rorty's Neo-Pragmatist Religion

Several times in the 1990s, Richard Rorty explicitly argued for the *privatization* of religious belief.[2] Drawing heavily on William James's *Varieties of Religious Experience,* Rorty contends that the only way for religious beliefs not to become an obstacle to social order is for them to be held privately—that is, excluded from the public square (Rorty 1999, 149). "The main reason religion needs to be privatized," he writes, "is that, in political discussion with those outside the relevant religious community, it is a conversation-stopper" (1999, 171). Rorty is not claiming that we need to abandon our religious commitments altogether; rather, we just need to recognize their proper sphere of relevance, and this sphere is separate from politics.

At first glance this seems a rather innocent and well-intentioned suggestion. Certainly we want to foster as much discussion and engagement as possible among the citizens of a country (or nations of the world) in an attempt to translate harmonious conversation into real political harmony. Since religious beliefs are among the most politically divisive ones that people can hold, removing them from the deliberative table is similar to asking gang members to check their weapons at the door in an attempt to cultivate a safe space for talking with each other. As Rorty argues repeatedly in *Contingency, Irony, and Solidarity,* and then echoes in *Philosophy and Social Hope:* "The search for private perfection, pursued by theists and atheists alike, is neither trivial nor, in a pluralistic democracy, relevant to public policy" (1999, 171). If Rorty's comments on religion were limited to statements advocating privatization, then the primary reason to engage him would perhaps be to argue for the legitimacy of religion in the public square (see the next chapter). However, as I have already suggested, Rorty's earlier separatist tendencies eventually gave way to reconstructivist ones.

Rorty's reconstructive project is best illuminated by looking at the main question that guides his 1997 essay, titled "Religious Faith, Intellectual Responsibility, and Romance." There he asks "whether the religious believer has a right to her faith—whether this faith conflicts with her intellectual responsibilities" (1999, 149). Rorty indicates that this question is really a question about justification. In opposition to W. K. Clifford, Rorty sides with William James regarding the obligation to justify one's beliefs. This obligation, Rorty emphasizes, "arises only when one's habits of action interfere with the fulfillment of others' needs." "Insofar as one is engaged in a private project," he continues, "that obligation lapses" (1999, 149). If Rorty were to stop here, then this claim could be read as a fairly sensible argument for the privatization of religious belief as the only means of maintaining both our public obligation to the needs of others and our widely divergent, private commitments to various conceptions of God. However, as with Janicaud's interpretation of phenomenology, Rorty smuggles in an argument for what sorts of beliefs a religious person *should* hold if she wants her public and private lives to be consistent with each other—i.e., consistent with Rorty's own account of pragmatically minded public discourse. If religious belief is to cohere with the other intellectual responsibilities of the believer, then it seems to need to be both *private* (so as to not interfere with the needs of others) and also *reconstructed* (so as to not interfere with the needs of the believer herself).

But, what sort of needs would the believer have in this regard? Rorty has already let the cat out of the bag by asking for consistency between religious beliefs on the one hand and what he terms "intellectual responsibility" on the other hand. According to Rorty, such consistency is possible only if certain sorts of religious commitments are abandoned. While describing "pragmatic theism," Rorty offers a list of what these problematic, or perhaps the better adjective would be *outdated*, beliefs would entail: "Pragmatic theists . . . do have to get along without personal immortality, providential intervention, the efficacy of sacraments, the Virgin Birth, the Risen Christ, the Covenant with Abraham, the authority of the Koran, and a lot of other things which many theists are loath to do without" (1999, 156). The key point here is that if one grants that epistemic consistency is an intellectual responsibility to oneself (and, I believe, one *should* grant this), then Rorty's contention is that beliefs that require accepting paradoxical propositions like those he mentions must be rejected in the name of overall coherence. It appears, then, that it is perfectly possible for a pragmatist to be a theist *if she reconstructs her theism in light of her pragmatism, but not vice versa.*

It could be argued that Rorty's reconstruction is only applicable to self-professed "pragmatic theists" and therefore does not commit him to a larger claim regarding *all* religious believers, but I want to point out two aspects of Rorty's thought that run counter this interpretation. First, ever since *Philosophy and the Mirror of Nature* (1979), Rorty has been a leading voice advocating the rejection of the appearance/reality distinction.[3] This move has both ontological and epistemological consequences: the idea of intrinsic essences must be overcome, and any correspondence theory of truth must be contested. Even though Rorty is deeply suspicious of theory (as we saw in chapter 1), these basic moves serve as the theoretical motivation for his attempt over the past several decades to *redescribe* truth, identity, and ethics as thoroughly "contingent," always held "ironically," and only deployed in the task of bringing about human "solidarity" (Rorty 1989).[4] This point is relevant to our concern here due to the idea that once the basic premises of Rorty's brand of antifoundationalism and behavioral contextualism are accepted, then, ironically, pragmatism ceases to be just a philosophical option and becomes the very condition for doing philosophy. Claiming that Rorty's comments about pragmatism are limited to pragmatists is undercut by his own *conviction* (could it ever be more than this for Rorty?) that pragmatism is the best way forward. So, to say that Rorty does not mean to include every religious believer in his comments really amounts to the claim that he is only addressing the clearest-thinking, most consistent, and most honest thinkers and not those who are self-contradictory, immature, and confused. This is hardly a promising line of defense. Rather, we should conclude that when Rorty says that pragmatists must abandon such paradoxical beliefs as the Virgin Birth and the Risen Christ, he really means that *any* clear-thinking person should do so.

The second point is a modification of the first. For Rorty, with the loss of foun-dationalism comes the loss of certainty with regard to the priority of one's com-mitments. When Rorty advocates reconstruction and redescription, he is really demanding a reconstruction *in the wake of pragmatism*. Just as Rorty claimed that democracy should always be understood to be prior to philosophy (1991a), when it comes to religion he indicates that one's pragmatism should be prior to one's re-ligious beliefs and practices. But, if Rorty's own claims are correct, then it appears that they are stripped of the justificatory warrant that would be required to give pragmatism itself such a priority (I will return to this point in chapter 11).

In *The Future of Religion,* Rorty offers the clearest example of his reconstructed neo-Pragmatist religion. In the midst of a consideration of Vattimo's *Belief,* Rorty claims that he understands the "holy" as "bound up with the hope that someday, any millennium now, my remote descendants will live in a global civilization in which love is pretty much the only law" (Vattimo and Rorty 2005, 40). He then says that the main difference between religious people like Vattimo, and non-religious people like himself, is really a difference between "unjustifiable gratitude and un-justifiable hope" (Vattimo and Rorty 2005, 40). This claim is reminiscent of his ear-lier "romantic" redescription of religious faith: "The kind of religious faith which seems to me to lie behind the attractions of both utilitarianism and pragmatism," he writes in 1997, "is . . . a faith in the future possibilities of moral humans, a faith which is hard to distinguish from love for, and hope for, the human community" (Rorty 1999, 160). Redefining religion as "romance" is, I believe, Rorty's attempt to make religion palatable to non-religious persons. Unfortunately, in the process Rorty makes religion unrecognizable to the vast majority of religious persons. The main problem with this reconstructed conception is that (like the notion of a "postmodern religious") it can amount to a patronizing and even condescend-ing view of religion itself while still deploying God-talk (see Clanton 2008). Reli-gion, he seems to say, is fine as long as it is stripped of anything that would con-test a pragmatic sensibility. Richard Rorty's pragmatic religion is devoid of paradox and struggle and, as I will argue below, thereby misses the key components of re-ligious life itself.

One of the major thinkers that Rorty depends on in the development of his thinking on religion is Ludwig Wittgenstein. Throughout *Contingency, Irony, and Solidarity,* Rorty appeals to Wittgenstein as one of the prime examples of how to "de-divinize the world" (1989, 21). This project of de-divinization, or more prosai-cally the redescription of the world as thoroughly contingent, is for Rorty a precursor of his own pragmatic project. And the pragmatic appropriation of Wittgenstein is not limited to Rorty. In his essay, "Faith: Themes from Wittgenstein, Kierkegaard and Nietzsche," Michael Hodges (2001) also appropriates Wittgenstein for similar purposes (see also Aikin and Hodges 2006). In the hands of Rorty, Wittgenstein allows for the de-divinization of the world, and this comes at the cost of the de-paradoxicalization of religion. Before explicitly contesting this reading of Wittgenstein, I want to outline the history of what Nietzsche and Heidegger diagnose as the demise of onto-theology. After providing this necessary context we will be in a good position to see how Wittgenstein's thinking in the *Tractatus* mirrors the general postmodern move from *transcendence* to *particularity* and from *necessity* to *contingency*.

I will suggest that, when read alongside Kierkegaard, Wittgenstein should be understood as deploying a notion of religious belief as an expression of the paradoxical reality that finite, existing human beings embody when they affirm a relation to divine Truth. Merold Westphal nicely expresses this situation as follows:

> The truth is that there is Truth, but in our finitude and fallenness we do not have access to it. We'll have to make do with the truths available to us; but that does not mean either that we should deny the reality of Truth or that we should abandon the distinction between truth and falsity. Moreover, the most we should claim for this claim itself is that it is true, that it is the best way for us humans to think about the matter. (Westphal 2001, 87)

The Failure of Onto-theology and the Opening of the Religious

Traditionally, the religious sphere has been defined by a *sub specie aeternitatis* viewpoint, a privileged position which looks down on the finite world of human history under the form or aspect of eternity. Religion has been understood to claim that since it is able to glean insight into how this view is constituted, it has knowledge and possession of Eternal or Absolute Truth. In a passage from *Overcoming Onto-Theology* that I often quote, Westphal notes that this approach made the claim "that we can occupy the divine perspective on the world, or at least peek over God's shoulder" (2001, 6).[5] Along with this perspective comes the thought that since God has created all that is, our rational capacity to understand the created world would also eventually lead us to a substantive knowledge of God. The Enlightenment's general take on natural theology was characteristically that God's existence and attributes can be made knowable through the rigorous application of rationality. For many working within the postmodern context (consider Heidegger's critique of onto-theology discussed earlier), this approach to religion requires that God become the conclusion to various arguments which lead toward the goal of theistic belief. A relationship to God would be, then, primarily a relationship to the truth of a proposition and/or to the outcome of dialectical thinking rather than to the God we worship and before whom we sing and dance. According to this critical interpretation, "God exists" is a proposition that remains true at all times and all that changes is our acceptance or denial of it. In the case of the latter, the hope remains that any rational person will eventually change her mind after fully considering the good arguments for theism.

In opposition to the vantage point of what we might call *transcendent externality*, the nineteenth-century work of such proto-existentialists as Kierkegaard, Dostoevsky, and Nietzsche, and the work of such diverse twentieth-century thinkers as James, Dewey, Wittgenstein, Heidegger, Kuhn, Foucault, Derrida, and Latour, is critical of any human claim to occupy such an external position. Kierkegaard's suggestion that Hegel built a crystal palace in the realm of ideas but forgot that he continued to live in a small house next door brings to light exactly what such a critique entails: in the attempt to talk of Truth and universal metaphysical structures, what gets lost is, to put it in the language of Marx, the historically situated social and material conditions of human existence (Marx and Engels 1970). With the birth of the postmodern age, claims to occupy the position of absolute transcendence are rejected in favor of a recognition of the inescapable situatedness of human existence. Nietzsche perhaps best represents this view in his short essay "On Truth and Lying in a Non-Moral Sense," when he describes "truth" as:

> A mobile army of metaphors, metonymies, anthropomorphisms, in short a sum of human relations which have been subjected to poetic and rhetorical intensification, translation, and decoration, and which, after they have been in use for a long time, strike a people as firmly established, canonical, and binding; truths are illusions of which we have forgotten that they are illusions, metaphors which have become worn by frequent use and have lost all sensuous vigour, coins which, having lost their stamp, are now regarded as metal and no longer as coins. (1999, 146)

Just as metaphors always presuppose a context in which they signify, truth requires a context in which it can be accepted as such.[6] The claim to view temporal existence "under the aspect of eternity" involves a bizarre illusion that covers over the situation in which one *historically* stands.

It might be concluded that this shattering of the symbolic mirror in which metaphysical religion viewed existence also destroys any claims to religious truth. For how could we still claim that God exists and possesses certain distinct attributes if to make such a claim is to again position ourselves outside of the conditions in which we necessarily live, move, and have our being? Attempting to dispel this worry in *After Christianity,* Vattimo claims that "postmodern pluralism has enabled . . . the recovery of the Christian faith. If God is dead, if philosophy has recognized that it cannot with certainty grasp the ultimate foundation, then philosophical atheism is no longer necessary" (2002, 5). "Only an absolute philosophy," he continues, "can feel the necessity of refuting religious experience" (2002, 5).

Following Vattimo and the work of those associated with the "theological turn," we have seen that moving toward particular contexts and away from absolutism need not represent one more nail in the coffin of religious belief. Rather, such a move opens the space in which religion could once again signify as a matter of lived existence rather than merely speculative thought. According to Vattimo, with the rejection of all metaphysical schemas comes the rejection of all specifically anti-religious metaphysical schemas as well. *Traditional atheism is just as metaphysically laden as traditional theism.* As Heidegger writes in the *Letter on Humanism:*

> Within the existential determination of the essence of man, therefore, nothing is decided about the "existence of God" or his "nonbeing," no more than about the possibility or impossibility of gods. Thus it is not only rash but also an error in procedure to maintain that the interpretation of the essence of man from the relation of his essence to the truth of Being is atheism. (Heidegger 1993, 253)

Heidegger's point is that theism and atheism both presuppose structures that postmoderns have abandoned. Thus, we now face the task of wrestling with what it would mean to be a "theist" or an "atheist" in light of these developments in postmetaphysical thinking. Nonetheless, "belief" in God is, "in the strong sense of the word," Vattimo says, "no longer possible" (2002, 8). While Vattimo's claim here could certainly be interpreted in ways that would cause me to distance myself from it, I take his point to be quite Kierkegaardian. Namely, faith does not stand in opposition to knowledge as certainty stands to uncertainty. In a postmodern world, faith must be re-thought, and so must the God in whom one puts one's faith.[7]

Before moving on to consider Wittgenstein's role in this history, I want to make clear that I am in no way advocating flippancy and vulgar relativism with regard to Christian belief. As I made clear in chapter 7, the contemporary tendency, all too prevalent in deconstruction, to reconstruct "the religious" while denying the specificity or uniqueness of the doctrines of determinate religions can be just as problematic as the pragmatic appropriations of religious discourse found in authors such as Richard Rorty and, as J. Caleb Clanton (2008) suggests, Cornel West as well.[8] Many contemporary postmodern and also pragmatic approaches to the philosophy of religion eliminate the struggle and risk that are so key to religious existence; *while pragmatism often makes faith too easy, postmodernism often makes it too vague.* I want to demonstrate how it is possible to both affirm the ontology of constitutive responsibility (which I have shown to be directly in line with a particular version of the postmodern critique of onto-theology / metaphysics) while still maintaining the distinctness of determinate religious traditions. Because of my focus, here, on Christianity in particular, let me suggest that it is only when we are able to do both that the struggle of religious life can be maintained as a radically passionate appropriation of the truth of the Christian narrative internal to one's lived contexts.

The Tragedy of the *Tractatus*

With this outline of my position in place, I will now turn to the "failure" of the *Tractatus* as reinforcing this basic post-metaphysical movement.[9] Wittgenstein opens the *Tractatus* with the claim: "The world is all that is the case" (1974, prop. 1). Or, restated in 1.1: "The world is the totality of facts." Importantly, in order to make such a claim, the judging subject must be located beyond the world itself—i.e., were the subject to be located within the world, such a judgment would be nonsensical due to the fact that the subject would fall within the domain of the judgment. Hence, Wittgenstein depends upon the metaphysical view described above. Simply put, the subject in the *Tractatus* is a subject beyond the world. Michael Hodges terms this perspective "transcendence," and notes: "From the beginning [Wittgenstein] speaks from the outside of the world as a whole—as a totality—given complete" (1990, 22). Now, this "transcendence" would not be a problem except that, according to Hodges, Wittgenstein ends up arguing that the *Tractatus* itself must be passed over in silence. That is, it represents unthinkable thoughts and unsayable propositions. Accordingly, it faces the very problem that it diagnoses.

The tragedy of the *Tractatus* is that it demands that "sense" be located *within* the world while its own propositions depend upon their being made from a position *outside* the world. According to its own logic, then, its propositions are nonsense. Hodges summarizes this nicely when he writes: "The 'transcendental point of view' is, of course, explicitly rejected in the doctrines of the *Tractatus,* so the positions expressed in it stand in dramatic conflict with the perspective the work takes" (1990, 24). Of course, that Wittgenstein did not realize this problem is doubtful, considering that Wittgenstein himself demands that "anyone who understands me eventually recognizes [my propositions] as nonsensical. . . . He must, so to speak, throw away the ladder after he has climbed up it. He must transcend these propositions, and then he will see the world aright" (Wittgenstein 1974, prop. 6.54).

How does this problem occurring internal to the *Tractatus* mirror the critique of onto-theological conceptions of God? The key is in how this problem is appropriated. For example, the positivists draw from the *Tractatus* a defense of the verification criterion. Since all religious claims would be examples of other-worldly propositions, they are rejected as nonsensical and thereby meaningless. A. J. Ayer expresses this position when he says of ethics: "We shall set ourselves to show that in so far as statements of value are significant, they are ordinary 'scientific' statements; and that in so far as they are not scientific, they are not in the literal sense significant, but are simply expressions of emotion which can be neither true nor false" (2007, 18). However, as Rorty himself successfully demonstrates in the introduction to *The Linguistic Turn,* the positivists fail to recognize that the claim of an absolute scientific criterion is itself a claim that is non-falsifiable.[10] On its own account, then, the positivist criterion must be rejected. That is, the standard by which positivists judge ethical and religious claims to be meaningless is the very standard that the *Tractatus* presupposes and then, by *reductio,* shows to be problematic.

Importantly, Wittgenstein does not fall prey to the misunderstanding of the positivistic appropriation. Rather, as Paul Engelmann writes:

> Positivism holds—and this is its essence—that what we can speak about is all that **really matters** in life. *Whereas Wittgenstein passionately believes that all that really matters in human life is precisely what, in his view, we must be silent about.* . . . [It] is not the coastline of that island which he is bent on surveying with such meticulous accuracy, but the boundary of the ocean. (Englemann 1967, 97; as quoted in Hodges 1990, 6; original emphasis)

Already in the *Tractatus* Wittgenstein is concerned with what he calls "the mystical" (6.522). Moreover, therein he claims that "God does not reveal himself in the world" (6.432). Religion is absolutely not excluded in Wittgenstein's thinking and, in fact, in the "Lecture on Ethics," Wittgenstein is explicit about this:

> I see now that these nonsensical expressions were not nonsensical because I had not yet found the correct expressions, but that their nonsensicality was their very essence. For all I wanted to do with them was just *to go beyond* the world and that is to say beyond significant language. My whole tendency and I believe the tendency of all men who ever tried to write or talk Ethics or Religion was to run against the boundaries of language. Ethics in so far as it springs from the desire to say something about the ultimate meaning of life, the absolute good, the absolute valuable, can be no science. What it says does not add to our knowledge in any sense. But it is a document of a ten-

dency in the human mind which I personally cannot help respecting
deeply and I would not for my life ridicule it. (Wittgenstein 1965, 11–
12; original emphasis)

Notice that here Wittgenstein continues to insist that religious significance
is located in its being "beyond the world" as he claimed earlier in the *Tractatus*.
However, he now shifts from a speculative language about "nonsensical expressions," to a discourse about the personal commitment of those who take meaningful religious life seriously. Wittgenstein does not give an argument for such a
transition, but is merely content to claim that he "personally cannot help respecting deeply" this religious "tendency in the human mind." Making a move that
anticipates the method and thinking of the *Philosophical Investigations*, Wittgenstein shifts, as Emyr Vaughan Thomas phrases it, "from detachment to immersion" (1999). We see here a proto-moment of the later Wittgenstein's concern for
the actuality of human engagement. With the failure of the metaphysics of the
Tractatus there does not come a critique of all religion, but instead a renewed engagement with religious life. In agreement with Wittgenstein, Richard Amesbury
claims that the "proper task of the philosopher of religion is to investigate the kind
of reality God has . . . by looking to see what roles talk of God plays in people's
lives" (2002, 162).

Echoing the criticism of onto-theology that one finds throughout postmodern
philosophy, M. O'C. Drury records Wittgenstein as saying:

It is a dogma of the Roman Church that the existence of God can be
proved by natural reason. Now this dogma would make it impossible
for me to be a Roman Catholic. If I thought of God as another being like myself, outside myself, only infinitely more powerful, then I
would regard it as my duty to defy him. (Drury 1984, 107–108)

Here we find Wittgenstein beautifully crystallizing the point that the death of
metaphysical religion does not mean that God is an illusion *à la* Freud or that religious belief is meaningless *à la* Ayer. Instead, it merely necessitates a re-articulation
of how we are to conceive the human relationship to God. If we have not caught
any fish, it perhaps only means that we need to cast our nets in a different direction.
The direction that Wittgenstein repeatedly proposes is away from metaphysical
speculation and toward an existential-phenomenological engagement with one's
linguistic context.

The Struggle of Religious Life

The move away from onto-theology is a move toward multiplicity. Rather
than search for one overarching criterion for truth, we must now look to various

and numerous practices in the attempt to locate a criterion which is specific to the examples (or language games) that we investigate/discover in the world.[11] Wittgenstein's resistance to any unifying metaphysical theory is made manifest when he claims that "the term 'language-*game*' is meant to bring into prominence the fact that the *speaking* of language is part of an activity or of a life-form" (2001, §23; original emphasis). Insisting that we "review the multiplicity of language-games," he suggests fifteen possible examples of how such a "game" could be construed. Wittgenstein uses this focus on the multiplicity of language-games to set in relief his mature opposition to "what logicians have said about the structure of language. (Including the author of the *Tractatus Logico-Philosophicus*)" (2001, §23). The relevance of this multiplicity to our concern here is that there must be as many criteria for epistemic adjudication as there are games in which such adjudication occurs.

On this point at least, Wittgenstein and Rorty are agreed: the standard by which we judge religious truth is unlikely the standard with which we judge scientific or historical truth. Amesbury pushes this even further when he notes that "religion" as such is far too large a category for a single language-game. As already noted by James in the 1890s, the recognition of the "varieties of religious experience" brings with it a variety of religious articulations.[12] And Wittgenstein seems to refer to this "variety" in a conversation with Drury: "The ways in which people have had to express their religious beliefs differ enormously" (Drury 1984, 93). To appeal to one definitive conception of the "religious" as occurring outside of the beliefs and practices of particular religions is, as Amesbury insists, "to suppose that these religions could *themselves* be evaluated in terms of some independent set of criteria" (2002, 167). Ignoring the singularity and independence of the various religious expressions would "return us to the confusion of thinking that the language in which claims to truth are made is itself a claim to truth" (2002, 167). Even though the *Investigations* make sparse reference to religion, it is while Wittgenstein is writing this text that Drury records him as saying, "I am not a religious man but I cannot help seeing every problem from a religious point of view" (Drury 1984, 79). For the Wittgenstein of *Philosophical Investigations,* the status of the philosophy of language and philosophy of religion are closely connected indeed.

In contrast to the neo-Pragmatist and positivistic appropriations of Wittgenstein, I contend that for Wittgenstein (as well as for the postmodern thinkers we have been considering in this book) it is actually the emphasis on lived existence, which arises in light of the deconstruction of onto-theology, that allows for the meaningfulness of religion to be able to be maintained. On this model, I suggest that Wittgenstein would contend that if there is no appeal to an overarching criterion outside all language games according to which theism can be affirmed or rejected, then it follows that the "scientific" truths of biology, archeology, and anthropology, say, can never contradict the truth of religion *as religious*. The criterion of judgment would always be internal to the activity of the game itself; the significance, and thus the meaning, of religion would be found within the activities of those persons claiming to operate within the domain of that game. Wittgenstein supports this interpretation of his work when in *Culture and Value* he claims:

> Queer as it sounds: The historical accounts in the Gospels might, historically speaking, be demonstrably false and yet belief would lose nothing by this: *not*, however, because it concerns "universal truths of reason!" Rather, because historical proof (the historical proof-game) is irrelevant to belief. This message (The Gospels) is seized on by men believingly (i.e., lovingly). *That* is the certainty characterizing this particular acceptance-as-true, not something *else*. A believer's relation to these narratives is *neither* the relation to historical truth (probability), *nor yet* that to a theory consisting of "truths of reason." (1980, 32; original emphases)

A point of clarification is in order here. We must be careful not to go too far with Wittgenstein regarding the radical independence of particular language games. It can be easy to slide from a sensible affirmation of contextualism to a problematic affirmation of a radical and unsustainable conception of relativism. The project of thinking after metaphysics and onto-theology can potentially move too far in the opposite direction, and once again strip religion of its significance. *What was initially a far too determinate attempt at description (metaphysical arrogance) can now be lost in a haze of relativity (postmodern subjectivism).* Though I am strongly resistant to the way in which Rorty places certain pragmatic limits on how we should reconstruct religious belief, in no way do I mean to advocate that there are not still *some* limits that should be rightly considered. Embracing contextualism does not mean that *just anything* can count as true (we will return to this in chapter 11 in relation to an objection to "Reformed epistemology"). Just because scientific evidence might not be able to straightaway refute a religious belief *as religious*, it does not mean that there will not be truth claims that are frequently *understood* as religious that should be viewed as remaining available for contestation in light of such evidence (and vice versa). For example, it is no longer plausible for someone to advocate a geocentric theory of the universe despite the fact that certain scriptures that were offered as evidence for such a theory in the past remain part of the Bible. Similarly, many of the beliefs that religious persons hold as a result of their having been raised in the American South, say—I should note that I have lived in the South all my life—might so thoroughly shape their appropriation of the Christian tradition that they currently hold to certain views on geological history, racial identity, or sexual orientation that advances in physics, genetics, and neuroscience might eventually make (or have already made) unsustainable.

That said, my Kierkegaardian appropriation of Wittgenstein is meant to demonstrate that such revisions simply illuminate the fact that the specific way in which these claims were understood, served to misplace their properly religious dimension. As such, the religious component of such beliefs—for instance, that God should be thought of as "creator," that all people are equally in need of salvation, and that one's sexual behavior is a matter of moral and religious concern—remain resistant to "scientific" objections. So, to fill this out a bit, though one might no longer be able to hold a "young Earth" view of literal six-day creation because of advances in carbon dating and evolutionary biology, this does not mean that such advances require abandoning a conception of God as "creator." Choosing to draw a religious line at whichever biological or astrophysical theory one happens to affirm is to misunderstand religious truth from the outset. By combining Wittgensteinian contextualization with a Kierkegaardian-Levinasian account of singularity, while yet guarding against the slide toward problematic relativism that threatens both notions, it becomes difficult to dismiss religion as nothing more than a failed meta-narrative that has been made obsolete by scientific advances.

In contrast to an emphasis on doctrinal commitment, and echoing Climacus's claim that to "know a creed by rote is paganism, because Christianity is inwardness" (CUP, 224), Wittgenstein suggests that "one of the things Christianity says is that sound doctrines are all useless" (1980, 53). Christianity says instead that "you have to change your *life*. (Or the *direction* of your life)" (1980, 53). While I certainly agree with the general Wittgensteinian (and Climacian) point here, I do think that it might go a bit too far. Though religion is certainly about *more* than belief and can never be *reduced* to propositions, it still requires affirming certain things as true and other things as false. In order to avoid the potentially patronizing vacuity that can eliminate the distinctiveness of a particular religious tradition in the name of "religion without religion," it is important that we not exclude the *epistemic* dimension of religion when we rightly attempt to emphasize its *lived* dimension. Moreover, we should realize that what one holds to be true serves as part of the context in which one lives. This is especially relevant when it comes to religion: altering the direction of one's life, as demanded by religious belief, is a transformation that must go all the way down to what Wittgenstein repeatedly calls "the depths."[13] Christianity must be appropriated with what, following Climacus, we might term the entire passion of one's subjectivity. Who I am must be *completely* altered in the light of this appropriation. "It strikes me that a religious belief could only be something like a passionate commitment to a system of reference," Wittgenstein remarks (1980, 64). "Hence," he continues, "although it's *belief*, it's really a way of living, or a way of assessing life. It's passionately seizing hold of *this* interpretation" (1980, 64).

Entering the "game" of religion is unlike entering any other game, though prior to one's making what Silentio calls the "movement of faith," it simply appears to be a game alongside many others. After making this "movement," however, the world in which one exists is radically otherwise than it was before. Imagine putting on a pair of sunglasses that cause everything in the field of vision to be tinted with a blue hue. Of course, one could object that we can always take off the sunglasses and everything will return to "normal." But Wittgenstein's point is that the religious "sunglasses" are more than a mere apparatus through which one sees: for the religious believer, religion is the medium (i.e., interpretation) through which one *is*. More than transforming the world, religion transforms those who inhabit it and then, in turn, the world is subsequently (or at least hopefully) made better.

Faith, Wittgenstein will repeatedly say, is a passion. In both wording and respect, Wittgenstein borrows this definition directly from Kierkegaard: "Wisdom is passionless. But faith by contrast is what Kierkegaard calls a *passion*" (Wittgenstein 1980, 53). Because religion is a passionate relationship to what Wittgenstein will term "authority," we begin to see why he characterizes religion fundamentally as a *struggle*. In an entry in *Culture and Values* dated 1949, Wittgenstein writes, "if you want to stay within the religious sphere you must *struggle*" (1980, 86; original emphasis). This claim is remarkably reminiscent of a statement made by Kierkegaard in his famous journal entry of 1 August 1835, where after a very long and personal account of his appropriation of and relation to religious truth he writes, "no doubt this road takes me into battle but I will not renounce it. . . . I will hurry along the path I have found and shout to everyone I meet: Do not look back as Lot's wife did, but remember that we are *struggling* up a hill" (JP, IA 75; emphasis added). What both of these passages portray is a conception of the religious life that is not at all that of a "light burden" and an "easy yoke" (Matthew 11: 30).

In the same journal entry, Kierkegaard continues on as follows:

> What I really need is to get clear about *what I am to do*, not what I must know, except insofar as knowledge must precede every act. What matters is to find my purpose, to see what it really is that God wills that *I* shall do; the crucial thing is to find a truth that is truth *for me*, to find *the idea for which I am willing to live and die* . . . (JP, IA 75; original emphases)

Kierkegaard realizes that Truth is constituted not in an objective assertion of "the way things stand," but instead in a subjective investment. My singular appropriation constitutes the truth of the True. For Kierkegaard's Climacus, truth is defined as an *"objective uncertainty, held fast through appropriation with the most passion-ate inwardness"* (CUP, 203; original emphasis). This definition of truth is crucial for understanding Wittgenstein because it insists upon the role of "subjectivity" (but *not* naïve subjectiv*ism*) for truth. Climacus even goes as far as to say that "subjec-tivity *is* truth" (CUP, 203; emphasis added); in other words, who I am is not inde-pendent of what I appropriate as true. Reminiscent of St. Augustine, the object of my love is actually determinant of who I am (Augustine 1974, esp. chap. 9).

Wittgenstein offers a similar conception when he writes: "Believing means submitting to an authority. Having once submitted, you can't then, without rebel-ling against it, first call it in question and then once again find it acceptable" (1980, 45). Wittgenstein's claim should be read as resonating with Silentio's notion of an "Absolute relation to the Absolute" (FT): the relation to God is a relation that is not contingent upon any other relation. Rather, it is a relation through which ev-ery other relational commitment must be viewed. For this reason, there can be a "teleological suspension of the ethical," *because* of the "absolute duty to God." In this way, faith is absolutely unique because of the degree to which it demands one's commitment.[14]

It is here that one sees the *struggle* of religious life. How is one to both recog-nize the contingency of all truth and yet stand, *truly,* in an Absolute relation to the Absolute? How does one realize that faith is not on the level of merely appropriat-ing historical factuality, while simultaneously insisting on the reality of the paradox of Christ as the God-man?[15] For Kierkegaard, the paradox of Christ is found in the truth of the claim that Christ did *historically* exist and yet the religious Truth of his existence is not historical.[16] So what are we to make of Wittgenstein's claim above that even if the Gospels were demonstrated to be historically false, it would not erase religious belief? Let me suggest that the power of Wittgenstein's claim lies in its insistence that if one has faith, then one stands in an entirely different relation to history than does someone without faith. History is not the sphere in which re-ligious truth is won or lost. But as my hesitancy to grant the absolute irrelevance of doctrine to living a religious life should indicate, I do contend that the relation to Christ fundamentally involves a relation to certain historical claims as religious insofar as they are also historical. Importantly, however, the status of these claims as religiously true is not contingent upon the truth of scientific discovery. Rather, everything hinges on the passionate appropriation of the singular individual. This is the paradox of faith! This is the struggle central to religious life! The religious person must somehow maintain the paradox that becomes so obvious when we realize that what is demanded is an Absolute relation that can only occur *within* contextualization.

This is where the bi-directional relationality of ethico-religious existence be-comes all the more profound, I believe, for the Christian. God is not merely "transcendent to the point of absence" as Levinas claims, but transcendent precisely *in* the radical historical proximity of God's kenotic revelation in the person and works of Jesus. Attempting to be faithful to God while working for justice for one's neighbor is something that is not, now, undertaken merely in relation to the ethico-religious encounter, but in relation to a particular theological narrative and its determinate social history. Affirming the ontology of constitutive responsibility does not prevent one from identifying as a member of a determinate religious tradition, but so identifying oneself does transform the way in which one understands the "God" before which one stands. So, for example, Levinas does not only understand God as "coming to mind" in the face of the Other because of his particular phenomenological perspective, but also because of the way he relates to his own Jewish tradition. Similarly, Marion's account of the Eucharist as an exemplary model of saturated phenomena owes, I believe, as much (or more) to his Catholic tradition as to his phenomenological commitments. Though one need not be determinately religious to advocate an ethico-religious encounter as constitutive of subjectivity, for those that are, there is more content available regarding what Westphal might term the "Truth" that one takes to be "true."

The essential paradox of religious life repeats the basic structure of the ontology of constitutive responsibility insofar as they both understand the self to be defined by the necessity of standing finitely in relation to the infinite. However, for the Christian, in particular, the centrality of the paradox is repeated in the very content of her account of God-in-time. Much more fully than Wittgenstein, Kierkegaard explains from the perspective of Climacus how this struggle with the paradox is to be understood:

> When subjectivity, inwardness, is truth, then truth, objectively defined, is a paradox; and that truth is objectively a paradox shows precisely that subjectivity is truth . . . The paradox is the objective uncertainty that is the expression for the passion of inwardness that is truth. . . . The eternal, essential truth, that is, the truth that is related essentially to the existing person by pertaining essentially to what it means to exist . . . is a paradox. Nevertheless the eternal, essential truth is itself not at all a paradox, but it is a paradox by being related to an existing person. (CUP, 204–205)

Following Westphal, we can see that the struggle here is due to the paradoxical status of *the truth of this Truth.* Accordingly, we must not miss the overall Kierkegaardian point that the Christian is not related to an *eternal objective universality* but to a *personal subjectivity who is involved in human history.* This shift of focus, which amounts to a radicalization of the self's relation to God, is the reason that faith is essentially a risk. In the relation to God, everything is at stake because it does not simply require an alteration in one's private existence while leaving one's public self untouched, but instead demands a radical reorientation of one's subjectivity.[17] As such, objectivity is only a possibility *for* subjectivity. And as is the case with all personal relationships, there is no value without risk. "Without risk," Climacus insists, there is "no faith" (CUP, 204). However, such a religious reorientation is always ethico-politically made in the context of one's being-in-the-world. Accordingly, religious existence is risky not only because there are no epistemic guarantees that accompany the movement of faith, but also because this movement before God is lived out in one's relationships with others. Singularity is always social *ethically* (I am only as a response to the Other) and *politically* (I am always in a historical context of other others).

Religious life should not be understood as primarily being an attempt at finding a justificatory principle that would eliminate the riskiness of faith (though as I have suggested earlier, this need not eliminate the possibility of an apologetic enterprise and, as I will demonstrate in the chapter 11, it does not mean that one should abandon a concern for justification).[18] Rather, religious belief is best understood as a "holding fast" or, as Wittgenstein says, a "trusting" (1980, 72).[19] Wittgenstein further emphasizes this understanding when he contends: "Religion says: *Do this!—Think like that!*" (1980, 29). Attempting to end the struggle—or in the language of Silentio, any attempt to make the "knight of faith" finally understandable to others—is to make faith itself "repellent." As struggle, as risk, Wittgenstein suggests that faith is found in its telling us: "Think like this! However strangely it may strike you" (1980, 29). And, reminiscent of what we saw in relation to the *Akedah* in part 1, Wittgenstein contends that faith implores us: "Won't you do this?—however repugnant you find it" (1980, 29). These notes of Wittgenstein's are a far cry from Rorty's pragmatic religion that decries whatever offends our rational sensibilities and rejects whatever is strange to our self-descriptions.

One could certainly object along with Drury that it is plausible that Wittgenstein would have resisted "Kierkegaard's frequent use of the words 'the paradox' and 'the absurd.'" For surely, as Drury notes, such references seem to be "an attempt to get beyond the barrier of language" (1984, 88–89). Yet, there are two rather serious problems with Drury's statement. First, he supposes that the reason Wittgenstein would have "disagreed" with Kierkegaard's conceptions is due to their falling back into a type of metaphysical schema that Wittgenstein rejects. But as I have suggested throughout this book, the Kierkegaardian paradox replaces traditional onto-theological metaphysics with an ontology of constitutive responsibility in which tension is perpetual and according to which life is always lived without guarantees. Without this ontological transition, Kierkegaard's very theory of paradox would not at all be paradoxical—it would be either straightforwardly contradictory or simply false. Hence, while it is certainly plausible that Wittgenstein just misunderstood Kierkegaard on this front, the reasons Drury gives for such a reading are, I believe, quite mistaken regarding Kierkegaard's own thinking. Second, the very idea of "the paradox" is Kierkegaard's way of attempting to give an account of an actual, we might say "phenomenological," experience. I do not think that it would be outside of the realm of possibility to contend that Wittgenstein's continued insistence on religion as providing a certain kind of "security" is his attempt to give a name to this same encounter. Religious (or ethico-religious) "security" should not be confused with epistemic certainty, however. Consider Wittgenstein's claim: "Religion is, as it were, the calm bottom of the sea at its deepest point, which remains calm however high the waves on the surface may be" (1980, 53). This metaphor bears a striking resemblance to one Climacus offers in the *Concluding Unscientific Postscript*: "I am 'out on 70,000 fathoms of water' and still have faith" (CUP, 204).

The result of the foregoing is that we now have a fuller notion of how religious existence constitutively involves a struggle to stand fast in one's singular trust in God, while always remaining particularly located. To say that the doctrinal claims of Christianity are no longer plausible is to keep in place the very modern hermeneutic and truth-structure that postmodernity rightly contests. Without a dynamism between what Westphal labels "truth" and "Truth," transcendence can easily become, to borrow from William Placher (1996), "domesticated." The wildness, as it were, of the personal relation to the Absolute Paradox implied in Christianity would thereby be tamed. For Kierkegaard and Wittgenstein, to tame Christianity would be to eliminate Christianity itself.

Conclusion: Maintaining the Paradox

In this chapter, I have offered a Kierkegaardian reading of Wittgenstein in the attempt to argue that we must go beyond the neo-Pragmatist religion advocated by Rorty and Hodges while simultaneously being wary of the vacuity that appears in many deconstructive readings.[20] In order to inhabit the space left open for theology and philosophy of religion after Wittgenstein (see Kerr 1986), while moving toward a postmodern ethico-religious subjectivity that allows for still identifying with a determinate religious tradition, we must maintain this particular account of tension as constitutive of religious life. We would be wrong to confuse Wittgenstein with Kierkegaard,[21] but if we can keep open the fertile cross-pollination of the intersecting ideas between them, then we may indeed be able to see the truth in Vattimo's claim that Christianity is again possible precisely *due* to the "death of God," and hopefully take a step closer to making room for a rigorously postmodern, while still robustly Christian, view of human existence.

I want to make clear, however, that although I am focusing on Christianity, in particular, I leave open the possibility of doing something similar to what I have done in this chapter with other determinate religious traditions. The most important upshot of this engagement between Wittgenstein and Kierkegaard, I believe, is that it demonstrates how it is possible to affirm postmodernism without thereby evacuating the determinate content of one's historical religion. Articulating a postmodern approach to Islam, Judaism, or Hinduism, for example, is something I find quite plausible even though it is not my own focus here. In conclusion, then, let me suggest that while Rorty's reconstructivism is too *reductive* and his privatization is *naïve,* the task of the postmodern philosopher of religion (of whatever determinate religious tradition), I believe, should be to think *dogma* without *arrogance* and *doctrine* without *certainty.*

Although I have focused on the tension between social existence and the relation to God, I do not mean to indicate that this is the only struggle which is important to religion. The tension between personal holiness and social justice, Christian ethics and democratic politics, and church and state, are all involved in the dynamism of religious life. This is why the pragmatic insistence on privatization and the reconstruction of religion is really a denial of religion itself. Relegating religion to so-called private spaces is to ignore the intrinsically political stakes of "the private" and the political influence of churches and households in the first place. As I will suggest in the next chapter, politics in light of the "theological turn" is best understood as an "ethico-political task" from which religion cannot be excluded.

TEN

The Political: Politics as an Ethico-religious Task—Reconsidering Religion in the Public Square

Epistemology and Responsibility

In a 1994 response to Stephen L. Carter's *The Culture of Disbelief,* published the year before, Richard Rorty suggests that, rather than be given a larger role in public discourse, religion should be "privatized." In a move that I have described as similar to Dominique Janicaud's attempt to keep theology out of phenomenology, Rorty's pragmatic-liberal commitment to keeping the conversation going leads him (at least in the late 1980s through the mid-1990s) to claim that the only justificative source to which citizens can legitimately appeal is a public reason that is independent of what Rawls would eventually term a "comprehensive doctrine." Rorty concludes his essay by claiming that religious belief is no more relevant in public discourse than a person's physical characteristics. Thus, he proposes that the burden of proof rests squarely on Carter's shoulders to demonstrate that "a speaker's depth of spirituality is more relevant to her participation in public debate than her hobby or her hair colour" (1999, 174).

It is important that we recall that Rorty slightly alters his view of religion and public discourse from this straightforwardly separatist perspective to one more akin to reconstructivism. Largely due to an engagement with Nicholas Wolterstorff (Rorty 2003; see also Rorty 2002), and further reinforced by a collaboration with Gianni Vattimo (Vattimo and Rorty 2005), Rorty eventually becomes much more receptive to the idea of religious belief and language in political debate. However, as I argued in the last chapter, this transition toward reconstructivism has its own problems. Namely, the only type of religious discourse that he finds productive in the public square is one that has been so reconstructed as to preclude the vast majority of religious believers from being able to recognize themselves *as* religious. Accordingly, the sort of beliefs that most religious people hold are, even on Rorty's more developed view, if not excluded still significantly marginalized (lest they conflict with the "intellectual responsibilities" religious believers have as public citizens).

Having spent quite a bit of time on Rorty's own account of neo-Pragmatist religion, I now want to turn to the explicitly political issue of how to conceive of religion's relation to public discourse and political policy. Crucially, Rorty is not alone in his occasional defense of separatism; this view remains quite prominent in contemporary political philosophy. Nonetheless, it is important to understand that separatism—also prominently advocated by Robert Audi (Audi and Wolterstorff 1997; see also Audi 2000),[1] John Rawls (2005), and others—is only one possibility for conceiving this crucial relationship between religious belief and public discourse. For example, in response to Audi, Nicholas Wolterstorff offers the alternative position of "consocial" impartiality (Audi and Wolterstorff 1997, 81, 114–15). Wolterstorff argues that although separatism attempts to instantiate governmental neutrality regarding religious organizations, in practice it serves to undercut it. The automatic exclusion of religious belief as a potentially legitimate justificative source for political action is not neutral, Wolterstorff contends, but actively biased against religion and the faith-commitments of religious believers. Similarly, Christopher Eberle (2002) and J. Caleb Clanton (2007) both suggest in various ways that religious beliefs, even if lacking all the secondary "secular" reasons that Rawls and Audi stipulate, should not be excluded as justificative sources for political commitments.[2]

What this very brief survey of various perspectives on the role of religion in the public square is meant to demonstrate is the way in which the debate has often been couched in terms of solidly epistemological concerns. All of these thinkers, despite their divergent positions, agree that the real issue regarding religion in the public square is about what should count as *justification* for political commitment and public policy. Whereas Carter, Wolterstorff, Clanton, and Eberle would argue that faith-claims should not be excluded, Audi, Rorty, and Rawls agree that they can only be admissible *if* they are supplemented by public reasons that are available to non-religious citizens as well.[3] As I will demonstrate in the next chapter, Continental philosophers of religion should be deeply engaged with such epistemological debates; and moreover, I believe that new phenomenology makes significant contributions to such debates. Nevertheless, I want to suggest that as long as the issue of religion in the public square is thought of as *primarily* epistemological, we will find it hard to break the philosophical deadlock that so often characterizes this issue: we will continue to speak past each other. This alone is reason enough to try and rethink the issue. But more worrisome still is that this philosophical impasse often reflects the global realities of political turmoil and sectarian violence that can accompany the question of how religion stands in relation to political theory and public policy.

In order to open a space in which this issue might be productively rethought in light of the ontology of constitutive responsibility, I will again bring Kierke-

gaard and Levinas together in order to suggest that they offer a way of constructively rethinking how to understand religious conviction in democratic politics. As
bi-directionally related to God and the Other, epistemological concerns that are
internal to political conversation are best thought of as ethico-religiously implicated. Rather than conceiving of the problem of political justification as merely a
variant of the classical problem of the criterion, the ontology of constitutive responsibility opens room for considering the demand for justification as more properly being an illustration of subjectivity as inherently social. To borrow a phrase
from Judith Butler (2005), "giving an account of oneself" is first and foremost a response to the call of the Other, and this call, as I have repeatedly noted, serves to
contest one's self-sufficiency. Drawing upon this insight, I will argue that, in light
of the notions of subjectivity expressed in the Kierkegaardian notion of "transparency" and the Levinasian conception of "exposure" (see chapter 4), political justification is an epistemic concern precisely because it is originally a manifestation
of the ethico-religious reality of obligation as constitutive of selfhood.

By looking first at the rethinking of religion in Kierkegaard's short essay, "The
Present Age," we will see how he offers a way to view religion as a corrective to political crises. According to this conception, religion should be viewed as always already politically invested.[4] Next, I will illustrate the way in which Levinas rethinks
politics as not religiously neutral, but rather as defined by the task of bringing
about a decidedly ethico-religious justice. In harmony with the argument of chapter 8 regarding the critical function of charity, Levinas's position leads to a rousing
defense of democracy as the most hopeful political structure because of its essential devotion to self-criticism. I will conclude by suggesting three ways in which
this ethical rethinking of the relationship between religion and politics might con-
tribute to the future of the debate surrounding religion in the public square.

Rethinking Religion with Kierkegaard

There are many places one could turn within Kierkegaard's expansive writings to contest the asocial readings of him which, as we have seen, are regrettably
prevalent, and to begin to discover his deep political relevance. Some of this work
has already been done in my reading of Johannes de Silentio's *Fear and Trembling*
and my discussion of the socio-historical import of paradox in Climacus, relative
to Wittgenstein. However, because I want to attribute the perspective that follows
to Kierkegaard *simpliciter,* and not obliquely through a pseudonym, I will focus on
Kierkegaard's short essay "The Present Age." Published in 1846 as the third part
of *Two Ages,* this piece carries Kierkegaard's own name and represents an early
example of his movement toward the decidedly polemical texts of the late 1840s
and early 1850s.

"The Present Age" is a sustained indictment of the social and political situation in mid-nineteenth-century Denmark in particular, and Europe in general. Kierkegaard's major contention is that his age "is essentially one of understanding and reflection, without passion" (PA, 33). He contrasts the "present" age with the "revolutionary" age: for Kierkegaard, the crucial aspect that differentiates these ages is the way in which the individual is understood in each. Due to its lack of passion, the present age makes everything external and, as such, subjectivity gets transmuted into an external relation rather than being understood as an interior constitution. "To be a subject," Kierkegaard writes, "has come to mean something quite different" than in the revolutionary age: "it means to be a *third party*" (PA, 44; original emphasis). Being rather snide, Kierkegaard concludes that selfhood has become, thereby, something that is formed by way of a committee. Indeed, he comments, "in the end the whole age becomes a committee" (PA, 44). What results from this evisceration of authentic subjectivity is Kierkegaard's realization that "a revolutionary age is an age of action; [whereas] ours is the age of advertisement and publicity" (PA, 35).

The self in the present age is no longer defined by its uniqueness (or we might say, its singularity), but by its relation to an abstraction that Kierkegaard names simply "the public." This "monstrous nothing," as he terms it, is now the star by which we set our course. Echoing J. G. Hamann's eighteenth-century references to "the Public, or Nobody," and anticipating Heidegger's twentieth-century discussion of "the They" (*das Man*), Kierkegaard notes that the self understands itself *as "the public" does*, desires *what "the public" desires*, and acts, affirms, appropriates according to the standards *set by "the public."* Illuminating his own personal conflict during the *"Corsair* affair" in 1846, a harsh set of exchanges between Kierkegaard and the editors of a satirical paper in Copenhagen, he views the press as being the mouthpiece of the public. The trouble with the press is that it speaks from the position of no one in particular: it is the voice of the generality, the nondescript, the mass. Operating from the perspective of the generality presents obstacles for real dialogue because you can't sit down for coffee with it and talk through contentious issues. Moreover, at what address does this generality (the mass) live, such that a written critique could be sent through the post? Hence, the rise of the nineteenth-century press as the medium of the public indicates, for Kierkegaard, the elimination of the singularity of individuals.

In light of the ontology of constitutive responsibility, the loss of singularity is tantamount to a loss of selfhood. For Kierkegaard, the present age does not merely threaten a particular *way* of living; it eviscerates the fundamental aspect of life itself. We should remember that the various "stages" or "spheres" of existence are only able to be properly understood in relation to despair (or lack thereof) when one assumes that the ethico-religious reality of standing be-for(e) God is taken as the fundamental reality of human existence. Accordingly, Kierkegaard's worry about the rise of the press is not primarily political (as if he were opposed to free speech, etc.); it is an ontological concern about the ethico-religious constitution of subjectivity. His worry is that by allowing oneself to be so essentially situated in relation to "the public" as spoken for by the press, the defining relation of selfhood is obscured. It is no longer bi-directional relationality that is taken as central; now "fitting in" with one's society is all that matters. In Heideggerian vocabulary, we might say that Kierkegaard is concerned about the usurpation of the ontological by the ontic.

This process of self-eradication is made more explicit with Kierkegaard's discussion of the phenomenon of "leveling." *Leveling* is the name Kierkegaard gives to the movement of society toward its lowest common denominator. Although concrete persons are the means by which leveling occurs, it is the product not of this or that individual but of the public as such. The process of leveling cannot have a distinct leader, Kierkegaard contends, because the leader must also be leveled in order for leveling to work with the impersonal anonymity that it requires. Again, the generality is a nondescript, nominal universality that affects one's existence—but does not itself have existence. Leveling is, thus, "the victory of abstraction over the individual" (PA, 53). In the present age, Kierkegaard claims, "people not only write anonymously, they sign their anonymous works: they even talk anonymously" (PA, 76). Being anonymous, the individual will not have to affirm herself in the anxiety of fear and trembling, but instead will be able to reach for a self-help guide on the shelf to eliminate any doubt about what to do and how to live. This situation ultimately leads Kierkegaard to say, perhaps as prophetically as polemically:

> In fact there are handbooks for everything, and very soon education,
> all the world over, will consist in learning a greater or lesser number
> of comments by heart, and people will excel according to their ca-
> pacity for singling out the various facts like a printer singling out the
> letters, but completely ignorant of the meaning of anything. (PA, 77)

I have claimed that Kierkegaard understood the key component of religious life to be the struggle with paradox. However, in the present age, religious life is nearly impossible because the struggles with meaning, interpretation, implementation, etc., that are so characteristic of human existence are eliminated in the name of the ease that comes with learning something by repetition according to a commonly accepted definition. The existential question with which one wrestles would no longer be "What is truth?" or "Why do I believe what I believe?" but now merely "Can I fit in with *them* and echo what *they* say?"

Importantly, Kierkegaard is aware that the stakes of politics are ontological. Consequently, he does not conclude that the crisis coordinated with an age of reflection and inactivity can be solved by merely instantiating a different political structure. Leveling is certainly a political problem, but it cannot be addressed merely with a political solution. Since leveling threatens singularity because it eliminates the central tension of lived existence, what is now required is a more robust account of subjectivity as singular and inescapably risky. For Kierkegaard, this account is found in the ontology of constitutive responsibility, which (given the priority he places on the relation to God) he understands in a decidedly "religious" way. "Man's only salvation," Kierkegaard insists, "lies in the reality of religion for each individual" (PA, 56).

Now, admittedly, this seems to be an odd sort of medicine for the sickness that has infected modern society. Wouldn't Rorty's suggestion that we need real, concrete answers for real, concrete problems be a more straightforward way to understand things? Aren't we again just making things unnecessarily hyperbolically complicated? Well, given that I have already argued for the political viability of hyperbole and considering that Kierkegaard understands politics as a name for the socio-historic space in which the individual lives out a relation to God, I find this ethico-religious diagnosis of his social situation to be quite appropriate. According to Kierkegaard, and similarly new phenomenology, standing in relation to God is not and could never be a relation that removes the individual from the political world. Indeed, it is this that makes such socio-historical embeddedness meaningful.

In contrast to my interpretation of Kierkegaard, many classic readings assume that Kierkegaardian religion consists of a worldless relation between the isolated self and God (see Mackey 1962; for replies see Ferreira, 1999; Walsh 1999). On such a reading, the perpetual tension that I have advocated between the relation to God and the relation to the Other would be finally settled. However, though it is right to view Kierkegaard as stressing the *priority* of the relation to God over the relation to the Other (i.e., religion over ethics), it is a misconception to understand his account of religion as *absolutely distinct from* his complicated and dynamic understanding of ethics. This is why I have encouraged that we view his account of subjectivity as "ethico-religious" rather than simply "religious"—which, I believe, has far too often obscured this important tension. And though there are important aspects of Kierkegaard that are helpfully illuminated in light of new phenomenology (and my overall interpretation of Kierkegaard owes much to such an engagement), one need not go further than Kierkegaard's own works to see support for my interpretation. Any acosmic reading of Kierkegaardian religion is already contested in "The Present Age," when Kierkegaard defines the "idea of religion" as being a reality in which the individual learns . . . before God to be content with himself, and learns, instead of dominating others, to dominate himself, content as priest to be his own audience, and as author his own reader, if he will not learn to be satisfied with that as the highest, because it is the expression of the equality of all men before God and of our likeness to others, then he will not escape from reflection. (PA, 57)

Kierkegaard's understanding of religion is clearly not a movement of escapism, but of *investment*. It does not yield arrogance, but *equality*. Indeed, "it is only after the individual has acquired an ethical outlook," resulting from the proper understanding of the "before God" relation, "that there can be any suggestion of really joining together" (PA, 79). Hence, we can see that within "The Present Age" Kierkegaard rethinks religion as not being primarily a principle of identity and exclusion that requires appeal to private justificative sources (i.e., religious reasons), but rather as an example of how selfhood is originally defined by a relation to God amid one's relation to others. The upshot is that religion is never separable from the public square: ethico-religious existence provides, for Kierkegaard (as for Levinas), the very *quasi-logical existential condition* of political life.

Hence, when Kierkegaard claims that he is "a religious author" and that his "work as an author is related to Christianity," he does not offer this as a *merely* theological explanation, but also as an intrinsically political one (PV, 5–6). In the same sentence where Kierkegaard announces that his whole authorship has been devoted to the "problem 'of becoming a Christian,'" he also notes that this project has carried with it "a direct or indirect polemic against the monstrous illusion we call Christendom" (PV, 6). This admission can only be taken as both ecclesial and social. In nineteenth-century Denmark, the reference to "Christendom" cannot be read according to the American notion of a structural split between church and state. For Kierkegaard, offering a critique of Christendom was tantamount to critiquing the established social order.[5]

Rethinking Politics with Levinas

In a 1986 interview Levinas expresses worry about the apparent lack of political traction in his thought:

If everything terminates in justice, why tell this long story about the face, which is the opposite of justice? The first reason is that it is ethics which is the foundation of justice. Because justice is not the last word; within justice, we seek a better justice. That is the liberal state. The second reason is that there is a violence in justice. When the verdict of justice is pronounced, there remains for the unique I that I am the possibility of finding something more to soften the verdict. There is a place for charity after justice. The truly democratic state finds that it is never democratic enough. It always wants to improve its institutions. The third reason is that there is a moment when I, the unique I, along with other unique I's, can find something else which improves universality itself. I think for example, that the abolition of the death penalty certainly results from that. (PM, 175)

Levinas gives three reasons here why his "long story about the face" is relevant to political discourse. First, Levinas insists on the priority that must be given to ethics over politics. It is the "foundation" of justice, he claims. This priority is never absolute in the sense of being unidirectional, however: justice always serves to critique the isolationism that can emerge in the ethical relation. Yet justice is never its own "last word." This is Levinas's way of saying that politics is not all-encompassing: there is a rupture within justice itself, namely, the face of the Other. Justice is always traumatized by ethics. This trauma results in the perpetual revolution which seeks to bring about an always "better justice." This better justice is a justice that is conscious of itself as always violent. The voice of singularity continues to be heard above the rumble of the generalized political crowd. Levinas calls this reality the "liberal state." When Levinas applauds liberalism he is really praising the liberal recognition of the incalculable value of each individual. "The liberal state," he contends, "is a state which holds justice as the absolutely desirable end and hence as a perfection. . . . consequently, I believe that it is absolutely obvious that the liberal state is more moral than the fascist state, and closer to the morally ideal state" (PM, 177). We might say that while Levinas stands as a critic of the classical liberal notion of the individual as prior to the community (for Levinas, subjectivity is always already social), he is nevertheless devoted to the principles in the name of which liberalism operates as a political reality. Hence, like Derrida and Vattimo, Levinas will champion democracy as the political system that is best suited to the promulgation and pursuit of justice. And this brings us to Levinas's second point.

For Levinas, and contrary to Rorty, the necessary generalization that occurs in politics is not simply *unfortunate,* it is *violent.* He moves beyond a simple pragmatic hope for a future in which suffering is lessened and, thereby, indicts politics as such rather than those forms of politics that do not suit his fancy. Democracy may indeed be more just than fascism, but it is never democratic enough to fulfill its ethical charge. For Levinas, democracy is the name we give to the recognition that politics can never be adequate to the ethical demand made upon it: no political system or social institution, even one that takes its name from "the people," can ever relate to every individual as a singular self. Democracies can strive for "justice for all," but can never attain to the higher ideal we might call "justice for each."

Levinas does not take democracy as such to be the final ideal, but rather understands it to be the best political option currently available for allowing the ideal of justice to be perpetually *held in view*. The value of democracy, as Derrida has so substantively argued, is that it is the only political system (of which we know) that is defined by its openness to self-criticism. Hence, democracy is seemingly required for democracy itself to be contested as unethical.[6] When Levinas claims that there is "a place for charity after justice," we should read this as a defense of democracy. It is by living in a state that champions the singularity of each individual (rather than merely her or his particularity) that we are able to realize the problems of contending that politics goes all the way down.

So what would this "charity after justice" look like? Consider the following situation that Levinas describes in an interview:

> Let us imagine . . . a matter of judging a man and rendering sentence. In order to determine this sentence, one finds oneself again face to face with the other, and one must look only at the face. But once the sentence is pronounced, once it is made public, one must be able to discuss, contest, approve, or combat it. Public opinion—other citizens and the press—can intervene and state, for example, that this sentence ought to be reviewed. Therein lies the very foundation of democracy. One can debate decisions; there is no human decree that cannot be revised.[7]

Here we see that the notion of an appeals process for convicts displays charity after justice insofar as it stands as a way of resisting finality and of always leaving open the possibility of revision internal to political decision. Extrapolating from Levinas's account of the liberal state, we might say that a politics that is guided by a concern for singularity will display the qualities of dialogical openness and perpetual criticism: *any democracy worth its name will operate with self-scrutiny, humility, and invitation.*

The third point is that occasionally there are political developments that further the cause of ethics. Levinas offers the example of abolishing the death penalty as a decision that continues to recognize the singularity of each person rather than merely working with a utilitarian conception of the whole. The practical consequence of democracy's constant struggle for a better justice is the reality of perpetually questioning the functionality and quality of the state's laws. As Levinas notes:

> Justice and the just State constitute the forum enabling the existence of charity within the human multiplicity. . . . Is this concern for reconsideration—for amelioration—not in effect the essence of de-

mocracy and of the liberal State, the sign of a mercy and charity that breathe there? An effort in view of an always better law. Is this not a striving to find an ever-improving law?[8]

Not only does Levinas offer an argument for democracy as the only structure that enables a "singular justice" (Perpich 1998), but he couples this with a moral vision of the legal system:

> Charity can accomplish a lot, even after a rigorous justice has been passed. Since justice constantly has a bad conscience, the demand of charity which precedes it remains and beckons it. And justice, the justice that deserves its name, does not forget that the law is perfectible. It leaves open the possibility of a revision of a judgment once pronounced. And this is very important. . . . This is why democracy is the necessary prolongation of the State. It is not one regime possible among others, but the only suitable one. This is because it safeguards the capacity to improve or to change the law by changing—unfortunate logic!—tyrants, these personalities necessary to the State despite everything. Once we choose another tyrant, we imagine, of course, that he will be better than his predecessor.[9]

It is only within Western democracies, Levinas says, that we find "an ideal for humanity which one would be wrong to consider contemptible." "When one has known other regimes and other modes of life," Levinas continues, "one can even consider this ideal a form of human perfection."[10] Wary of giving the indication that democracies are themselves perfect, Levinas quickly adds, "I believe in the force of liberalism in Europe. But I also have too many memories to be certain in my answer."[11] Because the face is never a strong foundation in the sense of an uncontestable rational principle, political certainty is never guaranteed: democracy is the best model we have for understanding politics as the interruption of state-processes by the ethical relation, *but it is also flawed.*

For all this, Levinas never offers anything like a detailed analysis of political life. When he is asked: "How do you tie your moral philosophy to the consideration of political questions?" Levinas responds: "Listen, I am a democrat. What more would you like me to say?" The interviewer then comes back with: "Nevertheless, when you posit democracy as the necessary prolongation of the State, this warrants further examination." Levinas replies: "Necessary but not natural. It is its ethical prolongation. . . . But how do you expect me to move from the absolute splendors of *hesed,* of charity, to an analysis of the state procedures at work in our democracies?"[12] Here we see that Levinas's philosophy should not be confused with the work of Ronald Dworkin or Cass Sunstein, say, but it crucially serves as an account of what such political philosophies require if they are to clarify how we *ought* to live and not simply how we *do*. In an interview with Richard Kearney, Levinas comments that: "If the moral-political order totally relinquishes its ethical foundation, it must accept all forms of society; including the fascist or totalitarian, for it can no longer evaluate or discriminate between them" (Levinas and Kearney 1986, 30). In order to understand the weight of Levinas's defense of democracy, we must constantly recognize the status that he gives to the ethical relation as both guiding, and yet constantly questioned by, the exigencies of political life.

Democracy, as Levinas understand it, is not primarily an existing social structure but the promise of an ever-increasing justice. Democracy is, thus, as Derrida repeatedly insists, always "to-come" (see esp. Derrida 2005, chaps. 7 and 8). As I have repeatedly claimed, however, this *to-come* occurs *here and now* at the level of legal reconsideration, "charity after justice," working to eliminate hunger, homelessness, the neglect and abuse of children, and so on.

With this understanding in place, we can see how Levinas makes a move similar to that of Kierkegaard. Levinas rethinks politics as not being a space of neutral intersubjective interaction, but instead as the space in which the ethico-religious task of justice presses upon us as a historical obligation. Accordingly, both thinkers are committed to the ontology of constitutive responsibility and both demonstrate its practical political viability: they demonstrate that being a democrat is not simply a matter of how one understands executive prerogative or legal constraints on the separation of powers; it is a matter of *living everyday toward the justice to-come.* It is in this qualified sense that I take both of them to be defenders of democracy. It is clear that Levinas is willing to go further in his support of democracy by defending the specifics of "the liberal state," while Kierkegaard resists such a move due to his worry about the "leveling" tendencies of such a political system. We might say that although both thinkers would endorse the "democracy to come," Levinas is decidedly more willing to also support "democracies here and now" as the best way currently available for moving toward such a goal.

Though Continental discourse is often guilty of the ethical and political formalism of which Rorty accuses Levinas, this is not due to the inherent uselessness or irrelevance of Continental ethics and philosophy of religion. Far from it. Having looked at a Kierkegaardian interpretation of religion and a Levinasian understanding of politics, we can see that Kierkegaard's account was already political and Levinas's was already ethico-religious. Moreover, both proposals were offered as a way of calling their respective political communities to display the necessary concern for the singularity of every person living within them. Consequently, before those of us working in Continental philosophy begin to feel haughty about our supposed philosophical sophistication (relative to non-Continental colleagues) and political correctness (relative to conservative neighbors), we should remember that unless we are constantly diligent (and probably even then) we will become blind to our repetition and perpetuation of the leveling that Kierkegaard warns against and the indifference that Levinas so stringently opposes. The perpetually self-critical gesture of recursive hermeneutics does not only apply to those who don't recognize its importance.

"The present age" is not isolated in nineteenth-century Denmark or twentieth-century France; "the present age" is the perennial temptation to allow the status quo to be satisfactory. Levinas's notion of "prophecy" is made politically relevant when we realize that, in relation to the ontology of constitutive responsibility, theory and practice are always co-implicated in society never being sufficiently just. As Levinas explains:

> In our times—is this its very modernity?—a presumption of being an ideology weighs on philosophy. This presumption cannot claim to be part of philosophy, where the critical spirit cannot content itself with suspicions, but owes it to itself that it bring forth proofs. This presumption, which is irrecusable, draws its force from elsewhere. It begins in a cry of ethical revolt, bearing witness to responsibility; it begins in prophecy. Philosophy does not become suspect at just any moment in the spiritual history of the West. To recognize with philosophy—or to recognize philosophically—that the real is rational and that the rational is alone real, and not to be able to smother or cover over the cry of those who, the morrow after this recognition, mean to transform the world, is already to move in a domain of meaning which the inclusion cannot comprehend and among reasons that "reason" does not know, and which have not begin in philosophy. A meaning thus seems to bear witness to a beyond which would not be the no-man's-land of non-sense where opinions accumulate. *Not to philosophize would not be "to philosophize still,"* nor to succumb to opinions. There is meaning testified to in interjections and outcries, before being disclosed in propositions, a meaning that signifies as a command, like an order that one signifies. (BPW, 147–48)

Religion and politics can never be separated not because of a fundamentally epistemological reality, but because of an ethico-religious one.

Before moving on, I want to make one clarification that I think will help avoid a rather prevalent confusion regarding the idea of a democratic political order never being sufficiently just. To say that justice is not something that one could *finally* claim to have achieved is not to say that we are unable to make distinctions between actions, institutions, etc., that are more or less just in relation to each other. To say that something is "just" should really be heard, in light of the ontology of constitutive responsibility, to simply mean that it is better than what came before. In no way does such a claim entail that there could not now continue to be, and need to be, improvement. We must realize that Levinas is not opposed to naming some things "just"—as is demonstrated in his opposition to the death penalty and praise of the appeals system, etc. The problem is not in saying that this or that policy is "just," but in thinking that such a proclamation ends the work that is to be done relative to our infinite responsibility to each and every other. Problems emerge when we think that proclaiming something "just" ends the task of recursive hermeneutics. For example, ending slavery, or giving women the right to vote, or ending oppression because of one's sexual orientation are all things that should be celebrated as "just." And yet—to look further at only the first example—while ending slavery in 1863 was "just," it did not and does not mean that racial equality has been achieved. The worries that many scholars and activists have recently expressed regarding the idea that the United States has entered a "post-racial" era due to the election of Barack Obama serve to express this basic point.

Unfortunately, those who work in Continental ethics and deconstructive political theory tend to be hesitant to ever admit that something is just. I believe that this hesitancy is motivated by a quite sensible belief that the to-come structure prevents ever arriving at the goal toward which one strives. Yet unless we are careful here, we can find ourselves falling back into the (now inverted) Rortian trap. As I claimed about Rorty, if everything is normative then nothing is normative such that we become unable to articulate what "better" would mean except as an expression of one's own interests. Similarly, if everything *equally* fails to be just (in light of infinite responsibility) then there is no way, at least ethically, to distinguish between slavery and civil rights, between patriarchy and universal suffrage, between fascism and representative democracy. This is an area in which I think that the otherwise productive hyperbole of Continental discourse might be a genuine obstacle to Continental philosophy's contribution to social progress. If a Levinasian-Derridean model of the political makes it impossible to ever say that something is just—so much the worse for that model. On my interpretation, however, we can avoid this powerlessness to proclaim something just while also avoiding the complacency that attends any view which loses the tension between the infinity of ethical obligation and the necessity of political decision.

Conclusion: Toward a Renewed Engagement

As a way of concluding this chapter, I want to highlight just a few points of resonance in Levinas and Kierkegaard with regard to the ethico-religious underpinnings of the political. This will then open spaces for considering how this Kierkegaardian-Levinasian conception can potentially make a fruitful contribution to contemporary debates concerning religion in the public square.

Though we would be wrong to simply equate Kierkegaardian religion and Levinasian ethics, since these thinkers disagree about the question of priority in such relationships, there are important structural points of convergence that underlie even this divergence. For both Kierkegaard and Levinas, the decisive thing is the way in which *religion and ethics are mutually interruptive.* For Levinas, God always stands between oneself and the Other in such a way as to constantly contest the potential isolation of a couple. Similarly, for Kierkegaard, the Other stands between oneself and God in such a way as to contest any retreat to monastic quietism. Claiming that Levinas offers a "teleological suspension of the religious" that serves as a counterpart to the Kierkegaardian "teleological suspension of the ethical," we would do well to *again* pay attention to the words of Merold Westphal when he writes: *"When the Other does not get in the way of my seeing God, God will end up getting in the way of my hearing the Other. That is what the teleological suspension of the religious is all about"* (1995a, 158; original italics). In contrast to Rorty, for both Kierkegaard and Levinas the sphere of the political is not all-inclusive. It may be impossible to stand outside of one's political location, but this does not mean that politics goes "all the way down."

Kierkegaard and Levinas alike demonstrate that politics receives its weight as the task of constant criticism in light of the reality of bi-directional relationality. This task finds its quasi-logical existential condition in ethico-religious obligation. Politics is the space in which we are required to engage in the practice of justification, adjudication, and calculation not on the basis of self-interest or mere social stability, but because we are concerned about justice. Due to the ethico-religious relationship that underlies political life itself, politics *is* the demand for justice *in history.* It is according to this framework that Kierkegaard and Levinas open a possible way to reanimate the problem of religion in the public square by repositioning the public square as itself always already ethico-religiously constituted.

Now, I admit that Kierkegaard and Levinas do not provide direct answers to the questions raised in contemporary debates surrounding the issue of religion in the public square that often arise from considerations of specific case studies. For example, they do not provide a specific answer for how to deal with the religious believer who refuses to allow medical treatment for her child. Further, they do not directly address how to establish criteria for scientific research that is viewed as morally reprehensible by many religious believers. Or again, they do not explicitly consider the inviolability of civil liberties relative to evolving concerns of national security. While these are all important questions, the fundamental benefit of how Kierkegaard and Levinas rethink religion and politics is the way in which the issue of religion in the public square is itself envisioned as being primarily *ethico-religious* rather than primarily *epistemological*.

First, following on from their challenge to the all-inclusivity of politics, the demand for discursive justification should not be understood as primarily being political, but instead as an ethico-religious requirement for all political structures. Just as I am called to give an account of myself in front of other people, so my nation is called to give an account of itself in front of its citizens and the world. This means that the justification is not primarily about *defending* oneself against criticism, but recognizing an obligation to others that calls for reason-giving.[13] This realization should give us pause when we easily "justify" the exclusion of certain voices from the public square. I do believe that there are times when such exclusion is *politically* justified, but what the distinction between ethics and politics provides is the ability to remain troubled by such exclusion—even when it is necessary. But in relation to those that we might claim should be excluded (or required to provide secondary, "secular" reasons for their beliefs), we should always remember that when "we" do not recognize the legitimacy of "their" appeals, it may well stand as an indictment of "our" mores and insensitivity rather than a reason for "them" to learn to speak "our" language.

Second, Kierkegaard's focus on the social embeddedness of the reality of religion (hence the centrality of struggle to the religious life, as discussed in relation to Wittgenstein), and Levinas's claim that the ethical relation is never separate from its political instantiation, illuminate the way in which appeals to "independent" criteria are always already problematic. To stand completely outside of a "comprehensive doctrine" is to stand outside of one's existence.[14] On the Kierkegaardian-Levinasian model I have outlined here, the right question is not how to leave comprehensive doctrines behind when we enter the public square, but rather how to make these doctrines constantly receptive to the call of others. Hence, the very demand for "public" justification is a recognition of this constitutive relationship by which selfhood is established and in which society is inextricably implicated. Moreover, in light of the constant demand for an ever-increasing justice, this singular and social task is unending. There can be no liberal utopia that would be ultimately adequate.

Finally, the content of Kierkegaard's religion and Levinas's democratic nation is in both cases an expression of self-contestation. To put structural limits on what sorts of reasons count in public discourse can often serve to restrict legitimacy to one's own view of public discourse. Openness and liberty are virtues of not only the deconstructive democracy to come, but of the classical conception of democracy upon which many societies have been founded. Hence, this openness is not something that *necessarily* occurs on the hither side of liberalism, but should serve to contest any suggestion we have fully gotten liberalism right and that our interpretation of openness is the best way to understand it.[15] There are many ways in which we can be open and many ways in which openness requires certain degrees of exclusion; so again, we *should* recognize that liberal democracies can be just— but they are never *sufficiently just*.

Here and now, in our day, and in relation to the specific problems that we face, we must continue to strive, with Levinas, for "charity after justice," and with Kierkegaard, against the dangers of "leveling." This is a struggle that cannot be closed off politically because it is a product of the constitutive responsibility that inaugurates selfhood. Therefore, what Levinas and Kierkegaard have shown is the way in which the question of religion in the public square is more than just an *epistemological or political problem*—it is an *ethico-religious task*.

Having laid out the way in which we must see the ethico-religious encounter as underlying the specific requirement of reason-giving in public discourse, we must be careful not to conclude that reason-giving is, thereby, unimportant. Accordingly, in the next chapter I will turn directly to the question of epistemic justification, especially as it stands in relation to political discourse. My suggestion will be that the ontology of constitutive responsibility should be read as operating according to a modest foundationalist account of justification.

ELEVEN

The Epistemological: Between Trust and Hope—Justification in a Deconstructive Democracy

> Risk is the very essence of trust.
> —Annette Baier, *Moral Prejudices*

> There is no society without faith, without trust in the other.
> —Jacques Derrida, *Deconstruction in a Nutshell*

Asking Unasked Questions

For ease of reference, let's call the philosophical position that defends the ontology of constitutive responsibility that I have advocated in this book, *Otherism.*[1] I suggest the following as its key tenets:

- ✧ The self is constituted in an ethico-religious encounter by the call of the God *and* the Other.

- ✧ This call inaugurates an infinite, bi-directional responsibility that must be undertaken as a political task.

- ✧ The ethico-religious encounter resists the primacy of traditional ontological and epistemological narratives, which is not to say that it is not still ontological in some sense (viz., as in the ontology of constitutive responsibility).

- ✧ The ethico-religious encounter with the Other/God is not something that occurs within chronological time, but instead in the "immemorial past" (Levinas) or "the moment" (Kierkegaard).

- ✧ The ethico-religious encounter is inescapably singular (first-personal) and does not allow for a universal, objective vantage point (third-personal perspective).

With this set of claims in place as definitive of Otherism, let me begin this chapter by asking a couple of questions that I find to be often overlooked or, more accurately, largely unasked in contemporary Continental philosophy.

First, if we no longer believe the traditional myth of reason's transcendent supremacy—i.e., that it operates beyond or above the fray of political subjectivities engaged in concrete existence (and perhaps serves as the condition for such an engagement in the first place)—then what are we to make of the demand for reasons in political life and moral philosophy? In other words, if substantially deflated of its claim to *de jure* force, what can reason-giving mean after the postmodern critique of reason? *Second,* if we move away from political theory as a debate about how to conceive of stability in the face of the fact of reasonable pluralism, say, and resituate it as discourse about the specific functioning of power structures, then what remains of the notion of "justification"? That is, isn't justification just another modification of power? When applied to Otherism, we might ask: what does it mean to say that one is "justified" in affirming Otherism as the best way forward for ethico-political or ethico-religious life? If the postmodern resistance to epistemology is understood as the reduction of epistemology to politics, as Richard Rorty contends, then it appears that to affirm Otherism is simply to do politics in a certain way, rather than allowing the ethico-religious encounter to inaugurate a radically different conception of the political. To concede that justification is impossible is to cede the day to Rorty, regarding political life; and this is a concession that I am unwilling to make, not just because I happen to disagree with Rorty, but because there are *good reasons* to do so.

These questions are frequently overlooked within Continental philosophy, I contend, because they have been primarily dealt with by reference to each other and, as such, are assumed to have already been answered. Moving in one direction, the problem of reason-giving is no longer a real problem once we realize that the political is best understood as a navigation of power structures. Reason-giving is not a distinct existential activity (whether political, ethical, or epistemological), but simply a particular way of describing one's location in particular "democratic" spaces. As Rorty might say, it is the name we give to the task of trying to get our interests publicly considered. Yet there are plenty of other ways to do this, and there is no longer a privileged mode of access for such a venture. Reason-giving is not the *primary* or *best* way to be heard and, accordingly, it deserves no exalted status in political discourse. So, the inescapability of power-play is able to account for reason-giving inasmuch as reason-giving is viewed as just another way of *playing*—whether such "play" is understood in a Rortian or a Derridean way.

Moving in the other direction, once reason is abandoned as a transcendental requirement for proper human sociality, justification seems to be no longer an appropriate thing to demand. That is, it becomes difficult to differentiate justification from explanation except along the lines of the social function that they respectively fill. This can easily be seen in the Nietzschean and Freudian conceptions of genealogy as ways of making sense of one's beliefs and commitments. The belief that p is not something that one needs to justify in order to demonstrate the rationality of holding p, but merely something that one needs to come to terms with and explain relative to one's own particular history in order to achieve particular social ends. On such a model, therapy might function as a stand-in for what was formerly allotted to epistemology. Indeed, if reason is no longer viewed as universal and justification is limited to being a local account of one's existential situation, then why continue to act as if such an account is required for social existence and philosophical activity? Perhaps philosophy is better understood as an accounting of the *failure* of justification.

In this chapter, I will attempt to spell out exactly why we should hesitate to move in such directions. In response to the questions above, I will argue for the following theses:

(A) Reason-giving is crucial even when reason is contextually localized.

(B) Justification is abandoned at our own peril.

(C) Justification considered in the context of Otherism can be articulated according to a notion of a postfoundationalist epistemology of trust.

(D) This epistemology of trust can be read as resonating with the work of such analytic philosophers as Nicholas Wolterstorff, William Alston, Alvin Plantinga, and Robert Audi.

I want to make clear that this chapter is intentionally meant as gestural—a mere indication of what I take to be a promising line of further inquiry, not a final account of all of the specifics of the epistemology of trust itself. I will claim that there are reasons to believe that a "modest," or "weak," or "minimal" foundationalism offers a plausible account of how to conceive of what might be considered a "deconstructive" notion of justification.[2] However, I will not go as far as arguing that this is the *only* way to understand the deconstructivist trajectory.[3] Instead, I will merely argue that Continental ethical and political philosophers should be more willing to admit the possibility that "epistemology" is a legitimate way of describing much of what we encounter in the work of Kierkegaard, Levinas, Derrida, Marion, and others. My suggestion is that a theory of justification which is internal to the postmodern commitments of Otherism is necessary if Otherism is going to be able to do the sort of work I called for in the introduction. Subsequently, I contend that Continental debates concerning these issues will be enriched through productive dialogue with those who work in analytic epistemology and philosophy of religion.[4] My goals in this chapter are thus: to clearly articulate the stakes of justification which are internal to contemporary Continental ethics; to get clear as to why philosophers like Derrida have been viewed as celebrating the demise of epistemology; and to make a case for epistemological debate as something that is needed in contemporary Continental philosophy of religion and ethico-political philosophy, by suggesting one possible account of how such a debate might proceed.

"Giving an Account of Oneself" . . . but with Good Reason?

In the introduction to *Driven Back to the Text*, Oona Ajzenstat claims that "many readers" find Levinas's claims regarding the fundamental responsibility to the Other to be "inadequately supported by evidence" (2001, 6). "Indeed," she continues, "Levinas's ethics must almost certainly appear to fans of evidence as naïve. But Levinas himself is not a fan of evidence" (2001, 6). Recognizing that this claim might seem to undermine her task of presenting a "defense" of Levinas's ethics, Ajzenstat bites the bullet and admits that she will "not attempt to adduce proof for his ethics drawn from experience or . . . display in the ethics an analytic coherence." Rather, she says: "I pronounce myself persuaded" (2001, 6). In *Infinitely Demanding*, Simon Critchley offers the following claim about Marx that seems to resonate, at least rhetorically, with Ajzenstat's approach to Levinas:

> Reading Marx on the genesis and emergence of capital and its political corollary, the modern representative state; reading him on the function of money as the universal, yet alienated, capacity of humankind; on commodity fetishism and the mystified nature of exchange value; on the massive structural dislocations of capitalist society and the yawning inequalities that it produces, *one is simply persuaded* of the massive prescience and truth of these analyses. (2007, 96; emphasis added)

What does it mean to be "simply persuaded" by something? Does persuasion require evidence? It seems that for Ajzenstat it does not, or her sheer pronouncement of being persuaded would be out of place. For Critchley it is unclear from this passage whether or not "simply" means that evidence is irrelevant or that the evidence provided by Marx for his claims is so strong that one is, *thereby*, "simply persuaded." Yet what counts as "evidence" in the first place? Does Ajzenstat's claim merely mean that there can be no deductive argument beginning from universally accepted premises in support of Levinasian ethics? If so, then Critchley seems to concur, but he applies the claim to ethics more generally:

> I don't think that it is the business of moral argument to be able to provide watertight proofs for its propositions. Ethical argument is neither

like logic, which is deductively true, nor science, which is inductively true. There is a point at which the rationality of moral argumentation gives way to moral recommendation, even exhortation, an appeal to the individual reader from an individual writer. (2007, 9–10)

Critchley's key claim is that there is "a point at which the rationality of moral argumentation gives way to moral recommendation," which consists of an "appeal" from one individual to another.

A couple of things are worth noting here. First, there appears to be a false dichotomy that frames Critchley's formulation: either we proceed by deduction/induction or by something like cajoling. Surely there are other options: pragmatic implicature, abductive inference, etc. Second, if we were to grant this expressed dichotomy, while denying the propriety of deduction/induction, as Critchley does, and conclude that to cajole is the only avenue open to us, then it becomes difficult to understand precisely what "an appeal" from one individual to another would mean in the context of "moral argument." It is easy to imagine what such an appeal would mean if one abandons the possibility of ethical argumentation altogether and instead relegates ethics to the "private" realm of encouragement and support between individuals who already, for the most part, agree—such agreement is often the basis for particular affiliations within social networks beyond the pale of public discourse. "Moral recommendation" might appeal to someone on the basis of considerations such as social acceptance (e.g., peer pressure occurring within a given social space), shared social goals (e.g., community groups organized around a particular issue), fear of ridicule (e.g., consider the way in which "new atheism" à la Dawkins, Hitchens, and Harris advocates a certain degree of ridicule as the best way of "persuading" religious individuals to give up their beliefs or at least remain silent about them in public debate),[5] or fear of punishment (e.g., as in the case of certain religious organizations).

For someone like Rorty, this deflationary conception of moral argumentation is not a problem at all. Indeed, his entire conception of "reason-giving" is best understood as a way of getting one's point across to those who can help you move forward toward shared goals. "If we occupy ourselves with practical measures to decrease suffering," Rorty writes, "we can safely forget about whether we are bringing man back to his true nature, or whether the institutions we establish are 'dictated by reason'" (Rorty 2006, 92). On this model, "justification" becomes more of a social praxis guided by contingent, and decidedly local, political interests than an epistemological conception used to differentiate legitimate beliefs from illegitimate ones. Indeed, for Rorty, what counts as "legitimate" is what *enough others* will let you continue to believe without serious repercussions. What counts as "illegitimate" is simply a belief that fails to be acceptable to those with whom one shares a community. "Some philosophers," Rorty claims, "see an important difference between logic and rhetoric, or between 'convincing' and 'persuading.' I do not" (2006, 70). "There is of course a difference between good and bad arguments," he continues. "An argument is good only for a public that accepts its premises" (2006, 70). Of course, Rorty does not intend to give up the notion of justification as such, but simply to locate it as an entirely social phenomenon that characterizes the way that individuals go about getting others to agree with them. In other words, we might say that *for Rorty, justification is best understood as a sociological notion and not an epistemological one*[6]—and moreover, it is certainly not an ethico-religious conception.

Importantly, however, Rorty's claim that an "argument is good only for a public that accepts its premises" might seem to indicate a vicious circularity at the heart of all public discourse. If an argument can only be good if one's interlocutors start by agreeing to its premises, then it looks like there is no distinction between "providing an argument" and "preaching to the choir." Many have objected to Rorty on precisely this point, claiming that his "postmodern bourgeois liberalism" is not "ethnocentric" in an innocuous manner. If one can only give good arguments to those that already agree, then it would appear that the only way to speak to those who *reject* one's premises is through *non-argumentative means of persuasion*. But then it would seem that one's interlocutor becomes not a true dialogical partner, but merely a straggler to be converted (by any means necessary?). In a certain sense, though it might sound perverse, Rorty's account of discourse (stripped of a real distinction between convincing and persuading) might strike some readers as a secular version of a particular sort of religious discourse—namely, a version of religion that does not open itself up to external critique and dialogue, but is motivated entirely by bringing others on board. And ironically, it is the anti-democratic political results of just such a "religious" vision that Rorty so adamantly opposes; as we have discussed, this is the basic rationale underlying his occasional suggestion that religion should be "privatized."[7]

Yet if Rorty's conception of when argumentation is possible is right, it seems that it would be nearly impossible to distinguish "public democratic discourse" from "privatized religious discourse" because, on his model, both of them would seemingly require previous assent from one's conversation partners. And it is the *lack of such consensus* that Rorty expects, or even requires, within a democratic *polis*—e.g., consider his general affirmation of Rawls's "fact of reasonable pluralism." So, two options seem to arise: (1) democratic dialogue is genuine, but thereby trivial (i.e., one is simply preaching to the choir), or (2) democratic discourse is not really an engaged consideration of various positions on the basis of strong argumentation, but reduces to a matter of public relations (i.e., one neither preaches nor argues, but instead attempts to woo converts through rhetorical "spin" or what Harry Frankfurt terms "bullshit").[8]

Now, if one finds Rorty's limitation of democratic life to be problematic on this front, as I do, then it seems that something more is needed than a dismissal of epistemological requirements and a deflationary conception of justification. "But," one might reply, "I am a Derridean (or Levinasian, or Kierkegaardian) and certainly not a Rortian. So, I don't need to be concerned." Well it is here that we should return to the claims of Ajzenstat and Critchley, which, when read in a particular way, seem to be quite close to what we find in Rorty. Both Ajzenstat and Critchley can be plausibly read as claiming that there is no way to convince someone of the truth of a Levinasian or Marxist position, but instead, in an almost religious or mystical way, one just *sees* the truth and is "simply persuaded." And again here, the voice of Dominique Janicaud might begin to rise from the background to protest against the "loaded dice" with which he takes Levinas to play. Janicaud's charge of a religious presuppositionalism at the heart of Levinasian phenomenology might gain plausibility in the light of Ajzenstat's pronouncement.[9] And similarly, unless it is supplemented by substantial supporting arguments, Critchley's comment that one is "simply persuaded" by the "massive prescience and truth" of Marx's analyses, goes a long way toward inviting Rorty's comment that "loyalty to Marx has become a fetish" (Rorty, Nystrom, and Puckett 2002, 18).[10] Must Continental philosophy, and Levinasian ethics in particular, resign itself to the mystical or fetishistic proclamation of its own presuppositions without room for receiving the real criticism of good arguments?

Diane Perpich directly addresses this concern when she notes:

> There is a subtle logic to Ajzenstat's position, since Levinas's thought explicitly attempts to render problematic any demand for arguments that would prove the "truth" of ethical responsibility. Nonetheless, insofar as such a view appears to set aside altogether the requirement to provide a defense of the ethical claims, it risks conceding that Levinas's thought can have a legitimate place in our religious or ethico-religious lives (understood as regions of private codes or beliefs) but denies Levinas a place in our public, philosophical lives—that is, in the sphere where justification is rightly demanded. In this respect, Ajzenstat's reading is fully concordant with Rorty's and Janicaud's. (Perpich 2008, 6)

It seems, then, that in order to argue for the specifically political relevance of the range of thinkers that advocate the ontology of constitutive responsibility, it is crucial that we not be complacent in the face of the apparent ease with which so many Continental thinkers have abandoned epistemology. As Perpich so rightly realizes, some sort of justificative account is required if Levinasian ethics—and I would add, Kierkegaard's notion of passionate inwardness, Derrida's notion of responsibility, Marion's conception of the interlocuted, Henry's dual conception of truth, Ricœur's proposal of hope, and Lacoste's liturgical reading of human existence, etc.—are not to be regarded as politically irrelevant.

Years ago, Rorty noted that there was a longstanding split in Derridean circles between those who "are content to admire his manner" and those who "want to say that the important thing is his matter—the truth that he has set forth" (Rorty 1991b, 119). While I grant that such a distinction is helpful for understanding in a very loose way the main branches of Derridean interpretation, I believe that this distinction is too quick. I would argue that it is precisely because of Derrida's *matter* that his *manner* developed as it did. With Derrida, the truth that *p* ("deconstruction is justice," say, or "deconstruction is undeconstructible") is not innocuously related to the style of writing in which one engages the truth that *p*. These complications notwithstanding, I am pretty firmly on the side of those who focus more on the "matter" of Continental philosophy than on the "manner" (e.g., Culler 1982; Norris 1987; Gasché 1986). It is crucial that the content being affirmed by Levinas's ethics, Derrida's notion of justice, and Marion's conception of revelation, for example, not be relegated to a private sphere of personal development, but are actually brought to bear, in a decidedly just way (i.e., not simply through cajoling, bargaining, bribery, etc.), on the task of making our shared social existence one that overcomes the problematic traditions and conceptions that have defined its history.

Essential to such a project, however, is the ability to justify one's commitment to the content of Otherism as a more promising way forward than other relevant alternatives. For example, if I am right that politics should be understood as an ethico-political task instead of primarily an epistemological one, even this claim requires justificatory support. Accordingly, my argument in the previous chapter should not be read as a rejection of epistemology, but as an attempt to resituate how the demand for justification operates internal to political life as ethico-religiously inaugurated. As Judith Butler asks, "if it is really true that we are, as it were, divided, ungrounded, or incoherent from the start, will it be impossible to ground a notion of personal or social responsibility?" (2005, 19). Notice that here she deploys the term "ground," which I read as functioning as a parallel term to "justify." In other words, following Butler, we might ask: if postmodernism has abandoned the things that have traditionally seemed to be required for justification (human nature, ontological essence, universal reason, objective truth, etc.) then is it possible to still justify our commitment to the ethico-religious encounter in the first place? Either way one answers this question, one needs to do so on the basis of something more robust than what is provided by Rorty or Ajzenstat and Critchley in the brief passages I have cited.

In order to lay out an account of how justification might, indeed, be possible in a postmodern context, we must first see exactly how Rorty and Derrida (for example) can appear to be so closely aligned regarding the demise of epistemology, and yet Derrida opens a space for understanding justification in a way that Rorty does not. The site at which this divergence appears, I will suggest, is in their variant notions of "justice." Justice is where the opportunity for a specifically "deconstructive," or "new phenomenological," or "Otherist" epistemology of trust begins to emerge in Derrida's postmodernism, while it cannot in Rorty's postmodernism.

Different Postmodernisms: Disentangling Rorty and Derrida

In *Philosophy and the Mirror of Nature*, Rorty claims that we must move "from epistemology to hermeneutics" (1979, 315).[11] Importantly, Rorty makes clear that he is "*not* putting hermeneutics forward as a 'successor subject' to epistemology, as an activity which fills the cultural vacancy once filled by epistemologically centered philosophy" (1979, 315). Rather, Rorty contends that "hermeneutics is an expression of hope that the cultural space left by the demise of epistemology will not be filled—that our culture should become one in which the demand for constraint and confrontation is no longer felt" (1979, 315). The key, Rorty claims, is that hermeneutics does not assume a "common ground" between individuals that would allow for a "commensurability" between divergent discourses; rather, there is a fundamental incommensurability between the various language games in which we are always already involved. "Thus," Rorty concludes, "epistemology proceeds on the assumption that all contributions to a given discourse are commensurable. Hermeneutics is largely a struggle against this assumption" (1979, 316).

As something of an epistemological version of the social problem that Locke's individuals faced in the "state of nature"—i.e., the need for an unbiased authority to which one could appeal in order to settle disputes—Rorty articulates the postmodern situation as not requiring some sort of ultimate arbiter (God, Reason, Nature, etc.), but rather as needing to overcome the dependence on (or even desire for) such an arbiter. This contestation of all final authorities seems very close to the Derridean notion of the constant "play" between signifiers that challenges all claims to "final" interpretations for particular texts:

> In the delineation of *différance* everything is strategic and adventurous. Strategic because no transcendent truth present outside the field of writing can govern theologically the totality of the field. Adventurous because this strategy is not a simple strategy in the sense that strategy orients tactics according to a final goal, a *telos* or theme of

domination, a mastery and ultimate reappropriation of the development of the field. (Derrida 1982, 7)

Despite the fact that Derrida recognizes that "the detours, locutions, and syntax" to which he often has recourse "will resemble those of negative theology,"[12] this strategic and adventurous play stands as a constant challenge to all conceptual and, as he makes explicit, theological authorities. *Différance,* Derrida insists, "governs nothing, reigns over nothing, and nowhere exercises any authority. It is not announced by any capital letter. Not only is there no kingdom of *différance,* but *différance* instigates the subversion of every kingdom" (1982, 22). In light of Derrida's much-cited claim in *Of Grammatology,* "there is no outside of the text" (*Il n'y a pas de hors-texte*), one might read his critique of authority as inviting what John Caputo will term the "radical translatability" which accompanies the "radical hermeneutical situation" that pertains after the demise of epistemology (Caputo 2005, 293).

It initially appears that Rorty's critique of the representationalism of the philosophical tradition and Derrida's resistance to the "metaphysics of presence" are really two ways of doing the same thing: viz., they both challenge the *privilege* and, following Nietzsche, *prejudice* of philosophers as somehow operating within a discourse that is more fundamental or more foundational than any other. Not only has epistemology been dislodged from its place as *prima philosophia* in modernity, but philosophy is no longer the foundation for *scientia* in the sense of the natural and social sciences. One scholar links Rorty to Derrida on precisely this point: "Siding with Derrida . . . over against Gadamer, Rorty in effect endorses Derrida's notorious claim: *Il n'y a pas de hors-texte;* there is nothing outside of textuality, outside of language. This in effect amounts to saying: 'There are no truths, only rival interpretations'" (Madison 2001, 72).[13] If such an interpretation is correct, then to claim that philosophy has some sort of unique access to truth would be a mistake. Moreover, to claim that there could be such a thing as the "justification" of a belief would be to forget the constitutively embedded and contextual reality of all of human existence. As Rorty says in an interview:

> I agree with the late Heidegger that the science/poetry/philosophy distinctions we have lived with are outmoded, and, in particular, the notion of philosophers as people who can provide the rest of culture with a framework. It seems to me that the demand that there be something for philosophy to be is unfounded. . . . Surely what the French philosophers and the Yale literary critics are doing is helping us to see how we live in story after story after story. (2006, 21)

Given such a challenge to the distinction of philosophical inquiry, it is a simple enough matter to also challenge the legitimacy of there being something like a "correct" or "adequate" or "true" account of the way things are—hence the anti-realism shared by Rorty and Derrida. And this is especially applicable to postmodern conceptions of God and religious/theological discourse. Throughout his recent work, Caputo builds upon this Derridean-Rortian trajectory and extends the postmodern resistance to epistemology into issues of concern to the philosophy of religion. As he writes in a review essay of Merold Westphal's *Overcoming Onto-Theology*:

> [Postmodernism] is not simply an epistemological way to delimit human knowledge here in time in order to make room for the world as it is eternally known by God; it shows us more mercilessly how exposed we are to the possibility that the world is not known comprehensively by anyone and that no one knows . . . [that] we are here. It does not dogmatically proclaim that, but it exposes us to that. Deconstruction is not only the continuous reminder that we are not God [as Westphal suggests], but it is the claim that the name of God is endlessly translatable into other names, like justice, and that we are in no position to stop this fluctuation. (Caputo 2005, 294)

Caputo's comment displays a continued opposition to anything like a notion of "justification" that could settle disputes regarding the "proper" or "correct" name of God. "Justification" for Caputo could no longer be a logical or even epistemological claim about the "legitimacy" or "warranted assertability" or "well-groundedness" of a belief—or the adequate truth-conduciveness of a practice, say—but would instead simply describe the way various people talk within their various cultural-historical situations. Such a contention is not far from Rorty:

> In my opinion what links the so-called postmodern philosophers to Davidson and Brandom, as well as to the later Wittgenstein, is a rejection of the idea that some discourses, some parts of the culture, are in closer contact with the world, or fit the world better, than other discourses. If one gives up this idea, then one will view every discourse—literary criticism, history, physics, chemistry, plumbers' talk—as on a par, as far as its relation to reality goes. (Rorty and Engel, 2007, 36)

Having thus demonstrated that Rorty and Derrida share in a general postmodern resistance to epistemology—and specifically, to the primacy of epistemology for inquiry—I now want to expose some dissonance between Rorty and Derrida which, I believe, will open the space for articulating a productive notion of justification within a Derridean-Levinasian legacy. This dissonance appears in their different conceptions of "justice."

Throughout much of his work from the mid-1980s onward, Rorty "argues" that justice should no longer be understood as some sort of transcendental ideal or postulate of practical reason—that is, as a "larger loyalty" beyond our contingent local commitments (see Rorty 2007, chap. 3; 1991a, 175–96). For Rorty, this conception of justice as some local loyalty that reflects a shared social hope follows from the failure of the Enlightenment projects that attempted to secure some firm foundation for obligation. Gone are the days when the encouragement to "be rational" and the encouragement to "be just" were two ways of saying the same thing. In our day, "to advise people to be rational," Rorty claims, "is . . . simply to suggest that somewhere among their shared beliefs and desires there may be enough resources to permit agreement on how to coexist without violence" (2007, 53–54). As I discussed in chapter 1, Rorty's view that there is a "priority of democracy to philosophy" depends heavily on his reading of the work of Michael Walzer and John Rawls (1991a, 175–96). Drawing on his reading of Walzer in particular, Rorty claims that "there is no such thing as a non-question-begging demonstration of the epistemic superiority of the Western idea of reasonableness" (2007, 49).

Though Derrida would certainly agree with Rorty that there is no universal rationality according to which the demands of justice could be objectively derived, he will part company regarding the way in which justice itself is, accordingly, understood. In contrast to the notion of justice as the local ties that bind, as it were, for Derrida justice names something much more unwieldy and paradoxical:

> Justice is an experience of the impossible. A will, a desire, a demand for justice whose structure wouldn't be an experience of aporia would have no chance to be what it is, namely, a call for justice. . . . Law (*droit*) is not justice. Law is the element of calculation, and it is just that there be law, but justice is incalculable, it requires us to calculate with the incalculable; and aporetic experiences are the experiences, as improbable as they are necessary, of justice, that is to say of moments in which the decision between just and unjust is never insured by a rule. (1992b, 16)

Here Derrida articulates the distinction between *law* and *justice* that will become all-important in his later philosophy. As Derrida claims in *Rogues*:

> Justice can never be reduced to law, to calculative reason, to lawful distribution, to the norms and rules that condition law, as evidenced by its history and its ongoing transformations, but its recourse to coercive force, its recourse to a power or might that, as Kant showed with the greatest rigor, is inscribed and justified in the purest concept of law or right. (2005, 149–50)

The distinction between law and justice depends on a set of oppositions:

Law	Justice
Calculation	Incalculability
Rational Norms	Aporia
Conditioned	Unconditionable
Rule-Based	Resistance to all Algorithms
Justifiable Force	Infinite Demand

For Derrida, these oppositions are not simply dialectical; the column on the right is always "prior" to the column on the left. Just as I have suggested with Levinas's distinction between ethics and politics, this priority is certainly not temporal, but instead is a "quasi-transcendental" or, as I have termed it, a "quasi-logical existential" conditionality. The "quasi-" is needed here because precisely what justice necessitates—namely, law—is what contests justice. That is, justice is the condition of possibility and the condition of impossibility for law. As Derrida makes clear, it is only because of the "experience of the undecidable" that there could ever be ethical decision:

> The structure I am describing here is a structure in which law (*droit*) is essentially deconstructible. . . . The fact that law is deconstructible is not bad news. We may even see in this a stroke of luck for politics, for all historical progress. But the paradox that I'd like to submit for discussion is the following: it is this deconstructible structure of law (*droit*), or if you prefer of justice as *droit*, that also insures the possibility of deconstruction. Justice in itself, if such a thing exists, outside or beyond law, is not deconstructible. No more than deconstruction itself, if such a thing exists. Deconstruction is justice. (Derrida 1992b, 14–15)

Justice is the condition for decision, and yet, my decision demands that I choose according to the categories of legality.[14] *Justice* is the ethical demand that inaugurates a responsibility before freedom; *Law* is the political situation in which I stand, freely, faced with the decision whether or not to be troubled by justice. Though I will return to this constitutive tension in chapter 13 and demonstrate how it need not grind ethico-political decision-making to a halt, but offers profound resources for such a task, for now what matters is that justice is absolute, for Derrida, it is undeconstructible, whereas all the historical manifestations human conceptions of justice (laws that are put in place, say) are "essentially deconstructible."

The main problem that Rorty has with Derrida's articulation of justice, as we observed in chapter 1, is that he finds the recourse to such hyperbolic and "religious" language to be simply unhelpful in the business of political life. Recall his claim that "it seems . . . pointless hype to dramatize our difficulties in knowing what to do by labeling our goal 'indescribable,' 'unexperiencable,' 'unintelligible,' or 'infinitely distant'" (Rorty 1996b, 42). Despite their seeming agreement on the futility of epistemology, they stand in stark contrast regarding what it is that underlies ethical decision itself. For Derrida, such decision is only possible as a result of affirming the aporetic experience of the undecidable; for Rorty, such decision becomes possible due to the historical relationships we have with other people in the context of certain shared social aspirations. Yet this is a difference that, I believe, makes all the difference. In the claim that justice is the very condition of deconstruction, Derrida demands that we invest ourselves in the narrative of selfhood articulated in the ontology of constitutive responsibility. Simply put, the Derridean conceptions of ethico-religious exposure, moral decision, ethico-political existence, and even the ability to name historical injustice, requires the fundamental belief that *tout autre est tout autre* (Derrida 1995). That is, all of these conceptions are grounded in the affirmation of the undeconstructibility of justice.

But how are we to understand this affirmation? I want to suggest that it is best understood as a gesture of *trust*. While it is clear that one could not "know" with certainty that justice functions in such a way, it is clear that one must invest oneself in the truth that it does in order to move forward in the way that Derrida recommends. Now, given Derrida's resistance to epistemological language—there is no confusing his work with William Alston's or Laurence Bonjour's, for example—and considering his deep dependence on the work of Kierkegaard, it might seem that there could be no way to "justify" such a fundamental belief. Surely Derrida—and even more so, Levinas—is a fideist when it comes to the relation to the Other, right?

While Rorty sees justice as a name for certain interests of one's own community, Derrida posits justice as the very condition for ethical life. Throughout new phenomenology, what one finds is that *trust in justice,* in the call of the Other, in standing transparently before God, is located as the basic commitment of the ethico-religious encounter and stands as the first move of philosophy—thus Levinas's claim, "ethics is first philosophy." If we are unable to give some epistemological account on which such trust is justified, then it seems that Rorty and Janicaud are correct to dismiss these gestures as religious fideism—and Ajzenstat is correct to simply pronounce herself "persuaded." However, I believe that a more robust account can be offered.

In the next section, I will suggest one possible contemporary epistemological perspective—a particular notion of foundationalism—which offers a model of justification that, I believe, can be productively applied to this deconstructive account. By bringing Otherism together with analytic epistemology I hope to demonstrate that, as Merold Westphal claims, "if the Enlightenment project is quintessentially modern, then . . . analytic philosophy in many of its current forms is as 'postmodern' as contemporary continental philosophy" (2001, 51). And, definitely more controversially but, I believe, more importantly, I will give support to Westphal's further suggestion that it is at least initially plausible to describe what many Continental ethicists and philosophers of religion are doing as, properly speaking, epistemological (2001, 51).[15] As W. Jay Wood correctly asserts: "postmodern philosophy has not altogether outgrown the need for epistemology" (1999, 13).

Not All Foundationalism is "Strong"

It is not entirely inaccurate to say that the postmodern resistance to epistemology amounts to a rejection of "foundationalism." As Westphal writes, "it is clear that where Rorty says 'epistemology' one might just as well say 'modernity' or, to be more precise, 'the Enlightenment project' or, to be still more precise, 'foundationalism'" (2001, 48). Or as Charles Taylor notes, on Rorty's model, "it is clear what overcoming epistemology has to mean. It will mean abandoning foundationalism" (1987, 465).[16] Even if we grant that it is really "foundationalism" that stands as the most appropriate target of postmodern ire, it is not exactly clear what this term means. As Evan Simpson writes, the concept of foundationalism "is often used in an untamed way. The word has become elastic, stretching easily to cover a variety of positions" (1987, 2). Robert Audi goes as far as to say that "foundationalism is one of the most widely misunderstood positions in philosophy" (1993, 2).

If "foundationalism" is "widely misunderstood" in contemporary epistemology, in Rorty's usage the confusions and equivocations accompanying this notion are legion. "By failing to distinguish the generic epistemological task from the specifically modern foundationalist projects," Westphal claims, "Rorty obscures the fact that hermeneutics is not the replacement of epistemology as such but the replacement of one type of epistemology with another" (2001, 49). I find that though "foundationalism" is far from prominent in the writings of Heidegger, Levinas, and Derrida, a similar sort of ambiguity plagues their work as well. Given the general lack of clarity surrounding this notion, and in order to lay out at least some of the ways in which this term has been deployed, I find Susan Haack's differentiation of the three ways in which it functions in Rorty's work to be quite helpful:

> Sometimes Rorty uses these expressions to refer to experientialist versions of the style of theory of justification characterized as "foundationalist"; sometimes to refer to the idea that epistemology is an a priori enterprise the goal of which is to legitimize the claim of science . . . to give us knowledge; sometimes to [refer to] what might less confusingly be called "epistemic objectivism," the thesis that criteria of justification require objective grounding. (1993, 186)

The first usage Haack writes, simply, "foundationalism," and she suggests that it is a "theory of justification distinguishing basic beliefs . . . and derived beliefs"; the second usage she writes *"foundationalism,"* and describes as a "conception of epistemology as an a priori discipline" that founds science; and the third she writes "FOUNDATIONALISM," and says that it is a "thesis that criteria of justification are not purely conventional but stand in need of objective grounding" (1993, 186). Importantly, Haack points out that

> FOUNDATIONALISM does not imply *foundationalism*, nor *foundationalism* foundationalism. It could be that though criteria of justification stand in need of ratification (as FOUNDATIONALISM holds), ratification is not to be achieved a priori (as *foundationalism* holds) but within, or with the help of, empirical knowledge. Or it could be that the way to ratify criteria of justification is (as *foundationalism* holds) a priori, but that the correct criteria are not foundationalist, but coherentist or foundherentist. (1993, 186)

Alhough Haack's analysis is specifically targeted at Rorty, her distinctions are helpful for more broadly understanding the "anti-foundationalism" that is so prevalent in postmodern philosophy: what unites all these usages of foundationalism is the notion of *privilege*. What Haack terms simply "foundationalism," we might call *epistemic foundationalism* and locate the privilege at work here in the very idea of "basic beliefs." Similarly, *"foundationalism"* might better be named *disciplinary foundationalism* according to which the privilege lies in the notion of epistemology itself as "first philosophy." And finally, "FOUNDATIONALISM" is perhaps better conceived as *metaphysical foundationalism,* due to the way in which it requires a grounding that lies outside or beyond the immanent trappings of human existence and linguistic practice (a God's-eye view, say). Anti-foundationalism, in its many varieties, asserts that there simply is not any sort of privileged perspective, position, standpoint, experience, access, or practice that can serve as *ground* in the way that foundationalism, in all its forms, requires.

So, what exactly is it that most postmodern philosophers (in a Derridean strain) are opposed to, when considered as "anti-foundationalists"? Is it a particular structure of justification (epistemic foundationalism), a view of epistemology itself as a philosophical practice (disciplinary foundationalism), or a notion of justification as transcendentally located (metaphysical foundationalism)? Due to the way in which many Continental philosophers have abandoned epistemological vocabulary altogether, answering this question is not easy. A term like 'foundationalism' is often deployed (if at all) as shorthand for everything that modernity stood for and "we postmoderns" have shed. Despite the lack of clarity on this issue in the contemporary Continental literature, I want to suggest that all Otherism needs to affirm is *anti-disciplinary foundationalism* and *anti-metaphysical foundationalism*. Yet, there may still be a place for *epistemic foundationalism* in Otherism.

Consider, again, the key tenets of Otherism that I outlined at the beginning of this chapter (I number them here for ease of reference):

(1) The self is constituted in an ethico-religious encounter by the call of the God *and* the Other.

(2) This call inaugurates an infinite, bi-directional responsibility that must be undertaken as a political task.

(3) The ethico-religious encounter resists the primacy of traditional ontological and epistemological narratives, which is not to say that it is not still ontological in some sense (viz., as in the ontology of constitutive responsibility).

(4) The ethico-religious encounter with the Other/God is not something that occurs within chronological time, but instead in the "immemorial past" (Levinas) or "the moment" (Kierkegaard).

(5) The ethico-religious encounter is inescapably singular (first-personal) and does not allow for a universal, objective vantage point (third-personal perspective).

Since (3) to (5) form the content of the claim that "ethics is first philosophy," this will be sufficient to challenge the privilege associated with disciplinary foundationalism. Yet, one might object: isn't the claim "ethics is first philosophy" itself an exemplary case of disciplinary foundationalism? Well, as the notion of disciplinary foundationalism was defined above, it is a thesis about the primacy of *epistemology* and not simply a claim that there is "first philosophy." If we wanted to broaden that definition then perhaps Otherism would be a model of disciplinary foundationalism, but such a discussion is beyond our concerns here.

Additionally, (1), (3), and (5) contest the crux of metaphysical foundationalism in that they reject the idea that there could be something like an objectivity internal to the ethico-religious encounter. While these claims are certainly "metaphysical" in the technical sense given to the term by Levinas, they are not claims to objectivity (the key characteristic of metaphysical foundationalism). Since such objectivity would only be possible internal to the "horizon of being," we might say, to require it as a condition of justification for the claims of Otherism would be either (a) to eliminate the possibility of justifying Otherism, or (b) to reinscribe the relation to the Other within the domain of being which it must transcend, according to Levinas's claim that it is "beyond being." If (a), then the attempt to make Otherism more than a matter of private edification is doomed, and if (b), then Otherism is fairly quickly seen as self-refuting.[17]

While disciplinary foundationalism and metaphysical foundationalism might be incompatible with Otherism (and thus, it is correct to label Levinas and Derrida "anti-foundationalists"), it is not clear that epistemic foundationalism has similar problems for Otherism. Indeed, when read as a claim about the *structure* of justification, there is nothing in (1) to (5) that would require epistemic foundationalism to be false. Now, that said, it is important to distinguish between different varieties of epistemic foundationalism;[18] as we will see, it is only a certain type of epistemic foundationalism that is compatible with Otherism.

The essential component of epistemic foundationalism in all its varieties is that it makes a distinction between "basic" and "nonbasic" beliefs. Basic beliefs are beliefs that are held non-inferentially—that is, they do not depend on other beliefs for their justification; nonbasic beliefs are beliefs that are held on the basis of other beliefs. Eventually, all nonbasic beliefs will, by inference, lead back to a basic belief, at which point the inferential regress stops. For example, if *r* is a nonbasic belief then, by definition, it is justified by another belief *q*, and if *q* is nonbasic then it is justified by some belief *p*, and so on until the chain of nonbasic beliefs leads to some basic belief *n*, which itself does not depend upon another belief. Audi summarizes this notion of (epistemic) foundationalism as follows:

> Foundationalism *as such*, taken as common to the various theorists who hold it, is above all a structural view. It says that a person's knowledge (or justified belief) has a foundational structure, but not what sorts of content the constitutive cognitions must have. In outline, the idea is that if one has any knowledge or justified belief, then, first, one has at least some knowledge or justified belief that is foundational, in the sense that it is not (inferentially) based on any further knowledge or belief and, second, any other knowledge or justified belief one has in some way rests on one or more of these foundational elements. This view does not imply that such foundational beliefs are, e.g., epistemically certain, or not themselves grounded in something else, such as perceptual experience. Thus, it is left open that, psychologically, the presence of these elements can be explained, and, epistemically, an answer can often be given to the question of what justifies them. What is ruled out is simply that they are justified, *inferentially*, by other beliefs. If they were, those beliefs would raise the same question, and we would either have to posit foundational ones or suppose . . . that our cognitive systems contain inferential circles or infinite regresses. (Audi 1993, 3; original emphases)

There are a number of important things to notice in Audi's account. First, all epistemic foundationalism involves is a claim about justificative structure—it neither presupposes nor entails metaphysical or ontological conclusions. Second, epistemic foundationalism is aimed at avoiding the charge of circularity or regress. In contrast to a coherentist focus on circularity—which attempts to demonstrate how circles might be virtuous, or perhaps deny that there are "circles," properly speaking, at all[19]—foundationalism focuses on regress and attempts to demonstrate that basic beliefs need not allow the regress to continue on *ad infinitum*. Third, and this is particularly important, epistemic foundationalism does not require any criterion of certainty or self-justification. Audi specifically suggests that a basic belief can be "grounded in something else"; all that is necessary for foundationalism to hold, is that this "something else" must not itself be a belief. Further, as Audi claims:

> A foundationalist need not posit any indefeasibly justified beliefs, and moderate foundationalists countenance at most a few such (e.g., beliefs of simple logical truths). Their point is not that other beliefs are *irrelevant:* some might strengthen, others destroy, the justification of foundational beliefs. The point is that the *source* of the justification of foundationally justified beliefs is not other beliefs. (1993, 8)

From this we can stipulate, fourth, that epistemic foundationalism does not require that basic beliefs be indefeasible. In other words, basic beliefs are not, themselves, uncontestable; they are essentially revisable in light of further experiences and evidence.

It is the last two points that raise the distinction between "strong" or "classical" foundationalism and what Audi terms "modest" foundationalism, which "posits only *movable* foundations" (2001, 30). It is clear that some of the main defenders of foundationalism in the history of philosophy have denied these latter claims and suggested that some basic beliefs are certain and indefeasible in some regard. As Alvin Plantinga writes:

> Ancient and medieval foundationalists tended to hold that a proposition is properly basic for a person only if it is either self-evident or evident to the senses: modern foundationalists—Descartes, Locke, Leibniz, and the like—tended to hold that a proposition is properly basic for S only if either self-evident or incorrigible for S. Of course this is a historical generalization and is thus perilous; but perhaps it is worth the risk. And now let us say that a *classical foundationalist* is any one who is either an ancient and medieval or a modern foundationalist. (1998, 135)[20]

Given Audi's clear articulation of "modest" foundationalism, which does not require these "classical" conditions, it is odd that so many philosophers continue to confuse "foundationalism" with "strong foundationalism"—that is, it is a frequent claim that foundationalism, as such, requires certainty and indefeasibility conditions for its basic beliefs. For example, despite the fact that Evan Simpson notes that there are many varieties of foundationalism, he then goes on to say that:

> Any pure foundationalism . . . supposes that genuine grounds for judgment are not merely confident assumptions but absolutely secure bases which are not subject to amendment, or are amendable only in the direction of greater accuracy. Only in this way could they serve as arbiters of rational judgment. This is the notion of a single, overarching, ahistorical standard against which any claim can be tested, so that it is possible in principle to decide between rival points of view. (1987, 2–3)

While it is possible that the term 'pure' here is meant to indicate "strong," Simpson's claim would require that "modest" foundationalism not really be foundationalism. Moreover, notice the way that Simpson's account slides between epistemic and metaphysical foundationalism; many other prominent epistemologists also suggest that incorrigibility and infallibility are necessary requirements for any belief that is to serve as a foundation (e.g., Lehrer 1974; Will 1974). It is only when we attend to these details that it becomes plausible that Otherism could be described as foundationalist, for on the account offered by Simpson it surely could not.

Audi is not alone in contending that foundationalism, as such, is not defeated just because "strong" or "classical" foundationalism is.[21] Audi's "modest" foundationalism bears striking resemblance to the "minimal" foundationalism of William Alston (1989). According to Alston, all that foundationalism in its most minimal and, thereby, most defensible version requires is that "every mediately justified belief stands at the base of a (more or less) multiplying branching tree structure at the tip of each branch of which is an immediately justified belief" (1989, 42). Choosing to speak about "weak, normative justification" rather than "basicality," Alston's account is properly foundationalist, and yet decidedly fallibilist.[22]

Although in the work of Nicholas Wolterstorff and Alvin Plantinga one will find such claims as "on all fronts foundationalism is in bad shape" and "our future theories of theorizing will have to be nonfoundationalist ones" (Wolterstorff 1984, 57), both thinkers offer accounts of justification that are in essential concord with the weak foundationalism offered by Audi and Alston. Despite presenting themselves as nonfoundationalists, both Wolterstorff and Plantinga are rightly termed "foundationalists," at least on a minimal or modest model. What Mark S. McLeod says of Plantinga could also be said of Wolterstorff: "The death of classical foundationalism does not signal the end of all foundational models of justification; Plantinga remains a foundationalist" (1993, 113).

For Plantinga, the notion of "properly basic belief" is central to his claim that Christian belief is rational even though it does not depend upon "evidence"— where "evidence" names a belief.[23] For Plantinga, the problem with "evidentialist" objections to Christian belief is that they assume that a belief is only justified if there is "evidence" for that belief. Plantinga suggests that a Christian belief such as "There is a God" can be justified without "evidence," but, as we will see shortly, this does not mean that the belief is "without grounds." The problem, as Plantinga sees it, is that the evidentialist objection actually depends upon a version of strong foundationalism, and since the claim "There is a God" is neither incorrigible, nor self-evident, nor evident to the senses, it does not count as a belief for which there is evidence. Similarly rejecting the evidentialist requirements for justified belief, Wolterstorff suggests that belief in God can be rational (justified) even if it lacks strong foundationalist status (see Wolterstorff 1983a; 1983b).

Although he will not use the specific terminology, Wolterstorff maintains the distinction between "basic" and "nonbasic" beliefs in his notion of "control beliefs" as distinguished from "data beliefs."[24] Whereas "data beliefs" can be understood as the things that we generally take to be the case—e.g., that I am now typing on my computer, that there is a brown leather chair to my right, and that Washington, D.C. is the capital city of the United States—Wolterstorff defines "control beliefs" as those beliefs that stipulate "what constitutes an acceptable *sort* of theory on the matter under consideration" (1984, 67). So, it is on the basis of one's control beliefs that one is able to count a belief as constituting data; yet it is not the case that we start with control beliefs and then, subsequently, arrive at data beliefs. Wolterstorff defends something that could be accurately compared to Heidegger's "hermeneutic circle." We always find ourselves already taking certain beliefs as data, and it is in coherence with this data that our control beliefs must accord (this is the basis for his rejection of "strong" foundationalism—that is, as control beliefs they exclude too many things as plausible contenders for data), and yet it is only as a result of some control belief regarding what will count as an acceptable theory and, accordingly, of data held internal to that theory, that data beliefs can be affirmed. In a passage which, couched in their respective vocabularies, could have been taken from *Being and Time, Truth and Method,* or *Of Grammatology,* Wolterstorff claims that "in weighing a theory one always brings along the whole complex of one's beliefs. One does not strip away all but those beliefs functioning as data relative to the theory being weighed. On the contrary, one remains cloaked in belief—aware of some strands, unaware of most" (1984, 66–67).

For Wolterstorff and Plantinga alike, certain Christian beliefs legitimately function as foundational: as either "control beliefs" or "properly basic beliefs." However, one might quickly object, as many have, that on such non-evidentialist (understood in a specific way) models of justification, it appears that *anything* could count as properly basic.[25] For example, Plantinga famously asks whether his account of proper basicality would allow a belief in the "Great Pumpkin" to count as "properly" basic. He replies that this objection

> betrays an important misconception. How do we rightly arrive at or develop criteria for meaningfulness, or justified belief, or proper basicality? Where do they come from? Must one have such a criterion before one can sensibly make judgments—positive or negative—about proper basicality? Surely not. Suppose I do not know of a satisfactory substitute for the criteria proposed by classical foundationalism; I am nevertheless entirely within my epistemic rights in holding that certain propositions in certain conditions are not properly basic. (1998, 150)

The method for arriving at a criterion of proper basicality, Plantinga says, is "broadly speaking, inductive" (1998, 150–51). Accordingly, "criteria for proper basicality must be reached from below rather than above; they should not be presented *ex cathedra* but argued to and tested by a relevant set of examples." And he continues: "But there is no reason to assume, in advance, that everyone will agree on the examples. . . . The Christian community is responsible to its set of examples," and not to the examples set by a different community (1998, 151). For Plantinga, a belief is justified for a person as properly basic if "(a) he is violating no epistemic duties and is within his epistemic rights in accepting it [at a given time], and (b) his noetic structure is not defective by virtue of his then accepting it" (1998, 152). Drawing on Chisholm's notion of "being appeared to" in a particular way (treely, greenly, etc.), Plantinga suggests that such experiences count as appropriate "grounds" for belief. These grounds are not beliefs and, therefore, do not violate the foundationalist requirement of stopping the regress of inference. "The central point," Plantinga concludes, "is that a belief is properly basic only in certain conditions; these conditions are, we might say, the ground of its justification and, by extension, the ground of the belief itself. In this sense basic beliefs are not, or are not necessarily, *groundless* beliefs" (1998, 153).[26]

Here we should return to the discussion in chapter 9 regarding the importance of Wittgenstein's account of language games for understanding postmodern Christianity. It might seem that, in light of Plantinga's "Great Pumpkin" objection, both Wittgenstein and Reformed epistemology are committed to a contextualist notion of belief similar to that of the Rorty-Sellars account of "we-intentions." If this were the case, then it would appear that I have done an awful lot of work to distinguish Otherism from Rorty only to bring them back into a comfortable unity (at least regarding the way in which contextualism serves to challenge the possibility of inter-community critique). In reply to such a worry, I want to make two points. First, in chapter 9, while considering passages from Wittgenstein, Vattimo, and Kierkegaard that made it seem as though ethico-religious struggle simply leads to a fideistic relativism, I noted that we should only go so far with them on this front. What matters in my appropriation of Wittgenstein and in Reformed epistemology is the fact that one only affirms certain things as true within particular socio-historical contexts. This is what gave rise to what I termed the historical manifestation of bi-directional relationality as the way in which religion requires the believer to, as Westphal says, affirm the truth that there is Truth.

Second, though the modest foundations articulated by Wolterstorff and Plantinga are not infallible, they are certainly not held "ironically," as Rorty suggests we must do. Accordingly, Rorty's appropriation of Sellars's notion of "we-intentions" serves not only to locate one's beliefs within a community of discourse (with which I have no problem), but to prescribe the way in which such claims must be affirmed. Wolterstorff and Plantinga rightly grant the contextualism of belief-formation and justification, but they also understand the particular religious beliefs that they take as central to their community's identity to be the *best* way of understanding reality (at least among the relevant options available to us), and not just *another* way of understanding it. That one affirms the truth that there is Truth does not mean that one does so with infallible certainty, but it does mean that one must then contest Nietzsche's claim that there is no Truth, only interpretations (and further, contest Vattimo's too-thorough embrace of Nietzsche in this respect), even if such a contestation still requires hermeneutic awareness and self-criticism.[27]

Otherism has quite a bit to offer to epistemology insofar as it articulates the way in which objectivity "happens," as it were, internal to subjective investment. It is here that reading Derrida with an emphasis on the *matter* and not just the *manner* (while recognizing the importance of bringing "how" and "what" together) is so important. For Rorty, as for certain interpreters of Wittgenstein, there are only limits on what one can believe because of the community in which one finds oneself (i.e., because of what language game one finds oneself playing). But for Kierkegaard, Levinas, Derrida, Wolterstorff, and Plantinga, all truth is certainly "relative" in the sense that one can never escape one's historicity and contextuality, but truth is *not* "relative" in the sense that *just anything* could count as true were one's context to change (as Rorty often, and Wittgenstein sometimes, seem to suggest).

Moving on, the final characteristic of this weaker epistemic foundationalism that I want to discuss is more appropriately applied to Plantinga, Wolterstorff, and Alston than it is to Audi. The idea is that "trust" is central to the experiential ground of basic beliefs. Plantinga, Wolterstorff, and Alston (more loosely) are affiliated with the recent, largely North American movement in philosophy of religion known as "Reformed epistemology." The movement receives its name from the connection of its proponents to the tradition of Reformed theology, and in particular, to the work of John Calvin. Though there are many areas where disagreement occurs within Reformed epistemology, one place where all of its proponents converge is the notion that the proper relation to God is one of trust rather than knowledge. That is, the claim that "There is a God," although perhaps properly basic, is not sufficient to express the relationship to God that such a belief is meant to convey. Wolterstorff expresses this centrality of trust when he claims:

> Central to Christianity, Judaism, and Islam alike is the conviction that we as human beings are called to believe in God—to trust in him, to rely on him, to place our confidence in him. To believe in God is our fundamental human obligation. . . . Presumably it is rational for a person to believe *in* God only if it is rational for him to believe various propositions *about* God—in particular, that there is such a being as God. The rationality of trusting someone presupposes the rationality of believing that that person exists. (1983b, 135)

The key here is that the trust in God is not something that excuses the believer from her epistemic duties. If it is irrational to believe that there is a God, then the notion of trusting God is similarly irrational. Hence, the fact that it is the experience of trusting God that might serve as the ground for belief, this trust, though itself not a belief, certainly involves specific beliefs—at least the belief that there is a God who exists in such a way that trusting God is possible. Drawing on the work of Rudolf Bultmann, Wolterstorff describes this trust-relationship as rooted in the New Testament notion of faith:

> The [Greek] term [*pistis*] . . . chosen to refer to what it is that God requires of man in man's relationship to him is a term whose root meaning, in its various grammatical forms in both classical and Hellenistic Greek, is trust (reliance, belief in, confidence). . . . The fact that faith, at its core, is trust in God comes to the fore especially in the great heroes of faith. (1983a, 11)

Crucially, then, Reformed epistemology attends to the fact that the belief that one holds as basic, internal to a Christian tradition / community, is not merely that God exists as an object of speculative knowledge, but as a subject with whom one stands in personal relationship. As we saw in relation to Wittgenstein's understanding of religion, the trust-relationship yields an obligation to obedience. To trust God is to not merely affirm the truth of the belief that "There is a God," but to live one's life in accordance with the obligations that result from such a relationship.

Toward a Modest, yet Deconstructive, Foundationalism

With this account of epistemic foundationalism—in its specifically modest or minimal version—let's now consider how Otherism might operate according to such a theory. Levinas is notoriously difficult to pin down when it comes to the idea of foundations. Diane Perpich and I have argued elsewhere (Simmons and Perpich 2005) that perhaps the best way to make sense of Levinas's notion of the "face of the Other" is as neither foundational nor anti-foundational. Our rationale was that Levinas offers conflicting accounts of how the relation to the Other is meant to be understood. Allow me to quote a passage from Levinas, a passage that we have already considered in relation to political criticism, which explicitly deploys a foundationalist sensibility:

> One can inaugurate the work of criticism only if one can begin with a fixed point. The fixed point cannot be some incontestable truth, a "certain" statement that would always be subject to psychoanalysis; it can only be the absolute status of an interlocutor, a being, and not of a truth about beings. An interlocutor is not affirmed like a truth, but believed. This faith or trust does not designate here a second source of cognition, but is presupposed by every theoretical statement. Faith is not the knowledge of a truth open to doubt or capable of being certain; it is something outside of these modalities, it is the face to face encounter with a hard and substantial interlocutor, who is the origin of himself, already dominating the forces which constitute him and sway him, a you, arising inevitably, solid and noumenal, behind the man known in that bit of absolutely decent skin which is the face, which closes over the nocturnal chaos and opens upon what it can take up and for which it can answer.[28]

Here it seems as though Levinas presents belief in the Other, faith in "a being" and not in some "truth about beings," as *foundational* for his noetic structure—notice the reference to the "absolute status of the interlocutor" and the claim that the face of the Other is "presupposed by every theoretical statement." However, elsewhere Levinas claims that "in the relationship of the one or the other, a rapport is traced that cannot be thought on the grounds of the rationality of a foundation."[29]

In Derrida, there occurs a similar ambiguity. In the texts where he describes justice as "undeconstructible," it seems as though it serves as a foundational presupposition for all other deconstructible claims. Yet Derrida will also directly challenge the idea of foundational perspectives: "For what is put into question is precisely the quest for a rightful beginning, an absolute point of departure, a principal responsibility. The problematic of writing is opened by putting into question the value of *arkhê*" (1982, 6). Accordingly, Derrida will eventually say that "the questioning of foundations is neither foundationalist nor anti-foundationalist" (1992b, 8). Given these ambiguities, I still think there are good reasons to describe the situation as Diane Perpich and I have done (Simmons and Perpich 2005). But while I do not want to ignore those places where Levinas and Derrida resist being identified as foundationalists, I do want to push a bit further and suggest that according to a more modest foundational account, stripped of all requirements of incorrigibility, certainty, self-evidence, and ties to metaphysical and disciplinary foundationalism, it is not incorrect to view Levinas and Derrida in particular, and Otherism in general, as affirming a form of *modest foundationalism*.

First, can Otherism be understood to deploy a distinction between basic and nonbasic beliefs? In a word, yes. The ethico-religious encounter is something that does not rest on other beliefs; in fact, it could be claimed that it *cannot* rest on other beliefs since it is the event that inaugurates subjectivity prior to the very possibility of belief. This is why Derrida's notion of justice is so important as distinguished from Rorty's: what Derrida calls "justice" might rightly be understood as the ethico-religious encounter that inaugurates the constant task of subjectivity to serve the Other. Certainly, then, justice would not itself be a belief; yet it is the "ground" of the basic belief that I am infinitely responsible. Further, this basic belief is the foundation for such non-basic beliefs as "law will never be absolutely just," "hospitality is better than exclusion," "choosing to ignore the Other is not to eliminate the call of the Other."

Now, for someone like Audi, the decidedly "religious" tenor of Otherism (and even of Reformed epistemology) might be viewed as problematic due to the way in which it suggests a transcendent ground (God/the Other) rather than a ground that is recognized as universal by all rational persons. Hence, for Audi, the "paradigms of basic grounds are sensory experience, introspection . . . , memory, and reason" (1993, 14; see also 2001, 16). Although Audi will admit that these might not be the only acceptable grounds, he does seem resistant to the specifically ethico-religious direction of Otherism (remember that Audi requires "secular" reasons for public discourse as well).[30] However, C. Stephen Evans demonstrates how the work of Kierkegaard provides a "fuller phenomenology of the ground of belief in God" by giving a "plausible, non ad hoc explanation of why belief in God lacks the universality of many types of properly basic beliefs, and also why many believers do not see belief in God as properly basic" (1988, 34). The key Kierkegaardian contribution (and something that I find to be shared in various ways and articulated in different vocabularies by Levinas, Derrida, Marion, and others) is the notion that all religious or ethico-religious understanding is "conditioned by what Kierkegaard calls 'inwardness' or 'subjectivity'" (1988, 34). Though Kierkegaard believes that all individuals are constituted as standing before God, not all of them "rest transparently" in this relation. It is, therefore, sensible to claim that there will be grounds available to some that are not available to others precisely because of the different way in which individuals invest themselves. Just because Audi might not recognize the ethico-religious encounter as a legitimate ground for basic beliefs does not mean that it cannot serve as a ground for others.

Second, although Otherism is certainly opposed to strong foundationalism, modest foundationalism does not require anything like incorrigibility or self-evidence. This allows for the possibility of "grounds" that stand behind the belief taken as basic without violating the conditions of foundationalist justification. The belief that "I am infinitely obligated to God and the Other" is one that is "grounded" in the ethico-religious encounter that Levinas terms "exposure" and Kierkegaard terms "transparency." Of course, the actual encounter is not itself a belief, but it nonetheless serves as the grounding condition for the beliefs about the encounter that then receive expression in the ontology of constitutive responsibility. As such, we can plausibly conclude that not only can Otherism be seen to depend upon basic beliefs, but those beliefs themselves are plausible contenders for "properly" basic belief due to their being non-arbitrary, well-grounded beliefs.[31]

Third, Otherism certainly requires revisability regarding the specific way in which basic beliefs are articulated. We might term this the "deconstructive" aspect of Otherism. Simply put, there is no way to end the recurrence of the hermeneutic task—even relative to these beliefs themselves. Now, the important point here, and this is the "foundational" aspect of Otherism, is that it is only on the basis of holding the five tenets of Otherism that one can motivate the constancy of recursive hermeneutics itself. To put this point more politically, Otherism demands constant revolution rather than the potential complacency invited by Rorty's account. This revolutionary gesture is something that is brought about by acting in accordance with the basic beliefs, and yet is what requires that these beliefs not be held infallibly. As Derrida says in *The Other Heading:* "These conditions can only take a negative form (without X there would not be Y). One can be certain only of this negative form. As soon as it is converted into positive certainty . . . one can be sure that one is beginning to be deceived, indeed beginning to deceive the other" (1992c, 80–81).

One might worry that even though this modest, deconstructive foundationalism has eliminated the criteria that accompanied "strong" or "classical" foundationalist accounts (viz., the requirement of infallibility, incorrigibility, and self-evidence), it still seems like it forces a rather perverse reading of such thinkers as Levinas and, especially, Derrida. If there is "nothing outside the text," then how is it possible to say that there is such a thing as a "properly basic belief" or a "well-grounded assumption" or a "control belief" that is not arbitrary? Even Westphal, though favoring the general notion of a deconstructive epistemological project, seems resistant to describing it as a "foundationalism": "Even if some hermeneutical turns are shaper, and thus more radical, than others, we should not lose sight of the common ground that unites the hermeneutical traditions as an alternative to those epistemologies that seek to locate knowledge in some Alpha or Omega point beyond interpretation" (2001, 74). While I take Westphal's claim seriously, and affirm its applicability to Otherism, I resist the idea that deconstructive foundationalism seeks to get "beyond interpretation."[32] Indeed, the very analytic epistemologists that we have considered as representatives of a more plausible foundationalism all resist (to varying degrees) the idea that interpretation stops when it comes to basic beliefs. For example, Wolterstorff displays a deep hermeneutic sensitivity internal to his foundationalism:

> The scholar never fully knows in advance where his line of thought will lead him. For the Christian to undertake scholarship is to undertake a course of action that may lead him into the painful process of revising his actual Christian commitment, sorting through his beliefs, and discarding some from a position where they can any longer function as control. It may, indeed, even lead him to a point where his authentic commitment has undergone change. We are all profoundly *historical* creatures. (1984, 97)[33]

To claim that the structure of justification operative in Otherism is "foundationalist" does not mean that it requires some truth-claim to be unavailable to revision, falsification, and abandonment. All it means is that at the base of all inferential beliefs is a belief that is not similarly inferred. It is to straw man these weaker versions of foundationalism to apply interpretive strictures to them that are really only applicable to strong foundationalist positions.[34]

Finally, Otherism resonates particularly well with the centrality of trust in Reformed epistemology. Levinas's claim above that "the fixed point cannot be some incontestable truth . . . it can only be the absolute status of an interlocutor, a being, and not of a truth about beings. An interlocutor is not affirmed like a truth, but believed," precisely demonstrates this aspect of Otherism. Namely, the face of the Other, or the trace of God, is not available for a third-personal account of objective fact, but only as a first-person gesture of subjective investment.[35] This model allows the Other to be a being that "counts as such." It is precisely because of the alterity of the Other as personal that the ethico-religious encounter is rightly described as "overflowing comprehension."[36] *Trust requires risk and, hence, strong foundationalism is a nonstarter.*

Further, also in accordance with Wolterstorff's conception of trust, Otherism is not simply a set of propositions to be believed, but an account of a relationship which, though involving certain propositional content, demands one's life be devoted to serving the Other. Taking Otherism as deconstructively foundational actually lays stress on the importance of linking trust, belief, and obedience. This is what Levinas conveys when he says that an interlocutor is not to be "affirmed like a truth, but believed." If Levinas really means to say that there is *no* propositional content, *no* "matter" to this "manner," then his claim that "the interlocutor is not to be affirmed . . . but believed" reduces to something no more coherent than "'Twas brillig, and the slithy toves / Did gyre and gimble in the wabe."

Importantly, Levinas never claims that the Other cannot be understood at all; only that the Other cannot be completely and finally understood. That is, the ethico-religious encounter is irreducible to the belief about the encounter—which would eliminate the foundationalist justificative structure by grounding basic beliefs in other beliefs. Nonetheless, this does not mean that the encounter does not stand as the ground of the basic belief *about* the Other. Additionally, it is the irreducibility that not only invites, but requires fallibilism and revisability regarding the way in which basic beliefs about the encounter and all beliefs based on these basic beliefs are articulated.

Given the way that Otherism can be read as resonating with the work of Alston, Audi, Plantinga, and Wolterstorff, we might avoid confusion if we term its distinctive perspective as "post-foundationalist"—as I did previously, in chapter 6. This way of phrasing it maintains the constructive ambiguity that accompanies the very notion of "post-foundationalism" or, for that matter, "post-modernism." That is, the "post-" can certainly be read as "anti-"—in this case, "anti-strong foundationalism"—but it need not be so read. It can also of course be understood as simply "coming after" or "following from," as postmodernism succeeds modernism while continuing to appropriate certain modernist traits and rejecting others, or in this case, as modest or minimal foundationalism follows from or comes after the demise of strong foundationalism, but without eliminating all the defining features of foundationalism as such.[37]

Before moving on, let me consider one final objection. In an interview, Plantinga rejects the idea that one is always in control of what beliefs one has. That is, he resists a strong notion of agency in belief-formation; his exact claim is that often, "you find yourself convinced" (Louthan 1996, 178). Though I have suggested that Otherism is compatible with a foundationalist model of justification, this claim by Plantinga might seem to suggest that instead of *denying* the sufficiency of being "simply persuaded" (Critchley), or simply presenting oneself as persuaded (Ajzenstat), what I have actually done is give a robust account of why this sort of move *is* epistemically legitimate. In a certain sense, I am willing to admit that this is not entirely an incorrect assessment. My worry about Ajzenstat's announcing herself persuaded is not that it suggests some sort of proper basicality that is non-inferentially based in a "well-grounded experience," but that she fails to recognize that something like this is actually going on. Indeed, I find that Ajzenstat and Critchley both depend on some sort of justificative structure (more implicitly Ajzenstat, more explicitly Critchley).

For example, having claimed that she is content to present herself persuaded, just a few pages later Ajzenstat writes that Levinas's critique of political systems is "the first to suggest that responsibility emerges from the disruption of system qua disruption, from difference, from what is uncommon in human beings, from what is unlike me in the other," and claims that "this is what has persuaded me of his ethics; or, to be precise, this is what has persuaded me that it is ethical to adopt his ethics" (2001, 9). Her claim here might be read as an admission that there are reasons, albeit of a particular sort, for being a Levinasian. She comes close to articulating these reasons as being located in the trust one has in the Other, as inaugurated in the face-to-face relationship: "Levinas undercuts the primacy of [political accounts] and offers an alternative: an ethics of each-to-each commenced in the face-to-face" (2001, 9).

Similarly, in *Infinitely Demanding* Critchley frequently replaces the vocabulary of "justification" with that of "commitment," which, I believe, occasionally invites misreading him as a defender of an ethics that stands indifferent to content as long as one invests oneself with vigor. However, to (mis)read Critchley in this way would be to force his thought into the problematic disjunction we considered earlier—either "what" or "how," either "matter" or "manner." A more charitable reading brings him very close to the post-foundationalist epistemology of trust that I have proposed here. Consider the following passage:

> Ethical experience *elicits* the core structure of moral selfhood, what we might think of as the existential matrix of ethics. As such, and this is what really interests me, ethical experience *furnishes an account of* the motivational force to act morally, of that by virtue of which a self *decides to pledge itself* to some conception of the good. My polemical contention is that *without a plausible account* of motivational force, that is, *without a conception of the ethical subject, moral reflection is reduced to the empty manipulation of the standard justificatory frameworks: deontology, utilitarianism and virtue ethics.* (Critchley 2007, 9; emphasis added)

What Critchley presents the reader with, here, is precisely something like the need for a justified account of moral and political life that would be sufficient for overcoming the "motivational deficit" that plagues contemporary liberalism. Notice that Critchley turns to "ethical experience" to supply such an account—i.e., to the encounter with the Other that I have claimed yields the properly basic belief that "I am infinitely obligated to the Other."

My concern is more precisely with the rhetoric of Ajzenstat and Critchley than with the philosophical accounts they offer. If their rhetoric of being "simply persuaded" is taken to reflect an arbitrary starting point which is as good as any other and which can only compete for an audience by preaching to the choir or engaging in the play of force by seeing all others as objects to be converted, then so much the worse for their philosophy (and for Levinas's, if they are right about him). But I do not think, at the end of the day, that this is what either of them intends. If it were, there would be no distinction between Levinasian ethics and Rortian ethics, and the latter, if justificatively equivalent to Levinas, might be viewed as a more plausible descriptive account of how things work in the messy world of political interests. In order to close down this possibility, those who attempt to defend a Levinasian perspective should avoid giving the indication that they have no reason for adopting this perspective.

If I am right that Otherism can be articulated according to a post-foundationalist epistemology of trust, then justification is not simply a matter of force, but of investment; not simply about political self-interest, but about Other-service; not merely a matter of private edification, but of public life. Whereas Otherism is compatible with this modest foundationalist account, Rorty's position is not. His rejection of foundationalism, as Haack demonstrated, is directed at not only metaphysical foundationalism and disciplinary foundationalism, but also at epistemic foundationalism. Because he is so quick to reduce epistemology to a deflationary hermeneutics, rather than seeing, as Westphal suggests, that hermeneutics actually functions as a kind of robust, though modest, epistemology, Rorty undercuts his own philosophical praxis. The irony, if that is indeed the word here, is that this makes Rorty's thought more akin to the private irony he attributes to Derrida and Levinas than to the public liberalism he admires in Rawls. In the end, admitting of a possible justificative framework according to which Otherism can be distinguished from Rorty's perspective allows for Otherism to be politically viable in a way that Rorty's account simply is not: *by erasing epistemology, Rorty ends up with a bad politics.*[38]

Now, I grant that even in its most modest or minimal form, foundationalism has numerous detractors within contemporary epistemology. Similarly, Reformed epistemology is not without its critics.[39] In no way to do I mean to suggest that we should ignore such objections. Indeed, it may be that Otherism faces the same sorts of obstacles and criticisms that continue to plague defenders of these weaker models of foundationalism. However, I see it as a step forward for Continental philosophers to become more engaged in issues such as those that surround contemporary foundationalism. It may turn out that there is another conception of justi-fication which would fit Otherism better than the modest foundational perspective I have suggested here; but without continued work in this area, such a possibility will remain unexplored.

As I suggested in the introduction to this book, being content to converse only with those who are already on board is problematic for ethical and political rea-sons. However, I would also contend, in line with my conclusions regarding the centrality of trust to Otherism, that if Otherism is right, then epistemology is it-self primarily an ethico-religious endeavor. As Butler rightly observes, giving an account of oneself depends on the recognition that one's interlocutor lays a claim upon the self—a claim that demands justification for one's actions and one's be-liefs (and perhaps for one's very existence). By opening the door to epistemological conversation across philosophical traditions, we are in a better position to illustrate the ethico-religious dimension of epistemology itself. Perhaps resonate with vir-tue epistemology on this front, Otherism is in a position to add decisively to the contemporary debates in this regard.

Conclusion: From Trust to Hope—Epistemology and Eschatological Politics

In an interview, Rorty summarizes his work at the intersection of episte-mology and political philosophy as follows: "I argued that if you have hope, it didn't really matter whether you believe that Christ was the son of God, or that there are universal human rights. The essential thing is to dream of a better world. Hope doesn't require justification, cognitive status, foundations, or anything else" (Rorty, Nystrom, and Puckett 2002, 58). Although I have challenged Rorty's per-spective throughout this chapter, I do not want to ignore places in his thought that could possibly serve as resources for Otherism.[40] One such place is his idea of "so-cial hope." While I certainly don't understand this idea to be simply a prolifera-tion of "we-intentions" in such a way that one's political life merely reflects the status quo of the "postmodern bourgeois liberalism" that characterizes Western democracy, I do think that there is something right about his claim that at the end of the day, it is a shared hope that motivates what Stephen Minister (2008) terms "works of justice."

When brought together with the modest-foundationalist beliefs of Otherism and the lives of invested service that should accompany them, Rorty's notion of social hope might be productively recast as an "eschatological" vision of a better tomorrow. Crucially, this vision is not something that can be achieved as a "liberal utopia," but instead serves to constantly call forth what Levinas will call an "ever-increasing justice." As Derrida writes:

The responsibility of what remains to be decided or done (in actuality) cannot consist in following, applying, or carrying out a norm or rule. Wherever I have at my disposal a determinable rule, I know what must be done, and as soon as such knowledge dictates the law, action follows knowledge as a calculable consequence: one *knows* what path to take, one no longer hesitates. The decision then no longer decides anything but is made in advance and is thus in advance annulled. It is simply deployed, without delay, presently, with the automatism attributed to machines. There is no longer any place for justice or responsibility (whether juridical, political, or ethical). (2005, 84–85)

Precisely because of the resistance to epistemology understood as metaphysical foundationalism or disciplinary foundationalism, Derrida is able to demand this ongoing and unfinished role of ethical decision—there is no rule that can objectively be found and infallibly followed. And Derrida is justified in affirming that such decision is constantly required, given the possible embrace of an epistemic foundationalism, modestly understood and with trust at the center, that I have suggested in this chapter. Ethico-political decision rests between trust and hope—*we trust* in the relation to the Other/God as the inaugural event that calls forth justice; *we hope* that we will have the fortitude to cultivate the solidarity required to live today toward an (un)expected tomorrow.

Once we recognize that bi-directional responsibility is the constitutive aspect of human existence, all of us, I believe, must live *between trust and hope.* Trusting the Other/God, we hope for a better tomorrow. This hope, however, should not be named simply a "liberal utopia," but is instead the expectation of a tomorrow in which an ethico-religious encounter actively defines the lives of all inhabitants of the global community. Appropriately grounded social hope does not contend that the "we-intentions" that define "our" community will now define all other communities, but that "our" community is defined by an extended hand of invitation, hospitality, and gratitude. Of course, trusting is always a risky gesture—but it is a risk that is *justifiably* worth taking. As we saw in our discussion of Ricœur's post-Hegelian Kantianism in chapter 5, living between trust and hope will require that we be theologically sensitive and philosophically rigorous; by bringing Otherism into conversation with contemporary epistemology, I believe we move toward being both.

Intersections and Applications

TWELVE

The Ethical: Expansive Relationality— Levinas, Community, and Climate Change

The relation to the Other has been primarily conceived in this book, as in the majority of the writings of Continental ethicists, as a relation to the other *person*. And yet, in a time of various environmental crises—deforestation, desertification, rampant extinction, unparalleled cases of industrial pollution, etc.—associated with generalized climate change, it is no longer adequate to consider moral (and even political) philosophy as something that concerns humans alone. For an ethical theory to be defensible, today, it must be able to speak to the reality of human obligations to non-humans. I consider this to be one of the spaces where Kierkegaard's and Levinas's concern for critically engaging the "present age" serves as an example we should follow in our own day. While Kierkegaard was worried about the loss of passion in nineteenth-century Demark and Levinas was concerned by the complacency and self-interest in twentieth-century Europe, we should be committed to challenging narrowly exclusivist notions of ethical and political relationships in a rapidly globalizing twenty-first-century society. Just because most of Otherism has been directed toward inter-*human* relationships and I have tended to characterize bi-directional relationality as a tension between God and other *people,* there is no reason things *must* be limited in this way. Therefore, in this chapter, I will still affirm a bi-directional model, but will expand the relationality that it rests upon and implies beyond merely human concerns. I will contend that Otherism, particularly as formulated by Levinas, provides profound resources for environmental philosophy and public policy. And accordingly, we will be able to see how the ontology of constitutive responsibility makes room not only for obligation to human others, but to non-human others as well.

Climate Change as a Meta-ethical Emergency

Although there is a vast history of *political* emergency situations, examples of such emergencies in ethical *theory* are far less common. Relevant here is Michael Walzer's notion of a "supreme emergency," which he develops in *Just and Unjust Wars* (1977, chap. 16). Walzer appropriates the phrase from Winston Churchill's account of Britain's situation in 1939. Walzer suggests that Churchill *implicitly* offers the following argument: "there is a fear beyond the ordinary fearfulness . . . of war, and a danger to which that fear corresponds, and . . . this fear and danger may well require exactly those measures that the war convention bars" (1977, 251). According to Walzer, there are a couple of requirements for supreme emergencies—"the first has to do with the imminence of the danger and the second with its nature" (1977, 251). These criteria are necessary conditions: (1) the danger must be very close and (2) radically, if not unprecedentedly, serious.[1] Walzer goes on to consider whether a situation that meets these criteria might lead us to override other moral intuitions and conventions, such as those that prohibit intentional attacks on civilians and noncombatants in the course of war. The specifics of his reflections are not important to my concerns here, but the structure of his basic framework is crucial. His question is not only one of *praxis* (e.g., when is it legitimate to do X or Y?) but of *theory* (i.e., when is it legitimate to affirm a new conception of legitimacy?). Walzer invites us to consider the possibility of a situation in which we must revise our commitment to a particular moral theory because it is inadequate to the demands of the situation in which one finds oneself.[2]

In the context of human-caused climate change and the ethical challenge that it presents, I contend that Walzer's conception of an ethical emergency situation has only gained in relevance; and as I will indicate, some of the most prominent theoretical contenders in contemporary environmental ethics are not able to countenance and adequately motivate a workable solution to this moral challenge.

In this chapter, I argue that for anyone who affirms that human-caused climate change is the overriding moral concern of our time, it serves to inaugurate a meta-ethical emergency situation.[3] I contend that this situation can most successfully be addressed if we pay particular attention to the unique relationship between temporality and ethics that climate change requires. That is, the moral considerations and particular obligations in light of human-caused climate change only exist as long as it continues to be something that can be affected by human action—I will term this *the challenge of limited time* and suggest that it stands in the place of Walzer's requirement of "imminent" danger. In light of this temporal concern, I contend that we should be willing to allow for the possibility that an anthropocentric approach to environmental ethics (once suitably formulated) might indeed be the most promising way forward for addressing the ethical challenges of human-caused climate change—I will term this *the challenge of anthropocentric requirements*.

I will defend the challenge of anthropocentric requirements by arguing that the challenge of limited time encourages a decidedly anthropocentric approach to environmental ethics that allows for a *hierarchy of ethico-political significance*. By allowing humans to be valued higher than non-humans, we will be able to respond, perhaps a bit more adequately, to human-caused climate change; but in light of the challenges faced by certain anthropocentric conceptions, I believe that a new anthropocentric model is called for. Allowing for the complex network of social and temporal relationships that results from considering humans and non-humans as part of the same "ethico-political community,"[4] I will draw upon the ontology of constitutive responsibility, especially as formulated by Levinas, and propose a *relational model of anthropocentrism*.

I will suggest that Levinas's philosophy provides important ways of reconciling responsibilities to presently existing individuals with obligations to future generations; and further, it offers an innovative notion of non-human value that opens important spaces for expanding the limits of our community. The specific way that this expansion should be worked out, in light of Levinas, is that non-human others are valuable only by virtue of the existence of the ethical relation between humans, but their value is not articulated in terms of human interests—i.e., *though it is not intrinsic, it is nevertheless non-instrumental*. This conception is inherently hierarchical and, in this sense, anthropocentric. Due to the anthropocentric perspective of this Levinasian vision, we are able to affirm a philosophically consistent and politically viable notion of human and non-human sociality in a context where climate change continues (or has only begun) to be an ethico-political challenge.

I will proceed as follows. First, I will begin by demonstrating how human-caused climate change meets the requirements of an emergency situation as set out by Walzer. This section will crucially illuminate two key obstacles that face moral theory in light of environmental crises. Second, I will demonstrate how non-anthropocentrism—and in particular, environmental egalitarianism—fails to overcome these obstacles. Third, I will outline those areas in Levinas's philosophy that I take to be critical resources for thinking through the notion of climate change as a meta-ethical emergency and articulating an adequate theoretical response to it. This section will show how Levinas's interrelated notions of diachronic temporality and heteronymous ethical subjectivity can provide the framework in which a relational model of anthropocentrism can be articulated. Finally, I will demonstrate that this model successfully overcomes the obstacles highlighted in the second section, raise and respond to possible objections, and conclude with a few suggestions for how Otherism also serves as an important guard against defeatism and resignation in political life.

Before proceeding, one prefatory clarification should be made: some might contend that my argument in what follows is an example of environmental pragmatism and, as such, faces similar problems and objections as does that approach (see Light and Katz 1996a). While I certainly think that a focus on transforming human practice should be an important goal of contemporary environmental philosophy—understood as an applied ethical concern rather than a *merely* speculative enterprise—and *to that extent* I am willing to be counted as a "metaphilosophical environmental pragmatist" (Light 1996a; 1996b), I am hesitant to *fully embrace* the "pragmatist" moniker for two reasons. First, I am decidedly *not* advocating pluralism and "tolerance" in light of human-caused climate change, but propose a particular moral theory that I find to be well suited to deal with its unique temporal challenge. Precisely because of the meta-ethical emergency that climate change represents, I do not think that we should continue to act as if certain moral theories are still viable options. Second, though I of course agree with the goal of "finding workable solutions to environmental problems now," I want to resist the idea that the real danger to progress is "theoretical delays" (Light and Katz 1996b, 4). Of course, Light and Katz might reply that the problem is not with theory per se, but with "delays" in action. In that case, I would contend that the encouragement of moral pluralism actually invites such delays, while my suggestion that we should (temporarily) adopt the relational model in order to effectively act in response to climate change eliminates delay while maintaining theoretical rigor and consistency.

Accordingly, I want to differentiate between *environmental pragmatism* and what I will call *philosophical activism*. While pragmatism raises the concerns I mention above, activism simply requires that our moral theory be politically viable. That is, in the context of a meta-ethical emergency, there is no time to advocate theories that do not have a good enough chance of motivating a reasonable public response to the crisis. If I am right that Otherism is able to successfully offer a model for environmental ethics that is likely to transform human action in light of climate change, then it becomes clear that Continental ethics (as expressed in new phenomenology) is able to meet the challenge of application that I laid out in the introduction to the book.

With that said, my argument runs as follows:

- Human-caused climate change is real.
- If human-caused climate change is real, then for any x, if x is a plausible moral theory, then it is not the case that x falls prey to the epistemic and ethico-political problems.
- So, for any x if x is a plausible moral theory, then x does not fall prey to the epistemic and ethico-political problems.
- Additionally, for any x if x is a plausible moral theory, then x is either non-anthropocentric or anthropocentric.
- But, for any x if x is non-anthropocentric, then x falls prey to both the epistemic and ethico-political problems.
- Hence, for any x if x is a plausible moral theory, then it is not the case that x is non-anthropocentric.

- Accordingly, for any x if x is a plausible moral theory, then x is anthropocentric.
- But, for any x if x is a plausible moral theory and x is anthropocentric, then it is not the case that x falls prey to political extremism.
- Yet, there exists an x such that x is anthropocentric and x falls prey to political extremism.
- It then follows that there exists an x such that x is anthropocentric and x is not a plausible moral theory.
- I then ask, does there exist an x such that x is a plausible moral theory?
- Well, for any x, if x is the relational model of anthropocentrism, then x is anthropocentric and it is not the case that x falls prey to political extremism.
- Thus, I conclude that given human-caused climate change, there exists an x such that x is a plausible moral theory—namely, the relational model of anthropocentrism.[5]

Serious and Imminent: The Challenge of Limited Time

I am not a climate scientist. Hence, when it comes to the science of climate change, I trust the experts. It is unnecessary to weigh in here on whether there is a "consensus" or exactly what a "scientific consensus" would require (see Romm 2008); there is a *general trend* within the scientific community that informs the following claims:

(1) Human-caused climate change is real and poses, at least potentially, unprecedentedly catastrophic threats to our future.
(2) The degree of severity of the consequences of human-caused climate change increases over time.
(3) Minimizing the consequences of human-caused climate change requires substantial, immediate action.
(4) There is a time coming (a tipping point) when the consequences of climate change will become both severe and unstoppable.

If these claims are accepted, *then* taken together, they present a challenge to contemporary moral and political philosophy. We have thus met the twofold condition that Walzer sets for something counting as a "supreme emergency." According to (1), we have satisfied the criterion of the threat's unprecedented severity; according to (3)–(4), we have satisfied the criterion of the threat's imminence. Importantly, the notion of "imminent" in this context is different than in the case of Germany's expansion in the late 1930s and early 1940s. The temporal component of climate change is *not* found in the closeness of its *consequences,* but in our proximity to the point at which our ethical responsibility in light of it terminates—i.e., the tipping point is close at hand and if it occurs then our responsibility to address climate change evaporates. Simply put, the ethical obligation to work to stop climate change is only a temporary obligation; it has an expiration date. Even though there is substantial debate in the scientific community regarding exactly when the tipping point will be reached, the *exact* timeline is less important than the fact that *there is* such a timeline.[6]

Let me give the claim that human-caused climate change counts as a meta-ethical emergency a bit more determinate shape by considering the way it contrasts with other situations that might seem to contend for such a designation. For example, what about the obligation to care for one's ailing grandmother? In this case, we do meet the imminent requirement because once she dies, the obligation to care for her will have passed (in a similar way as the obligation to address climate change will have passed once we reach the tipping point). However, though the death of my grandmother is a serious matter for my family, say, this situation fails to meet the necessary scope for eventual consequences—as Walzer will say, "supreme emergencies" only apply to the potential death of a community itself. This is not merely a calculation of quantitative impact, but also of qualitative severity. Human-caused climate change threatens not only countless numbers of individual humans and non-human organisms, numerous species and entire ecosystems with extinction, but may also, arguably, require a substantial rethinking of what we even understand existential fulfillment and individual flourishing to mean in a radically transformed ecosphere.

As a second possibility, consider the very plausible obligation to work toward the eradication of nuclear weapons. It seems that if we were able to eliminate all nuclear weapons and put in place international structures that ensured they would never be produced again, then we would have both a serious threat and also a similarly limited time frame, as in the case of human-caused climate change. Wouldn't that meet the sort of standards that I have articulated relative to meta-ethical emergencies? Here we have indeed met the requirement of severity—a post-nuclear-war world would certainly yield the sorts of quantitative and qualitative consequences that are required by the unprecedented scope-condition for emergencies. However, while it is true that our obligation to eliminate nuclear weapons only exists as long as there are such weapons, it does not follow that the end of such obligation is temporally pressing (the imminence-condition). It could be that we continue to have weapons and, accordingly, continue to work to get rid of them for decades and centuries to come. So, while there would be a limited duration to the obligation, it is not at all clear that the end of this particular obligation is close at hand. Moreover, the relation of our action to this situation is exactly the opposite of what it is in the case of human-caused climate change. With climate change, the tipping point and, subsequently, the severe consequences occur *if we do nothing*. Alternatively, with nuclear armaments, doing nothing only continues to leave their grave *potential* of destruction as a possibility. It is certainly plausible to believe that the world could continue to have stockpiles of weapons and never make use of them. Thus, though there are situations in which the mere potential for nuclear cataclysm could turn into an imminent threat—the Cuban Missile Crisis or Chernobyl, say—this example fails relative to the necessary requirement of imminence.

Since I am assuming (1) to (4), above, because of my trust in the current scientific evidence and prevailing interpretations of that evidence, I can claim that human-caused climate change is real, threatens unprecedented types of collective destruction, and presents an imminent challenge to moral life. Moreover, as long as we assume that ought implies can (at least to some extent) then it is trivial to say that there is only an obligation to address human-caused climate change while it is addressable—i.e., only as long as what James Hansen terms an "alternative scenario" remains a possibility (see note 9, above). So, we should add the following:

(5) I am only obligated if I can do something to address the obligation (at least partially).[7]

(6) I could only be obligated by the event of human-caused climate change prior to our reaching the tipping point.

From (5) to (6) we can conclude that human-caused climate change does seem to yield the challenge of limited time. But what reasons do we have for affirming that this would lead one to advocate the relational model of anthropocentrism— if only for a limited time?

Well, in order to view (1) to (4) as yielding moral consequences, we need to add:

(7) Human-caused climate change is not just an overriding social problem but an overriding ethical one; moreover, though this is contestable, it is not unreasonable to claim that it is the most pressing moral issue of the contemporary world.

We can introduce (7) without any problem because my argument is not that climate change *does* present us with specific obligations, but that *if* we grant the immediate obligation of it, *then* certain things follow. If one is committed to the need for ethical theory—i.e., one is not a moral particularist, say (e.g., see Hooker and Little 2001; Dancy 2006)—then it becomes ridiculous to affirm that human-caused climate change is the most pressing moral concern of one's existential situation while denying that we should affirm the moral theory best able to account for it. So, we can also introduce:

(8)   Given (7), we should affirm that ethical theory which is best able to account for the specific moral problems raised by human-caused climate change.

Of course, it could be the case that there is an ethical theory that best addresses this situation (let's call it X), but raises other significant ethical problems in the process. In that case, we would not be morally required to affirm X because in the totality of ethical considerations it fails to be a legitimate contender even though it is appropriate for the specific challenges of climate change. So, we should revise (8) to now read:

(8*) We should affirm that ethical theory which is best able to account for the specific moral problems raised by human-caused climate change, unless there is reason to believe that this theory would yield unacceptable moral consequences in other areas to the extent that it no longer remains the most sensible overall ethical theory for the totality of one's moral context.

Following from (7) and (8*), we must now ask what ethical theory we should adopt. Since I am unable, here, to consider all of the contenders in contemporary environmental ethics, let me simply present what I take to be the two overriding obstacles that any ethical theory has to overcome if it is to be a contender in light of climate change.

First, there is what I will term an *epistemic problem:* if a moral theory fails to close off the possibility that working to address human caused climate change is not ethically required, then it is not a reasonable contender. Second, there is an *ethico-political problem:* if a theory fails to provide good reason to motivate behaviors that are required to address climate change, then it too fails as a promising way forward. Because of the challenge of limited time (as expressed in (1) to (6)), we cannot advocate anything like an ethical perfectionism: we must act to address human-caused climate change and we have a limited time to do so; hence, we must be pragmatically aware and politically sensitive. In meta-ethical emergencies, political viability affects ethical theory in a way that might not be operative in other times. With this in mind, I assert that *in our contemporary global context, non-anthropocentric approaches to environmental ethics are nonstarters because they fail to overcome the ethico-political problem.* Non-anthropocentrism requires global citizens to hold views that it is highly unlikely that they will adopt any time soon. In general, the global political situation is not yet at the place where the fate of a particular species of bear or beetle is popularly viewed as even in the same league as the fate of a single human being.

Martin Schönfeld gives voice to this situation. "Even if we grant that animals deserve moral consideration," he notes, "environmental policy, for better or worse, will operate with a nonegalitarian, hierarchical approach. Egalitarian approaches, by which animals and humans are equal right-holders generate problems in legislation and do not work in policy" (2008, 51). Andrew Light makes a similar claim:

> Environmental philosophy evolved out of a concern about the state of the growing environmental crisis and a conviction that a philosophical contribution could be made to the resolution of this crisis. If environmental philosophers spend most of their time debating non-human-centered forms of value theory, they will arguably never be able to make such a contribution. (2002, 428)

Now, I do not think that we should grant the absolutism that Light conveys— viz., that non-anthropocentrism will "never be able to make" a contribution to political life. For this reason, I encourage us to hear Schönfeld's claim that non-anthropocentric approaches "do not work in policy" as a historically contingent descriptive claim, not an absolutely normative one. Perhaps eventually political realities will have changed enough for non-anthropocentrism to be plausible; until then, philosophical activism should cause us to recognize a "motivational deficit"[8] in non-anthropocentrism when it is deployed in our contemporary political context.

Given this situation, then, should we fully endorse anthropocentrism? Not exactly. We should recognize that certain anthropocentric approaches are themselves extremely troubling when considered in light of the ethico-political problem. As Ned Hettinger points out,

> although anthropocentric values are of crucial importance in environmental policy, I believe it is dangerous to limit our defense of nature to arguments based on its usefulness to us. This is especially true if what one wants to defend is a wild, autonomous nature. Humans often find technologically enhanced and controlled nature of most use to them. (2008, 122)

In other words, though anthropocentrism might motivate political action, the action it motivates may be too morally problematic and thereby fail to overcome the required qualification added in (8*). Going a bit further, it could be said that anthropocentric ethics fails to close down a potential speciesist political extremism. Holmes Rolston expresses this concern as follows: "There is something subjective, something philosophically naïve, and even something hazardous in a time of ecological crisis, about living in a reference frame where one species takes itself as absolute and values everything else in nature relative to its potential to produce value for itself" (2008, 119). Rolston here cautions that if, in our terminology, anthropocentrism overcomes the ethico-political problem but fails to overcome the epistemic problem, then we have not gained much.

In addition to worries regarding political extremism, Rolston also suggests that anthropocentrism is too narrow ethically: "There is something overspecialized about an ethic, held by the dominant class of *Homo sapiens,* that regards the welfare of only one of several million species as an object and beneficiary of duty" (1992, 135). With Rolston, I want to suggest that if anthropocentrism as such commits us to such a perspective, we should be wary of adopting it. However, these worries, which are certainly appropriate critiques of some kinds of anthropocentric ethics, need not be seen to apply to *all* anthropocentric accounts. One can hold the relational model, I will suggest, while consistently rejecting the notion that humans are the *"only one* of several million species" that are worthy of consideration. We should appreciate that Rolston's charge of ethical narrowness challenges any latent arrogance in our theorizing. However, my argument in what follows is meant to demonstrate that we need not abandon anthropocentric approaches to maintain such a caution regarding arrogance. Part of why I find Otherism to be so helpful in environmental thinking is because it locates epistemic and ethical humility as a key component of our relations to others, be they human or not.

Before moving on to offer a model of anthropocentrism that it is both epistemically and politically viable, I want to spend a bit more time laying out why non-anthropocentrism seems to be untenable in light of climate change. In the next section, then, I will consider a particular characteristic of some non-anthropocentric models—viz., those endorsing egalitarianism—and show how such notions fail to successfully respond to the epistemic problem.

The Epistemic Problem with Environmental Egalitarianism

I want to make clear at the outset that I do not intend to wade very deeply into the technical scholarship regarding various types of environmental ethical theory. In what follows, I will be stipulatively defining my terms in order to reflect what I take to be general trends in environmental philosophy; however, many of the terms (especially internal to the distinction between individualism and holism) are slippery within the literature, so being entirely precise is difficult.

The non-anthropocentric environmental ethical theories that I find inadequate to the epistemic problem are those that agree on the equality of moral status for human and non-human inhabitants of the earth. We could better refer to these theories as "strict egalitarianism," since egalitarianism as such need not hold that all beings have the same status in a restricted sense—e.g., that they all have the *same* rights. Rather, egalitarianism really only needs to be committed to the notion that they all count for moral consideration according to an accepted metric. So while the pain of a dog is morally considerable, it need not be identically morally considerable to the pain of a human child. However, since I take all non-anthropocentrism to fail in relation to the ethico-political problem, in what follows I will use "egalitarianism" to refer to "strict egalitarianism." As an example of this stricter notion of egalitarianism, consider Paul Taylor's account of biocentrism. Taylor contrasts biocentric views with anthropocentric views by claiming that:

> According to the latter, human actions affecting the natural environment and its nonhuman inhabitants are right (or wrong) by either of two criteria: they have consequences which are favorable (or unfavorable) to human well-being, or they are consistent (or inconsistent) with the system of norms that protect and implement human rights. From this human-centered standpoint it is to humans and only to humans that all duties are ultimately owed . . . We have no obligation to promote or protect the good of nonhuman living things, independently of this contingent fact. (1981, 139; see also Taylor 1986)

For Taylor, anthropocentricism introduces a conception of "human superiority" which should be stringently rejected. "Rejecting the notion of human superiority," he continues, "entails its positive counterpart: the doctrine of species impartiality. One who accepts that doctrine regards all living things as possessing inherent worth—the *same* inherent worth, since no one species has been shown to be either 'higher' or 'lower' than any other" (1981, 152).[9] However, even within the egalitarian schema, there are substantially different versions for working out the specifics.

One area, in particular, where there are differences of opinion within non-anthropocentric accounts concerns the limitation of moral considerability to "living things." In contrast to *bio*centrism, just discussed, we find *eco*centrism, which can affirm egalitarianism in such a way as to focus on the wellbeing of the ecological whole rather than just the *living* organisms within it. While ecocentrism deploys an inherently holistic value theory, biocentrism can be conceived as either being individualistic (i.e., holding that the unit of moral concern is the individual organism), or, at least to some extent, as being holistic (i.e., holding that the unit of moral concern is larger than the individual; it might be located at the level of species, say).

As an example of how the distinction between individualism and holism yields significant consequences internal to egalitarianism, consider the notion of eradicating invasive species from a particular ecosystem. For the ecocentrist, such eradication is not a problem since it fosters the overall health of the whole. The same might be said for the biocentric holist, insofar as she could claim that such eradication promotes the continued thriving of the other species in the particular ecosystem. However, because of egalitarian commitments, it is not clear that such a claim holds up. Namely, why is it that the value of the native species trumps the value of the invasive species? For the biocentric individualist, the problems are even more obvious: how are we to legitimate trading off the lives of *these* individuals for the lives of *those*? On this front, the biocentric species-holist does seem to have more resources at her disposal. Consider, for instance, the familiar situation in which wolves or deer, as a species, are best sustained in a given region when the packs or herds are occasionally thinned out. For the species-holist, the killing of individual wolves or deer, here, would not be morally problematic, so long as it serves to promote the wellbeing of the species as a whole; for the individualist, however, the same option is not available.

Following from these considerations, ecocentric holism initially might seem to be the strongest contender for the best way to relate to the overall flourishing of the global environment itself. A concern for the *environment* is clearly something different than a concern for *lions,* say. The problem with anything less than ecocentrism, one might argue, is that being obligated to care for one thing (or group of things—e.g., the majestic Redwood forests of North America) need not entail being obligated to care for anything else. Continuing on, to decide in favor of any single organism is not to be *entirely* environmentally concerned, but instead to be only *partially* environmentally concerned. Such a partial concern would appear to be powerless to close off the danger of sliding from an otherwise sensible biocentricism, say, to a mosquito-centric or fish-centric position. However, notice that though ecocentrism can initially seem to be quite egalitarian, it can also end up being quite un-egalitarian. And this might be viewed as the overall problem with holism in general: namely, it treats individuals as minimally being replaceable and perhaps even contemptible (when they get in the way of the flourishing of the whole). It is from this general perspective that there arises the specter of "eco-fascism," which has become a bugbear for both environmental philosophy and also for conservative interpretations of environmentalism as a political movement. With this problem in mind, I will argue that even a robust ecocentric holism (e.g., as found in deep ecology) is unable to overcome the epistemic problem in light of climate change (i.e., it fails to motivate workable solutions) precisely because it is unable to close off such extremist possibilities.

Further, judging what is best for the whole depends upon a conception of what the "good" for the whole would be; but there could be many different accounts of what "good" should mean here. For example, ecocentrism could affirm that a good action is one that contributes to the *harmony* of the ecological community, or it could be one that allows for the *persistence* of that community, or one that increases the *complexity* of the community, or one that expands the *diversity* of its constituents, etc. Any answers to questions of how to proceed relative to an egalitarian theory are going to assume a particular account of what the ecosphere or biosphere *should* look like; but there are many alternative accounts of how to understand this "should."[10] This becomes especially troubling in light of climate change.

Even if we allow global temperature increases to go unchecked such that the earth becomes a radically different place, we would still have an ecosphere and biosphere of one form or fashion. As such, egalitarianism seems to face problems explaining why a post-climate change earth is *worse* than the one that we have now. In response, one might contend that the relevant criterion, here, is functionality: if a post-climate change world would be less habitable for the living entities therein, then we are morally obligated to attempt to prevent it from coming about. Moreover, to be consistent with egalitarianism, one could argue whatever the ecosphere or biosphere looks like, our moral obligation is to care for it as best we can. Thus, one's obligation is to care for the ecosphere or biosphere as it *currently* exists; i.e., we are not obligated to care about what might or might not exist at some point in the future. However, the problem with such replies becomes clear when we consider situations that egalitarianism seems unable to give sufficient reasons to avoid. For example, it could be argued that although climate change might greatly threaten many non-human species, it could also potentially reduce the human population to numbers that are more beneficial for the long-term thriving of these other species (as we considered earlier, regarding wolves and deer), and especially beneficial for the functionality of the ecosphere as a whole.[11] In this respect, given the potentially problematic growth of the human population, it might be better to allow climate change to go unchecked. But this would be a disastrous conclusion for any ethical model that desires to transform human behavior in political contexts. In other words, the general strains of misanthropic environmentalism are extreme cases of the incapacity to address the ethico-political problem.

Not only does non-anthropocentric environmental egalitarianism potentially *fail to motivate* ethical reasons to work to address climate change, we have seen how, in its extreme forms, it could even potentially be deployed as *a reason for advocating* climate change and encouraging some of the most severe consequences (viz., substantially reduced human population) in the name of the ecocentric or biocentric "good" itself. Thus, on an egalitarian model of non-anthropocentrism, one is not required to affirm (7), which stated:

> Human-caused climate change is not just an overriding social problem but an overriding ethical one; moreover, though this is contest-

able, it is not unreasonable to claim that it is the most pressing moral issue of the contemporary world.

Even more troubling, it looks like the environmental egalitarian could even be inconsistent in affirming this claim.

In light of the preceding arguments, I therefore suggest that we view non-anthropocentrism, in general, as incapable of coherently motivating transformed behavior and sustainable public policies. *Thus, non-anthropocentrism fails with respect to the ethico-political problem.* Further, I propose that egalitarianism, in particular, is unable to motivate ethical norms that would be required for considering human-caused climate change as something that should be addressed in the first place. *Thus, non-anthropocentric environmental egalitarianism fails with respect to the epistemic problem.*

From Bi-directional Responsibility to a Relational Model of Anthropocentrism

Holmes Rolston claims that "the challenge of environmental ethics is a principled attempt to redefine the boundaries of ethical obligation" (1992, 135). In this section, I will draw upon Levinas as a resource for constructing an environmental ethical theory that redefines such boundaries while remaining epistemically and politically viable.[12] Importantly, this Levinasian anthropocentric model also successfully avoids the problems of political extremism and ethical narrowness that are faced by some anthropocentric accounts. I will refer to this account as a "relational model of anthropocentrism" because I consider it to be an expansion of the core idea of bi-directional relationality.

The following are the definitive claims that I propose for the relational model of anthropocentrism:

(A) All living organisms (and even some non-living, but metaphorically expansive communities of living organisms—e.g., ecosystems) are either *intrinsically* valuable or *non-instrumentally* valuable by virtue of the existence of intrinsically valuable beings.

(B) All humans are intrinsically valuable, and no non-human is intrinsically valuable.

(C) There is a hierarchy regarding the ethico-political status of all the valuable organisms.

(D) At the top of the hierarchy are human beings.[13]

(E) This hierarchy is contextually situated in a complex network of relationships between organisms.

(F) This network is spatially and temporally constituted. That is,

Intersections and Applications

future and past generations of humans and non-humans are valuable.

(G) The justification for (C) and (D) is not simply based on the intrinsic value of humans, but also because humans are ontologically constituted as not only being *responsive to,* but also *responsible for* this complex socio-temporal network of relationships.

(H) There is no immediate preference given to the presently existing generation (or subsequent generations in close proximity to the present), but there might be occasions that require such preference.

With these basic commitments in place, we can see that, as stated above in (A), (E), and (F), there is what we might call an "expansive relationality," both ontologically and temporally, at the heart of the relational model. This model does not give exclusive consideration to humans as morally considerable, and moreover, it does not give immediate priority to presently existing generations—though it allows that such priority might be granted in specific cases. Now, the relationship between temporality and obligation is notoriously complex.[14] In Otherism, one finds a possible conception of how time and ethics are always already implicated in one another. Recall from the last chapter that the fourth tenet of Otherism is:

> The ethico-religious encounter with the Other/God is not something that occurs within chronological time, but instead in the "immemorial past" (Levinas) or "the moment" (Kierkegaard).

The ethical (or ethico-religious) relation is, thus, not one that proceeds according to a *chronological* progression. Obligation does not operate with reference to the time tracked by clocks. In other words, there was not a first instant of obligation that could be marked on one's calendar. Instead, ethical time is described by Levinas as a "diachrony."

The obligation to the Other arises from an "encounter" with the Other, but this encounter did not occur yesterday or the day before yesterday, but in a "past that was never present." What Levinas realizes is that if ethics is really going to be "first philosophy," there could be no "moment" prior to the ethico-religious encounter because then ethics would still cede the day (literally) to traditional ontology rather than opening the space for an ontology of constitutive responsibility that maintains the reality of diachrony. Levinas suggests that the "time of ethics" (or "time of the Other") and the "time of being" (or "time of the Same") are not identical (see TI, 56–58). Simply put, ethics is not an *"arche"* (beginning) of the progression of being, but instead is "an-archic" in that it both challenges the ease with which we deploy notions of "firstness" and contests the structure that we take to be operative in our speculative endeavors and our political projects. Ethics arises "in a time without beginning" (OTB, 51). So how does such an an-archic event signify in the space/time of ontological description? Levinas introduces the notion of the "lapse" as a way of representing that which resists representation (OTB, 51). In the context of the relational model of anthropocentrism, this "lapse" or lack of simultaneity between myself and the Other provides substantial philosophical resources for thinking our responsibility to those others who have gone before and those others who are not yet. On the one hand, according to the ontology of constitutive responsibility, my responsibility *precedes* my status as a free being: I am already obligated "before" I arrive on the scene, as it were. On the other hand, and extending in the opposite direction, the relational model does not immediately privilege the interests of the present generation: my responsibility extends far beyond my own lifetime to those who are literally "to come." Thus, diachronic temporality should be recognized as an asset in dealing with questions regarding obligations to future generations.

Otherism understands obligation to be something that does not arise from a discrete instant, but that troubles *all* instants. This perspective allows us to begin to take valuable steps toward expanding our conception of how to negotiate the complicated issue of being responsible *now* for something that has a *limited duration* in which the obligation occurs, and yet is something that has *extremely distant* impacts on persons with whom I will never share *a present time.* Now, by definition human-caused climate change brings geological time to bear on our moral calendar, as it were, but in so doing it requires an alternative conception of how to understand the relationship of obligation and temporality from the outset. According to Otherism and the relational model of anthropocentrism that I am constructing in light of it, there is always a recognition of the lapse of temporal adequation between oneself and the object of one's moral concern. The ontology of constitutive responsibility fractures the commonplace notion that we have a greater obligation to those with whom we share the present. Receiving impetus from the notion of diachrony, the relational model is able to countenance such an imperative and, thereby, provides a way to move forward today toward a better tomorrow.

Although Levinas begins to address the question of time and ethics early in his authorship, in *Totality and Infinity* his attempt to work out the notion of the "time of the Other" receives a particular shape relative to a conception of subjectivity. As I discussed in chapter 4, the metaphors deployed throughout this text are ones of interruption, contestation, and challenge. His overall narrative in *Totality and Infinity* is one of a self going along untroubled until the Other shows up and ruptures the security of self-sufficiency: "We name this calling into question of my spontaneity by the presence of the Other ethics" (TI, 43). The problem with such an account, as Levinas quickly realizes, is that ethics is still seemingly secondary to the ontological constitution of subjectivity. Subjectivity does not name responsibility from the first, but responsibility attempts to countenance the failure of subjectivity to proceed unchecked. And moreover, how is the encounter with the Other even possible if this Other is *absolutely other (L'absolument Autre)* (TI, 39)?

Levinas's answers to these difficult questions are worked out throughout the rest of his life, but of particular note is the way in which he shifts, in *Otherwise Than Being*, from a narrative of interruption to one of original dispossession. His metaphors describing the ethical encounter in the later work and the subjectivity that results are ones of constitutive trauma. Consider this passage from early in *Otherwise Than Being:*

> Vulnerability, exposure to outrage, to wounding, passivity more passive than all patience, passivity of the accusative form, trauma of accusation suffered by a hostage to the point of persecution, implicating the identity of the hostage who substitutes himself for the others: all this is the self, a defecting or defeat of the ego's identity. And this, pushed to the limits, is sensibility, sensibility as the subjectivity of the subject. It is a substitution for another, one is the place of another, expiation. (OTB, 15)

Here we see the extreme stakes of a responsibility that precedes freedom and, as such, "goes beyond being" (OTB, 15). But, how does one speak about that which is beyond the space of discourse? How are we to *be* if we *are* "beyond essence"? Put in slightly less abstract terms, we might ask the quite sensible question to which Rorty continues to draw our attention: how is one supposed to *live* the ethics that Levinas describes?

With this question, we must again take seriously the transition from the realm of *ethics,* or what I have suggested we understand as *ethico-religious* (the relation to an incomparably and incalculably singular Other) to that of *politics* (justice; the relation to multiple others in which we must engage in comparison and calculation). Crucially, for Levinas and for most of those working in new phenomenology, it appears that within the ethical relation the Other is always a *human* other. The problem with this, of course, is that it seems that non-human others are relegated to a strictly derivative status and, if considered at all, can only be considered as instrumentally rather than intrinsically valuable. However, I want to contend that a *derivative status need not entail instrumentalism.* With the move from ethics to politics, there is room for expanding our relational context to potentially include non-human others as valuable internal to an *ethico-political community* in ways that do not narrowly articulate their value according to human interests (as do most other anthropocentric theories).

According to Otherism, my moral worth is not a product of my ontological standing, but arises from an original obligation: I am "me" only in the response to the call of God and the Other. One possible way of understanding this notion is that we are always already in the context of an *ethico-religious* relation (I am always already *with* or be-for(e) God and the Other); that is, there is only individuality in the context of a prior sociality. Sociality is not merely one possible mode for self-hood, but the name of the very condition of selfhood. If we begin with a social-ity that is always prior to individuality (i.e., I am always "too late" to catch up to the Other; God has always already "passed by"), then we arrive at new ways for re-thinking the intrinsic value of humans as always *contextual,* and here "contextual" should be heard in its etymological sense of being "woven together."

What *heteronomy* means for Levinas is that when it comes to moral standing, there are not individual threads that are then brought together, but the weaving is always prior to that which is woven. For Levinas, something is only "of itself" in the space of engagement with others. Obligation is the very space in which social standing is possible. "Glorious humility, responsibility, and sacrifice," Levinas says, are the very "condition for equality itself" (TI, 64). Notice that Levinas stringently resists any conception of instrumentality here: the Other is not morally valuable because of some sort of utility relative to my interests. Equality and rationality are not the basis for moral sentiment, but instead the responsibility to the Other is the backdrop against which we are all able to stand as equals who are called to the practice of reason-giving. It is the radical asymmetry of ethico-religious soci-ality (the relation to God and the Other) that makes possible theories of equality and reciprocal responsibility in political society (the relation to other others). As Levinas will note, "the other is from the first the brother of all the other men. The neighbor that obsesses me is already a face, both comparable and incomparable, a unique face and in relationship with faces, which are visible in the concern for jus-tice" (OTB, 158). It is in this second, political, relation that there is, I believe, room for environmental concern.

For Levinas, the ethical status of a non-human is a result of the responsibility that is inaugurated in relation to the human face. Accordingly, only humans are "intrinsically valuable," we might say, since human value does not require the exis-tence or non-existence of any other non-human being (though it does presuppose the contextuality of ethico-religious sociality). However, merely given the fact that it is the human face that potentially opens the face of the dog, for example, it is by no means clear that the dog's face (or the face of the tree, spider, or swamp) will *not* signify ethically as well. All that seems clear is that whatever ethical status a non-human other has, it has because of the primary intrinsic value of the human face. We might say, then, that Levinas leaves room for non-human others to have "secondary" ethical status. I do not believe that such a description would necessarily be in error, but I have chosen not to refer to the situation in these terms because I find too many problems to accompany the notion of *secondary ethical value*. For example, Levinas often indicates that the face of the (human) Other signifies as infinitely valuable "of itself." If we take this infinite, and we might say immediate, value as the key characteristic of the ethical (or ethico-religious) relation, then it seems difficult to speak of a "secondary" ethical relation at all. In other words, if something is an other *ethically*, then it looks as if that other is always immediately Other *without reference* to anything else. But we have already stipulated that non-human others can only be others by virtue of the intrinsic value of the human face.

On the one hand, it looks to be more correct to simply say that something either has ethical status or it does not; but on the other hand, there are clearly places in Levinas's authorship that indicate something like a notion of secondary worth. For example, when recounting a story from his time in the prison camps during World War II, Levinas notes that a dog "Bobby," who greeted the downtrodden prisoners as they walked out to the fields to work, was "the last Kantian in Nazi Germany" (DF, 153). By referring to this dog as a "Kantian," Levinas indicates the way in which the dog saw the faces of these men in a way that their captors did not. And in light of this passage, it seems hard to conclude that Levinas is unwilling to recognize *any* value in the dog's face. In an attempt to accommodate those passages in Levinas's authorship where non-humans are apparently recognized as others (of some sort), while not having to contest the necessity of "immediacy" for ethical standing, I think we need to deploy a different terminology than "secondary" ethical worth. To that end, I propose that we simply speak about non-humans as having *ethico-political* value.[15] Though it is likely that Levinas would choose to term this as merely "political value," I resist this way of phrasing things because I want to maintain the important relation/tension between ethics, politics, and religion that I have been arguing for as the hallmark of Otherism throughout this book. That is, I have moved away from merely *ethical* or *religious* domains and instead argued for the *ethico-religious* as the best descriptor for the original relation by which selfhood is constituted (hence bi-directional responsibility). However, as I have argued, the ethico-religious relation only signifies as situated and implicated in political life (hence the ethico-religious task of political existence itself). Accordingly, I propose that we refer to an "ethico-political community," which stands in constant tension with "ethico-religious sociality," as the space in which calculation and adjudication occurs as required by existential decision.

Although Levinas resists an *equality* of ethical and political standing between Bobby and his fellow prisoners/neighbors walking beside him, it seems that Levinas opens the door for an expansive conception of value that nevertheless includes Bobby as part of the ethico-political community where responsibility signifies as an existential task and in which we are all, whether human or non-human, *woven together*.[16] I contend that when it comes to problems such as environmental degradation, it is not essential to finally determine whether non-humans are part of our community as "ethical" or "ethico-religious" others. As part of the ethico-political community, even if Bobby is not worthy of *ethico-religious* consideration, he can still be worthy of *ethico-political* concern.

Though claims of other humans still carry a special weight, this recognition is not problematic because we can easily admit of primary and secondary value according to the hierarchies that function internal to our ethico-political decision-making processes (which is a distinction we could not maintain internal to the asymmetrical ethico-religious relation, as such). While the ethico-religious relation might require that *all* others signify *absolutely and infinitely*, the ethico-political allows for others (both human and non-human) to signify in finite circumstances and always *in relation to each other*—this is what ethico-political calculation as an ethico-religious requirement is all about.

We can now return to the issue of instrumentalism. Importantly, I maintain that according to Otherism, animals, trees, mountain ranges, local ecosystems, etc., need not have intrinsic ethico-religious value in order to still be considered non-instrumentally—i.e., according to what flourishing would mean for them independent of human interests, though still in relation to the ethico-political community that includes humans as well.[17] This is the upshot of the notion of original ethico-religious sociality when it is brought to bear on political life (and, as a reminder, it is only internal to the ethico-political sphere that this prior relation can signify as such). The good of the Other is not considered in terms of some larger category—rationality, say. Levinas's re-articulation of humanism as a "humanism of the Other" is precisely an expression of this point. Concern for the Other must be articulated in terms of the flourishing *for the Other* and not in terms of what counts as flourishing *for me* even though the Other's flourishing must, in the ethico-political sphere, be considered in relation to the existence of all other others. As Levinas writes in "Is Ontology Fundamental?" in 1951, the Other "is a being and counts as such" (BPW, 6). The Other does not count according to my interests or my categories. The inclusion of non-human ethico-political others, who all "count" according to their own terms and not merely derivatively of my good or the good of my species, serves as a constant challenge to the arrogance of automatically deciding in favor of one's own (or one's species') desires. The flourishing of both human and non-human others occurs in the context of an ethico-political community that includes us all.

Let me conclude this section by summarizing the important ways in which the relational model of anthropocentrism is able to provide the basis for an adequate theoretical response to human-caused climate change. First, due to the way in which diachrony opens new avenues for thinking about intergenerational justice (expressed as (F) and (H) above) we are able to account for the potential victims of climate change as morally considerable, here and now. Second, according to the constructive rethinking of non-human value provided by the notion of heteronymous subjectivity coupled with an extrapolative reading of the move from ethics to politics, now understood as a move from the ethico-religious to the ethico-political, we are now presented with a way of viewing non-human others as neither valuable only due to their relation to human projects nor because of an isolated ontological standing. Instead, their contextual location in a shared world is such that they also politically call to me as valuable on their own terms (articulated in (A) and (E)). Third, the qualified hierarchy recognized by Levinas—that is, it only operates internal to an expansive context of relationality—makes room for an ethico-political community that contests any claims to human interests as automatic "trump cards," as it were (see (C), (D), and (E)). Rather than being ethically narrow, as Rolston contends anthropocentrism to be, the epistemic humility and ethical hospitality of Otherism infuses the relational model with an Other-directedness rather than a self-concerned egoism or speciesism (see (F) and (G)).

It may seem that while this sort of argument serves as a propaedeutic to a Levinasian or Otherist environmental ethics, it fails to go so far as offering one. So I should note that in light of the increasing data about climate change there have been proposed responses to the problem that range from deep and immediate transformation of our daily lives and public policies, to slowing down and gathering more information, to throwing up our hands and praying that technological breakthroughs and the market economy will work out a solution. Although I am convinced that there are reasons to view particular strategies as more viable than others in light of the relational model of anthropocentrism that I am proposing, my concern in this chapter is not which *political policy* we should advocate to address human-caused climate change, but instead what *ethical theory* is the most sensible to affirm in light of the challenge of limited time such that questions of effective policy could then be considered. Importantly, insofar as Otherism encourages a critique of ontology in the name of justice, it invites us to reconsider the relation between theory and practice. Hence, rather than just a speculative exercise, my project here should turn out to be a crucial part of moving forward toward a better future for all organisms. That said, this theoretical work is the first step in articulating an applied solution and not merely a precondition for such a solution.

The Relational Model of Anthropocentrism as a Promising Way Forward

I will now consider whether the relational model successfully overcomes the *epistemic* and the *ethico-political* obstacles that arise in light of the meta-ethical emergency of human-caused climate change. In order to see if it can respond to the epistemic problem, we should now ask whether it is able to affirm (7) without arriving at an inconsistency; immediately, we can see that it can. For example, drawing on the work of contemporary social scientists, it is increasingly clear that within human society human-caused climate change will affect the global poor most significantly.[18] Within (D) and (E) we have resources for allowing poverty to factor into our considerations. Moreover, although there are signs of climate change's impact already being felt across the globe by both humans and non-humans, many of the most substantive effects will be faced by distant future generations (though some serious effects might be felt much sooner). Hence, a workable theory should be able to account for this temporal delay. Since (E) is not temporally indexed and (H) denies a *prima facie* priority to the concerns of present generations, the relational model of anthropocentrism is well suited to address the long-term ethical obligations that human-caused climate change demands we consider. Hence, unlike environmental egalitarianism, the relational model can indeed affirm (7) without any inconsistencies arising with its other commitments.

It remains to be shown that the relational model of anthropocentrism is equally successful regarding the ethico-political problem. When faced with the motivational deficit of non-anthropocentric approaches generally, the way in which the relational model builds upon hierarchical norms that are more common among the global populace enables it to gain the traction required to affect political will and public policy in a way that non-anthropocentric approaches simply do not. The same is the case regarding problematic notions of anthropocentric ethics. Here we should return to the concerns about anthropocentrism raised by Hettinger and Rolston that were considered above at the end of the second section. Does the relational model successfully overcome the objections that (a) anthropocentrism yields a morally problematic notion of political action and (b) anthropocentrism invites a speciesist political extremism?

First, notice that Hettinger (who is not alone in this) fails to adequately differentiate between anthropocentricism and instrumentalism. As I have argued, the relational model is not an instrumentalist approach; rather, it is a theory that affirms the non-instrumental value of non-human organisms, but then positions those organisms in a hierarchical relation to human value. Internal to the relational model, there is no species egoism, but only species preference in the context of an extremely complex network of relationships (both spatial and temporal). As such, Hettinger's worry, while valid for many rival accounts of anthropocentric ethics, is not valid regarding the relational model.[19] Second, in response to Rolston's worry about political extremism, I simply want to deepen my reply to Hettinger. The relational model is always already situated inside a network of relationships such that failing to be concerned about non-human others would fail to be properly ethico-politically concerned in the first place. It is certainly true, though, that due to this complex relational network, the relational model must not be limited to the sphere of individual human action, but actually requires a serious rethinking of such wide-reaching and interrelated domains as economics, politics, domestic norms, legal theory, consumption, consumerism, etc. For example, the relational model is not meant to close down questioning into the meaning and stakes of "sustainability," but instead serves as a theoretical framework in which we might reconsider these stakes in the first place.

Accordingly, it allows for everything that we require while simultaneously avoiding the problems faced by non-anthropocentric models as well as the excesses of some anthropocentric conceptions in which non-human interests and the interests of future generations fail to signify.

We can, thus, conclude that

(9)   The relational model of anthropocentrism is a sensible ethical theory to affirm, at least temporarily, given the overriding moral obligations arising from human-caused climate change.

Now, this conclusion must be situated in the context of climate change understood as a meta-ethical emergency situation. It is because of the challenge of limited time (which inaugurates the state of emergency) that the *activist* concerns such as political motivation, transformed public policy, and plausible speed of effective implementation, continue to press.

Conclusion: A Fragile Hope

The distinction between the ethico-religious and the ethico-political invites complicated questions. Simply put, since there is a host of other persons, I have to judge between my obligation to all of them: Whom will I choose to care for? It is here that choosing to feed domesticated animals or livestock while there are starving humans presents a problem; but alternatively, choosing to feed humans and ignoring the animals in human care or in the wild is also problematic in its own way. Despite the fact that serious questions remain, by drawing upon Levinas's allowance for *a hierarchy which recognizes the non-instrumental value of non-human others,* we have been able to articulate a conception of environmental ethics that countenances human uniqueness as well as the constitutive interconnected-ness of an ethico-political community that is composed of more than just human members.[20]

Importantly, though, for Levinas,

> justice remains justice only, in a society where there is no distinction between those close and those far off, but in which there also remains the impossibility of passing by the closest. The equality of all is borne by my inequality, the surplus of my duties over my rights. The forget-ting of self moves justice. (OTB, 159)

We can see that the engine of a politics concerned about "an ever-increasing jus-tice" is the humble recognition of a seemingly overwhelming task. While it is cer-tain that I will not, nor could I ever, succeed in fulfilling the demands made upon me by the host of living others, this does not mean that I abandon hope and give in to quietism or resignation. What Otherism makes clear is that *while I might al-ways be guilty, I am never defeated.* The necessity of finitely accepting an infinite ob-ligation allows for the present to be defined by an open-ended relation to the fu-ture (see Simmons 2010). It is for this reason that Levinas opens *Totality and Infinity* with a discussion of "eschatology," Ricœur encourages us to think freedom in "the light of hope," and Derrida articulates the democracy "to come" according to the structure of "messianism." Given the political realities of human existence, ethics is never a *telos* to be finally achieved but a future to be constantly expected. I exist in the time of expectation—this is how we stand, here and now, in the lapse. Yet this expectation is not a passive awaiting of the future (i.e., "come what may . . .") but an active engagement with the world in the name of social justice (i.e., "take my hand; what can I / we do?"). When politics is no longer about me / us and my / our interests (as it necessarily is for Rorty), then we begin to move ever closer to jus-tice *for all* and *for each*. Our sphere of influence and our context of engagement are larger than our moral imagination might attest. It is here that we can see that there should be no confusion between, on the one hand, the meta-ethical emergency of human-caused climate change and the specifically Levinasian way forward that I suggest, and on the other hand, the conceptions of sovereignty and hegemonic power that are too often found in contemporary political discourse.

The relational model of anthropocentrism stands as an invitation to inhabit the world otherwise—not *simply* anthropocentrically and not *simply* non-anthro-pocentrically.[21] It does not operate in the name of my / our interests, but from a commitment to others, whether human or not. Accordingly, while it is hier-archical, the relational model refuses to recognize the false dichotomy of humans / non-humans as if they were in a zero-sum game of supremacy. An Otherist ap-proach to anthropocentrism ruptures the ease with which our political task is conceived and the limits by which it is constrained, and further, it opens spaces for a continued hope for progress. When faced with the seemingly impossible task of correcting the disastrous trends of global greenhouse gas emissions, it is easy to become defeated and resign oneself to the inevitability of failure—this is perhaps one of the most troubling motivational problems faced by current environmental thought. However, the distinction between the infinity of the ethico-religious and the finitude of the ethico-political allows us to continue to work for a better tomorrow—or as Levinas will say, "an ever-increasing justice"—without being cowed by the magnitude of the task before us. Though we continue to hope for a future in which the direst consequences of human-caused climate change will have been averted, the expansive relationality that is operative at the heart of Otherism reminds us that our task is best expressed as being faithful to God while working for justice for both human and non-human others. When we reorient ourselves in this way, success becomes more likely precisely because we are not defeated by the likelihood of failure: we continue to press on, here and now, toward the eschatological vision of justice.

THIRTEEN

The Ethico-political: Following Postmodern Exemplars

On the Importance of Existential Traction

In his influential text *Ethics After Babel*, Jeffrey Stout says of the frequently abstract discourse of "ethical reflection" that "abstractions all count for nothing if they are not brought down from the tower, back to earth" (1988, 8). In the last few chapters, I have attempted to show how it is that the ethico-religious thought of new phenomenology, when read against the backdrop of an ontology of constitutive responsibility as articulated by Kierkegaard and Levinas, is able to come "back to earth," as it were. I have suggested that a deconstructive vision that maintains the tension between the bi-directional responsibility to God and to the Other (now understood expansively to make room for relations to non-human others as well) and that recognizes the important distinction between the infinite demand of the ethico-religious and the necessary calculation of the ethico-political, is politically efficacious due to its sustainable notions of critique (as linked to the idea of *kenosis*) and justification (drawing on "modest foundationalist" theories which allow for the centrality of trust). Additionally, I argued that this general new phenomenological perspective yields illuminative new directions for debates concerning religion in the public square and even offers insights for dealing with the problem of climate change. Moreover, we have seen how Continental philosophy of religion also makes room for a decidedly postmodern conception of Christianity.

The argument could still be made, however, that I face a similar problem as the person mentioned by Wittgenstein in the *Philosophical Investigations* who could not remember what the word "pain" meant and so "constantly called different things by that name" (2001, §271). One could suggest that it is only because there is a certain degree of consistency in the usage of our terms and the meanings of our conceptions that our private thoughts gain traction in the social world. Accordingly, one might worry that what I mean by "efficacy"—whether ethical, religious, political, or philosophical—is not what is meant by a person in the midst of everyday life who asks for guidance in addressing particular problems. Granting that philosophical terminology often stretches the bounds of common vernacular, it might seem plausible to try and evade this objection by protesting that one is guilty of merely an *academic* offense resulting from semantic complexity. However, I think that such a strategy misses the substance of this possible objection: namely, discussions of ethics and politics should have at least some relevance to what goes under the heading of *ethics* and *politics* in our shared social discourse and engagements. Moreover, evading such an objection serves to eliminate the possible gains to be made by taking it seriously and developing a direct response to it.

I have argued that much of the efficacy of the ontology of constitutive responsibility derives from its decidedly *critical* function, which I have suggested is found both in the task of recursive hermeneutics and also in the notion of *kenosis*. Certainly, criticism has a crucial role to play in political life. Socrates and Marx are examples of how philosophy's political task can be for the most part *negative*. Socrates' challenge to the Athenian senate was that their corruption prevented them from pursuing justice; Marx's notion of ideological criticism was intended to oppose the far-too-apparent legitimacy of the dominant political order. Regarding this notion of critique, some commentators have even suggested that Kierkegaard's politics have a certain Marxist tendency.[1] Therefore, if the objection that my notion of "efficacy" is detached from the historical and material conditions of human existence is to stick, it must be about something other than the way I illuminate the critical task as central to political life.

With this said, I take it that the actual site of contention is that whereas Marx supplemented his criticism with a positive account of a just society, it appears that Kierkegaard, Levinas, and other distinguished voices in Continental philosophy of religion simply leave us with a recognition of the failures of our political institutions, but without any clear sense of what better ones would look like. It could be claimed that for a philosophy to be "politically efficacious," say, it should offer an account of *effective* politics and not simply show how the political itself, of necessity, fails to be adequately just (and the same could be said for ethics, religion, etc.). As Jim Wallis writes: "saying no is good, but having an alternative is better" (2005, 45).

Although I have demonstrated how Kierkegaard, Levinas, Derrida, Vattimo, and others offer resources for quite substantially responding to the charge of political irrelevance leveled by Richard Rorty, in this concluding chapter I want to go still a bit further in this direction and sketch a possible positive alternative regarding what ethical, political, or religious "guidance" might look like after the "theological turn." Having shown how maintaining the tension between God *and* the Other calls for constant diligence and engagement, I will now consider whether it can offer anything other than a problematically utopian vision for the future of social life. What would it mean to give some content to the democracy to-come such that we might be able to live toward the future here and now? Is such an attempt even possible? I believe that it is and, by drawing on Edith Wyschogrod's

(1990; see also 2006)[2] notion of "postmodern saints" (which I have alluded to earlier) and Susan Wolf's (1982) critique of "moral saints," I will suggest that such positive content is not to be found in an abstract principle or moral code, but in the lives of people who embody the tension between the ethico-religious and the ethico-political. After considering the problems that can arise when this tension is forgotten, I will briefly summarize the positions of Wyschogrod and Wolf before discussing several individuals whom I consider to be ethico-political exemplars.[3] The first few, Dietrich Bonhoeffer and Corrie and Betsie Ten Boom, are offered as historical examples. But in order to demonstrate that Rorty is right to consider literary texts as productive sites for expanding one's moral imagination, I will suggest that ethico-political exemplars can also be found in literature and film. Thus, although Oskar Schindler was of course a historical person, the last exemplar I will focus on is the *character* of Schindler as presented in the film *Schindler's List* (Spielberg 1993).

From Protests to Alternatives: Mark Dooley as a Case Study in Continental Politics

Although the attention paid to the political relevance of recent Continental philosophy of religion has been on the rise over the past decade, much of this literature fails to go beyond *a challenge to* traditional moral and political philosophy and actually attempt to think through the complicated questions of how *to move forward* differently—especially after the "theological turn."[4] Though there are notable exceptions, much of the literature in this area does not do much to assuage Rorty's worry of ethical (and we might say political) formalism. As I suggested in chapter 1, this should trouble us precisely because of the key commitments involved in Otherism— namely, obligation is what constitutes the self in the first place.

Within the Kierkegaardian literature that occurs in light of deconstruction, Mark Dooley's *The Politics of Exodus* (2001a) stands out as one of the most sustained treatments of the possible political relevance of Kierkegaard's thought. Dooley claims that by arguing in favor "of both Kierkegaard and Derrida as thinkers whose scrupulous attention to the needs of singularity does not stop them from holding a concrete political philosophy," he is able to "show how Kierkegaard's insights can have practical political utility" (2001a, xxiv). However, the account of how one moves from Kierkegaard's philosophy to such "practical political utility" meets with substantial difficulties.

For example, consider Dooley's considerations of the notions of gift, hospitality, and forgiveness that are prominent in the final pages of his text. As I have argued in previous chapters, these conceptions are crucial for working out the political upshots of Otherism. To this extent, then, Dooley does a service to the literature by giving extended consideration to these ideas in the context of working out a Kierkegaardian political theory. Despite these beneficial dimensions of Dooley's account and his important (and quite correct) contention that these ideas are politically viable, he stops short when it comes to the difficult questions of application. Now, no one text can do everything and answer all possible questions in a given area. That said, I do not want to simply critique Dooley's project in that book, but rather to point out that unless Dooley's account is supplemented by an account of, for example, how we are to forgive *absolutely* and yet continue to live with the scars and memories of past atrocities, how to *actualize* the gift without erasing its significance, and how *to be infinitely hospitable* and yet deal with the problems of immigration, threats to national security, and economic and educational challenges that such hospitality would create, we have to cede too much to Rorty's claim that Continental ethics are of *no real use* in the messy business of political existence. Even if Dooley were to claim that the "to-come" structure of deconstruction contests his ability to address such specifics (and in this, I believe, fall prey to the temptation I have discussed regarding the claim that *nothing* can be labeled "just"), he does not adequately consider whether it would then be "just" to advocate the to-come structure itself.

It is here that I find Dooley's resistance to Levinas to be especially troubling. By linking Kierkegaard to Derrida without Levinas serving as a sort of mediator between them, Dooley downplays, I believe, the important ontological stakes of ethics and politics. Or to be more Levinasian about it, Dooley does not seem to recognize the ethico-religious stakes of all ontology. Fearing what he takes to be the "religious" aspects of Levinas's thought, Dooley actually, whether intentionally or not, aligns himself with Rorty in denying Levinas's political relevance due to the "religious" abstraction introduced by the notion of absolute alterity, and so on. To illustrate this alignment, let me again quote the following passage from Dooley:

> For a pragmatist, Levinas's Judaically charged ethics is at best idealistic. This is so because pragmatists in the mode of Rorty believe that ethics ought to take the form of concrete responses to pressing dilemmas. In suggesting that "the word of God speaks through the glory of the face and calls for an ethical conversion or reversal of our nature," Levinas, on a pragmatist reading, is simply indulging in hyperbolic rhetoric. Ethics demands practical projects which aim at relieving unjustifiable misery and suffering, and this is achieved through a manipulation of sentiment in which we come to see strange people as fellow-sufferers. (Dooley 2001b, 36–37)

While I applaud Dooley's "pragmatic" concern for political efficacy, I think that his resistance to the "religious" dimensions in Levinas serves to downplay the possibility of retooling a viable Kierkegaardian model of political theory. In the end, I am unable to see how his own Derridean reading of Kierkegaard demonstrates the latter's viability relative to "practical projects which aim at relieving unjustifiable misery and suffering." I would suggest that Dooley would be better served to draw upon the very sorts of "religious" gestures he has suggested we need to abandon, and then show how they can be made applicable to the complicated issues of existential reality (which is what I have tried to do in this book). Without such a move, one might propose that the choice to turn to Kierkegaard (whose work, I would argue, is substantially more dependent on God-talk than is Levinas's) as a viable voice in contemporary political discourse seems odd indeed. Consider the final paragraph of *The Politics of Exodus*:

> Kierkegaard's notion of a community of neighbors, one founded on self-sacrificing love, challenges the inhospitable "perfect community" (*communio*) in which individuals, in loving the other, seek only their own. The former is a community in which universality gives way to the requirements of singularity, and one in which justice, compassion, and mercy keep the law from becoming unremitting and cruel. It is, to appropriate the words of Caputo once again, "constituted by bonds that do not bind up and constrain, by links of love that do not constrain, by the spontaneities of love, by which, over and above accusation, which puts me in the accusative of obligation, the least of God's children is the object of my love."[5] In such a community, "the law articulates with difficulty," but "love speaks the word plainly."[6] For Kierkegaard, Derrida, and Caputo, the "infinite renunciation" which is *Gelassenheit* is the way "to love and trust and seek justice, to seek the kingdom, which is here and now, which is for the lame and the leper, the outcast and the sinner, the widow and the orphan."[7] Such indeed amounts to a politics of exodus, a politics of conviction and responsibility in the name of those whose only aspiration is for a room, no matter how modest, at the inn. (2001a, 246)

There is certainly much in the above passage with which I agree—the emphasis on invitation, the notion that seeking justice must be done here and now, and the insistence on perpetual openness to contestation. Hence, I again want to stress that we should not miss the importance of Dooley's reading of Kierkegaard. Yet when it comes to how his reading of Kierkegaard is able to avoid the idealism and decidedly religious aspects that he found so problematic in Levinas and, thus, stands as relevant to "practical projects" in a way that might assuage the pragmatic worries Dooley notes, I remain at a loss. In this way, I take Dooley's book to illustrate the speculative detachment that can far too often vitiate Continental considerations of ethics and politics.[8] Dooley's last sentence calls for a "politics of exodus," a "politics of conviction and responsibility," and urges that these be conducted in the name of "those whose only aspiration is for a room, no matter how modest, at the inn." Surely this is a noble goal, but its nobility is circumscribed by the political realities in which such aspirations occur. Moreover, even the language of aspiration, by itself, is difficult to reconcile with the more than tens of thousands of children who die daily of malnutrition, starvation, and unsanitary living conditions. It would seem that debilitating poverty would demand more than a mere "room at the inn," or if we read "the inn" to be a metaphor for the material needs of existing humans, this still neglects the fact that there are complicated decisions about distribution and, at least theoretically, sheer limits on the available resources. So, while it may be true that a dollar a day can feed a starving child, any given dollar will only feed one and leave many others still starving. Further, unless there *is* that dollar, just the fact that it *could* feed the child does not put food in her mouth. While I am deeply appreciative of Dooley's worries about the lack of political traction in Levinas, which is a concern that I have considered and attempted to respond to in this book, I also worry that this critique is applicable not only to his own account of a Kierkegaardian-Derridean alternative, but to much of Continental philosophy.

Thinking in light of the "theological turn," I believe, calls for a renewed engagement between theoreticians and practitioners, between philosophers and activists. In other words, simply calling for political criticism, when this is conceived as a purely negative operation, is not enough. *Critique must translate into activity.* This is why the Derridean democracy to-come is not utopian even though it cannot be actualized. As Levinas, Derrida, Reinhold Niebuhr, and others demonstrate,[9] impossible ideals are not necessarily politically irrelevant; but as I have tried to show in the preceding chapters, such ideals need to be supplemented with rigorous argumentation and practical activism regarding how their relevance might be instantiated in the world. This is how it is possible to avoid the temptation to give into the problematic idealism Dooley is rightly concerned about, while also recognizing that the cultivation a certain kind of critical idealism is perhaps the best model for achieving positive practical results. Although we should be wary of algorithmic claims of how best to act in the world or arguments claiming finality regarding the best public policy approach for a given topic, the tension between the ethico-religious and the ethico-political should continually motivate a conversation as to how best to translate "impossible" ideals into practical results (even if always fallibly). Intrinsic to this tension is also the urgency with which such translation must occur. To say that we must wait to act until the proper theorization can be achieved is to fail to engage the tension itself. While certainly drawing on the important work that Dooley and many others have done, I have tried in this book to go a bit further, if only slightly, and work out not only the theoretical stakes of Continental ethics and philosophy of religion by articulating the ontology of constitutive responsibility, but also the possible "practical political utility" (to borrow Dooley's phrase) of such a perspective for such issues as postmodern religious identity, religion in the public square, political justification, and environmental ethics. That said, I recognize that I have not gone anywhere near far enough. There is much more work to be done, and I hope that this book stands as a step in the right direction though it has clearly not crossed the finish line.

The Continued Threat of Formalism: Conversing with Caputo

The distinction that Otherism offers between the ethico-religious and the ethico-political should stand as a challenge to our ordinary vocabulary: politics is not something public as opposed to the private sphere of ethics, it is not what we do as communities or nations in distinction from what we do as individuals. Rather, politics contains both the questions of how to treat my neighbor or my family and also the questions of dealing with international affairs and legal statutes. "Politics" is the name for what we *normally* call both "ethics" and "politics," and this is part of why I have suggested that *ethico-political* is a better term. This is important because it allows us to understand that when we ask about "political" alternatives, we should include the issue of how to conceive of right action in whatever existential modality we would be inclined to investigate. I mention this because the question of practical alternatives demands that we attempt—or at least includes the desire for making the attempt—to articulate what the best course of action is given the relevant alternatives available. It is a question that seeks not only answers, but at least some sort of guidance for ethico-political decision-making.

But, hasn't Derrida (e.g., 1995; 1997; 2002; 2008) persuasively demonstrated the egotistical underbelly of such a desire for guidance? If we are to be ethical, shouldn't we stop trying to ask for instruction from above or below? Perhaps negative responses are the only ones that can be given to the sorts of messy situations that confront us in our daily lives? If this is indeed the case, then it would seem that deconstructive political theory is concerned with justice *in name only,* since it can never give any sort of indication as to what justice would look like here and now (again, even if always only partially). Demanding that we act in the name of the marginalized and then saying that all actions will fail to meet the absolute and infinite ethical requirement may just sound to many like an overly complicated way of making Rorty's point that we should try the best we can without asking for supernatural skyhooks or blessed assurances.

When faced with the need to go beyond critique and actually propose alternatives, it becomes exceedingly difficult to find such alternatives ready-to-hand. John Caputo expresses the situation that seems to confront us here:

> I have gone on record against ethics, against both the Categorical Imperative and *Sittlichkeit,* against Virtue and against Being's binding *nomos,* against Kant, Hegel, and Heidegger, against all ethicists and originary ethicists. I have even dared to speak against Levinas's ethics of infinity, against the absolutely, infinitely Other. I love Levinas dearly, but I would love him more dearly still if, instead of singing the praises of ethics and infinity, he would admit that it is necessary to deconstruct ethics, or better, necessary to see that ethics undergoes deconstruction, right before our eyes. (1993, 123)

While I agree with Caputo regarding the limits that face the majority of classical ethical theories, I want to resist a quick identification between my project and Caputo's stand "against ethics" for two reasons.

First, I find that Caputo gives entirely too much credit to the seeming limitlessness of deconstruction. For Derrida, deconstruction always stands in relation to (and indeed even operates because of) the un-deconstructible—viz., justice. However, for Derrida, even justice can never be taken as a given—it is always followed by the phrase that operates as a question-mark: "if there is such a thing." Nonetheless, only by premising the reality of justice and then simultaneously contesting any claims to absolute certainty regarding this reality can deconstruction even get off the ground. This is why I have suggested that Otherism operates according to a *modest* foundationalist theory of justification, rather than according to a strong foundationalism. I do not find Caputo to leave space for such a distinction. This can be seen when we read the following two passages side by side:

> ❧ Ethics is always already political, even as it would be a disaster were politics to inure itself to ethics. When I say I am against ethics I am saying that, rather than maintaining an impossible duality between a (pure) ethics and a (dirty) *Realpolitik,* I would rather have a more sensible, a more delimited, deconstructed idea of ethics to begin with . . . (1993, 123)

> ❧ Obligations happen, like faint flickers of flesh against a black expanse, lights against a great night. Obligations happen; they happen because they happen; they happen for the while that they happen. Then the cosmos draws a few more breaths, the little star grows cold, and the animals made of flesh have to die. The snow

falls faintly through the universe on all the living and the dead. Life is justified not as an aesthetic phenomenon but as a quasi-ethical one. (1993, 247–48)

Although I agree with Caputo that ethics can never be understood except as interrupted by politics, unless we give some (albeit non-absolute) priority to ethics we cannot understand the political as necessarily involved in the task of justice. Therefore, Caputo's dichotomy between a "pure" ethics and a "dirty" politics is at least too easy; and it may be simply false. Recognizing the ethico-religious encounter as the very quasi-logical existential condition of politics need not commit us to a *pure* ethics that stands as some sort of transcendent standard against which we judge our flawed reality. This is the very point of the *existential* dimension of such conditionality. Nonetheless, I understand Caputo to be making a point that I have also affirmed: namely, when ethics is understood as universal normativity, social convention, or even pragmatic prudence, we should resist it as missing the point of obligation.

My second point of distance from Caputo has to do with the idea of what a deconstructed ethics would look like. Consider the following passage from the beginning of *Against Ethics:*

> Obligation happens. It is a fact, as it were, but it is not a necessary truth. Obligation calls, but its call is finite, a strictly earthbound communication, transpiring here below, not in transcendental space (if there is such a thing). Obligation calls, and it calls for justice, but the caller in the call is not identifiable, decidable. I cannot make it out. I cannot say that the call is the Voice of God, or of Pure Practical Reason, or of a Social Contract "we" have all signed, or a trace of the Form of the Good stirring in our souls, or the trace of the Most High. I do not deny that these very beautiful hypotheses of ethics would make obligation safe, but my impiety is that I do not believe that obligation is safe. (1993, 15)

Again, I contend, we see Caputo offering an oversimplified dichotomy: *either* safety and clarity *or* non-identifiable risk. Though I agree with Caputo that the desire for "safety" can itself be an un-ethical desire reflecting little more than a selfish concern for one's own good conscience, I think that we should build upon this fact and understand that even the *realization* of the selfishness of this desire illuminates the ethico-religious constitution of selfhood as fundamentally (be)for-e God and the Other—that is, that we *take* this desire to be "selfish" is an *indictment* of its focus. Although Caputo might worry that this is too solid a conception of the self for a deconstructive framework, I would counter that unless this ontology of constitutive responsibility is presupposed we are unable to even hear the call of obligation as a "call for justice." Obligation's lack of safety arises because we can never be certain that our notion of justice is correct or that obligation itself is not pervaded by egotistical inclinations. Obligation is dangerous in that it demands constant diligence without offering recourse to any *final* security (i.e., modest foundations are always fallible and revisable).

In the attempt to continue a conversation with Caputo's and Dooley's important trajectories, let me suggest that the positive political alternative offered by the thinkers we have discussed in this book is not to be found in some sort of code, principle, imperative, standard, or set of virtues that stand outside or above or beyond history. Since it is only in lived-experience that the ethico-religious task can confront us, it is only in lived-experience that we can look for goodness. Rather than look to rationality for paradigms of piety and metaphysics for forms of the Good, we should look to the lives that are lived around us which exemplify the constitutive responsibility that defines us all. Since the task of justice always involves a certain kind of risk, albeit a fine one, we are not able to go to some non-risky source for instruction on how to proceed; the danger is persistent. Once we realize this we are better able to see how critique, when guided by the demand for recursive hermeneutics, can itself serve as a *positive* contribution to contemporary moral and political discourse.

The deconstructive political theory I advocate is not one that simply breaks with and breaks down all political institutions, it is one that also continuously inaugurates new debate about how to re-construct them ever anew. Kierkegaard, Levinas, Derrida, Vattimo, Marion, Lacoste, Henry, and Chrétien, etc., do not merely chastise others for bad ideas. Instead, they invite them to more productive conversation as we all search for good (or at least better) ideas. To demonstrate how Otherism can support the search for positive alternatives while still being committed to the constancy of the critical task, I will turn now to the notion of a "postmodern saint" as developed by Edith Wyschogrod.

Wyschogrod and Postmodern Saints

In her 1990 book, *Saints and Postmodernism,* Edith Wyschogrod claims: "A postmodern ethic must look not to some opposite of ethics but elsewhere, to life narratives, specifically those of saints, defined in terms that both overlap and overturn traditional normative stipulations that defy the normative structure of moral theory" (1990, xiii). Wyschogrod's contention here is that the only place to look for ethico-political guidance is not outside the social realities of historical existence but within the lives of those individuals who transform those realities by serving other people. Terming such individuals "saints," Wyschogrod is quick to dissociate her conception from any latent theism. She defines a saint as,

> One whose adult life in its entirety is devoted to the alleviation of sorrow (the psychological suffering) and pain (the physical suffering) that afflicts other persons without distinction of rank or group or, alternatively, that afflicts sentient beings, whatever the cost to the saint in pain or sorrow. (1990, 34; original emphasis)

I want to alter Wyschogrod's definition slightly by adding the following caveat in the language of the present work: *The saint's life performs the tension between God and the Other and between the ethico-religious and the ethico-political by transforming justification from an excuse for not doing more into a constant recognition that one has not done enough.* What the saint does is reject the notion that he or she has adequately acted, such that his or her moral duty is finally discharged. The infinity of ethics and the immediacy of politics can never be separated and the saint constantly walks this existential tightrope. This does not mean that the saint has somehow figured out a way to transcend the human condition. Precisely the opposite is the case. The saint embraces her full humanity by not allowing humanity to be reduced to naturalistic (or liberal) competition. Saints realize that humans are most fully human when they contest their own "natural" constitution.[10] Saints refuse to let Hobbes have the last word on the status of social life. That the world is *not* simply a war of all against all, but instead *is* the site of sacrificial decision, is not just a platitude: this is the daily reality of the saint's social interaction.

It is by looking to the lives of saints we are able to see how Otherism does not eliminate the possibility of moral guidance. A life lived be-for(e) God and the Other is a life that is modeled daily by saints around the world. "What legitimates antinomian saintly practices," Wyschogrod importantly claims, "is not theological or social concepts but rules of thumb immanent to the lived life itself" (1990, 29). What I take Wyschogrod to suggest is that we should not get too distracted by delimiting the criteria according to which one would be able to judge who is and who is not a saint, which is always simply a preliminary step and not really the most important one, but instead we should look directly at particular lives and allow the criteria to emerge from within such a relationship.

One might object here that the implication of Otherism is not the possibility of moral perfection but the necessity of moral failure, such that Otherism would make saints impossible not in a productively deconstructive way, but in a simply useless one. Consequently, to look to any other person for guidance would seem to involve the blind leading the blind. Well, here I want to respond by noting a couple of things. First, Wyschogrod's notion of the saint is not simply of a "moral saint" as such, but of a *"postmodern* saint." This adjective requires a transition in our understanding of sainthood as well as of moral guidance. We do not look to exemplars of perfection, but instead to lives well lived. We do not see someone a saint because she or he is more than human, but because of how exemplary they are at understanding the human condition and living in light of it. It is not a matter of finding people who never fail, but of finding people who fail in the right ways. Second, moral guidance should not be understood as an algorithmic stratagem for one's own right action. If the postmodern saint becomes simply another name for practical reason, say, then the decision (which Kierkegaard, Levinas, and Derrida all emphasize so strongly) which is essential to justice would be eliminated. One looks to the postmodern saint not as a guide in the sense of appealing to an absolute standard (as one might do with Kant's categorical imperative and/or Rawls's original position), but as a guide in the sense of following in the footsteps of one who has gone before (as one might do when listening to the wisdom of one's grandmother). Following postmodern saints does not guarantee that one will live a good life and does not ensure that one will make things better for others. However, it does at least help one to focus on what really matters—namely, the constitutive tension that demands risky investment and historical action—and to recognize that singularity (when understood as inherently social) does not rule out solidarity. Abraham might have had to walk alone, and we all may indeed have to answer for our own singular relation to God and the Other, but it is a mistake to think that we cannot learn from those who have walked their own path in a way that we would like to walk our own.

Even though I want to appropriate Wyschogrod's proposal, I should note one place where I find her account to potentially go too far. Wyschogrod's definition of the "postmodern saint" as someone "whose adult life in its entirety" is devoted to the Other is simply untenable. Though I certainly appreciate the hyperbole functioning in her definition as a way of resisting some sort of limit beyond which one would move from obligatory acts to superogatory acts, if we take her claim hyper-literally all sorts of problems arise.[11] For example, the classic example of "giving the bread from one's own mouth" would quickly lead to starvation and end the ability of the saint to continue serving others. Further, if one's "entire" life is spend in such service, then even going to sleep at night (rather than continuing to work for the good of the Other) would be unethical. In her classic essay "Moral Saints," Susan Wolf (1982) argues that any moral theory that demands saintliness is a theory we should reject. "I believe," Wolf writes, "that moral perfection, in the sense of moral saintliness, does not constitute a model of personal well-being toward which it would be particularly rational or good or desirable for a human being to strive" (1982, 419). "In other words," she says, "there seems to be a limit to how much morality we can stand" (1982, 423). For Wolf, the moral saint is someone "whose every action is as morally good as possible" (1982, 419). When understood in this way, Wolf concludes that "the ideal of moral sainthood should not be held as a standard against which any other ideal must be judged or justified. . . . In other words, a person may be *perfectly wonderful* without being *perfectly moral*" (1982, 435–36; original emphasis).

I take Wolf's essay to stand as something of a litmus test for Otherism. Unless Otherism is able to respond to her concerns regarding saintliness, then it seems that it is a disastrous model for contemporary moral and political theory. Moreover, unless Wyschogrod's account can be understood as withstanding Wolf's objections, appropriating her as a helpful lens through which to consider postmodern moral guidance would be problematic. In response to Wolf, I want to offer two ways in which I take Wyschogrod (and Otherism) to be resistant to Wolf's quite legitimate challenge to the ideal of moral saints. First, it is crucial that we see the distinction between Wolf's location of the moral saint's goodness at the level of "action" and Wyschogrod's reference to "adult life in its entirety." While "every action" would certainly raise the sorts of difficulties I outlined above regarding the impossibility of living the saintly life, Wyschogrod's definition allows for a bit more flexibility. Though I find the caveat "in its entirety" to be regrettable because it is one of those moments of hyperbole in Continental ethics that invites misunderstanding, let me suggest that it is plausible to interpret this phrase as simply meaning "on the whole." That is, the postmodern saint is someone who has so significantly worked for the good of others that those around her would proclaim her to be saintly "all things considered."

Hence, Wyschogrod would not require that a saint never sleep, but simply that a saint not be someone for whom self-interest is the primary motivation. However, when read a bit more loosely, in this way, the postmodern saint might not seem to be a very high standard at all: many people are "on the whole" devoted to serving others, right? This is where I think that my addition to Wyschogrod's definition is helpful. By considering the postmodern saint to be the person who "on the whole" or "all things considered" spends her life in service to the Other *and also as* the person who exemplifies the lived tension between the ethico-religious and the ethico-political, then we begin to see that postmodern sainthood is not something that is very common after all. It is the conscious recognition of doing all one can and yet realizing that one has not done enough that distinguishes the postmodern saint from generally good people.

Second, as I noted above regarding the problem of a postmodern notion of guidance, it is important to appreciate the "postmodern" qualifier to Wyschogrod's notion. That is, her account is one that thoroughly locates the saint in the context of fallible, flawed, finite, and frail human existence. Part of what Wolf so rightly rejects is the idea that the moral saint would be a moral exemplar, and yet be someone whose life is quite plausibly unlivable. Wyschogrod's account of the postmodern saint requires that the saint's life be one that is able to be historically emulated by others; and this, incidentally, is why she is so opposed to the notion of the "imitation of Christ." Although I have stressed the possible political importance of "impossible" demands, as I noted in chapter 8, when it comes to providing possible exemplars for postmodern political existence, I do not think Christ is the best candidate for precisely the sorts of reasons Wyschogrod offers. That said, I find Wyschogrod to already address Wolf's worry and to structurally incorporate it into her notion of saintliness. In other words, the postmodern saint could never be self-recognized (as seems possible for Wolf's "moral saint"), but would be the person who continues to try, and fail, and try again. When expressed in this way, I do not believe that *postmodern* saintliness needs to be seen as problematic in the way Wolf might contend regarding other conceptions of saints.

Following Wyschogrod's lead while fully appreciating Wolf's reservations, I will now turn to four people I take to be good contenders for postmodern saints or, as I will term them, *ethico-political exemplars*. All of the following people demonstrate the way in which infinite obligation is not an obstacle to ethico-political action, but precisely the prerequisite for it. I admit that this may be a less than satisfactory answer to some who demand clear and certain answers to political questions, but as I have argued throughout, what a constitutive relation to alterity serves to do is challenge such clarity and certainty as already un-ethical *if* they stand as a replacement for a continued interrogation of our understanding of the complicated task of sharing the world with a host of others. What follows is my, however brief and tentative, attempt at demonstrating that just because we resist *easy* clear and distinct political answers, we need not arrive at a vacuous incapacity to speak to the real political situations that confront us. Crucially, I want to maintain the weight with which these situations continue to press upon us, which might be said to be the ethico-political upshot of Lessing's famous choice.[12]

Ethico-political Exemplars

"We Can Do Otherwise": Dietrich Bonhoeffer (1906–1945)

A celebrated pastor and distinguished theologian, Dietrich Bonhoeffer's life, and ultimately his death, is a testament to the struggle to work out one's salvation with fear and trembling while living humbly before God and others. Bonhoeffer received early renown for his commitment to the idea that Christian faith could not be reduced to some sort of easy way of life. Echoing Kierkegaard and anticipating Derrida, he demonstrates that to imitate Christ is to risk everything: to follow the path of Christ is to walk toward Golgotha. In his early book, *The Cost of Discipleship*, Bonhoeffer clearly differentiates between what he calls "cheap grace" and grace that is "costly." "Cheap grace," Bonhoeffer writes, "means grace as a doctrine, a principle, a system. It means forgiveness of sins proclaimed as a general truth, the love of God taught as the Christian 'conception' of God" (1959, 45). Reminiscent of Kierkegaard's irritation with the notion that Christianity could be something one was "born into," Bonhoeffer refuses to allow faith to be reducible to intellectual assent to some sort of rationally verifiable objectivity. On such a model, faith would be simply an added predicate to an otherwise unchanged subject. Anticipating postmodern Christianity, Bonhoeffer embraces the idea of a faith that cannot be confused with a weak form of knowledge by arguing that the relation to Christ can only be had in a life of constant struggle toward Christ's calling:

> Such grace is *costly* because it calls us to follow, and it is *grace* because it calls us to follow *Jesus Christ*. It is costly because it costs a man his life, and it is grace because it gives a man the only true life. It is costly because it condemns sin, and grace because it justifies the sinner. Above all, it is *costly* because it cost God the life of his Son . . . and what has cost God much cannot be cheap for us. (1959, 47–48; original emphasis)

It would be wrong to conclude from the above passage that the path one follows when following Christ is *clearly* defined. Part of the risk of faith is attempting to walk daily as Christ would walk while not knowing exactly what that would entail. Life demands decision—to lay this decision off on someone else (be it the church, reason, the state, the elders, tradition, or public opinion) is to evade one's own calling. There cannot be forgiveness without repentance, baptism without discipline, or communion without confession (1959, 47); but how one is to live a life of repentance, discipline, and confession is not predetermined. Contrary to Luther, Bonhoeffer insists that the proclamation, "Here I stand, I can do no other," is "simply untrue, or it is unpardonable frivolity and pride."[13] Far too often, Bonhoeffer contends, we simply "hide behind this statement." What we must realize is that "We *can* do otherwise!"[14] Bonhoeffer's point is that even such moralistic, or pietistic, stances are far too often a form of callous indifference. Every decision at every moment in every situation is always one among many. To choose to go one way instead of another is always to affirm that this is the *best* way. But there can never be a guarantee that a wise choice has been made—thus the need for fear and trembling.

Imitating Christ (and we might add, postmodern saints) may not yield the *specific* instruction that we desire. What exactly, then, is the content of discipleship? Bonhoeffer offers the following suggestion:

Intersections and Applications

Follow me, run along behind me! That is all. To follow in his [Christ's] steps is something which is void of all content. It gives us no intelligible programme for a way of life, no goal or ideal to strive after. It is not a cause which human calculation might deem worthy of our devotion, even the devotion of ourselves. . . . The disciple is dragged out of his relative security into a life of absolute insecurity. . . . Again it is no universal law. Rather is it the exact opposite of all legality. (1959, 62–63)

Bonhoeffer's words about the absolute insecurity demanded by costly grace will turn out to be tragically prophetic regarding his own life. Convinced that he could not be an effective contributor to the reconstruction and restoration that a post–World War II Germany would require if he had not suffered with the German people, Bonhoeffer gave up his professorship at New York's Union Theological Seminary in 1939 and returned to his homeland. And this decision to return to Germany was certainly not made without intense personal turmoil. Although Bonhoeffer continued to be hopeful that Germany would emerge quickly from the abyss of human degradation into which Hitler was leading it, he was a firm realist in his recognition that his return would interrupt, if not eliminate, his ability to continue his work—and more seriously still, would invite serious threats to his own person. Although the choice to go back in an attempt to help others was clear, Bonhoeffer struggled to find some sort of divine affirmation of his decision. Ultimately he concluded:

The reasons that one gives for an action to others and to one's self are certainly inadequate. One can give a reason for everything. In the last resort one acts from a level which remains hidden from us. So one can only ask God to judge us and to forgive us. . . . At the end of the day I can only ask God to give a merciful judgment on today and all its decision. It is now in God's hand.[15]

The absolute insecurity of which Bonhoeffer had written many years earlier was now made personally manifest. He echoes this undecidability—and yet the necessity for a decision—in a letter to Reinhold Niebuhr dated July 1939:

Christians in Germany will face the terrible alternative of either willing the defeat of their nation in order that Christian civilization may survive, or willing the victory of their nation and thereby destroying our civilization. I know which of these alternatives I must choose; but I cannot make that choice in security.[16]

His decision to privilege the needs of those suffering in Germany, which of course included non-Christians and Christians alike, at the cost of his own well-being certainly qualifies Bonhoeffer as a saint according to Wyschogrod's definition. Yet the task of converting the infinite responsibility to God and others into specific political action came to a climax in Bonhoeffer's decision to become involved in the resistance movement, which tried to assassinate Hitler. The tension that should not be overlooked here is that since his early friendship with Jean Lasserre and his deep study of Christ's Sermon on the Mount, Bonhoeffer had been a convinced pacifist (see Bethge 1970, 153ff.). His commitment to figuring out how Christianity could be politically effective through non-violent means led Bonhoeffer to closely study the example set by Gandhi—who invited Bonhoeffer to India in 1934.

For Bonhoeffer there was no justification for violence within the Christian framework, and yet he was convinced that *not* putting a stop to Hitler's reign was also unjustifiable. Caught between the demand to see even Hitler as covered by the commandment not to kill and included in the instruction to "bless those that curse thee" (*Luke* 6: 28), and the realization that eliminating Hitler was the only way he could stand up for the battered and broken victims of National Socialism, Bonhoeffer was again faced with the necessity to act without guarantees. One would be hard-pressed to find a better example of someone painfully aware of the tension between ethico-religious obligation and ethico-political necessity. Bonhoeffer's decision, a decision that was not "made in security," was to stand for those who could not stand for themselves, all the while asking God to "judge and forgive" him.

Bonhoeffer's decision would eventually lead to his arrest and execution, after a period of imprisonment. Of Bonhoeffer's last moments the camp doctor wrote the following:

> On the morning of that day between five and six o'clock the prisoners, including Admiral Canaris, General Oster, . . . and state attorney Dr. Sack were taken from their cells and the verdicts of the court martial read out to them. Through the half-open door in one room of the huts I saw Pastor Bonhoeffer, before taking off his prison garb, kneeling on the floor praying fervently to his God. I was most deeply moved by the way this unusually lovable man prayed, so devout and so certain that God heard his prayer. At the place of execution, he again said a short prayer and then climbed the steps to the gallows, brave and composed. His death ensued after a few seconds. In the almost fifty years that I worked as a doctor, I have hardly ever seen a

man die so entirely submissive to the will of God. (Fischer-Hüllstrung 1966, 232; cit. Bethge 1970, 927–28)

The apparent impossibility of infinite obligation did not grind Bonhoeffer into a state of wretched indecision, but propelled him forward in the bold service of others. His martyrdom is an example that I would hope no more will have to imitate *in extremis,* but the nobility with which he faced the reality of his situation and his sheer fortitude in preferring his neighbor over himself should cause us to look to him as a model for how to conceive of a world in which self-interest is overcome by generosity. Although martyrs might be, by definition, exemplary, Bonhoeffer's life need not be read as removed from the gritty everyday decisions that each of us must make. Bonhoeffer shows how to stand in humility while still being quite discriminating regarding that for which one chooses to stand.

"Show Them That Love Is Greater": Corrie and Betsie Ten Boom

Raised primarily by their father, Casper Ten Boom, Corrie and Betsie were taught from a young age that to love God is to serve those in need. When the Nazis began to overrun Holland, the Ten Booms built an additional space onto one of their upstairs bedrooms. This "hiding place" would save the lives of many Jews and other individuals involved in the resistance movement. When ultimately arrested and interrogated, Casper was offered freedom due to his advanced age; the only condition placed upon his freedom was that he would "not cause any more trouble" (Ten Boom 1971, 137). Casper Ten Boom's reply was immediate and firm: "If I go home today . . . tomorrow I will open my door again to any man in need who knocks" (1971, 138). Surely this is what radical hospitality looks like when it is lifted out of philosophy books and placed in the midst of existence. In his response, abstraction decidedly comes back to earth.

Because of the aid they offered to Jews and others, Corrie and Betsie were sent to a penitentiary in Scheveningen and then eventually transferred to the Ravensbruck concentration camp. The horrors that Corrie details in her memoir include being exposed to bitter cold, confined in overcrowded transport trains without food or water, malnutrition, physical and psychological abuse, humiliation, depersonalization, lice, fleas, and the constant witnessing and threat of death. Corrie's father Casper and sister Betsie would both eventually die as a result of Nazi cruelty. Her description of Betsie's body graphically depicts the realities of their situation:

> I reached the window and cupped my eyes to peer in. A nurse was standing directly between me and Betsie. I ducked out of sight, waited a minute, then looked again. A second nurse had joined the first, both now standing where I wanted to see. They stepped to the head and

foot of the bed: I gazed curiously at what lay on it. It was a carving in old yellow ivory. There was no clothing on the figure; I could see each ivory rib, and the outline of the teeth through the parchment cheeks. It took me a moment to realize it was Betsie. (1971, 218)

While one might quite plausibly suggest that such a situation would legitimate vengeance and the severest retribution, the response of Betsie to her captors, and Corrie to her sister's murderers, is strikingly *not* one of reciprocity. Consider the above description alongside the following horrifying passage that recounts an event that occurred just a short time prior to Betsie's death:

One dark morning when ice was forming a halo around each street lamp, a feeble-minded girl two rows ahead of us suddenly soiled herself. A guard rushed at her, swinging her thick leather crop while the girl shrieked in pain and terror. It was always more terrible when one of these innocent ones was beaten. Still the *Aufseherin* continued to whip her. It was the guard we had nicknamed "The Snake" because of the shiny dress she wore. I could see it now beneath her long wool cape, glittering in the light of the lamp as she raised her arm. I was grateful when the screaming girl at last lay still on the cinder street. (1971, 209)

When faced with this awful scene, Corrie asked her sister, "what can we do for these people? Afterward I mean. Can't we make a home for them and care for them and love them?" To which Betsie replied, "Corrie, I pray every day that we will be allowed to do this! To show them that love is greater!" Corrie goes on to note that "it wasn't until I was gathering twigs later in the morning that I realized that I had been thinking of the feeble-minded, and Betsie of their persecutors" (1971, 209). Betsie never stopped viewing her persecutors as also being children of God (or as Kierkegaard would say, she never stopped seeing them as "neighbors"). She continued to love them even as they killed her. Betsie is a modern exemplar of the love demonstrated by Stephen, the Christian martyr, who prayed, "Lord, do not hold this sin against them" as he was stoned to death (*Acts* 7: 54–60; NIV); and of Christ who looked down from the cross and asked God to "forgive them, for they do not know what they are doing" (*Luke* 23: 32 (NIV)). Betsie Ten Boom gives the lie to any supposition that the im-possibility of forgiveness means its dissolution. Her actions might rightly be considered "mad" according to the retributionist logic of human society and its laws, but the example that she sets translates an "impossible possibility" into a way of life.

Being released on a clerical error in the same month that her sister had died, Corrie narrowly missed becoming one of the ninety-six thousand women who were murdered at Ravensbruck. After the war, she followed her sister's instruction to "tell people" about what they had experienced in order that she might transform the world in which such atrocities could be committed. From 1946 to 1960, Corrie operated a home and place of restoration for those who had suffered under the Nazis. Working well into her eighties, Corrie reached out to whomever she could in over sixty-one countries. And her efforts were not confined to victims of the Holocaust. Like Levinas, she recognized that inhumanity to one's fellow man must be resisted in all its forms; it was to this resistance that she dedicated her life, *in its entirety*.

"I Didn't Do Enough": The Filmic Character Oskar Schindler

Ethico-political exemplars are not confined those who are living or have actually lived. Literature, drama, poetry, and art are replete with individuals and narratives that should inspire us here and now to envision better futures. In order to demonstrate the way in which ethico-political exemplars can be found in fiction as well as real life, I want to look to an example from film. Although Oskar Schindler was a historical individual, I will focus on the way in which he was represented in Stephen Spielberg's *Schindler's List*.[17] This *character* Oskar Schindler nicely demonstrates the way in which a guilty conscience presents not an impasse for ethical life, but is actually internal to it. After having been nonchalant about his ethical role for the majority of the film, at the very end, Schindler is presented with a token of the appreciation of those whose lives he saved. On behalf of many, the character Stern gives Schindler a gold ring inscribed with a Hebrew phrase: "Whoever saves one life, saves the world."[18] What follows is what I find to be the most powerful scene of the entire film. Allow me to quote it at length:

> SCHINDLER: I could've got more out . . . I could've got more . . . if I'd
> just . . . I don't know, if I'd just . . . I could've got more . . .
> STERN: Oskar, there are twelve hundred people who are alive because
> of you. Look at them.
> SCHINDLER: If I'd made more money . . . I threw away so much money,
> you have no idea. If I'd just . . .
> STERN: There will be generations because of what you did.
> SCHINDLER: I didn't do enough.
> STERN: You did so much.
> SCHINDLER: This car. Goeth would've bought this car. Why did I keep
> the car? Ten people, right there, ten more I could've got. . . . This
> pin. Two people. This is gold. Two more people. He would've
> given me two for it. At least one. He would've given me one.

The Ethico-political   301

One more. One more person. A person, Stern. For this. One more. I could've gotten one more person I didn't. (Zailian 1993)

Wholly absent from this scene is any sense of Rorty's self-contented bourgeois liberalism. The very ethicality of Schindler's actions is emphasized by the fact that he does not presume that he has "done his duty." His example has normative bite precisely because he is not motivated by some sort of desire to do what is required of him so that he can subsequently be at peace. He sets into relief that there is no limit to the call of obligation—this call defines him as a self. The task cannot be completed, but this does not prevent his commitment to determinate activity. Thinking politics in light of Otherism overturns the assumption that the goal is to finish the race and obtain the prize; by maintaining the tension between the ethico-religious and the ethico-political, we are able to see that one of the worst things that can be done is to do nothing. As Norman Geras (1998) persuasively argues, nothing is as dangerous as indifference. The rationale that Geras offers is that active violence is always able to be contested as long as there are those who continue to live saintly lives in opposition to it. The truly terrifying thought is that if these saints disappear—if everyone simply turns their backs in selfishness or mere apathy—then violence itself ceases to be horrific.

Crucially, *the status of violence is just as fragile as goodness.* Only by speaking up against the violence that continues to occur can we keep naming the violent as violent, rather than allowing it to become a mere commonplace. As Levinas might say, if we forget the radicality of evil then we are unable to affirm the infinity of goodness; and as Hannah Arendt (1985) is right to say, what is so shocking about evil is the way in which it often presents itself as *banal.* What I see as exemplary about Schindler is not just that he saved twelve hundred people, but the way in which he relates to his own activity. Much like Bonhoeffer's insistence that we must humbly act and then ask for forgiveness for not having done enough, Schindler finally realizes that the goodness is only something that is made manifest as long as we continue to struggle to bring it to presence. Crucially, however, this does not mean that the saving of people is a mere trifle. Nothing could be further from the truth. This is not some sort of deontological ethics of intention: there is no abstract duty that stands removed from the corporeal faces of my neighbors. Yet it is the relation *between* the actions and how one understands oneself as a political agent that matters. Schindler shows how Kierkegaard's notion of living forward while understanding backward can be politically instructive.

Resting on one's laurels depends on having first received them. But again, if the goal is not to finish the race but to keep on running, then laurels are not something that can ever properly be given or received. This is not to deny the possibility of laudation, however: it has been my intention to sing the praises of the above people because I consider them worthy of emulation. What I find worth modeling after them is the way in which none of them considered themselves to be exemplary—they simply did the best they could with what they had where they were, and then contested the idea that they had done enough.

An Open-ended Conclusion

Let me now return to the central question that I asked in the introduction:

> Can a philosophical concern for the question of God actually enrich and undergird an ethico-political concern for others in the world—while also opening spaces for Continental thought to participate in debates in the larger philosophical literature?

In light of this question, we should hear Roger Burggraeve's suggestion that

> Levinas' philosophy of responsibility, peace, justice, and human rights is far from simplistic or easy. It is a thinking which tries to both disclose foundations and, on that basis, do justice to interpersonal and social reality. Above all, his views on the relationship between love of neighbor and justice for human rights offers interesting potential for new and paradoxical ways of thinking about political peace and human rights. (2002, 185)

Consistent with Burggraeve, in this book I have attempted to show that the philosophical presuppositions, the ethico-religious stakes, and the political ramifications of Kierkegaard, Levinas, and other voices in Continental philosophy are profoundly important for contemporary social existence.

Deconstructive ethics and politics are not lacking in content just because they always contain an element of the un-decidable. The political conversation such a perspective encourages is essentially invitational, absolutely hospitable, perpetually focused on singularity, and always self-critical. It is democratic and dialogical and yet despite being "welcoming to the enemies of democracy" (as Derrida says), still recognizes the necessity of potentially excluding some voices in the name of maintaining the very possibility of democracy. Derrida himself admits of this potentially necessary exclusion in *Of Hospitality* (and elsewhere) when he notes that if one simply gives over one's house to the stranger who knocks at the door, then one has eliminated the possibility of continuing to be hospitable. This potential exclusion is only "justified" inasmuch as we continue to contest the final legitimacy of such exclusion by looking for "charity after justice." Accordingly, consider the following warning from Shakespeare's *A Winter's Tale*:

> Be certain what you do, sir, lest your justice
> Prove violence . . . (Act II, sc. 1)

The exemplars we have discussed in this chapter, as well as Kierkegaard, Levinas, Derrida, Vattimo, and many others in new phenomenology, all help us to understand that this search for certainty—that our "justice" not prove to be violence—is never a task that could be completed. *The very risk of ethico-political life is that our justice may prove to be violence.* The recursive project of constantly saying and unsaying, acting and then offering criticism, projecting new alternatives and then finding ways to improve on them, is not a depressing fate of always seeking but never coming to the knowledge of the truth (see *2 Timothy* 3: 7). It is the realization that the truth may best be found in the ethico-political engagement that is always singular in its very sociality.

I want to quote, finally, from a sermon by Martin Luther King, Jr.—a figure who represents the critical and emancipatory potential of religious conviction in modern democratic politics—which he preached on Sunday, 4 February 1968. This was shortly before he was murdered. I take these words to be a beautiful example of how it is that one can humbly devote oneself to serving the Other:

> If any of you are around when I have to meet my day, I don't want a long funeral. And if you get somebody to deliver the eulogy, tell him not to talk too long. . . . Tell them not to mention that I have a Nobel Peace Prize. That isn't important. Tell them not to mention that I have three or four hundred other awards. That's not important. Tell them not to mention where I went to school. I'd like somebody to mention that day, that Martin Luther King, Jr. tried to give his life serving others. I'd like for somebody to say that day, that Martin Luther King, Jr. tried to love somebody. I want you to say that day that I tried to be right on the war question. I want you to be able to say that day, that I did try to feed the hungry. And I want you to be able to say that day that I did try in my life to clothe those who were naked. I want you to say on that day, that I did try in my life to visit those who were in prison. I want you to say that I tried to love and serve humanity. (cit. Bennett 1976, 241–42)

Notice that King never says that he did these things (though he clearly did do them), but that he *tried* to. Postmodern saints understand that our justice *can* prove to be violence, and that even when we are just, our justice has not been *sufficiently* just: we all have more work to do. Propelled toward action, but suspicious of perfection, this should be the way we all attempt to live as we continue to stand in relation to God *and* the Other.

NOTES

Introduction

1. I should note that in light of the important work by Wolterstorff (Audi and Wolterstorff 1997), Eberle (2002), and Clanton (2007), among many others, arguments for such privatization have recently, and rightly, had to be reconsidered. I will return to this in chapter 7.

2. There are many other "Continental" strains that also have begun to dip into what Anglo-American philosophers would refer to as "philosophy of religion"—consider psychoanalysis, critical theory, French feminism, eco-theology, etc. However, in this book I will focus on the notion of the postmodern God that emerges internal to the debates of those working primarily within a phenomenological inheritance.

3. For just a few examples: Diane Perpich (2008) and John Davenport (2008) have both brought Continental ethics into conversation with contemporary debates in non-Continental ethical theory; Stephen Minister (2008), William Paul Simmons (2003; 2000; 1999), Martin Matuštík (2008; 1995; 1993), and especially Chantal Mouffe (2006; 2005; 2000) have offered substantive considerations of Continental thought in relation to post-Rawlsian political philosophy. Especially in environmental philosophy there is an emerging Continental voice that poses serious questions about how to address the crises that we face as a global community—see David Wood (2007; 2003), John Llewelyn (2004), and Edelglass, Diehm, and Hatley (forthcoming).

4. Importantly, this concern for the oppressed can only go so far. Surely there is a distinction between the person who is oppressed for her race, for instance, and the person who is excluded from public discourse because she is a racist who advocates violence.

5. For critical responses to Nussbaum's essay on Butler (and Nussbaum's rejoinder to her critics), see Hedges, Spivak, Benhabib, Fraser, et al. (1999). See also p. 307n15 below.

1. *The Problem*

1. As we will see in chapter 4, along with Michel Henry, Levinas is widely recognized as a source of the "turn."

2. For a different take on the engagement between Levinas and Rorty, see Visker 1997. Although interesting, Visker's argument is peripheral to my thesis here. The literature is also extremely limited regarding Levinas and Pragmatism generally; for a couple of exceptions, see Rosenthal 2003; Simmons 2010.

3. Regarding Rorty's reading of Derrida, see Bell 1992.

4. These criteria are: "(1) She has radical and continuing doubts about the final vocabulary she currently uses, because she has been impressed by other vocabularies, vocabular-

ies taken as final by people or books she has encountered; (2) she realizes that argument phrased in her present vocabulary can neither underwrite nor dissolve these doubts; (3) insofar as she philosophizes about her situation, she does not think that her vocabulary is closer to reality than others, that it is in touch with a power not herself" (Rorty 1989, 73).

5. The inclusion of Foucault here is rather interesting considering Rorty's essay, "Method, Social Science, Social Hope," in which he announces that the projects of Dewey and Foucault are essentially the same (in Rorty 1982). I should note that he goes on to say that the difference between Dewey and Foucault is really a matter of their ways of relating to the same basic insights. Perhaps this difference in relation is enough to class Foucault with Nietzsche and Derrida as private ironists, but if the basic point for Foucault is the same as for Dewey—who is consistently Rorty's public liberal *par excellence*—then his classification here is a bit awkward.

6. It is important to keep in mind that the Dewey one discovers in Rorty's texts is often very different from the one who is encountered in Dewey's works. This disconnect is not specifically relevant to my consideration of Rorty above, but I do want to note that any references to the "neo-Pragmatist" or "pragmatic" view I ascribe to Rorty is not intended to represent a vision shared by all those who are identified as Pragmatists or neo-Pragmatists. Whether Dewey's *Ethics* is able to do what Rorty's ethics is not is an interesting question which I want to intentionally leave open (see Dewey 1989).

7. See Rorty 1979, esp. chap. 8. Therein, Rorty draws a distinction between "systematic" and "edifying" philosophers, and claims that those that seek to edify do so because they have given up on any "appearance/reality" distinction and thus realize that epistemology is really a matter of hermeneutics and not of justification according to first principles. That Rorty is right in this division is contestable. Several of the thinkers that Rorty puts into the "edifying" camp do not as easily depart from a process of justification as he would like to think: for example, Derrida and the later Wittgenstein are both committed to something like "first philosophy," even though it is not articulated in a classically foundational form. Regardless, what matters to my argument above is that for Rorty there is not, and could not be, any appeal to anything exterior to the process of deliberation and our social practices themselves. What this amounts to is a claim about the impossibility of transcendence (for an extremely provocative account of the history of phenomenology as it relates to the question of transcendence, see J. Smith 2002). Although Rorty develops his critique of correspondence throughout his authorship, an important group of essays are collected together in section 2 of Rorty 1999. Similarly, in a 2004 review of Richard Wolin's *The Seduction of Unreason* (2004), Rorty also offers a positive account of how antifoundationalism can be politically relevant (Rorty 2004). See also, Gutting 2003.

8. See Rorty's introduction to *Philosophy and Social Hope,* titled "Relativism: Finding and Making" (1999).

9. This will turn out to be a problematic description given Rorty's own admission and even advocacy of "ethnocentrism." See "The Priority of Democracy to Philosophy," "Postmodernist Bourgeois Liberalism," and "On Ethnocentrism: A Reply to Clifford Geertz," all in Rorty 1991a. Rorty's introduction to that collection is also helpful regarding this rather thorny issue.

10. Rorty's alternations between the terms "ethics" and "justice" do not seem to convey any real conceptual difference; in most cases, either term seems to be applicable to and even interchangeable with the other. The context of his discussion and the language of the critic to whom he is responding appear to determine his usage more so than any philosophical matter. However, if there is a distinction to be made, I contend it is nothing more than numerical for Rorty. Ethics refers to the decisions made in one-on-one situations, whereas justice is applying the wisdom and experience gained from those "ethical decisions" to a larger social context. The above quote illustrates the difficulty of radically trying to push a wedge between the terms: that is, "justice" is defined by looking to both public situations (the judge) and private encounters (the parents).

11. For a consideration of Rorty's understanding of hermeneutics as it relates to his democratic politics, especially as influenced by Gadamer, see Warnke 2003.

12. I would like to thank John Stuhr for illuminating this point for me.

13. Rorty even says at one point that he is sure that his "tone"—i.e., sarcastic, casual, laidback, and nonetheless weighty and pointed—is a large part of the reason so many people get frustrated with his writing (Rorty, Nystrom, and Puckett 2002, 34).

14. Of course, this statement makes it seem as if the members of labor unions and the congressional representatives did not go to college.

15. It should be noted that Rorty's claim that leftist theory is detached from political reality is not one that originates with him. Feminists have been saying similar things since the mid-1980s. For example, Wendy Brown goes so far as to suggest that such liberal doctrines as "universal equality, liberty, suffrage, and opportunity" have actually contributed to the exclusion of large groups of individuals making up liberal society: "Due to the abstract nature of these doctrines [and] their grounding in the concept of the individual rather than in the concrete content of an individual's life circumstances and endeavors," she writes, "the exclusion of women and others from basic civil and political rights had a blatantly illogical and untenable quality about it" (1988, 3). For a more recent example of Brown's political critique of leftist "moralism," see 2001, esp. chap. 2.

16. Speaking of one of President Clinton's State of the Union Addresses, Rorty says, "I don't see why there shouldn't be sixteen initiatives, each of which in one way or another might relieve some suffering, and no overall theoretical integration" (Rorty, Nystrom, and Puckett 2002, 46).

17. Jean Bethke Elshtain makes a similar point regarding Rorty's rejection of argument and his process of redescription: "Because his arguments are often slippery and difficult to engage . . . Just when you think you've come up against something solid, it turns squishy" (2003, 139).

18. And crucially, this redescription should not just expose potential difficulties, but potential injustice. As Maria Lugones (1987) illustrates, to even suppose that all language-games are translatable is to give a default status to the rules laid down by the socially privileged. That is, some languages, groups, or individuals may be essentially non-integratable into the dominant liberal framework in which Rorty operates. An implicit contention that underlies much of this book is that ethics already obligates us to not simply encounter the other on "my" or "our" terms, but to try as much as possible to, as Lugones says, "world-

travel." Politically, this may function as a continual recognition of the limitations of all institutions and theories; that is, an ethical politics will be one that perpetually seeks to critique its own injustices.

19. Rorty claims that he is quite taken by those Derridean texts that are specifically directed toward private concerns. As an example, Rorty discusses the "Envois" section of Derrida's *The Post Card* (1987). It is this text, Rorty writes, "which best illustrates what I take to be Derrida at his best," it "differs from *Glas* in being readable, and also in being moving" (1989, 126). That it "moves" him, Rorty attributes to the way in which it abandons all theory in favor of a personal engagement with one's own history and heritage. On Rorty's reading, there is no claim to objectivity in this Derridean text, rather, a subjective encounter is laid before us for us to take from it what we will. For Rorty, this is the highest that a private ironist can aim to do, and Rorty suggests that Derrida does it as well as anyone else in contemporary philosophy.

20. Mark Dooley (2001b) also contends that we should disentangle Derrida from Levinas (I will return to his claim on this front in chapter 13). The crucial difference between Dooley and Rorty on this point is that whereas Rorty advocates such a separation in the name of Derrida's private importance, Dooley does so because of what he takes to be Derrida's political importance.

21. Rorty makes this explicit in *Contingency, Irony, and Solidarity* where he writes: "Abandoning universalism is my way of doing justice to the claims of the ironists whom Habermas distrusts: Nietzsche, Heidegger, Derrida. Habermas looks at these men from the point of view of public needs. I agree with Habermas that as *public* philosophers they are at best useless and at worst dangerous, but I want to insist on the role they and others like them can play in accommodating the ironist's *private* sense of identity to her liberal hopes" (1989, 68).

22. It should be noted that such statements sometimes make it seem as if Rorty were ignorant of the horrors of the twentieth century. To suggest that ethics and politics can be reduced to such "banal" conversations overlooks the extraordinary ways in which the "banality of evil" (as Arendt (1985) would say) can manifest in history.

23. Support for this is evident in Rorty's own thinking. Consider the way in which he advocates a move away from "argument" toward what he terms "redescription" in *Contingency, Irony, and Solidarity* (1989, 44ff.). There, Rorty says that his "strategy" will be to change the subject, rather than "meeting . . . criticisms head-on" (1989, 44).

24. Rorty's most explicit and sustained consideration of the power of such imaginative storytelling is found in Rorty 1998a. The chapters in *Contingency, Irony, and Solidarity* (1989) that deal with Orwell and Nabokov are also important examples of this position.

25. The reference to "moral progress" is as follows: "The view I am offering says that there is such a thing as moral progress, and that this progress is indeed in the direction of greater human solidarity" (Rorty 1989, 192).

26. These quotes from Rorty are not originally directed at Levinas, but I feel they capture the overall position of Rorty's demand on those who read Levinas.

27. Simon Critchley says something similar to this (1999, 237): Levinasians must contend with the charge of "empty formalism" that Rorty levels at Levinas.

28. For a sustained argument for why Pragmatism in general might be incompatible with pluralism, see Talisse 2007.

29. Norman Geras (1995) persuasively argues that Rorty's thought is unintelligible without the idea of some conception of human nature.

2. Hearing Divine Commands and Responding to the Call of the Other

1. For a sustained consideration of Rorty's reading of Kierkegaard, see Simmons forthcoming.

2. Consider Rorty's claim: "When people develop private vocabularies and private self-images, people like Nietzsche, Kierkegaard, and Derrida, it's very unclear what impact, if any, this will ever have on public discourse. But over the centuries, it actually turns out to have a certain impact" (2006, 50).

3. In recent years, there has been a significant amount of attention paid to developing a conversation between Levinas and Kierkegaard (see especially Simmons and Wood 2008). The work of Merold Westphal has been particularly important on this front—see Westphal 1992b; 1995a; 1995b; 2000; 2002; 2008a; 2008b. For other engagements between Kierkegaard and Levinas, see Ferreira 2001; Robbins 1999, esp. chap. 6; de Vries 2002, esp. chap. 2; Weston 1994, esp. chap. 7; Dooley 1999 and 2001, esp. 206ff.; Caputo 1993; Treanor 2001; Kemp 1997; Butin 1999; Prosser 2002; and Minister 2003.

4. For a general overview of the predominant interpretations of *Fear and Trembling,* see Greve 2000.

5. Merold Westphal has argued for a similar conclusion and I am deeply indebted to his work on the relation between these thinkers. However, for Westphal, in order to find such an ethical resonance between Kierkegaard and Levinas we must go to *at least* to the work of Johannes Climacus, if not to Kierkegaard's explicitly social focus in *Works of Love* (see Westphal 1995b, 2000, 2004, and 2008b). Although I would agree entirely that we must go to such texts as *Works of Love, Practice in Christianity,* and *Judge for Yourself!* if we want to find more determinate content for how to relate to other people on the basis of standing "before God" *(for Gud / coram Deo)*, in what follows I will be supplementing Westphal's account by arguing that the basic structure of relationality which is explicitly articulated in these later texts is already implicitly present in *Fear and Trembling.*

6. I should note, however, that I am not denying that there are consequences for soteriology, as Green contends. My point is that if the book is indeed a "modern discussion of the classical Pauline-Lutheran theme of justification by faith" (1993b, 192), it need not necessarily conflict with my claims here except to the extent that Green suggests that it is really the "book's essential concern" (1993b, 191). In his response to Green's essay, Gene Outka does a nice job of demonstrating that although Green's interpretation might have some merit, it "receives insufficient support from the text itself" to warrant the narrow reading Green suggests (1993, 211). Instead, Outka rightly locates Green's reading as a possible "supplement" (1993, 211) to the otherwise ethical focus of *Fear and Trembling.* See also Green's reply to Outka (Green 1993a).

7. This is not to say that Kierkegaard is not helpful for the task of constructing a nor-

mative ethics, however; for a good example of how such a normative project might arise from within Kierkegaard, see Warren 1982. My point is simply that such a project could only be undertaken in light of this constitutive relation itself.

8. For a good defense of this claim see Merold Westphal's essay "Abraham and Hegel," included in 1991. Additionally, for considerations of Kierkegaard's relation to Hegel, see M. Taylor 2000, Thulstrup 1980, and Stewart 2003.

9. For a detailed analysis of Hegel's notion of ethics, see A. Wood 1990.

10. I do not mean to be reductive here. I recognize that Judge William also anticipates certain "existentialist" trajectories. However, the point is simply that, for the most part, the ethical framework operative in the second volume of *Either/Or* is a matter of existing social relations and not of laws of practical reason.

11. C. Stephen Evans (2004) also argues for a Hegelian understanding.

12. For examples of Kantian readings, see Goodman 1996, Mooney 1991, Cohen 2003, and Glenn 1974. For a good critique of Kantian interpretations, see Stack 1977.

13. One other possible option, which I find simply inadequate, is Brand Blanshard's conclusion that "Kierkegaard had little grasp of ethical theory" (1969, 114–15).

14. For other considerations of Kierkegaard's relation to Kant, especially as it centers on the issues of ethics and faith, see Green 1992; Schrader 1968; and Perkins 1981a.

15. See Evans (2004, 67–9) for an expanded articulation of this distinction between rationality and sociality as the key factor in Silentio's understanding of ethics.

16. Indeed, on this point Silentio might comment that at least Kant is consistent, since he challenges the idea that acting on such a divine command is ever properly within the domain of ethical life (see Kant 1960, 174–75). As Silentio repeatedly points out, for Hegel to be true to his own ethical standard, he must condemn Abraham rather than elevating him as the father of faith (see FT, 55, 68–69, 82).

17. Although Mackey is one of the only commentators who takes adequate account of the "if," it should be noted that in his classic essay, "The Loss of the World in Kierkegaard's Ethics" (included in Mackey 1986), he equates the "Kierkegaardian ethical" with an individualistic and acosmic existentialism that is in direct opposition with the sort of ethical understanding that I find in *Fear and Trembling*. For a very good response to the acosmic reading of Kierkegaard, see Ferreira 1999, and Walsh's reply 1999.

18. As an example, see Anthony Rudd's discussion of "Kierkegaardian ethics" (1993, 69–114). Rudd claims to "have attempted sympathetically to reconstruct Kierkegaard's argument for the ethical" (1993, 115). Additionally, Alasdair MacIntyre speaks of the "conservative and traditional character of Kierkegaard's account of the ethical" as one of the main "features" of *Either/Or* (1984, 43). For both thinkers, Judge William is taken largely to speak for Kierkegaard.

19. New spaces for doing philosophy in light of new phenomenology and deconstruction are most likely to occur when such traditional "dogmas" as these begin to be overcome. I try to do something of this sort in chapter 11 when I propose a notion of a "deconstructive foundationalism," which I recognize will sound like an oxymoron to many philosophers (regardless of the tradition in which they work).

20. One could object that my account of a decidedly Levinasian notion of ethics al-

ready being present in *Fear and Trembling* would fall prey to this same critique; this is not the case, however, because what matters is the *telos* within which ethics moves. The conception of ethics that I advocate below does not operate according to the standards of universality (which is a trait that divine command theory shares with *Sittlichkeit*), but instead according to singularity. The *telos* that is operative in Silentio's account of faith is the same as that which is operative in my re-reading of ethics in *Fear and Trembling*. This is why the conception of ethics that I find under the surface of the text stands in constant tension with religion rather than somehow competing with it. It could never be "teleologically suspended" by religion because the *telos* is the same: the recognition of responsibility as constitutive of subjectivity.

21. Richard Cohen makes a related claim regarding the similarities between the singularity of Kierkegaard's religious sphere and the particularity of his aesthetic sphere. Both resist the category of the "general" that is characteristic of the ethical sphere. Without this notion of generality, Cohen finds it problematic to distinguish between piety and impiety since both are for the most part a matter of interiority and hence are private concerns. "In the end," he writes, "having rejected any standard as merely 'general,' the faith of Kierkegaard is indistinguishable from personal inclination, which means it is indistinguishable from unfaith or impiety" (2003, 23–24).

22. It is important to note that although Schaeffer is highly critical of Kierkegaard, he at least recognizes that the irrationality that is attributed to him may be somewhat misdirected. For this reason, Schaeffer's critical comments are often directed at "Kierkegaardianism" rather than at Kierkegaard himself. That said, Schaeffer's reading of Kierkegaard (and Kierkegaardianism) should, I believe, ultimately be viewed as quite superficial even given this contextual explanation.

23. For an alternative "Aristotelian" defense of Kierkegaard against the charge of irrationalism, see Lillegard 2002.

24. M. Jamie Ferreira (1998) also argues that the "Kierkegaardian leap" need not be considered as irrational as it is often presented. Although her focus is slightly different than mine, it can be read as complementary to it. By looking to the way in which Climacus deals with the leap as a "pathos filled qualitative transition," she suggests that the volitional prerequisite that is required for Blanshard's and MacIntyre's critiques to hold is not present throughout the texts themselves.

25. For further elaboration on how the paradox is paradoxical precisely due to its relation to human existence, see Westphal 2004, 205; and 1991, chap. 6.

26. Consider Anthony Rudd's claim: "In the Kierkegaardian world—and I believe that it is our world—there are no guarantees. The desire for the absolute, the 'infinite longing' of which Kierkegaard speaks so eloquently, may be delusive; the leap into the religious may be a leap into thin air. We must either give up the infinite longing or transcend the merely ethical; but there is nothing that can tell us which is the right choice to make" (1993, 139–40). With this assessment Edward Mooney is in some agreement: ". . . the infamous 'teleological suspension of ethics' marks a moment when justification falls away" (1991, 66).

27. For a consideration of how this singularity is manifested as a political reality, see Matuštík 1995.

28. As I have already mentioned, Evans (2004) also challenges a narrow reading of the Kierkegaardian individual.

29. I use the terms 'individuality' and 'particularity' interchangeably.

30. This should not be read as an instrumentalist claim. The role of Isaac cannot be read as simply a moment along the way to the articulation of some larger point. All I am stressing is that without Abraham's singular relation to Isaac, we are unable to make sense of his ordeal. Abraham's relation to Isaac is central to Abraham's relation to God—and importantly, vice versa.

31. For more on how this hospitality shows up as both a political and also religious notion, see chapter 8.

32. This passage is too often overlooked in the literature. An exception to this trend is Jerome Gellman's consideration of it (2003, 54). See also Gene Outka's (1973) discussion of Abraham's love for Isaac.

33. I do not use the term 'fundamentalism' lightly. I am not saying that all who describe themselves as religious fundamentalists fall within the purview of my discussion here. Certainly, being traditional and dogmatically orthodox need not involve the sort of violence I am worried about. Rather, I use this term to describe various groups of individuals who have used the banner of "divine revelation" to propagate some of the most horrific crimes in human history.

34. For a very good collection of essays that explore the relationship between gift and sacrifice, see Wyschogrod, Goux, and Boynton 2002.

35. It is here that the main difference between Kierkegaard and Levinas begins to appear: for Levinas, it is within the relation to the Other that we encounter the trace of God. The difference between the thinkers is, thus, primarily a difference of emphasis and priority rather than of structure and content. However, the results that follow from this difference may turn out to be very significant.

36. See Derrida 1995 and 1992a. See also, Caputo and Scanlon 1999, and Horner 2001. For a consideration of the "logic of gift" in Kierkegaard, see Kangas 2000.

37. I use Outka as an example here, but it should be noted that at the end of the same essay Outka goes on to sketch the possibility of an alternative, and "more modest," interpretation of *Fear and Trembling* in which "religious duty can but need not conflict with our ordinary antecedent judgments of right and wrong" (1973, 250). Nonetheless, this alternative interpretation still understands ethics in the way that I have suggested is contested by the text itself.

38. Other scholars have noted such parallels. George L. Stengren (1977) claims that Kierkegaard and Aquinas offer similar conceptions of "connatural" knowledge as opposed to the objectivity that characterizes "speculative" thought. Brian Stiltner (1993) suggests that although Kierkegaard and Aquinas are often viewed as divergent in their conceptions of how to relate morality to God's will (voluntarist and rationalist respectively), upon closer examination their positions begin to converge on how believers can "affirm a conception of God who both acts and is worthy of worship" (1993, 223). Stiltner does not collapse Kierkegaard into Aquinas or the reverse, but rather sees the potential resonance between their thought as opening the space for a more productive disagreement.

39. Evans also reads *Fear and Trembling* as attributing epistemic certainty to Abraham: "It is noteworthy that *Fear and Trembling* does not discuss the question as to how Abraham came to know that God had asked him to perform the act. The book simply assumes that Abraham knows this and knows it with certainty" (2004, 310).

40. As I pointed out in note 37 above, Outka does offer a "more modest" interpretation of *Fear and Trembling* at the end of the essay under consideration here. It is important that he notes that such an alternative conception is not completely at odds with a possible interpretation of Aquinas as well. I mention this to simply say that since I am unable to consider Aquinas's account with the depth and precision that it requires, I am entirely open to the possibility that there might be interpretations of Aquinas that would converge with my reading of *Fear and Trembling* here. The differences between Aquinas and Kierkegaard are not my primary concern; rather, I am simply trying to point out that as long as we take Kierkegaard to affirm a "traditionally" Thomistic conception of divine obligation and moral duty then it is extremely difficult to maintain the anxiety that Silentio is so concerned about.

41. It may turn out that we need to contest Silentio's usage of the term "know" rather than merely rethink it. Because of the difficulties inherent in attempting to keep faith (understood as risk) separate from simply falling back into a form of "weak knowledge"—i.e., one claims to have faith because she just doesn't have the evidence (justification) to convert it into full-fledged knowledge yet—it is possible that religious "knowing" is not primarily about *knowledge* at all in this sense, but, as will be made clear in chapters 9 and 11, more about *trusting*. Similarly, "certainty" may turn out to be inextricably wedded to a problematic conception of knowledge and, hence, should perhaps be replaced by "confidence" or "assurance." As such, it might be that what is required is not a certainty without ordinary sorts of knowledge, but a lived confidence in the God in whom I place my trust.

42. For more on how Bonhoeffer stands as a crucial example of what postmodern ethics and politics might look like, see chapter 13.

3. Bi-directional Relationality

1. It is certainly the case that orthodox Judaism also affirms a personal God (a fact that Levinas often seems to neglect in his own thought, see Westphal 2008b). The central distinction I am trying to draw here is about the way in which one understands and lives out the relation to God (amid others), more than about specific doctrines of God operating in various theologies.

2. See, for example, Pailin (1981) which discusses the various readings of Genesis 22 arising in the seventeenth and eighteenth centuries.

3. For a consideration of Kierkegaard's relation to the Jewish tradition, see Steinberg 1960.

4. Green's claim about the exceptional status of Kierkegaard's reading is not limited to the Jewish tradition. Indeed, he goes on to say that Kierkegaard's presentation is "enormously eccentric" even within the Christian tradition (1988, 122).

5. Interestingly, it seems as if Levinas's engagement with Genesis 22 is due primarily to his reaction against Kierkegaard rather than its being a primary concern of his own. As

far as I know, Levinas does not spend substantial time working through the Genesis account except in relation to Kierkegaard's reading of it.

6. For a decidedly different take on Levinas's reading of the *Akedah,* see Cohen 2003. Therein, Cohen attempts to offer a critique of Kierkegaard's conception of the religious as somehow beyond ethics. In response, Cohen clearly favors the reading of Levinas in which religion is only a possibility within ethics. As much of what follows will demonstrate, I find this reading to be extremely problematic. For another example of a reading of the *Akedah* that challenges the Kierkegaardian interpretation in a similar way to Cohen's, see Katz 2005. For a very good consideration of sacrifice in general as it stands in relation to Christian theology, see Coakley forthcoming.

7. Levinas, "Loving the Torah more than God," in DF.

8. Levinas, "Loving the Torah more than God," in DF, 145.

9. During a lecture at Florida State University in 1998, Wiesel said that throughout his authorship there were critiques of God. Yet, he immediately added, these critiques never stood alone; they were always followed by some form of prayer. The point is simply that in order to cry out to God (in anger or in adoration) you must first recognize God as someone to whom or at whom one could cry out.

10. On Evans's (2004) account of divine command theory, it is necessary that he distinguish between the obligations that arise out of social relationships to other people (which do not immediately stand as "moral" obligations) and those that result from divine imperative—which is what adds the "moral" dimension. It might seem that this would be fundamentally at odds with Levinas's location of moral obligation in the face of the Other, and in many ways I think that it is. However, as I suggested in the last chapter, divine command and human nature can be rethought in a deconstructive way, and accordingly it might be that Evans's model is quite consistent with Levinas's. That is, there are places in Levinas's authorship where it seems that it is the trace of God's passing (the height) that orders me to care for the Other (the low). Perhaps this is a different vocabulary for expressing the key aspect of Levinas's insight regarding the identity of these duties. My suspicion, though, is that Evans (perhaps rightly) would resist the identity of these obligations and suggest that something is lost on the Levinasian model because it is less able to distinguish between moral and nonmoral obligations to other people. The position I am advocating here is not one of identity, but of a perpetual tension between priorities. This tension would be impossible if one were not able to differentiate between the duty to God and the duty to the Other, and this is why I propose that Kierkegaard and Levinas must be read *together.*

11. Levinas, "A God 'Transcendent to the Point of Absence,'" in GDT.

12. For a discussion of human sacrifice in the period of Abraham, see Goodman 1996, esp. chap. 1: "The Logic of Monotheism."

13. Consider Silentio's claim: "The one knight of faith cannot help the other at all. Either the single individual himself becomes the knight of faith by accepting the paradox or he never becomes one. Partnership in these areas is utterly unthinkable" (FT, 71).

14. See also OTB, 149, 152, 185; "Truth of Disclosure and Truth of Testimony," in BPW, 105–106; "God and Philosophy," in BPW, 144–45.

15. For considerations of Abraham's silence, see Wren 1981 and M. Taylor 1981.

16. On the link between responsibility, normativity, and discourse, see Korsgaard 1996, and Perpich 2008, esp. chap. 2.

17. For an extremely good critical response to Derrida and Levinas on this point, see David Wood 2002, esp. chaps. 8 and 9.

18. I have worked through these differences somewhat more thoroughly elsewhere (Simmons 2008). Westphal rightly diagnoses the locus of the different priorities when he claims that "for Levinas, recognizing the infinity of the neighbor is an essential prior condition to recognizing the infinity of God, while for Kierkegaard it seems to be the other way around" (1995b, 273). For more considerations of the relation between Levinas and Kierkegaard, see Simmons and Wood 2008.

19. One might protest that I am constructing a straw man here. However, I have heard this suggested by several quite distinguished Levinas scholars. Since they have never put this idea in print, however, I have chosen to let the comment remain anonymous and put it in the mouth of an imagined interlocutor.

20. Philip L. Quinn suggests that *Practice in Christianity* be read along with *Works of Love* as examples of the "new ethics" (1998, 368ff).

21. I find this to be quite similar to Levinas's claim at the beginning of *Totality and Infinity* that the infinite only shows up (as a rupture) within the totality of history.

22. Accordingly, a deconstructive re-thinking of divine command theory would require locating such commands as only possible *after* the movement of faith and never before it. Why this would be a radical notion is that the movement of faith, as I have argued, never allows for there to be a relation to God that is detached from the relation to other people. Hence, the "command" of love is actually inscribed into what it means to be a self in the first place—as Evans (2004) rightly contends. To understanding this command *as a* command is to recognize the relation to God that makes it possible.

23. For a good consideration of the relation between love and sacrifice in Kierkegaard, see Agacinski 1998.

24. For a deconstructive appropriation of the WWJD mantra, see Caputo 2007.

4. An Ontology of Constitutive Responsibility

1. Two points of clarification are needed here. First, by "religious" I do not mean *non-philosophical*. As I will make clear in part 2, I do not consider the "theological turn" to be a turn to theology and away from philosophy. Instead, I will describe it as a deepening of the phenomenological impulse originally articulated by Husserl. The sustained engagement with Rorty's ambiguous relation to theory in chapter 1 was meant to demonstrate that the political worry about Levinasian ethics is really one directed toward the "religious" dimensions of Levinas's philosophy. That said, those dimensions need not be seen as explicitly religious at all, but more rightly as being ontological rather than reductively political (as I contend is the case in Rorty, Hardt and Negri, the early work of Foucault, etc.). Second, I want to make clear that my discussion of the ontological stakes of politics is not meant to suggest that somehow Levinas and Kierkegaard are the only ones to recognize this. Similar sorts of ontological considerations are found, for example, in Charles Taylor's (1989) discussion of how selfhood occurs in the context of socio-cultural communities, Nussbaum's

(2000; 2006) neo-Aristotelian version of liberalism, and Sandel's (1998; 2006; 2009) critique of (while deeply appreciating) Rawls in the name of a more plausible account of justice. What the ontology of constitutive responsibility offers to political theory that these other alternatives do not, I believe, is the bi-directional notion of relationality that is opened by the tension between a constitutive relation to God and to the Other. Although a comparative analysis of these ontologies is something I hope to return to in the future, in this book my task is simply to argue for the ethical and political relevance of the such a relationality (and ontology), in light of Rorty's critique, but not to contend for its absolute uniqueness.

2. I want to distinguish what I am doing here from Carol Gould's (1988) account of "social ontology." Gould claims that her notion overcomes the difficulties faced by the other three political versions: (1) Liberal Individualism, (2) Pluralist Political Democracy, and (3) Holistic Socialism. Resisting both the isolationist tendencies of the former and the totalizing characteristics of the latter, Gould proposes a "coherent ontology in which individuality is given its full due but not at the cost of regarding individuals as isolated and abstract egos, standing in only external relations to each other; at the same time, in this ontology, internal relations are seen to obtain in a way that preserves the importance of sociality, but not at the cost of an overarching totality or whole of which individuals are mere parts or functions" (1988, 105). The "fundamental entities" that populate this ontological narrative are "individuals-in-relations, where these individuals are human beings and their relations are social relations." Although I am strongly in support of the overall direction that she offers in this text—namely, the attempt to overcome the liberal/communitarian divide—I want to differentiate between her conception of "social ontology" and what I am calling an "ontology of constitutive responsibility." The basic difference is that her entire account *already lies* in the realm of politics. The human beings that she considers are political entities and as such are themselves problematically taken-for-granted. What I am trying to offer here is not a *political* conception of ontology, but an ontology that would open the space for an *ethico-religious approach to politics.* Her notion may indeed be the best alternative for how to understand the sociological or empirical realities of political life, but it does not give an adequate explanation for how to conceive of politics as an ethico-religious task. To put it succinctly, if Heidegger's account of *Mitsein* is taken as the basic structure of political life, then Gould's notion would be perfectly reasonable as an account of how being-with others is constitutive for *Dasein.* But just as there are specifically ethical problems with *Mitsein,* so there are ethical problems with Gould's "social ontology." Being in a society may indeed mean that we are always already about the task of justifying ourselves to others, as Christine Korsgaard (1996) suggests. Nonetheless, this process of justification can always be conducted in line with egoism: I justify myself in order to make greater room for my own possibilities. I convince others that I have, as Levinas says, "a right to be" so that I can more fully actualize my specific desires and wants. Normativity can still be unethical; this is the whole point of Kierkegaard's *Fear and Trembling.* The work that I am suggesting ontology should do is to contest egoism from the start—i.e., egoism is challenged from within my own interiority. Hence, I find Gould's "social ontology" to be too late, as it were, for the real questions that confront any ethico-religiously minded politics. In another vein, the phrase "social ontology" is also used by Robert D'Amico to describe Georg Lukacs's conception of

how sociology has replaced ontology in Continental philosophy (1999, 121ff.). There are two reasons that D'Amico's comments are outside of my concern here: (1) Whether rightly or not, D'Amico uses the phrase to describe the way in which Lukacs sidesteps ontological questions in favor of mere historical descriptions. This is far from what I mean by an ontology of constitutive responsibility. (2) D'Amico does not offer an extended discussion of the phrase itself and so leaves the reader to wonder whether a more appropriate description might be something like "sociological reductionism." And finally, Michael Theunissen (1984) also uses the phrase "social ontology," but in a way that is still distinct from what I am advocating here.

3. For a good analysis of this paragraph, as well as a reading of *The Sickness Unto Death* as a whole that is largely in line with the interpretation I will offer below, see Crites 1992. Therein, Crites discusses the implications of what he calls a "relational self."

4. Elsewhere I have given extended consideration of this Levinasian reading of Kierkegaard, especially as influenced by Jean Wahl (Simmons 2008).

5. Anti-Climacus will repeat this claim repeatedly throughout the text: ". . . the self is healthy and free from despair only when, precisely by having despaired, it rests transparently in God" (SUD, 30); ". . . the formula for the state in which there is no despair at all: in relating itself to itself and in willing to be itself, the self rests transparently in the power that established it" (SUD, 131).

6. Stephen Crites will differentiate these aspects as referring to the "self given" and the "self potentiated" (1992, 155ff.).

7. This passage should be read in tandem with Kierkegaard's famous Gilleleje journal entry of 1 August 1835 (JP, IA, 75).

8. Hent de Vries also uses this terminology in his description of the Levinasian "Ethical-Religious" Other (2005, esp. chap. 7).

9. Levinas, "Is Ontology Fundamental?" in BPW, 10.

10. Levinas and Richard Kearney, "Dialogue with Emmanuel Levinas.," in Cohen 1988, 13–33, 21–22.

11. When Wyschogrod (2000) and Peperzak (1997) deploy the term "ethical metaphysics," they are close to what I term an "ontology of constitutive responsibility." Regarding this idea of ethical metaphysics, Peperzak writes: "Although Levinas himself sometimes calls his 'first philosophy' an ethics . . . he does not deny that it is at the same time a metaphysics, and he calls it that more than once. Like Plato's thought, Levinas's philosophy is a metaphysical ethics or an ethical metaphysics" (1997, 223).

12. Importantly, I am specifically attributing this problematic notion of ontology to *Platonism* rather than to *Plato*. There is much debate regarding exactly how Plato understood the self and it is not unimportant that Levinas found Plato to be one of the moments in philosophy where the Good is grasped "beyond Being"—i.e., ethics is conceived in Plato outside of ontology. Thus, Levinas himself distinguishes between Plato and Platonism—see "Meaning and Sense," in BPW. For Levinas's conception of the Platonic Good, see TI, 103, 218, 293; OTB, 19; AT, 61.

13. Levinas will speak of this absent signification in various ways: as trace, lapse, a past that was never present, diachrony, and also by using the example of skepticism. Consider

also Levinas's parallel discussion of a God who is "transcendent to the point of absence," in GDT.

14. Levinas, "Is Ontology Fundamental?" in BPW, 6; TI, 51.

15. Although it is slightly beyond the purview of my discussion here, it could be argued, legitimately I believe, that transparency does display such an ambiguity when it comes to the Kierkegaardian notion of God-in-time (i.e., Christ). It is essential for Kierkegaard that God was incarnated in the lowliest of persons. This exposes more than simply the kenotic status of God's relation to humanity: it demonstrates the agapic love of God as expressed by radical humility. This expression of love, this relation, would be such that in the person of Christ, God is also transparent. When considered in this way, the difference between God's transparency and that of the single individual would be tied up with the notion of "resting": Christ never rests transparently in us, although we rest transparently in Christ. The reason for this is that the single individual is never the "power that constitutes" the original relation, but merely the one who takes it up as definitive of her existence. Interestingly, by tracing these apparent differences between Kierkegaard and Levinas, we arrive at another interesting congruence: namely, both thinkers understand the constitutive relation to be asymmetrical. However, without being able to adequately develop the thought here, I would suggest that because Kierkegaard inserts God as the middle term between the individual and the other person, he has the resources to overcome the problems that arise when asymmetry is taken to exist between individuals. The very way I give to God would be to take up my obligations to other people; but although singularly constituted as responsible and irreplaceable, I am also equal to every other because they too stand before God, whether reflectively or not. As Dietrich Bonhoeffer (1954) will say in *Life Together,* the cross of Christ does not only illuminate the suffering of God, thus calling my gaze upward; rather, it illuminates the suffering of all the others standing beside me, thus calling me to care for my neighbor. This would be an equality without egoism, and I am unsure if Levinas is able to offer anything comparable.

16. Levinas, "Peace and Proximity," in AT, 139–40.

17. For Kierkegaard, that the other person can possess this dual status is made possible through Christ's paradoxical existence.

18. As Levinas will write: "If the same would establish its identity by simple *opposition to the other,* it would already be a part of a totality encompassing the same and the other" (TI, 38).

19. See also, "Is Ontology Fundamental?"

20. Levinas, "Language and Proximity," in CPP, 121.

21. Accordingly, we might ask whether Kierkegaardian "faith" and Levinasian "substitution" are not structurally equivalent relative to both thinkers' vocabularies and formulations.

22. Levinas repeats this later in the text when he is discussing the fundamental asymmetry between the self and the Other: the "inequality" between myself and the Other "does not appear to the third party who would count us" (TI, 251).

23. As C. S. Lewis might say in this regard, we can only look "along the beam" and never "at the beam" (see 1970, 212–15).

24. Levinas, "Language and Proximity," in CPP, 115; emphasis added.

25. Here Simone Weil's (2005) discussion of force provides a helpful articulation of the way in which force views others as "things."

26. Levinas, "Language and Proximity," in CPP, 199.

27. Levinas, "Language and Proximity," in CPP, 124.

28. Emmanuel Levinas, Luc Ferry, Raphaël Hadas-Lebel, and Sylvaine Pasquier, "In the Name of the Other," in RTB, 192.

29. This formulation can be found in his work as early as 1947's *Time and the Other:* "nous ne 'pouvons plus pouvoir'" (TO, 74).

30. For a good consideration of this point, see Hughes (1998). Additionally, for a discussion of whether war or peace is primary in Levinas, see Atterton 1992; D. Wood 2005.

5. Levinasian Subjectivity and Political Critique

1. Not to mention the difficulties that occur at the level of expression with the persistent challenge of self-refutation pointed out by Derrida in "Violence and Metaphysics" (in Derrida 1978). See also Aikin and Simmons 2009. For good discussions of the relationship between Levinas and Derrida, see Bernasconi 1986, 1991, and 1997; Critchley 1999; Llewelyn 1988 and 2002; Wyschogrod 1989; and Manning 1998.

2. The same could be said regarding the metaphor of vision and having the proverbial "eyes to see" (see Simmons 2009).

3. We would be right to question the adequacy of this explanation when disengaged from its theological implications. Levinas does admit that the Other, "in his signification prior to my initiative, *resembles* God" (TI, 293; emphasis added). Yet how far this resemblance is from identification is an open question. Adriaan Peperzak notes that this ambiguity is more than just superficial; he goes so far as to suggest that Levinas begins by identifying "The Other" as the "other human being," but in his later formulations uses the term to "stand for God" (1997, 4).

4. This is reminiscent of Gianni Vattimo's statement, "Thanks to God, I am an atheist," which will be discussed in detail in chapter 8. See also Vattimo 1999, 2002; Vattimo and Rorty 2005.

5. Levinas, "Freedom and Command," in CPP, 21.

6. Levinas, "The Ego and the Totality," in CPP, 29.

7. Levinas, "Philosophy and the Idea of Infinity," in CPP, 54.

8. Levinas, "Substitution," in BPW, 91.

9. Levinas, "Substitution," in BPW, 91.

10. Levinas, "The Ego and Totality," in CPP, 41.

11. The way Levinas's sentence is constructed, it gives the impression that these options are simply two ways of expressing the same problematic understanding of the fixed point; I want to suggest that his claim only makes sense if we separate the two as distinct. Certainly something could be an "incontestable truth" without being available to psychoanalysis, and something could be claimed as "certain" without being incontestable or true. In the first instance, we might locate the basic laws of logic—(A = A), ~(A & ~A), etc.— and in the second, we could find certainties that define an individual's psyche but do not

extend to the realm of universality. For example, someone's "certainty" that swimming or wading in water is terrifying if not deadly may be due to a childhood trauma at a pool. Neither of these examples would qualify as instances of the "fixed point" for Levinas, and so I conclude that we must read this passage as bracketing out these distinct contenders.

12. Levinas, "Is Ontology Fundamental?" in BPW, 6.

13. For a good collection of essays dealing with the relationship between negative theology and contemporary Continental philosophy, see Scharlemann 1992—especially the essays by David E. Klemm, Mark C. Taylor, and Edith Wyschogrod. For a consideration of the difficulties that alterity poses for language and theory, see J. Smith 1997, 2002.

14. I will return to this claim as it relates to epistemology in chapter 11.

15. This is the substance of Levinas's task of thinking "escape" (l'évasion) without at all making it a movement from this world to another; see OE.

16. Following Rorty, we should also mention Sellars, Quine, and Davidson as making similar moves within analytic philosophy.

17. The main proponent of a "transcendental" reading of Levinas is Theodore de Boer (1997). See also Levinas's response to a question de Boer asks about method (in GWCM, 86–90). Although I am influenced by de Boer's reading of Levinas, I depart from it when it comes to the way in which he understands what a "transcendental ethical philosophy" would actually be. De Boer's formulations retain a conception of deduction that is far too rooted in logical certainty. In what follows I will try to articulate a vision of the transcendental method that is already critical of itself and in this way build upon de Boer while also sharply diverging from him. Jeffrey Dudiak extends and deepens this transcendental reading in conversation with de Boer and Bernasconi (Dudiak 2001, chap. 7). Jeffrey Bloechl also advocates understanding Levinas as offering a "transcendental analysis of human being which takes into account a dimension which can not be reduced to any form of self-interest" (2002, 201).

18. Another example of this is in contemporary worldview studies. Worldviews are said to be products of culture, and yet they are the very "frames" through which we are able to engage, understand, and participate in culture. Elsewhere, I argue that this paradoxical status is promising for deconstructive social and political thought rather than being an obstacle that should motivate us to eliminate the term and concept from philosophical discussion (Simmons 2006).

19. Diane Perpich and I have suggested (Simmons and Perpich 2005) that the face of the Other is best understood as neither foundational nor anti-foundational. While I still think this is basically right, I am now inclined to say that there are better ways of conceiving it; see chapter 11 below.

20. Levinas specifically claims that the "presentation and the development of the notions employed [in *Totality and Infinity*] owe everything to the phenomenological method" (TI, 28). In 1975, Levinas revisits this claim and says that "it is not the word 'transcendental' that I would retain, but the notion of intentional analysis" (GWCM, 87).

21. David Roochnik (1990) argues that such an aporetic structure can be seen throughout the dialogues of Plato, and suggests that this "tragedy of reason" calls for a certain amount of humility to temper philosophical rigor. Nevertheless, that this is the case calls

for rigorous and rational demonstration—the situation that confronts all philosophizing after Socrates.

22. For another important consideration of Derrida as a transcendental or quasi-transcendental philosopher is Gasché 1986. For a critique of Gasché, see Rorty's "Is Derrida a Transcendental Philosopher?" (in Rorty 1991b, 119–28).

23. Levinas, "Subjectivity as An-Archy," in GDT, 175.

24. Levinas will define phenomenology as giving voice to the concrete (TI, 28).

25. Again, I want to stress that this is *not* a claim that this is the *only* viable ontological account. There is much that seems right to me about the communitarianism of Sandel, MacIntyre, and Taylor, as well as the neo-Aristotelianism of Nussbaum. Those working in Continental ethics and political theory should avoid the temptation to view their particular thinker of choice—Levinas or Derrida, Butler or Kristeva, say—as promising everything to everyone. I simply want to present a strong argument in favor of the ontology of constitutive responsibility as a substantive alternative to many other contenders in contemporary political philosophy.

26. Levinas, "Is Ontology Fundamental?" in BPW, 6.

27. For a rather interesting discussion of the implications and possibilities of such an idea see Derrida's essay "The Right to Philosophy from the Cosmopolitical Point of View" (in Derrida 2002). Also, for an introduction to this notion and its progression throughout Derrida's thought, see Patton 2007.

28. There is much to be said about the way in which Rorty and Levinas differ in their understandings of "utopia" (see Simmons 2010). For a good example of Levinas's thoughts on utopia, see "Place and Utopia," in DF (see also Horowitz and Horowitz 2006).

6. Mapping Twists and "Turns"

1. This list is not meant to be exhaustive. Although I will be focusing on these figures, other names that might be mentioned here are Jean-François Courtine, Paul Ricœur, René Girard, and to a lesser degree, perhaps even Jean-François Lyotard.

2. For just a few examples, see Bloechl 2002, 2003; Benson 2002; Benson and Wirzba 2008, 2010; Caputo and Scanlon 2007.

3. Although these Derridean notions are extremely complicated and deserve to be considered in the context of the entire Derridean corpus, for our purposes here they can be understood simply as attempts to philosophically maintain the structures of religious experience (hope, anticipation, devotion, patience, etc.) while abandoning the specific doctrinal content of determinate religious traditions.

4. Žižek's relation to phenomenology is complicated and cannot be given adequate consideration here; however, for Žižek's primary considerations of religion, see 2003; 2001; 2000.

5. For essays on the specifically phenomenological strain of contemporary Continental philosophy of religion, see Janicaud et al. 2000; de Vries 1999; Caputo 2002; Jonkers and Welten 2005; Westphal 1997; and Long 2003, esp. chap. 9. For broader considerations of Continental philosophy of religion, see Goodchild 2003, 2002; Caputo and Vattimo 2007, especially the introduction by Jeffrey W. Robbins; Derrida and Vattimo 1998; Bloechl 2003; Wrathall 2003; and Long 2007, 2003, esp. chaps. 15, 20, 21, and 23.

6. Because there have been many very good technical essays written regarding the religious turn in phenomenology, this chapter is intentionally written for those without a substantial background in phenomenology (or even Continental philosophy). The reader should of course not assume that my accounts of various thinkers are the final word on their thought, but instead receive them as invitations to consider what might be a foreign area of philosophical study as nonetheless being worthy of further investigation.

7. For more on Husserl's reductions, see Føllesdal 2006.

8. For a good account of not only the progression of the notion of horizon, but of Husserl's thought in general, see Mohanty 1995.

9. Russell makes very clear that this particular conception of the lifeworld is only one among several possibilities. Distinguishing between the "thick" and "thin" interpretations, Russell leaves the open the question of which is more appropriate to the intention of the text (2006, 194).

10. It is reminiscent of Climacus's claim in *Philosophical Fragments* that when it comes to Christianity, God would have to not only provide an occasion for truth, but the conditions for being able to receive it as such.

11. Janicaud is not alone in this, and neither is he the first: Bernard Prusak suggests that Jean Hering's 1925 text *Phénoménologie et philosophie religieuse* raises similar concerns (Prusak 2000, 4).

12. Although discussions of God appear frequently in Levinas's authorship, for some of the more prominent examples see GWCM and GDT, part 2. For good commentaries on Levinas's philosophy of religion see Kosky 2001; Bloechl 2000; Peperzak 1995; and Purcell 2006.

13. An exception being Merleau-Ponty's consideration of the "invisible," for which Janicaud expresses admiration due to its always being intimately concerned with phenomenality (see Janicaud 2000, 22–28). I will return to this in the next chapter.

14. Prusak points out that Janicaud's rigid commitments to a very specific interpretation of Husserl leave him "vulnerable to the charge that he ignores Husserl's development and turns Husserl's method into a doctrine" (2000, 7).

15. For example, see Jonkers and Welten 2005; Housset 1997. For a classical consideration of Husserl's thoughts on God, see Q. Smith 1979.

16. When asked about his own religious perspective, Derrida said that he "rightly passed" as an atheist.

17. As I mentioned in the section introduction to part 2, I have chosen to focus on these overarching themes rather than on individual figures because although others have already written very good introductory essays on certain new phenomenologists (see Jonkers and Welton 2005), considerations of the movement as a whole are less prominent (one exception would be de Vries 1999). What I consider to be the best introduction to the movement as a whole is actually a fairly technical essay by Merold Westphal (2007), which focuses primarily on Marion but still nicely raises issues that are central for many of the main figures of new phenomenology. Of course, my strategy at present has certain drawbacks—at times, my references to particular figures will have to be more suggestive than explicative. Nonetheless, such a thematic focus has the benefit of more easily allowing us to see lines

of possible engagement between new phenomenology, political philosophy, and contemporary Anglo-American philosophy of religion. Importantly, although they will allow for a general introduction to the key notions developed by the major players in the movement, these themes are not meant to be applicable in the *same* way to *all* new phenomenological thinkers. Instead, they are intended to be broad ways of seeing the basic lines of argumentation that loosely connect these otherwise varied philosophers. I should note that Lacoste is an interesting case, however. Although primarily recognized as a theologian, his work under consideration here, *Experience and the Absolute* (2004), is, I contend, more appropriately viewed as a philosophical work.

18. Additionally, it should be noted that some American appropriators of new phenomenology have begun to be more comfortable with self-consciously crossing into theology (see Caputo 2006).

19. Any consideration of *kenosis* in Continental philosophy of religion should involve the work of Gianni Vattimo, who has done more work on this notion than anyone else in contemporary Continental philosophy (see Vattimo 1999; 2002). However, since Vattimo is outside the community of new phenomenology, though intimately related to it, I will not explore his thought here, but instead return to it in chapter 8.

20. It should be noted that Caputo's 2006 text is perhaps more a work of theology than philosophy and depends as much upon process theology (in particular, the work of Catherine Keller) as it does upon phenomenology. Also, I do not want to give the impression that new phenomenology need be committed to the specifics of Caputo's formulations. As I will suggest in chapter 13, when it comes to ethics and philosophy of religion, quite a bit more can be, and I believe should be, said on the topic than Caputo does.

21. For an excellent introduction to Rawls's philosophy, see Freeman 2007.

22. For a slightly different, but very productive, model of religious engagement in political debate, see Eberle 2002. Moreover, for a collection of essays that represents many different perspectives on this issue, see Weithman 1997.

23. For a classic collection of essays on the politics of difference, see Benhabib 1996.

24. Importantly, Wolterstorff does engage Derrida and Ricœur in his work and I take this to be a model of the sort of conversation I am advocating here.

25. For just a couple of further examples of this general trajectory in philosophy of religion, see Plantinga and Wolterstorff 1983; and Phillips 1988.

26. For good considerations of religious belief and skepticism, see Alston, Audi, Penelhum, and Popkin 1992; and Gutting 1982.

27. For just a few examples, see the work of Merold Westphal, John D. Caputo, Bruce Ellis Benson, James K. A. Smith, Jeffrey Kosky, John Davenport, Stephen Minister, Jeffrey Hansen, Drew Dalton, and Jeffrey Bloechl.

7. Reconstructive Separatism

1. This fact leads Welten to write: "Phenomenologically speaking, such 'theological remains' land Marion in trouble in *God without Being*" (2005b, 198). However, as I claimed in the previous chapter, it seems entirely sensible that the same thinker could write texts that are philosophical and also texts that are theological. I see no reason that a person should

be required to do *only* one *or* the other. Kierkegaard, Levinas, and Caputo are other examples of important modern philosophers who write explicitly, on occasion, as constructive theologians (alternatively, Lacoste is primarily a theologian who occasionally writes as a phenomenological philosopher). This does not jeopardize their status as philosophers, but it does require that readers carefully distinguish the sort of work they are doing in particular texts.

2. I am indebted to J. Caleb Clanton for some of this terminology. He applies the terms "separatist" to thinkers like Rawls who advocate an elimination of religion from the public square, and "reconstructivist" to those like Rorty and Cornel West who allow religion back in, but on the provision that it is effectively stripped of its doctrinal particularity (Clanton 2007). Robert Audi and Nicholas Wolterstorff also use the term "separatist" to describe the predominant liberal attitude regarding religion in the public square (1997).

3. For a couple of examples of such presuppositionalist thinkers, see Van Til 2003; Schaeffer 1976.

4. It could be argued that this decidedly religious concern is only present in Derrida's later writings, and hence, that Sneller's contention is rightly more applicable to Derrida's later work. Although I cannot adequately consider this division in Derrida's authorship here, it should be noted that an argument can be made for understanding the religious aspect of Derrida's thought as more properly being an ethico-political trajectory. If this is indeed the case, then Derrida's contestation of an ethico-political turn in his thought is strikingly relevant. As Derrida writes in *Rogues*: ". . . there never was in the 1980s or 1990s, as has sometimes been claimed, a *political turn* or *ethical turn* in 'deconstruction,' at least not as I experience it. The thinking of the political has always been a thinking of différance and the thinking of différance always a thinking *of* the political, of the contour and limits of the political, especially around the enigma or the autoimmune *double bind* of the democratic" (2005, 39).

5. Clanton (2008) makes a similar charge regarding the "prophetic pragmatism" of Cornel West. Elsewhere I have attempted to bring West and Levinas together regarding the notion of an "impossible politics" (see Simmons 2010).

6. I am not saying that one must be a Christian, say, to appropriate Christian themes. Rather, I am simply saying that borrowing from a tradition can often mask an unwillingness to engage that tradition on its own terms (this can be the case even for someone who personally identifies with that tradition).

7. It should be noted that it might be possible to rethink natural theology in postmodernism without thoroughly rejecting it. For example, Adriaan Peperzak argues for the continued relevance of "natural theology" in a postmodern context (1999, esp. chap. 5).

8. For good examples of what a positive trajectory might entail see the following: Westphal 2001; J. Smith 2002; Baker and Maxwell 2003; and Olthuis 1997.

8. Is Continental Philosophy Just Catholicism for Atheists?

1. Here I am referring to the irony of prominent God-talk given the atheism of some of the more important Continental thinkers. For example, Sartre claims that there is either "God or freedom," Freud suggests that religion is an "illusion" out of which we need to be

"educated," Nietzsche famously announces that "God is dead," and Marx characterizes religion as an "opiate of the masses." And though not often viewed as located in the tradition of Continental philosophy, the influence of nineteenth-century attempts to demythologize the life of Jesus could also be considered as a contextual backdrop for such thinkers as Nietzsche, Freud, and Heidegger (see, e.g., Strauss 1994; Renan 1991). For good collections that deal with the relation between postmodern philosophy and religion, see Westphal 1999a, Baker and Maxwell 2003, Derrida and Vattimo 1998, Caputo 2002, and Caputo et al. 2001.

2. Having said that the God-talk under consideration here is primarily tied to the Jewish and Christian religions, let me say again that I am entirely open to the possibility of arguing for non-Christian and non-Jewish God-talk in postmodernism.

3. The interview between Rorty and Vattimo included in *The Future of Religion* was conducted in 2002, and Rorty's essay also originally appeared in 2002 (see Rorty 2002). For an expanded version of Rorty's "reconsideration" of religion in the public square, see Rorty 2003.

4. James K. A. Smith (2002) goes so far as to suggest that incarnational theology might be the condition for philosophical discourse itself.

5. This is what Slavoj Žižek means by Christ's "Uncoupling" (2000, 123ff.).

6. For more on how Christ's claim "I am the truth" can be deployed as an impetus to ethical existence, see Henry 2003.

7. Consider also the hyperbolic quality of Jesus' instruction in Matthew 18: 21–22 (NIV): "'Then Peter came to Jesus and asked, 'Lord, how many times shall I forgive my brother when he sins against me? Up to seven times?' Jesus answered, 'I tell you, not seven times, but seventy-seven times.'"

8. Another way to understand this claim is that, for humans, there simply is no "view from nowhere" (Nagel 1986).

9. Consider the wonderful title of a new collection of essays, *Nietzsche and Levinas: After the Death of a Certain God* (Stauffer and Bergo 2009).

10. Consider Vattimo's claim: "I accept that there is a sort of cutoff point in history: BC before and AD after" (Vattimo and Rorty 2005, 63).

11. Heidegger's relationship to religion, and especially to Christianity, is widely recognized as being philosophically and biographically complex. For good accounts of these complexities, see Kovacs 1990 and Macquarrie 1994. For a discussion of the way in which Heidegger informs the contemporary debates in Continental philosophy of religion, see Jonkers 2005.

12. As in part 1, I draw here on Robert Bernasconi's suggestion that there exists an irresolvable tension between ethics and politics in Levinas's thought (1999). However, as I argued earlier, ethics must be granted a certain priority for this tension to even exist.

13. Importantly, in *Works of Love* Kierkegaard will suggest that the very possibility of viewing the other person as "neighbor" requires a theological gesture. For very helpful considerations of Kierkegaard's reflections on this front in relation to Levinas, see Ferreira 2001; 2008; and Dudiak 2008.

14. Though tapping into this archive in no way requires that one commit oneself to a specific set of religious beliefs, one should continue to pay careful attention to the specifics

of the determinate traditions themselves (i.e., it is important to be on guard against the potential patronizing tendencies of reconstructivism). Importantly, this list includes a Catholic (Marion), a Jew (Levinas), a Catholic-trained atheist, well-versed in patristic, medieval, and Protestant theology (Heidegger), a person who claims that he "rightly passes as an atheist" (Derrida), and one who affirms Christianity and yet says, "Thanks to God, I am an atheist" (Vattimo). Additionally, although it is beyond the scope of this chapter, I want to note that recently such thinkers as Alain Badiou, Slavoj Žižek, as well as many others associated with Radical Orthodoxy have tapped the Christian theological archive for political resources. For the central texts in this area see Badiou 2003; Žižek 2000, 2001, 2003, and 2006; Žižek et. al. 2005; and Davis et al. 2005.

9. The Religious

1. Theological appropriations of Wittgenstein are widespread, especially in post-liberal religious thought. The majority of these appropriations share a dependence on Wittgenstein's conception of the contingency of all language-games and tend to use him as an important figure for thinking the unavoidability of tradition and communal practice for all religious communities. For examples of such post-liberal appropriations of Wittgenstein, see Hauerwas 2001, and 2004, 120–29; Lindbeck 2002; Murphy 1994, 233–36, and 1996, esp. chap. 5. Additionally, for an interesting biographical discussion of the joint impact of Kierkegaard and Wittgenstein on the intellectual development of Hauerwas, see Hauerwas 1997.

2. See, "Religion as Conversation Stopper" and "Religious Faith, Intellectual Responsibility, and Romance," both in Rorty 1999. See also Hardwick and Crosby 1997.

3. Other good examples of the same sorts of argument include the essays, "Truth without Correspondence to Reality," "A World without Substances or Essences," and "Ethics without Principles," all included in Rorty 1999. See also the introduction to Rorty 1991a, as well as the following essays in the same collection: "Solidarity or Objectivity?" "Science as Solidarity," and "The Priority of Democracy to Philosophy."

4. For a consideration of redescription relating to patriotism and American identity, see Rorty 1998a.

5. Westphal repeats this claim later in the book: "I remind you that it is not just Nietzsche but also Kierkegaard's Climacus who wages a sustained polemic against claims that human knowledge can operate *sub specie aeterni*, can peek over God's shoulder and see things from the divine perspective" (2001, 79).

6. For an interesting study on the significance of "metaphor" in the thought of Wittgenstein, see Gill 1996.

7. Two excellent collections of essays in this vein are Ward 1997, and 2001. There are many other good examples of how this project might be undertaken (although some are more convincing than others). For just a few examples, Jean-Luc Marion (1991; 2002b; 2008) argues for a radical conception of God as love and yet "without Being" (*sans l'être*). Richard Kearney (2001) contends for God to be thought as a certain kind of openness to possibility and futurity. John Sanders (2007) argues that we can maintain the idea of a radically personal God, but that we need to rethink the idea of temporality in relation to God

and thus contest the idea of divine omniscience when it comes to personal decision. John Caputo (1993) offers a conception of faith that is radically invitational and yet "against ethics" and has recently begun to bring deconstruction together with process theology (2006). Catherine Keller (2003) attempts to rethink Christian faith and especially the biblical creation narrative in light of postmodernism and contemporary feminism.

8. For a general critical consideration of Pragmatism that also makes gestures in this direction, see Talisse and Aikin 2008.

9. For a discussion of Wittgenstein's later understanding of his own early writing, see Malcolm 1986.

10. Regarding the debate between both religious and nonreligious philosophers on this issue, see Flew and MacIntyre 1955. See also, Lewis 1960. Similar in some respects to what I am suggesting here, Lewis argues that there must be a transformation from one conceptual scheme to another.

11. Importantly, as Nietzsche (1994) repeatedly demonstrates, the claim to "discovery" is also always a claim to "invention."

12. That Wittgenstein was deeply influenced by James is explicitly noted by Drury: Wittgenstein was "early influenced by William James's *Variety of Religious Experience*. This book he told me had helped him greatly. And if I am not mistaken the category of *Varieties* continues to play an important part in his thinking" (1984, 93). For an excellent discussion of precisely this topic, see R. Goodman 1994.

13. Consider the following claims: "One keeps forgetting to go right down to the foundations. One doesn't put the question marks *deep* enough down" (Wittgenstein 1980, 62). Also: "Getting hold of the difficulty *deep down* is what is hard" (Wittgenstein 1980, 48).

14. For a good account of Wittgenstein's struggle with his own complex religious heritage, see Edmonds and Eidinow 2001, esp. chaps. 9 and 11.

15. Of course, one could go to work on exactly how to understand the paradox of Christ and attempt to explain it by means of symbolism and metaphor and in this way defuse the problematic I have outlined; but to do so, as I will attempt to explain below, eliminates exactly what one was trying to save in such an explanation.

16. For example, how could one "observe" Christ's divinity? That which would be available for scientific or historical verification is precisely what is *not* at stake in the *religious* truth of his identity claims. However, without the historical aspect—that it really was a physical person standing before crowds at particular times making these claims—there is no paradox.

17. Wittgenstein makes a quite striking personal claim that captures this idea of the risk of faith when he writes, "I cannot kneel to pray because it's as though my knees were stiff. I am afraid of dissolution (of my own dissolution), should I become soft" (1980, 56).

18. Wittgenstein: "A proof of God's existence ought really to be something by means of which one could convince oneself that God exists. But I think that what *believers* who have furnished such proofs have wanted to do is give their 'belief' an intellectual analysis and foundation, although they themselves would never have come to believe as a result of such proofs" (1980, 85). Also: "God's essence is supposed to guarantee his existence—what this really means is that what is here at issue is not the existence of something" (1980, 82).

19. The passage reads: "Religious faith and superstition are quite different. One of them results from *fear* and is a sort of false science. The other is a trusting."

20. For essays on the debate between deconstruction and Pragmatism in the shadow of Wittgenstein, see Nagl and Mouffe 2001. See also, Staten 1984.

21. For sustained considerations of the two thinkers in conversation, see Creegan 1989; Mulhall 2003; Schonbaumsfeld 2007.

10. *The Political*

1. In this later work, Audi does not oppose a person's having religious grounds for action, but does suggest that there must be "secular reasons" that are available to all rational citizens in order for public policy to limit freedom. We might term this a "revised separatism" since it maintains the requirement of public reason, but does not exclude religious belief *as such* from political life. However, the key aspect of separatism is maintained—that is, as with Rawls, Audi does not think that "religious reasons" are sufficient sources of political justification.

2. For an excellent collection of essays representing the wide diversity of views on the topic of religion in the public square, see Clanton 2009.

3. Of course, Rorty will not appeal to anything like "public reason" as an objective category in quite the way that Audi and Rawls seem sometimes to do. For Rorty, the notion of the "public" is simply something that expands our conversational context. As such, religious reasons are problematic because they unnecessarily, and unhelpfully, limit the scope of possible conversation partners.

4. For just a few recent examples of literature arguing for Kierkegaard's political relevance, see Westphal 1991; Dooley 2001; Wirth 2004. Similarly, for a few examples on Levinas, see Bernasconi 1999; Burggraeve 2002; Cohen 2003, 1996; Critchley 1999, 2007.

5. I want to briefly address the possible concern that by focusing only on this one text in Kierkegaard's complex authorship, I have not given due consideration to the troubling religious individualism that seems so marked in texts such as *Either/Or, Stages on Life's Way, Concluding Unscientific Postscript*, and foremost in *Fear and Trembling*. Haven't I forgotten that there is supposed to be a religious "suspension of the ethical," rather than an ethico-religious conception of the political? In light of this question, let me simply repeat the basics of my argument in chapter 2. I suggested there: (1) the ethical in much of Kierkegaard's pseudonymous work is offered as an example of a Hegelian interpretation and does not necessarily reflect Kierkegaard's own conception; (2) in *Fear and Trembling* the relation between Abraham and Isaac serves to contest any interpretation of Kierkegaardian religion as simply being an asocial relation between Abraham and God; and (3) ultimately, the relation to other people is a constitutive part of the life of faith. I do not want to downplay the fact that there are texts within Kierkegaard's corpus that appear to offer substantive challenges to the claim that he was concerned with more straightforwardly ethical and political matters. However, let me again stress that there are also many texts that problematize an exclusive focus on Kierkegaard's supposed religious individualism. I have already mentioned *Works of Love* as such a text, but for further support one could also look at *Practice in Chris-*

tianity, *For Self-Examination*, and *Judge for Yourself!*, and the late essays that constitute his *Attack on Christendom*. To link these writings up with our discussion above, it should be noted that Kierkegaard states on the original title pages of *For Self-Examination* and *Judge for Yourself!* that they are works "Recommended to the Present Age" (FSE/JFY, 220, 242).

6. I take this to be a fundamentally Platonic point. That is, the *Republic* can be read as presupposing democracy as the very condition that would allow for the conversation which is contained in the dialogue (and the other Platonic dialogues) to occur. Although this interpretation challenges the received view of Plato as being essentially undemocratic, this democratic reading of Plato has recently been gaining some popularity in the literature. Gerald M. Mara writes: "Socrates' democratic conversations are conducted in such a way as to be neither vitiated by exclusions nor corrupted by empowerments. Through these conversations, Socrates articulates criticisms of and alternatives to, not only democratic politics, but also politics in general. Yet these critical and alternative views are also voiced within, and to a certain extent enabled by, a democratic culture. . . . Alternatives to democratic political institutions are thus articulated within a democratic political context" (1997, 3). David Roochnik not only concurs with Mara's contention, but goes further by suggesting that "only in a democracy, it seems, is it possible to imagine a regime that runs entirely against the grain of the one in which it is imagined." "In other words," he continues, "a democracy allows fundamental self criticism. This simple observation is the key to understanding the Republic as a qualified and cautious defense of democracy" (2003, 79). For much more modest versions of this thesis, see Monoson 2000; Saxonhouse 1996, esp. chap. 4; Euben 1990, esp. chaps. 7 and 8. Additionally, though she does not mention democracy directly here, Debra Nails nicely articulates what is at stake in the democratic foundations of Plato's thought: "Plato's greatest achievement, his breakthrough from pre-Socratic, sophistic, and rhetorical precedent, was the thoroughgoing application of a doubly open-ended philosophical method, leading Plato to criticize most effectively even the beliefs he may have cherished most deeply. Plato's dialogues are and were in Plato's lifetime occasions to philosophize further, not dogmatic treatises" (1995, 3). For the classic anti-democratic reading of Plato, see Popper 1971, and for a contemporary restatement of Popper's basic interpretation, see Samaras 2002.

7. Levinas and Roger Pol-Droit, "The Awakening of the I," in RTB, 183.

8. Levinas and Augusto Ponzio, "Responsibility and Substitution," in RTB, 230.

9. Levinas, Luc Ferry, Raphaël Hadas-Lebel, and Sylvaine Pasquier, "In the Name of the Other," in RTB, 194.

10. Levinas and Pol-Droit, "The Awakening of the I," in RTB, 185.

11. Levinas and Pol-Droit, "The Awakening of the I," in RTB, 186.

12. Levinas, Ferry, Hadas-Lebel, and Pasquier, "In the Name of the Other," in RTB, 195.

13. Consider Derrida's rethinking of Europe along exactly these lines (1992c).

14. Of course, this basic claim is also found, in various ways, in many communitarian critiques of liberalism.

15. Although a good case could be made that it might require, as Robert Talisse (2005) suggests, opening a space for "democracy *after* liberalism."

11. *The Epistemological*

1. Scott Aikin and I (Aikin and Simmons 2009) have used this term to describe the philosophy of Levinas in particular, but here I want to expand it to include Kierkegaard and the new phenomenologists.

2. In what follows, I will refer primarily to a "deconstructive" notion of justification as a loose way of referring to the work of those who affirm Otherism. This is not meant to suggest that all thinkers described as "deconstructionists" will therefore exemplify the model of justification I will articulate. Nor is it meant to suggest that all advocates of Otherism are involved in the technical project of "deconstructionism." It is simply deployed here as a loose way of naming the trajectory I am describing.

3. It seems to me that, in particular, the coherentist notion of self-trust offered by Keith Lehrer (1997) and the foundherentism of Susan Haack (1993) are also possibly compatible with Otherism—or at least worth exploring in connection to Otherism. It has even been suggested by W. Jay Wood (1999) that postmodernism should be read in line with the virtue epistemology of such thinkers as Sosa (2007; 2009), Zagzebski (1996), and Monmarquet (1993). Further, I am thankful to Scott Aikin for suggesting to me that the "infinity" of the demand of the Other might open space for infinitism as a possible justificatory framework, as defended by some contemporary epistemologists (see Aikin 2005, 2008; Fantl 2003; Klein 2003, 2005, 2007).

4. Occasionally, one finds suggestions that this engagement between analytic and Continental philosophy on matters of epistemology is a productive way forward, but in general, these suggestions are not sustained. For example, Merold Westphal (2001, chap. 3) attempts to read Heidegger, Gadamer, and Derrida as epistemologists; and similarly, C. Stephen Evans (1988) puts Kierkegaard and Plantinga into conversation. Further, W. Jay Wood (1999) offers a broad-strokes analysis of how postmodernism might productively intersect with virtue epistemology; and James K. A. Smith (2005) has suggested in footnotes that there is reason to believe that deconstruction operates according to a very similar epistemological structure to "Reformed epistemology," though he has not suggested exactly how. For essays offering specifically Christian accounts of how postmodernism and epistemology might be jointly considered, see Evans and Westphal 1993. Gary Brent Madison (2001) defends a notion of postmodern epistemology that draws heavily on the hermeneutic tradition of Gadamer, but is quite critical of any epistemological value in Derrida. Similarly, Frederick Ferré (1998) advocates a "constructive postmodern epistemology," but draws primarily on the process philosophy of Whitehead while being quite critical of Derrida. Perhaps the most common way that certain Continental and analytic thinkers are brought together on epistemological matters concerns what is perceived as their shared "anti-foundationalism" and "anti-epistemology" (see Simpson 1987; Baynes, Bohman, and McCarthy 1987; McCarthy 1990; and Luntley 1995).

5. Importantly, it is not the case that shaming someone for a belief that she holds is always immoral. As one can learn fairly quickly from Socrates, a certain type of ridicule, which properly deployed, can serve moral ends. The sticking point concerns what we are

to count as "proper" deployment. It would appear that for such a rhetorical maneuver to be morally legitimate, it would need to be undergirded by argument.

6. In "A Self-Defeat Problem for the Rhetorical Theory of Argument," Scott Aikin offers two arguments for why perspectives such as Rorty's are self-defeating (unpublished manuscript).

7. Concerning Rorty's own suggestion of privatization, we should not forget that he eventually revises this position after an engagement with Wolterstorff (see Wolterstorff 2003; Rorty 2003).

8. Others have offered criticisms of Rorty along similar lines, see Wolterstorff 2003; Bernstein 2003; Comay 1987.

9. As a personal note: at a recent conference, I attended a session on Levinas and one of the speakers, whom I will leave anonymous, claimed that "when it comes to Levinasian ethics, one simply gets it or simply doesn't." When pressed, the speaker compared affirming Levinasian ethics to being religiously converted.

10. See also Rorty's essay "A Spectre is Haunting the Intellectuals: Derrida on Marx" (in Rorty 1999).

11. For more on how Pragmatism in general approaches epistemology, see Talisse and Aikin 2008, chap. 2.

12. Nonetheless, Derrida explicitly resists any actual tie to negative theology: "And yet those aspects of *différance* which are thereby delineated are not theological, not even in the order of the most negative of negative theologies, which are always concerned with disengaging a superessentiality beyond the finite categories of essence and existence, that is, of presence, and always hastening to recall that God is refused the predicate of existence, only in order to acknowledge his superior, inconceivable, and ineffable mode of being. Such a development is not in question here, and this will be confirmed progressively. *Différance* is not only irreducible to any ontological or theological—ontotheological—reappropriation, but as the very opening of the space in which ontotheology—philosophy—produces its system and its history, it includes ontotheology, inscribing it and exceeding it without return" (1982, 6).

13. Westphal claims something similar when he says that, for Derrida, "the whole world is a text, or better, a library of texts" (2001, 70)

14. Moreover, as I suggested in the last chapter, we must be able to differentiate between "just" laws and "unjust" laws—or at least, between more just and less just laws. Such a distinction need not require final certainty, but if we are unable to say that laws protecting civil rights are just in a way that laws promoting segregation are not, then this makes a hash of ethico-political judgment. While I understand the reasons that Continental ethicists give for saying things like "no laws are just"—and perhaps that is correct, in an extremely technical sense—such comments threaten to undercut the defensibility of Continental ethics. Moreover, it forces individuals into self-defeating positions: a critical race theorist who is unable to defend civil rights legislation as just; a feminist who is unable to label laws that promote equal rights for women as just, etc.

15. Westphal's comments regarding this "initial plausibility" of a Continental epistemology is directed to the work of Heidegger, Gadamer, and Derrida.

16. For Taylor, the quintessential example of this sort of abandonment is the work of Quine.

17. For a consideration of how Levinas faces the possible challenge of self-refutation, see Aikin and Simmons 2009.

18. In no way have I exhausted the different varieties of foundationalism. For just a few other examples, see Audi (1993) in which he distinguishes between psychological foundationalism and axiological foundationalism, and Aikin (2007) in which he claims that we must be careful not to confuse foundationalism as a meta-epistemic theory and foundationalism as an evaluative theory.

19. For a classical account of the coherence theory, see Bonjour 1976; for an account of how circularity might still allow for justification, see Cling 2002.

20. This quote is from Plantinga's 1983 essay, "Reason and Belief in God" (in Plantinga and Wolterstorff 1983). All citations to this essay will be to the version reprinted in Plantinga 1998.

21. Similarly, as perhaps the clearest indication that Rorty critiques strong foundationalism when he refers to foundationalism, consider his claim that foundations are "representations which cannot be gainsaid" (1979, 315).

22. Recently, Alston (2005) has suggested that we go "beyond justification" and instead focus on "epistemic desiderata."

23. Dewey Hoitenga explains how "evidence" functions for Plantinga: "Evidence and grounds both function as *justification,* but they do this in substantially different ways. The difference is that evidence consists of *beliefs* on the basis of which other, nonbasic beliefs are held (and thereby justified), whereas grounds are not beliefs at all, but *conditions* or *circumstances* that occasion properly basic beliefs, and thereby justify them *without being formulated as beliefs*" (1991, 87–88).

24. Wolterstorff will also introduce the notion of a "data-background belief," which he describes as "a large set of beliefs such that one's holding them is a condition of one's accepting as data that which one does" (1984, 67).

25. A similar charge is that Reformed epistemology is simply fideism; for a discussion of this objection and a defense of Reformed epistemology against it, see K. Clark 1990, 155–56.

26. Related to this notion of how justification will operate relative to grounds—and eventually constitute knowledge—is Plantinga's notion of warrant understood as "proper functionalism." Although I want to leave room for debate, I find this to be one area where Otherism is likely to part company with Plantinga due to the inherently teleological conception of human nature that Plantinga requires. For more on proper functionalism, see Plantinga 1993a, 1993b, 2000; Feldman 1993.

27. This does not mean, however, that one can ever get beyond interpretation and stand in a direct relation to the Truth. This is what modest foundationalism recognizes and strong foundationalism does not.

28. Levinas, "The Ego and Totality," in CPP, 41.

29. Levinas, "Signification as Saying," in GDT, 157. It is, of course, possible that Levinas is wrong about his own theory: his theory could be foundationalist, while his theory about his theory—viz., that it is non-foundationalist—is simply false.

30. This is especially clear in Audi's debates with Wolterstorff (Audi and Wolterstorff 1997).

31. I recognize that there is much more to be said about how this works, and I hope to return to this question in future. For now, my claim is simply that there is reason to think that this dependence between basic beliefs (e.g., "Justice is undeconstructible") and the experience of the relation to the Other's alterity might operate in a foundational way.

32. See note 27, above.

33. Regarding the historical and cultural contextuality of belief, consider also the following by Wolterstoff: "Rationality of belief can only be determined in context—historical and social contexts, and, even more narrowly, personal context. It has long been the habit of philosophers to ask in abstract, nonspecific fashion whether it is rational to believe that God exists, whether it is rational to believe that there is an external world, whether it is rational to believe that there are other persons, and so on. Mountains of confusion have resulted. The proper question is always and only whether it is rational for this or that particular person in this or that situation, or for a person of this or that particular type in this or that type of situation, to believe so-and-so. Rationality is always *situated* rationality" (1983b, 155).

34. I am not claiming that Westphal does this. I am simply saying that if one were to actually affirm that *all* versions of foundationalism require a belief that is held "beyond interpretation," this would fall prey to the sort of equivocation so present in the anti-foundationalist literature. In other places, as when Westphal contends that Derrida is best thought of as a "natural law theorist," he comes close to recognizing this foundationalist structure as being operative in deconstruction (see Westphal 2001, chap. 11).

35. For a suggestion of how first-personal accounts might more readily allow for legitimate trust, see Hasker 1993. Alston's work on "Christian experience" is also helpful here, see Alston 1983. And though I am unable to pursue the thought here, I believe that recent work in the epistemology of testimony by prominent analytic epistemologists (e.g., Lackey and Sosa 2006) might yield productive avenues of inquiry when considered alongside Otherism's first-personal conception of the ethico-religious encounter—especially given Levinas's suggestion that truth is better understood as "testimony" than as "disclosure."

36. Levinas, "Is Ontology Fundamental?" in BPW, 6.

37. Importantly, I also find the language of a "post-foundationalist" epistemology to allow for more options regarding the specific theory of justification one defends. For example, Lehrer's coherentist account also depends on the centrality of trust (in particular self-trust) in his conception of rationality and justification (Lehrer 1997). Interestingly, modest foundationalism is not necessarily opposed to finding support in coherentist approaches. Audi allows for the possibility that coherence might play "a significant role in justification, so long as non-inferentially justified belief is a necessary element in it" (2001, 30). Similarly, Wolterstorff asks whether "the time has come for us to discard the supposition that the foundationalist/coherentist dichotomy is an illuminating principle of classification" (1983b, 172). As one possible illustration of how this post-foundationalism might display aspects of modest foundationalism and aspects of coherentism, consider Simon Critchley's *Infinitely Demanding*. Therein, Critchley claims that "all questions of normative justification, whether with reference to theories of justice, rights, duties, obligations or whatever, should be re-

ferred to what I call 'ethical experience'" (2007, 8–9). By itself, this claim bears a striking resemblance to Alston's minimally foundationalist notion of "Christian Experience" (Alston 1983). Elsewhere in the text, however, Critchley fills in the notion of "ethical experience" by claiming that its two components, "demand" and "approval," are "virtuously circular" (2007, 16–18); this conception of "virtuous circularity" certainly has a coherentist aspect and appeal.

38. One could reply that when it comes to the notion of force, Otherism does not fare any better than Rorty: both seem to be deploying force from *within* their own community of discourse. The key difference is that Rorty's deployment abandons any attempt to offer justificative reasons for such a necessity while Otherism has good reasons for why force might, at least occasionally, be politically necessary. Further, for Otherism, this force (violence) is always necessarily *contested* from within the basic beliefs that operate in the community of discourse deploying it—this is the importance of the priority of ethics to politics, or justice to law. Rorty does not allow for any similar sort of necessity.

39. For a classic set of essays critical of Reformed epistemology, see Zagzebski 1993.

40. For other critical considerations of how Rorty stands in relation to contemporary ethics, politics, and religion, see Dann 2008; Voparil 2006; Fabbri 2008; and Frazier 2006.

12. *The Ethical*

1. In particular, Walzer articulates this severity-requirement as having to do with the "death of a community."

2. In no way, of course, do I support all historical or future actions taken in times of, or simply in the name of, disaster. Far too often, emergencies serve as excuses for violence and retrenchment of power rather than for critical engagement with the complicated tasks of political life. And in particular, I want to express my deep concern about political theories that turn to a strong conception of executive sovereignty regarding the declaration and duration of emergencies. For example, Carl Schmitt and Leo Strauss, though in slightly different ways, both propose conceptions of "the political" that I find to be quite at odds with the Levinasian conception I am operating with, and advocating, here. For a good attempt to think at the intersection of Strauss and Levinas, see Batnitzky 2006.

3. I want to make the important point here that this conception of meta-ethical emergency is one that I take to be motivated by a commitment to justice, while the alteration in our theoretical commitments is required in order to better enact justice in a radically changed context. This notion *must not* be reframed as a "suspension" of justice in the name of political hegemony or the maintenance of particular power structures.

4. For various positions on questions of competition between human and non-human interests, see Rolston 2003; Attfield 2003.

5. Importantly, I do not claim that this is the *only* plausible theory, but simply that the relational model of anthropocentrism is a viable contender as one such theory.

6. For a few examples of some of the scholarly estimates consider the following. In May 2007, an international team of climate scientists (led by James Hansen) suggested that in order to achieve the "alternative scenario" that avoids "dangerous" consequences, significant steps had to be taken within the next ten years. That is, if we continue "business as

usual" for more than ten more years then "it becomes impractical to achieve the alternative scenario." This ten-year time frame is not offered as a date for crossing the "tipping-point," but instead as a date at which our trend toward the tipping-point becomes nearly inevitable. As Gavin Schmidt notes, these projections should be viewed as "advisory speed limits," but, he continues: "What should be the target for mugging old ladies? You want to minimize the number, regardless" (Spotts 2007). A similar projection regarding a ten-year timeline for change is offered by Peter Smith. In 2006, Smith claimed that: "The scientific opinion is that we have a ceiling of 440 parts per million of atmospheric carbon before there is a tipping point, a step change in the rate of global warming. . . . The rate at which we are emitting now, around 2ppm a year and rising, we could expect that the tipping point will reach us in 20 years' time. That gives us 10 years to develop technologies that could start to bite into the problem" (in Jha 2006). He continues on to say that by century's end a society free of fossil fuels will "not just be an option, it will be a necessity." "To reach that goal," he continues, "we need to be infinitely more ambitious than we are at the moment" (in Jha 2006). The situation is grave. As Peter B. deMenocal warns, "the magnitude of what we're talking about greatly, greatly exceeds anything we've withstood in human history" (Eilperin 2006). Regarding the urgency required to deal with the current situation, John Holdren urges that "it is still possible to avoid an unmanageable degree of climate change, but the time for action is now" (O'Driscoll 2007). Despite these widely accepted (if not heeded) scientific projections, many continue to emphasize their uncertainty and the continued debate about the potential level of consequence. For example, John H. Marburger III—former President George W. Bush's chief science advisor—claimed in 2006 that "there's no agreement on what it is that constitutes a dangerous climate change . . . we know things like this are possible, but we don't have enough information to quantify the level of risk" (O'Driscoll 2007). In response to such hesitancy to adjust political policy and recognizing the economic realities that often underlie such policy, Stephen H. Schneider claims that for the small island nation of Kirbati "the tipping point has already occurred. . . . As far as they're concerned, it's tipped, but they have no economic clout in the world" (O'Driscoll 2007).

7. Given my Levinasian commitments, it might seem odd that I am depending upon the truth of "ought implies can" here. However, as I have argued throughout this book, though it is certainly true that Levinas resists the idea that ethical obligation is able to be finally discharged or the demands of morality fully met, he does expect that we can and must do something. Im-possible demands, at least for Levinas and Derrida, should not be read as *ridiculous* expectations to do that which we cannot do, but rather as *unending* expectations that continue to challenge all assumptions of adequacy.

8. I borrow this phrase from Critchley (2007); he argues that contemporary liberalism faces a "motivational deficit."

9. It is perfectly possible that one could introduce a hierarchy that does not have humans at the top, and thereby still be non-anthropocentric. If one were to affirm such a non-anthropocentric and yet non-egalitarian (i.e., hierarchical) model, then the problems mentioned above regarding the ethico-political obstacle still hold.

10. J. Baird Callicott shows how the assumptions from which we operate allow for different perspectives to emerge even regarding the same moral theory. Discussing Leopold's

"Land Ethic," Callicott suggests that it arises from "a Copernican cosmology, a Darwinian protosociobiological natural history of ethics, Darwinian ties of kinship among all forms of life on earth, and an Eltonian model of the structure of biocenoses all overlaid on a Humean-Smithian moral psychology" (2008, 178). The theory only makes sense, Callicott contends, with these commitments in the background. That said, he is able to claim that the land ethic is "self-consistently both" deontological and prudential, but which of these options we affirm depends more on the perspective from which we consider it—"from the inside, from the lived, felt point of view of the community member with evolved moral sensibilities, it is deontological. . . . From the outside, from the objective and analytic scientific point of view, it is prudential" (2008, 185).

11. Callicot argues that such readings of ecocentric holism are wrongheaded: the holism of the land ethic, for example, "happily, implies neither inhumane nor inhuman consequences" (2008, 183). However, he notes that "human beings are equally subject to the same subordination of individual welfare and rights in respect to the good of the community as a whole" (2008, 183). It is this notion of subordination that I find to be so problematic. In light of the rampant species loss (and incalculable loss of individuals) that climate change could potentially bring about, it is difficult to say that there might not be benefits for the overall ecological community by substantially reducing the number of humans inhabiting the earth. So while I concede that such ecocentric positions might not *necessarily* be "inhumane" or "inhuman," a problem remains for such positions when it comes to affirming that human-caused climate change stands as an overriding ethical challenge.

12. For an alternative account of a possible Levinasian approach to environmental ethics, see Llewelyn 1991a.

13. We might now suggest that this hierarchy could be viewed as what Trusted terms a "restricted speciesism" (1992, 20). However, I think that "speciesism" is a term that is difficult to use without some negative connotation; and hence, I prefer the notion of a "hierarchy" because it does not say "only these and no others," but instead simply maintains an ordering of moral value among decidedly valuable beings.

14. As a couple examples of contemporary debates wrestling with this relationship, one might look at the "futurity problem" as considered by Gregory Kavka 1978 (see also Wenz 2001, chap. 2), the "identity problem" addressed by Derek Parfit 2008, or a moral "discount rate" discussed by Gower 1992. For collections of essays on the question of responsibilities to future generations, see Partridge 1980; Sikora and Barry 1978; and Pojman and Pojman 2008, sec. 6.

15. For more on how animals and the environment might achieve political importance in Levinas, see Perpich 2008.

16. There has been much scholarly debate about Levinas and animal ethics. For just a few examples, see D. Clark 1997; Diehm 2003; Steeves 2005; Guenther 2007; Llewelyn 1991b. See also Derrida 2008; Wolfe 2003; Calarco and Atterton 2004; Steeves 1999.

17. Here I am reading Levinas in conversation with Martha Nussbaum's "capabilities approach" and then attempting to apply such a notion to environmental concerns (Nussbaum 2006).

18. For just a few examples, see IPCC 2008; Neumayer and Plümper 2007; and McGhie et al. 2006. For a consideration of the question of obligations to the poor as it relates to environmental concerns, see Trusted 1992.

19. Here Bryan G. Norton's distinction between "strong" and "weak" anthropocentrism is helpful in distinguishing between those versions of anthropocentrism that "dictate that nature will be used in an exploitative manner" and those that allow for "a basis for criticism of value systems which are purely exploitative of nature" (2003, 165).

20. Potential objections could be raised regarding whether Levinas actually introduces some sort of moral-capacity requirement for inclusion. In particular, does Levinas make the ability of moral responsibility the prerequisite for having status in a moral community? So does the case of Bobby actually count as an instance that demonstrates this capacity-requirement? Or is this merely an example of creative attribution of human characteristics to non-humans, which does nothing to alter their valued status? Although I cannot even begin to address these concerns here, I do believe that there is at least an ambiguity within Levinas on how to understand the capacity for responsive engagement.

21. Here we should also consider James Sterba's compatibilist account:

> Regarding the members of all species as equals still allows for human preference in the same way that regarding all humans as equals still allows for self preference. First of all, human preference can be justified on grounds of defense. . . . Second, human preference can also be justified on grounds of preservation. . . . For these reasons, the degree of preference for our own species found in the principle of human preservation is justified even if we were to adopt a nonanthropocentric perspective. (2008, 254–55)

While I am sympathetic to Sterba's approach and believe that there are many points of intersection between his theory and that which I am proposing here, I do find it to still allow for a problem at the level of ethico-political activism. That is, I worry that his compatibilism allows for language that is still *close enough* to non-anthropocentrism to interfere with its political efficacy. Admittedly, this is more of a sociological concern than it is a philosophical objection.

13. *The Ethico-political*

1. Of course, this parallel only goes so far; regarding their conception of the individual and the crowd, for instance, Kierkegaard and Marx could hardly be further apart. For possible lines of connection between Marx and Kierkegaard, see Westphal 1991, esp. chaps. 3 and 7; and Kirmmse 1992. For a good consideration of the striking differences between Kierkegaard and Marx, see Malantschuk 1980.

2. For an excellent collection of essays considering the impact and influence of Wyschogrod, see Boynton and Kavka 2009.

3. The inclusion of the filmic depiction of Oskar Schindler is meant to indicate that ethical exemplars might be found in literature, drama, art, or film. What is essential is that all these exemplars are concerned with the struggles of ethico-political existence. That ex-

emplars have actually lived makes them in some sense more compelling, but that others exist even in the imaginations of authors, artists, and directors demonstrates that fiction and existence are never as far apart as some might otherwise be inclined to think.

4. For just a few examples, see Critchley 2007; McQuillan 2007; Horowitz and Horowitz 2006.

5. Caputo 1997b, 228; cit. Dooley 2001a, 246.

6. JP, III, 2404; cit. Dooley 2001a, 246.

7. Caputo 1995, 235; cit. Dooley 2001a, 246.

8. It should go without saying that Continental philosophy does not have the patent on speculative detachment, but since my own focus is the political viability of this tradition, my criticism is primarily focused on the internal difficulties it faces.

9. Representing the pragmatic tradition, Cornel West (1989) might also be added to this list because of his notion of "prophetic pragmatism." For a consideration of West and Levinas, see Simmons 2010.

10. Importantly, however—as chapter 12 should have made clear—this does not preclude the recognition of obligation to non-human others. The saint's life may be, and, I believe, should also be devoted to the alleviation of the sorrow and pain of animals and the degradation of the environment.

11. The question of whether Otherism is able to countenance superogatory acts is one I want to leave open here. It seems that for Otherism to be viable as an ethical theory it would have to allow for such a notion, but the very "infinity" of the obligation to the Other makes it difficult to see how this idea would be possible.

12. The choice is between having all truth offered on the one hand, and having the perpetual task of striving for truth offered on the other. Lessing indicates that he would humbly choose the striving, and importantly, he recognizes that the task of striving will necessarily involve making errors.

13. Cit. Bethge 1970, 237; *Dietrich Bonhoeffer Werke*, 12: 423–25.

14. Cit. Bethge 1970, 237, emphasis added; *Dietrich Bonhoeffer Werke*, 12: 423–25.

15. Bonhoeffer, "Diary entry of June 20, 1939," in Kelly and Nelson 1995, 472.

16. Bonhoeffer, "Letter to Reinhold Niebuhr from July 1939," in Kelly and Nelson 1995, 479–80.

17. I am not saying that what follows would not also apply to the historical Schindler, but I am content to leave such application aside here.

18. All quotes from *Schindler's List* are taken from the screenplay as written by Steve Zaillian as contained in The Internet Movie Database, www.imsdb.com. Further citations will simply be to Zailian 1993.

BIBLIOGRAPHY

Adams, Robert. 1999. *Finite and Infinite Goods.* Oxford: Oxford University Press.

Agacinski, Sylviane. 1998. "We Are Not Sublime: Love and Sacrifice, Abraham and Ourselves." In Rée and Chamberlain 1998, 129–50.

Agamben, Giorgio. 2005. *State of Exception.* Trans. Kevin Attell. Chicago: University of Chicago Press.

Aikin, Scott F. 2005. "Who Is Afraid of Epistemology's Regress Problem?" *Philosophical Studies* 126, no. 2 (November): 191–217.

———. 2007. "Prospects for Skeptical Foundationalism." *Metaphilosophy* 38, no. 5 (October): 578–90.

———. 2008. "Meta-Epistemology and the Varieties of Epistemic Infinitism." *Synthese* 163, no. 2 (July): 175–85.

Aikin, Scott F., and J. Aaron Simmons. 2009. "Levinasian Otherism, Skepticism, and the Problem of Self-Refutation." *Philosophical Forum* 40, no. 1 (Spring): 29–54.

Aikin, Scott F., and Michael P. Hodges. 2006. "Wittgenstein, Dewey, and the Possibility of Religion." *Journal of Speculative Philosophy* 20, no. 1: 1–19.

Ajzenstat, Oona. 2001. *Driven Back to the Text: The Premodern Sources of Levinas's Postmodernism.* Pittsburgh: Duquesne University Press.

Alston, William P. 1983. "Christian Experience and Christian Belief." In Plantinga and Wolterstorff 1983, 103–34.

———. 1989. *Epistemic Justification: Essays in the Theory of Knowledge.* Ithaca, N.Y.: Cornell University Press.

———. 2005. *Beyond "Justification": Dimensions of Epistemic Evaluation.* Ithaca, N.Y.: Cornell University Press.

Alston, William P., Robert Audi, Terence Penelhum, and Richard H. Popkin. 1992. *Faith, Reason, and Skepticism.* Ed. Marcus Hester. Philadelphia: Temple University Press.

Amesbury, Richard. 2002. "The Truth of Religion and Religious Truths." *International Journal for Philosophy of Religion* 51: 271–77.

Aquinas, St. Thomas. 1947. *Summa Theologica,* vol. 2. Trans. Fathers of the English Dominican Province. New York: Benziger Brothers.

Arendt, Hannah. 1985. *Eichmann in Jerusalem: A Report on the Banality of Evil,* rev. edition. New York: Penguin.

Atterton, Peter. 1992. "Levinas and the Language of Peace: A Response to Derrida." *Philosophy Today* 36, no. 1 (Spring): 59–70.

Attfield, Robin. 2003. "Saving Nature, Feeding People, and Ethics." In Light and Rolston 2003, 463–71.

Audi, Robert. 1993. *The Structure of Justification*. Cambridge: Cambridge University Press.
———. 2000. *Religious Commitment and Secular Reason*. Cambridge: Cambridge University Press.
———. 2001. *The Architecture of Reason: The Structure and Substance of Rationality*. Oxford: Oxford University Press.
Audi, Robert, and Nicholas Wolterstorff. 1997. *Religion in the Public Square: The Place of Religious Conviction in Political Debate*. Lanham, Md.: Rowman and Littlefield.
Augustine, Saint. 1974. *The Essential Augustine*. Ed. Vernon J. Bourke. Indianapolis: Hackett Publishing.
Ayer, A. J. 2007. "A Critique of Ethics." In *Ethical Theory: An Anthology*. Ed. Russ Schafer-Landau. Oxford: Blackwell, 18–24.
Badiou, Alain. 2003. *Saint Paul: The Foundation of Universalism*. Trans. Ray Brassier. Stanford, Calif.: Stanford University Press.
Baier, Annette C. 1995. *Moral Prejudices: Essays on Ethics,* new edition. Cambridge, Mass.: Harvard University Press.
Baker, Deane-Peter, and Patrick Maxwell, eds. 2003. *Explorations in Contemporary Continental Philosophy of Religion*. Amsterdam: Rodopi.
Barber, Benjamin. 1975. "Justifying Justice: Problems of Psychology, Politics, and Measurement in Rawls." In *Reading Rawls: Critical Studies on Rawls' A Theory of Justice*. Ed. Norman Daniels. Stanford, Calif.: Stanford University Press, 292–318.
Batnitzky, Leora. 2006. *Leo Strauss and Emmanuel Levinas: Philosophy and the Politics of Revelation*. Cambridge: Cambridge University Press.
Baynes, Kenneth, James Bohman, and Thomas McCarthy, eds. 1987. *After Philosophy: End or Transformation?* Cambridge, Mass.: MIT Press.
Bell, Roger. 1992. "Rorty on Derrida: A Discourse of Simulated Moderation." In Dallery and Scott 1992, 283–300.
Benhabib, Seyla, ed. 1996. *Democracy and Difference: Contesting the Boundaries of the Political*. Princeton, N.J.: Princeton University Press.
Bennett, Lerone, Jr. 1976. *What Manner of Man: A Biography of Martin Luther King, Jr.* Chicago: Johnson Publishing.
Benson, Bruce Ellis. 2002. *Graven Ideologies: Nietzsche, Derrida, and Marion on Modern Idolatry*. Downers Grove: InterVarsity Press.
Benson, Bruce Ellis, and Norman Wirzba, eds. 2008. *Transforming Philosophy and Religion: Love's Wisdom*. Bloomington: Indiana University Press.
———, eds. 2010. *Words of Life: New Theological Turns in French Phenomenology*. New York: Fordham University Press.
Bernasconi, Robert. 1986. "Levinas and Derrida: The Question of the Closure of Metaphysics." In Cohen 1986, 181–202.
———. 1991. "Skepticism in the Face of Philosophy." In Bernasconi and Critchley 1991, 149–61.
———. 1997. "The Violence of the Face: Peace and Language in the Thought of Levinas." *Philosophy and Social Criticism* 23, no. 6: 81–93.

———. 1999. "The Third Party: Levinas on the Intersection of the Ethical and the Political." *Journal of the British Society for Phenomenology* 30, no. 1 (January): 76–87.

———. 2002. "What is the Question to which 'Substitution' is the Answer?" In Bernasconi and Critchley 2002, 234–51.

Bernasconi, Robert, and David Wood, eds. 1988. *The Provocation of Levinas: Rethinking the Other.* London: Routledge.

Bernasconi, Robert, and Simon Critchley, eds. 1991. *Re-Reading Levinas.* Bloomington: Indiana University Press.

———, eds. 2002. *The Cambridge Companion to Levinas.* Cambridge: Cambridge University Press.

Bernstein, Richard J. 2003. "Rorty's Inspirational Liberalism." In Guignon and Hiley 2003, 124–38.

Bethge, Eberhard. 1970. *Dietrich Bonhoeffer: A Biography.* Rev. and ed. by Victoria J. Barnett. Minneapolis: Fortress Press.

Blanshard, Brand. 1969. "Kierkegaard on Faith." In *Essays on Kierkegaard.* Ed. Jerry H. Gill. Minneapolis: Burgess Publishing, 113–26.

———. 1975. *Reason and Belief.* New Haven, Conn.: Yale University Press.

Bloechl, Jeffrey, ed. 2000. *The Face of the Other and the Trace of God: Essays on the Philosophy of Emmanuel Levinas.* New York: Fordham University Press.

———. 2002. "A New Philosophy for Theology?" In Burggraeve 2002, 193–201.

———. 2003. *Religious Experience and the End of Metaphysics.* Bloomington: Indiana University Press.

Bonhoeffer, Dietrich. 1954. *Life Together.* Trans. John W. Doberstein. New York: Harper.

———. 1959. *The Cost of Discipleship,* rev. edition. Trans. R. H. Fuller, rev. Irmgard Booth. New York: Macmillan Publishing.

Bonjour, Laurence. 1976. "The Coherence Theory of Empirical Knowledge." *Philosophical Studies* 30: 281–312.

Boyd, Gregory. 2000. *The God of the Possible: A Biblical Introduction to the Open View of God.* Grand Rapids: Baker.

Boynton, Eric, and Martin Kavka, eds. 2009. *Saintly Influence: Edith Wyschogrod and the Possibilities of Philosophy of Religion.* New York: Fordham University Press.

Brown, Wendy. 1988. *Manhood and Politics: A Feminist Reading in Political Theory.* Lanham, Md.: Rowman & Littlefield.

———. 2001. *Politics Out of History.* Princeton, N.J.: Princeton University Press.

Buber, Martin. 1947–1948. *Tales of the Hasidim.* New York: Schocken.

Burggraeve, Roger. 2002. *The Wisdom of Love in the Service of Love: Emmanuel Levinas on Justice, Peace, and Human Rights.* Milwaukee: Marquette University Press.

Butin, Gitte W. 1999. "Encounter with the Other: A Matter of Im/Mediacy." *Kergma und Dogma* 45 (October–December): 307–16.

Butler, Judith. 2005. *Giving an Account of Oneself.* New York: Fordham University Press.

Calarco, Matthew, and Peter Atterton, eds. 2004. *Animal Philosophy: Essential Readings in Continental Thought.* London and New York: Continuum.

Callicott, J. Baird. 2008. "The Conceptual Foundations of the Land Ethic." In Pojman and Pojman 2008, 173–85.

Caputo, John D. 1993. *Against Ethics: Contributions to a Poetics of Obligation with Constant Reference to Deconstruction*. Bloomington: Indiana University Press.

———. 1995. "Instants, Secrets, and Singularities: Dealing Death in Kierkegaard and Derrida." In Matuštík and Westphal 1995, 216–38.

———, ed. 1997a. *Deconstruction in a Nutshell: A Conversation with Jacques Derrida*. New York: Fordham University Press.

———. 1997b. *The Prayers and Tears of Jacques Derrida*. Bloomington: Indiana University Press.

———, ed. 2002. *The Religious*. Oxford: Blackwell.

———. 2005. "Methodological Postmodernism: On Merold Westphal's *Overcoming Onto-Theology*." *Faith and Philosophy* 22, no. 3 (July): 284–96.

———. 2006. *The Weakness of God: A Theology of the Event*. Bloomington: Indiana University Press.

———. 2007. *What Would Jesus Deconstruct? The Good News of Postmodernism for the Church*. Grand Rapids: Baker Academic.

Caputo, John D., and Gianni Vattimo. 2007. *After the Death of God*. Ed. Jeffrey W. Robbins. New York: Columbia University Press.

Caputo, John D., Mark Dooley, and Michael J. Scanlon, eds. 2001. *Questioning God*. Bloomington: Indiana University Press.

Caputo, John D., and Michael J. Scanlon, eds. 1999. *God, the Gift, and Postmodernism*. Bloomington: Indiana University Press.

———, eds. 2007. *Transcendence and Beyond; A Postmodern Inquiry*. Bloomington: Indiana University Press.

Carter, Stephen L. 1993. *The Culture of Disbelief: How American Law and Politics Trivialize Religious Devotion*. New York: Basic.

Chrétien, Jean-Louis. 2000. "The Wounded Word: Phenomenology of Prayer." Trans. Jeffrey L. Kosky and Thomas A. Carlson. In Janicaud et al. 2000, 147–75.

———. 2002. *The Unforgettable and the Unhoped For*. Trans. Jeffrey Bloechl. New York: Fordham University Press.

———. 2004. *The Call and the Response*. Trans. Anne A. Davenport. New York: Fordham University Press.

Ciaramelli, Fabio. 1991. "Levinas's Ethical Discourse Between Individuation and Universality." In Bernasconi and Critchley 1991, 83–105.

Clanton, J. Caleb. 2007. *Religion and Democratic Citizenship: Inquiry and Conviction in the American Public Square*. Lanham, Md.: Lexington Books.

———. 2008. "Religion in the Public Square? A Critical Response to Cornel West." *Philosophy in the Contemporary World* 15, no. 1 (Spring): 82–93.

———, ed. 2009. *The Ethics of Citizenship: Liberal Democracy and Religious Convictions*. Waco, Tex.: Baylor University Press.

Clark, David. 1997. "On Being 'The Last Kantian in Nazi Germany': Dwelling with Animals After Levinas." In *Animal Acts: Configuring the Human in Western History*. New York: Routledge, 165–98.

Clark, Kelly James. 1990. *Return to Reason: A Critique of Enlightenment Evidentialism and a Defense of Reason and Belief in God*. Grand Rapids: William B. Eerdmans.

Cling, Andrew D. "Justification-Affording Circular Arguments." *Philosophical Studies* 111: 251–75.

Coakley, Sarah. Forthcoming. "In Defense of Sacrifice." In *The Broken Body: Israel, Christ, and Fragmentation*. Oxford: Blackwell.

Cohen, Richard A., ed. 1986. *Face to Face with Levinas*. Albany: State University of New York Press.

———. 1996. "Justice and the State in the Thought of Levinas and Spinoza." *Epoché* 4, no. 1: 55–70.

———. 2003. "'Political Monotheism': Levinas on Politics, Ethics and Religion." In *Essays in Celebration of the Founding of the Organization of Phenomenological Organizations*. Ed. Cheung, Chan-Fai, Ivan Chvatik, Ion Copoeru, Lester Embree, Julia Iribarne, and Hans Rainer Sepp. Web-published at www.o-p-o.net.

Coleridge, Samuel Taylor. 2000. "Selections from *Biographia Literaria*." In *The Norton Anthology of English Literature,* 7th edition, vol. 2. Ed. M. H. Abrams and Stephen Greenblatt. New York and London: W.W. Norton & Co., 467–86.

Comay, Rebecca. 1987. "Interrupting the Conversation: Notes on Rorty." In Simpson 1987, 83–98.

Connell, George B., and C. Stephen Evans, eds. 1992. *Foundations of Kierkegaard's Vision of Community: Religion, Ethics, and Politics in Kierkegaard*. New Jersey and London: Humanities Press.

Cooper, David E., and Joy A. Palmer. 1992. *The Environment in Question: Ethics and Global Issues*. London and New York: Routledge.

Creegan, Charles L. 1989. *Wittgenstein and Kierkegaard: Religion, Individuality, and Philosophical Method*. London and New York: Routledge.

Critchley, Simon. 1996. "Deconstruction and Pragmatism—Is Derrida a Private Ironist or a Public Liberal?" In Mouffe 1996, 19–41.

———. 1999. *The Ethics of Deconstruction: Derrida and Levinas,* 2nd edition. Edinburgh: Edinburgh University Press.

———. 2007. *Infinitely Demanding: Ethics of Commitment, Politics of Resistance*. London and New York: Verso.

Crites, Stephen. 1992. "*The Sickness Unto Death:* A Social Interpretation." In Connell and Evans 1992, 144–60.

Culler, Jonathan. 1982. *On Deconstruction*. Ithaca, N.Y.: Cornell University Press.

Dallery, Arleen B., and Charles E. Scott, eds., with P. Holley Roberts. 1992. *Ethics and Danger: Essays on Heidegger and Continental Thought*. Albany: State University of New York Press.

D'Amico, Robert. 1999. *Contemporary Continental Philosophy*. Boulder, Col.: Westview Press.

Dancy, Jonathan. 2006. *Ethics Without Principles*. New York and Oxford: Oxford University Press.

Dann, Elijah. 2008. *After Rorty: The Possibilities for Ethics and Religious Belief.* London: Continuum.

Davenport, John J., and Anthony Rudd. 2001. *Kierkegaard After MacIntyre: Essays on Freedom, Narrative, and Virtue.* Chicago: Open Court.

Davis, Creston, John Milbank, and Slavoj Žižek, eds. 2005. *Theology and the Political: The New Debate.* Durham, N.C.: Duke University Press.

Dawkins, Richard. 2006. *The God Delusion.* New York: Houghton Mifflin.

de Boer, Theodore. 1986. "An Ethical Transcendental Philosophy." In Cohen 1986.

———. 1997. *The Rationality of Transcendence: Studies in the Philosophy of Emmanuel Levinas.* Amsterdam: J. C. Gieben.

de Vries, Hent. 1999. *Philosophy and the Turn to Religion.* Baltimore and London: Johns Hopkins University Press.

———. 2002. *Religion and Violence: Philosophical Perspectives from Kant to Derrida.* Baltimore: Johns Hopkins University Press.

———. 2005. *Minimal Theologies: Critiques of Secular Reason in Adorno and Levinas.* Baltimore: Johns Hopkins University Press.

Dennett, Daniel. 2007. *Breaking the Spell: Religion as a Natural Phenomenon.* London: Penguin.

Derrida, Jacques. 1978. *Writing and Difference.* Trans. Alan Bass. Chicago: University of Chicago Press.

———. 1982. *Margins of Philosophy.* Trans. Alan Bass. Chicago: University of Chicago Press.

———. 1987. *The Post Card: From Socrates to Freud and Beyond.* Trans. Alan Bass. Chicago: University of Chicago Press.

———. 1992a. *Given Time: I. Counterfeit Money.* Trans. Peggy Kamuf. Chicago: University of Chicago Press.

———. 1992b. "Force of Law: The 'Mystical Foundation of Authority.'" In *Deconstruction and the Possibility of Justice.* Ed. Drucilla Cornell, Michel Rosenfeld, and David Gray Carlson. New York: Routledge, 3–67.

———. 1992c. *The Other Heading: Reflections on Today's Europe.* Trans. Pascale-Anne Brault and Michael B. Naas. Bloomington: Indiana University Press.

———. 1994. *Specters of Marx: The State of the Debt, the Work of Mourning, & the New International.* Trans. Peggy Kamuf. New York and London: Routledge.

———. 1995. *The Gift of Death.* Trans. David Wills. Chicago: University of Chicago Press.

———. 1996. "Remarks on Deconstruction and Pragmatism." In Mouffe 1996, 77–88.

———. 1997. *Politics of Friendship.* Trans. George Collins. London and New York: Verso.

———. 1999. *Adieu to Emmanuel Levinas.* Trans. Pascale-Anne Brault and Michael Naas. Stanford, Calif.: Stanford University Press.

———. 2000. *Of Hospitality: Anne Dufourmantelle Invites Jacques Derrida to Respond.* Trans. Rachel Bowlby. Stanford, Calif.: Stanford University Press.

———. 2001. *Cosmopolitanism and Forgiveness.* Trans. Mark Dooley and Michael Hughes. London and New York: Routledge.

———. 2002. *Ethics, Institutions, and the Right to Philosophy.* Trans. and ed. Peter Pericles Trifonas. Lanham, Md.: Rowman & Littlefield.

———. 2005. *Rogues: Two Essays on Reason.* Trans. Pascale-Anne Brault and Michael Naas. Stanford, Calif.: Sanford University Press.

———. 2008. *The Animal That Therefore I Am*. Ed. Marie-Louise Mallet. Trans. David Wills. New York: Fordham University Press.

Derrida, Jacques, and Gianni Vattimo, eds. 1998. *Religion*. Stanford, Calif.: Stanford University Press.

Dewey, John. 1989. *The Later Works, 1925–1953: Volume 7—1932: Ethics*. Ed. Jo Ann Boydston. Carbondale: Southern Illinois University Press.

Diehm, Christian. 2003. "Natural Disasters." In *Eco-Phenomenology: Getting Back to the Earth Itself*, ed. Ted Toadvine and Charles S. Brown. Albany: State University of New York Press, 171–85.

Dooley, Mark. 1999. "'The Politics of Exodus: Derrida, Kierkegaard, and Levinas on 'Hospitality.'" In *International Kierkegaard Commentary: Works of Love*. Ed. Robert L. Perkins. Macon, Ga.: Mercer University Press, 167–92.

———. 2001a. *The Politics of Exodus: Kierkegaard's Ethics of Responsibility*. New York: Fordham University Press.

———. 2001b. "The Civic Religion of Social Hope: A Response to Simon Critchley." *Philosophy and Social Criticism* 27, no. 5: 35–58.

Drury, M. O'C. 1984. "Conversations with Wittgenstein." In *Recollections of Wittgenstein*. Ed. Rush Rhees. Oxford and New York: Oxford University Press, 97–171.

Dudiak, Jeffrey. 2001. *The Intrigue of Ethics: A Study of the Idea of Discourse in the Thought of Emmanuel Levinas*. New York: Fordham University Press.

———. 2008. "The Greatest Commandment? Religion and / or Ethics in Kierkegaard and Levinas." In Simmons and Wood, 2008, 99–121.

Dupré, Louis. 1968. "Husserl's Thought on God and Faith." *Philosophy and Phenomenological Research* 29, no. 2 (December): 201–15.

Eberle, Christopher J. 2002. *Religious Conviction in Liberal Politics*. Cambridge: Cambridge University Press.

Edelglass, William, Chris Diehm, and Jim Hatley, eds. Forthcoming. *Faces of Nature: Levinasian Ethics and Environmental Philosophy*. Pittsburgh: Duquesne University Press.

Edmonds, David, and John Eidinow. 2001. *Wittgenstein's Poker*. New York: Harper Collins.

Eilperin, Juliet. 2006. "Debate on Climate Shifts to Issue of Irreparable Change." *Washington Post*. January 29. Online at http://www.washingtonpost.com/wp-dyn/content/article/2006/01/28/AR2006012801021. Accessed 21 March 2008.

Elshtain, Jean Bethke. 2003. "Don't Be Cruel: Reflections on Rortyan Liberalism." In Guignon and Hiley 2003, 139–57.

Englemann, Paul, ed. 1967. *Letters from Ludwig Wittgenstein with a Memoir*. Ed. B. F. McGuinness. Trans. L. Furtmuller. Oxford: Blackwell.

Euben, J. Peter. 1999. *The Tragedy of Political Theory: The Road Not Taken*. Princeton, N.J.: Princeton University Press.

Evans, C. Stephen. 1981. "Is the Concept of an Absolute Duty toward God Morally Unintelligible?" In Perkins 1981b, 141–51.

———. 1983. *Kierkegaard's* Fragments *and* Postscript: *The Religious Philosophy of Johannes Climacus*. Atlantic Highlands: Humanities Press.

——. 1988. "Kierkegaard and Plantinga on Belief in God: Subjectivity as the Ground of Properly Basic Religious Beliefs." *Faith and Philosophy* 5, no. 1 (January): 25–38.

——. 1993. "Faith as the *Telos* of Morality: A Reading of *Fear and Trembling.*" In *International Kierkegaard Commentary: Fear and Trembling and Repetition*, vol. 6, ed. Robert L. Perkins. Macon, Ga.: Mercer University Press, 9–27.

——. 2004. *Kierkegaard's Ethic of Love: Divine Commands and Moral Obligations.* Oxford: Oxford University Press.

Evans, C. Stephen, and Merold Westphal, eds. 1993. *Christian Perspectives on Religious Knowledge.* Grand Rapids: William B. Eerdmans.

Fabri, Lorenzo. 2008. *The Domestication of Derrida: Rorty, Pragmatism and Deconstruction.* London: Continuum.

Fantl, Jeremy. 2003. "Modest Infinitism." *Canadian Journal of Philosophy* 33, no. 4 (December): 537–62.

Feldman, Richard. 1993. "Proper Functionalism." *Nous* 27, no. 1 (March): 34–50.

Ferré, Frederick. 1998. *Knowing and Value: Toward a Constructive Postmodern Epistemology.* Albany: State University of New York Press.

Ferreira, M. Jamie. 1998. "Faith and the Kierkegaardian leap." In *The Cambridge Companion to Kierkegaard.* Ed. Alastair Hannay and Gordon D. Marino. Cambridge: Cambridge University Press, 207–34.

——. 1999. "Other-Worldliness in Kierkegaard's *Works of Love.*" *Philosophical Investigations* 22, no. 1 (January): 65–79.

——. 2001. *Love's Grateful Striving: A Commentary on Kierkegaard's* Works of Love. Oxford and New York: Oxford University Press.

——. 2008. "Kierkegaard and Levinas on Four Elements of the Biblical Love Commandment." In Simmons and Wood 2008, 82–98.

Fischer-Hüllstrung, H. 1966. "A Report from Flossenbürg." In *I Knew Dietrich Bonhoeffer: Reminiscences by His Friends.* Ed. Wolf-Dieter Zimmermann and Ronald Gregor Smith. Trans. Käthe Gregor Smith. New York: Harper & Row.

Flew, Antony, and Alasdair MacIntyre, eds. 1955. *New Essays in Philosophical Theology.* London: SCM Press.

Føllesdal, Dagfinn. 2006. "Husserl's Reductions and the Role they play in his Phenomenology." In *A Companion to Phenomenology and Existentialism.* Ed. Hubert L. Dreyfus and Mark A. Wrathall. Oxford: Blackwell, 105–14.

Frankfurt, Harry G. 2005. *On Bullshit.* Princeton, N.J.: Princeton University Press.

Frazier, Brad. 2006. *Rorty and Kierkegaard on Irony and Moral Commitment: Philosophical and Theological Connections.* London: Palgrave Macmillan.

Freeman, Samuel. 2007. *Rawls.* London and New York: Routledge.

Gasché, Rodophe. 1986. *The Tain of the Mirror: Derrida and the Philosophy of Reflection.* Cambridge, Mass.: Harvard University Press.

Gellman, Jerome. 2003. *Abraham! Abraham! Kierkegaard and the Hasidim on the Binding of Isaac.* Aldershot: Ashgate.

Geras, Norman. 1995. *Solidarity in the Conversation of Humankind: The Ungroundable Liberalism of Richard Rorty.* London and New York: Verso.

———. 1998. *The Contract of Mutual Indifference: Political Philosophy After the Holocaust*. New York: Verso.

Gill, Jerry H. 1996. *Wittgenstein and Metaphor*. New Jersey: Humanities Press.

Glenn, John D., Jr. 1974. "Kierkegaard's Ethical Philosophy." *The Southwestern Journal of Philosophy* 5, no. 1: 121–28.

Goodchild, Philip, ed. 2002. *Rethinking Philosophy of Religion: Approaches from Continental Philosophy*. New York: Fordham University Press.

———, ed. 2003. *Difference in Philosophy of Religion*. Aldershot: Ashgate.

Goodman, L. E. 1996. *God of Abraham*. Oxford: Oxford University Press.

Goodman, Russell B. 1994. "What Wittgenstein Learned from William James." *History of Philosophy Quarterly* 11, no. 3 (July): 339–54.

Goud, Johan. 2005. "'This Extraordinary Word': Emmanuel Levinas on God." Trans. Lydia Penner. In Jonkers and Welten 2005, 96–118.

Gould, Carol C. 1988. *Rethinking Democracy: Freedom and Social Cooperation in Politics, Economy, and Society*. Cambridge: Cambridge University Press.

Gower, Barry S. 1992. "What Do We Owe to Future Generations?" In Cooper and Palmer 1992, 1–12.

Green, Ronald M. 1988. *Religion and Moral Reason: A New Method for Comparative Study*. Oxford: Oxford University Press.

———. 1992. *Kierkegaard and Kant: The Hidden Debt*. Albany: State University of New York Press.

———. 1993a. "A Reply to Gene Outka." *Journal of Religious Ethics* 21, no. 2 (Fall): 217–20.

———. 1993b. "Enough is Enough! *Fear and Trembling* Is *Not* About Ethics." *Journal of Religious Ethics* 21, no. 2 (Fall): 191–209.

Greve, Wilfried. 2000. "Abraham in Kierkegaard Research." *Kierkegaardiana* 21: 7–18.

Guenther, Lisa. 2007. "*Le flair animal*: Levinas and the Possibility of Animal Friendship." *PhaenEx* 2, no. 2 (Fall/Winter): 216–38.

Guignon, Charles, and David R. Hiley, eds. 2003. *Richard Rorty*. Cambridge: Cambridge University Press.

Gutting, Gary. 1982. *Religious Belief and Religious Skepticism*. Notre Dame, Ind.: University of Notre Dame Press.

———. 2003. "Rorty's Critique of Epistemology." In Guignon and Hiley 2003, 41–60.

Haack, Susan. 1993. *Evidence and Inquiry: Towards Reconstruction in Epistemology*. Oxford: Blackwell.

Hall, Amy Laura. 2002. *Kierkegaard and the Treachery of Love*. Cambridge: Cambridge University Press.

Hannay, Alastair, and Gordon D. Marino, eds. 1998. *The Cambridge Companion to Kierkegaard*. Cambridge: Cambridge University Press.

Hardwick, Charley D., and Donald A. Crosby, eds. 1997. *Pragmatism, Neo-Pragmatism, and Religion: Conversations with Richard Rorty*. New York: Peter Lang.

Harris, Sam. 2004. *The End of Faith: Religion, Terror, and the Future of Reason*. New York and London: W.W. Norton & Co.

————. 2006. *Letter to a Christian Nation*. New York: Alfred A. Knopf.

Hart, Michael, and Antonio Negri. 2000. *Empire*. Cambridge, Mass.: Harvard University Press.

Hasker, William. 1993. "Proper Function, Reliabilism, and Religious Knowledge: A Critique of Plantinga's Epistemology." In Evans and Westphal 1993, 66–86.

Hauerwas, Stanley. 1997. "How to Go On When You Know You Are Going to Be Misunderstood, or How Paul Holmer Ruined My Life, or Making Sense of Paul Holmer." In Stanley Hauerwas, *Wilderness Wanderings: Probing Twentieth-Century Theology and Philosophy*. Boulder, Col.: Westview Press, 143–52.

————. 2001. "Vision, Stories, and Character." In *The Hauerwas Reader*. Ed. John Berkman and Michael Cartwright. Durham, N.C.: Duke University Press, 165–70.

————. 2004. *Performing the Faith: Bonhoeffer and the Practice of Nonviolence*. Grand Rapids: Brazos Press.

Haverkamp, Anselm. 1995. *Deconstruction is/in America: A New Sense of the Political*. New York: New York University Press.

Hedges, Warren, Gayatri Chakrovorty Spivak, Seyla Benhabib, Nancy Fraser, et al. 1999. "Marcha C. Nussbaum and Her Critics: An Exchange." *The New Republic* 220, no. 16 (April 19): 43–45.

Hegel, G. W. F. 1967. *Hegel's Philosophy of Right*. Trans. T. M. Knox. Oxford: Oxford University Press.

————. 1991. *The Encylopaedia Logic*. Trans. T. F. Gareats, W. A. Suchting, and H. S. Harris. Indianapolis: Hackett.

Heidegger, Martin. 1993. *Basic Writings*, rev. and exp. edition. Ed. David Farrell Krell. San Francisco: HarperSanFrancisco.

————. 1996. *Being and Time*. Trans. Joan Stambaugh. Albany: State University of New York Press.

————. 1999. *Contributions to Philosophy (From Enowning)*. Trans. Parvis Emad and Kenneth Maly. Bloomington: Indiana University Press.

————. 2002a. "Phenomenology and Theology." In Caputo 2002, 49–66.

————. 2002b. "The Onto-theo-logical Constitution of Metaphysics." In Caputo 2002, 67–75.

————. 2003. *Four Seminars: Le Thor 1966, 1968, 1969, Zähringen 1973*. Trans. Andrew Mitchell and François Raffoul. Bloomington: Indiana University Press.

Henry, Michel. 1973. *The Essence of Manifestation*. Trans. Girard Etzkorn. Dordrecht: Springer.

————. 2003. *I am the Truth: Toward a Philosophy of Christianity*. Trans. Susan Emanuel. Stanford, Calif.: Stanford University Press.

Hettinger, Ned. 2008. "Comments on Holmes Rolston's 'Naturalizing Values.'" In Pojman and Pojman 2008, 120–23.

Hitchens, Christopher. 2007. *God Is Not Great: How Religion Poisons Everything*. New York and Boston: Twelve Books.

Hodges, Michael P. 1990. *Transcendence and Wittgenstein's Tractatus*. Philadelphia: Temple University Press.

———. 2001. "Faith: Themes from Wittgenstein, Kierkegaard, and Nietzsche." In *Wittgenstein and Philosophy of Religion.* Ed. Robert L. Arrington and Mark Addis. London and New York: Routledge.

Hoitenga, Dewey J., Jr. 1991. *Faith and Reason From Plato to Plantinga: An Introduction to Reformed Epistemology.* Albany: State University of New York Press.

Hooker, Brad, and Margaret Little, eds. 2001. *Moral Particularism.* New York and Oxford: Oxford University Press.

Horner, Robyn. 2001. *Rethinking God as Gift: Marion, Derrida, and the Limits of Phenomenology.* New York: Fordham University Press.

Horowitz, Asher, and Gad Horowitz, eds. 2006. *Difficult Justice: Commentaries on Levinas and Politics.* Toronto: University of Toronto Press.

Houe, Poul, Gordon D. Marino, and Sven Hakon Rossel, eds. 2000. *Anthropology and Authority: Essays on Søren Kierkegaard.* Amsterdam: Rodopi.

Housset, Emmanuel. 1997. *Persone et sujet selon Husserl.* Paris: Presses Universitaires de France.

Hughes, Cheryl L. 1998. "The Primacy of Ethics: Hobbes and Levinas." *Continental Philosophy Review* 31: 79–94.

Husserl, Edmund. 1970. *The Crisis of European Sciences and Transcendental Phenomenology.* Trans. David Carr. Evanston, Ill.: Northwestern University Press.

———. 1982. *Ideas Pertaining to a Pure Phenomenology and to a Phenomenological Philosophy: First Book.* Trans. F. Kersten. The Hague: Kluwer Academic Publishers.

———. 1999. *Cartesian Meditations.* Trans. Dorion Cairns. Dordrecht: Kluwer Academic Publishers.

IPCC. 2008. *Climate Change 2007: Impacts, Adaptation, and Vulnerability: Working Group II Contribution to the Fourth Assessment Report of the IPCC.* Cambridge: Cambridge University Press.

Jacobs, Louis. 1981. "The Problem of the *Akedah* in Jewish Thought." In Perkins 1981b, 1–9.

James, William. 1985. *The Varieties of Religious Experience.* Cambridge, Mass.: Harvard University Press.

Janicaud, Dominique. 1991. *Le tournant théologique de la phenomenology française,* Combas: Editions de l'éclat.

———. 2000. "The Theological Turn of French Phenomenology." Trans. Bernard G. Prusak. In Janicaud et al. 2000, 16–103.

Janicaud, Dominique, Jean-François Courtine, Jean-Louis Chrétien, Jean-Luc Marion, Michel Henry, and Paul Ricœur. 2000. *Phenomenology and the "Theological Turn": The French Debate.* New York: Fordham University Press.

Jha, Alok. 2006. "Energy Review Ignores Climate Change 'Tipping Point.'" *The Guardian.* September 4. Online at http://www.guardian.co.uk/environment/2006/sep/04/greenpolitics.science/print. Accessed 21 March 2008.

Jonkers, Peter. 2005. "God in France: Heidegger's Legacy." In Jonkers and Welten 2005, 1–42.

Jonkers, Peter, and Ruud Welten, eds. 2005. *God in France: Eight Contemporary French Thinkers on God.* Leuven: Peeters.

Kangas, David. 2000. "The Logic of Gift in Kierkegaard's *Four Upbuilding Discourses* (1843)." In *Kierkegaard Studies Yearbook*. Berlin: de Gruyter, 100–20.

Kant, Immanuel. 1960. *Religion Within the Limits of Reason Alone*. Trans. Theodore M. Greene and Hoyt H. Hudson. New York: Harper Torchbooks.

———. 1987. *Critique of Judgment*. Trans. Werner S. Pluhar. Indianapolis: Hackett.

Katz, Claire Elise. 2005. "The Responsibility of Irresponsibility: Taking (Yet) Another Look at the Akedah." In *Addressing Levinas*. Ed. Eric Sean Nelson, Antje Kapust, and Kent Still. Evanston, Ill.: Northwestern University Press, 17–33.

Kavka, Gregory. 1978. "The Futurity Problem." In Sikora and Barry 1978, 186–203.

Kearney, Richard. 2001. *The God Who May Be: A Hermeneutics of Religion*. Bloomington: Indiana University Press.

Keller, Catherine. 2003. *Face of the Deep: A Theology of Becoming*. London and New York: Routledge.

Kelly, Geffrey B., and F. Burton Nelson, eds. 1995. *A Testament to Freedom: The Essential Writings of Dietrich Bonhoeffer*, rev. edition. San Francisco: HarperSanFrancisco.

Kemp, Peter. 1997. "Another Language for the Other: From Kierkegaard to Levinas." *Philosophy and Social Criticism* 23, no. 6: 5–28.

Kerr, Fergus. 1986. *Theology after Wittgenstein*. Oxford: Basil Blackwell.

Kierkegaard, Søren. All references are located in the list of abbreviations at the front of this volume.

Kirmmse, Bruce. 1992. "Call Me Ishmael—Call Everybody Ishmael: Kierkegaard on the Coming-of-Age Crisis of Modern Times." In Connell and Evans 1992, 161–82.

Klein, Peter. 2003. "When Infinite Regresses Are 'Not' Vicious." *Philosophy and Phenomenological Research* 66, no. 3 (May): 718–29.

———. 2005. "Infinitism's Take on Justification, Knowledge, Certainty, and Skepticism." *Veritas: Revista de Filosofia* 50, no. 4 (December): 153–72.

———. 2007. "Human Knowledge and the Infinite Progress of Reasoning." *Philosophical Studies* 134, no. 1 (May): 1–17.

Korsgaard, Christine M. 1996. *The Sources of Normativity*. Cambridge: Cambridge University Press.

Kosky, Jeffrey L. 2000. "Translators Preface: The Phenomenology of Religion: New Possibilities for Philosophy and or Religion." In Janicaud et al. 2000, 107–20.

———. 2001. *Levinas and the Philosophy of Religion*. Bloomington: Indiana University Press.

Kovacs, George. 1990. *The Question of God in Heidegger's Phenomenology*. Evanston, Ill.: Northwestern University Press.

Lackey, Jennifer, and Ernest Sosa, eds. 2006. *The Epistemology of Testimony*. Oxford: Clarendon Press.

Lacoste, Jean-Yves. 1994. *Expérience et Absolu: Questions disputes sur l'humanité de l'homme*. Paris: Presses Universitaires de France.

———. 2004. *Experience and the Absolute: Disputed Questions on the Humanity of Man*. Trans. Mark Raftery-Skehan. New York: Fordham University Press.

Lehrer, Keith. 1974. *Knowledge*. Oxford: Clarendon Press.

———. 1997. *Self-Trust: A Study of Reason, Knowledge, and Autonomy*. Oxford: Clarendon Press.

Levinas, Emmanuel. All references are located in the list of abbreviations at the front of this volume.

Levinas, Emmanuel, and Richard Kearney. 1986. "Dialogue with Emmanuel Levinas." In Cohen 1986, 13–34.

Lewis, C. S. 1960. "On Obstinacy in Belief." In Lewis, *The World's Last Night and Other Essays*. San Diego, New York, and London: Harcourt, 13–30.

———. 1970. "Meditation in a Toolshed." In Lewis, *God in the Dock: Essays on Theology and Ethics*, ed. Walter Hooper. Grand Rapids: William B. Eerdmans, 212–15.

Light, Andrew. 1996a. "Environmental Pragmatism as Philosophy or Metaphilosophy? On the Weston-Katz Debate." In Light and Katz 1996a, 325–38.

———. 1996b. "Compatibilism in Political Ecology." In Light and Katz 1996a, 161–84.

———. 2002. "Contemporary Environmental Ethics from Metaethics to Public Philosophy." *Metaphilosophy* 33, no. 4 (July): 426–49.

Light, Andrew, and Eric Katz, eds. 1996a. *Environmental Pragmatism*. London and New York: Routledge.

———. 1996b. "Introduction: Environmental Pragmatism and Environmental Ethics as Contested Terrain." In Light and Katz 1996a, 1–18.

Light, Andrew, and Holmes Rolston III, eds. 2003. *Environmental Ethics: An Anthology*. Oxford: Blackwell.

Lillegard, Norman. 2002. "Passion and Reason: Aristotelian Strategies in Kierkegaard's Ethics." *Journal of Religious Ethics* 30, no. 2 (Summer): 251–73.

Llewelyn, John. 1988. "Levinas, Derrida and Others Vis-à-vis." In Bernasconi and Wood 1988, 136–55.

———. 1991a. *The Middle Voice of Ecological Conscience: A Chiasmic Reading of Responsibility in the Neighborhood of Levinas, Heidegger, and Others*. London: Palgrave Macmillan.

———. 1991b. "Am I Obsessed by Bobby? (Humanism of the Other Animal)." In Bernasconi and Critchley 1991, 234–45.

———. 2002. *Appositions of Jacques Derrida and Emmanuel Levinas*. Bloomington: Indiana University Press.

Lindbeck, George A. 2002. *The Church in a Postliberal Age*. Ed. James J. Buckley. Grand Rapids: William B. Eerdmans.

Long, Eugene Thomas. 2003. *Twentieth-Century Western Philosophy of Religion 1900–2000*. Dordrecht: Kluwer.

———, ed. 2007. *Self and Other: Essays in Continental Philosophy of Religion*. Dordrecht: Springer.

Lugones, Maria. 1987. "Playfulness, 'World-Traveling,' and Loving Perception." *Hypatia* 2, no. 2 (Summer): 3–19.

Luntley, Michael. 1995. *Reason, Truth, and Self: The Postmodern Reconditioned*. London and New York: Routledge.

Luthan, Stephen. "On Religion—A Discussion with Richard Rorty, Alvin Plantinga, and Nicholas Wolterstorff." *Christian Scholars Review* 26, no. 2 (Winter): 177–83.

MacIntyre, Alasdair. 1984. *After Virtue: A Study in Moral Theory,* 2nd edition. Notre Dame, Ind.: Notre Dame University Press.

Mackey, Louis. 1962. "The Loss of the World in Kierkegaard's Ethics." *The Review of Metaphysics* 15, no. 4 (June): 602–20.

———. 1986. *Points of View: Readings of Kierkegaard.* Tallahassee: Florida State University Press.

Macquarrie, John. 1994. *Heidegger and Christianity.* New York: Continuum.

Madison, Gary Brent. 2001. *The Politics of Postmodernity: Essays in Applied Hermeneutics.* Dordrecht: Kluwer.

Malantschuk, Gregor. 1980. *The Controversial Kierkegaard.* Trans. Howard V. Hong and Edna H. Hong. Ontario: Wilfrid Laurier University Press.

———. 2003. *Kierkegaard's Concept of Existence.* Ed. and trans. Howard V. Hong and Edna H. Hong. Milwaukee: Marquette University Press.

Malcolm, Norman. 1986. *Nothing is Hidden: Wittgenstein's Criticism of his Early Thought.* Oxford: Basil Blackwell.

Manning, Robert John Sheffler. 1998. "Derrida, Levinas, and the Lives of Philosophy at the Death of Philosophy: A Reading of Derrida's Misreading of Levinas in 'Violence and Metaphysics.'" *Graduate Faculty Philosophy Journal* 20/21, no. 1/2: 387–405.

Mara, Gerald M. 1997. *Socrates' Discursive Democracy: Logos and Ergon in Platonic Political Philosophy.* Albany: State University of New York Press.

Marion, Jean-Luc. 1991. *God Without Being.* Trans. Thomas A. Carlson. Chicago and London: University of Chicago Press.

———. 1998. *Reduction and Givenness: Investigations of Husserl, Heidegger, and Phenomenology.* Trans. Thomas A. Carlson. Evanston: Northwestern Illinois Press.

———. 2000. "The Saturated Phenomenon." Trans. Thomas A. Carlson. In Janicaud et al. 2000, 176–216.

———. 2002a. *Being Given: Toward a Phenomenology of Givenness.* Trans. Jeffrey L. Kosky. Stanford, Calif.: Stanford University Press.

———. 2002b. *Prolegomena to Charity.* Trans. Stephen E. Lewis. New York: Fordham University Press.

———. 2008. *The Visible and the Revealed.* Trans. Christina M. Gschwandtner and others. New York: Fordham University Press.

Marx, Karl, and Frederick Engels. 1970. *The German Ideology.* Ed. C. J. Arthur. New York: International Publishers.

Mason, H. E. 1988. "The Many Faces of Morality: Reflections on *Fear and Trembling.*" In *The Grammar of the Heart: New Essays in Moral Philosophy and Theology,* ed. Richard H. Bell. San Francisco: Harper & Row, 131–48.

Matuštík, Martin J. 1993. *Postnational Identity: Critical Theory and Existential Philosophy in Habermas, Kierkegaard, and Havel.* New York and London: Guilford Press.

———. 1995. "Kierkegaard's Radical Existential Praxis, Or Why the Individual Defies Liberal, Communitarian, and Postmodern Categories." In Matuštík and Westphal 1995, 239–64.

———. 1998. *Specters of Liberation: Great Refusals in the New World Order*. Albany: State University of New York Press.

———. 2008. "'More Than All the Others': Meditation on Responsibility." In Simmons and Wood 2008, 244–56.

Matuštík, Martin J., and Merold Westphal, eds. 1995. *Kierkegaard in Post/Modernity*. Bloomington: Indiana University Press.

McCarthy, Michael H. 1990. *The Crisis of Philosophy*. Albany: State University of New York Press.

McGhie, John, Katy Migiro, Anjali Kwatra, Andres Pendleton, Judith Melby, Dominic Nutt, Sarah Wilson, and John Davison. 2006. "The Climate of Poverty: Facts, Fears, and Hope: A Christian Aid Report." Online at http://www.reliefweb.int/rw/lib .nsf/db900sid/RURI-6PUL34/$file/cha-gen-may%2005.pdf?openelement. Accessed 21 May 2008.

McLeod, Mark S. 1993. *Rationality and Theistic Belief: An Essay on Reformed Epistemology*. Ithaca, N.Y.: Cornell University Press.

McQuillan, Martin, ed. 2007. *The Politics of Deconstruction: Jacques Derrida and the Other of Philosophy*. London: Pluto Press.

Minister, Stephen M. 2003. "Is There A Teleological Suspension of the Philosophical? Kierkegaard, Levinas, and the End of Philosophy." *Philosophy Today* 47, no. 2 (Summer): 115–25.

———. 2008. "Works of Justice, Works of Love: Kierkegaard, Levinas, and an Ethics Beyond Difference." In Simmons and Wood 2008, 229–43.

Mohanty, J. N. 1995. "The Development of Husserl's Thought." In *The Cambridge Companion to Husserl,* ed. Barry Smith and David Woodruff Smith. Cambridge: Cambridge University Press, 45–77.

Moltmann, Jürgen. 1967. *The Theology of Hope*. Trans. J. W. Leitch. New York: Harper & Row.

Monoson, S. Sara. 2000. *Plato's Democratic Entanglements: Athenian Politics and the Practice of Democracy*. Princeton, N.J.: Princeton University Press.

Monk, Ray. 1990. *Ludwig Wittgenstein: The Duty of Genius*. New York: Penguin.

Montmarquet, James A. 1993. *Epistemic Virtue and Doxastic Responsibility*. Lanham, Md.: Rowman and Littlefield.

Mooney, Edward F. 1991. *Knights of Faith and Resignation: Reading Kierkegaard's* Fear and Trembling. Albany: State University of New York Press.

Mouffe, Chantal, ed. 1996. *Deconstruction and Pragmatism*. With Simon Critchley, Jacques Derrida, Ernesto Laclau, and Richard Rorty. London and New York: Routledge.

———. 2000. *The Democratic Paradox*. London and New York: Verso.

———. 2005. *On the Political*. London and New York: Routledge.

———. 2006. *The Return of the Political*. London and New York: Verso.

Mulhall, Stephen. 2003. *Inheritance and Originality: Wittgenstein, Heidegger, Kierkegaard*. Oxford and New York: Oxford University Press.

Murphy, Nancy C. 1994. *Reasoning and Rhetoric in Religion.* Valley Forge: Trinity Press International.

———. 1996. *Beyond Liberalism and Fundamentalism: How Modern and Postmodern Philosophy Set the Theological Agenda.* Valley Forge: Trinity Press International.

Nagel, Thomas. 1975. "Rawls on Justice." In *Reading Rawls: Critical Studies on Rawls' A Theory of Justice,* ed. Norman Daniels. Stanford, Calif.: Stanford University Press, 1–16.

———. 1986. *The View from Nowhere.* New York: Oxford University Press.

Nagl, Ludwig, and Chantal Mouffe, eds. 2001. *The Legacy of Wittgenstein: Pragmatism or Deconstruction.* Frankfurt am Main: Peter Lang.

Nails, Debra. 1995. *Agora, Academy, and the Conduct of Philosophy.* Dordrecht: Kluwer.

Neumayer, Eric, and Thomas Plümper. 2007. "The Gendered Nature of Natural Disasters: The Impact of Catastrophic Events on the Gender Gap in Life Expectancy, 1981–2002." *Annals of the Association of American Geographers* 97, no. 3 (September): 551–66.

Niebuhr, Reinhold. 1963. *An Interpretation of Christian Ethics.* San Francisco: HarperSanFrancisco.

Nietzsche, Friedrich. 1994. *On the Genealogy of Morality.* Ed. Keith Ansell-Pearson. Trans. Carol Diethe. Cambridge: Cambridge University Press.

———. 1999. *The Birth of Tragedy and Other Writings.* Ed. Raymond Geuss and Ronald Speirs. Cambridge: Cambridge University Press.

———. 2001. *The Gay Science.* Ed. Bernard Williams. Trans. Josefine Nauckhoff. Cambridge: Cambridge University Press.

Norris, Christopher. 1987. *Derrida.* Cambridge, Mass.: Harvard University Press.

Norton, Bryan G. 2003. "Environmental Ethics and Weak Anthropocentrism." In Light and Rolston 2003, 163–74.

Nussbaum, Martha C. 1999. "The Professor of Parody: The Hip Defeatism of Judith Butler." *The New Republic* 220, no. 8 (February 22): 37–45.

———. 2000. *Sex and Social Justice.* Oxford and New York: Oxford University Press.

———. 2006. *Frontiers of Justice: Disability, Nationality, Species Membership.* Cambridge, Mass.: Belknap Press/Harvard University Press.

O'Driscoll, Patrick. 2007. "Study: 'Tipping Point' for Climate Is Near." *USA Today.* 27 February. Online at http://www.usatoday.com/tech/science/2007-02-27-global-warming_x.htm. Accessed 21 March 2008.

Olthuis James H., ed. 1997. *Knowing Other-wise: Philosophy at the Threshold of Spirituality.* New York: Fordham University Press.

Oord, Thomas Jay. 2010. *The Nature of Love: A Theology.* St. Louis: Chalice Press.

Outka, Gene. 1972. *Agape: An Ethical Analysis.* New Haven, Conn.: Yale University Press.

———. 1973. "Religious and Moral Duty: Notes on *Fear and Trembling.*" In *Religion and Morality: A Collection of Essays,* ed. Gene Outka and John P. Reeder, Jr. Garden City: Anchor, 204–54.

———. 1993. "God as the Subject of Unique Veneration: A Response to Ronald M. Green." *Journal of Religious Ethics* 21, no. 2 (Fall): 211–15.

Pailin, David A. 1981. "Abraham and Isaac: A Hermeneutical Problem Before Kierkegaard." In Perkins 1981b, 10–42.

Parfit, Derek. 2008. "Energy Policy and the Further Future: The Identity Problem." In Pojman and Pojman 2008, 364–73.

Partridge, Ernest, ed. 1980. *Responsibilities to Future Generations: Environmental Ethics.* Buffalo: Prometheus Books.

Paton, H. J. 1955. *The Modern Predicament: A Study in the Philosophy of Religion.* New York: Collier.

Patton, Paul. 2007. "Derrida, Politics, and the Democracy to Come." *Philosophy Compass* 2 (November): 766–80.

Peperzak, Adriaan T., ed. 1995. *Ethics as First Philosophy: The Significance of Emmanuel Levinas for Philosophy, Literature, and Religion.* New York and London: Routledge.

———. 1997. *Beyond: The Philosophy of Emmanuel Levinas.* Evanston, Ill.: Northwestern University Press.

———. 1999. *Reason in Faith: On the Relevance of Christian Spirituality for Philosophy.* New York: Paulist Press.

Perkins, Robert L. 1981a. "For Sanity's Sake: Kant, Kierkegaard, and Father Abraham." In Perkins 1981b, 43–61.

———, ed. 1981b. *Kierkegaard's* Fear and Trembling: *Critical Appraisals.* University, Ala.: University of Alabama Press.

Perpich, Diane. 1998. "A Singular Justice: Ethics and Politics Between Levinas and Derrida." *Philosophy Today* 42 (Supplement): 59–70.

———. 2008. *The Ethics of Emmanuel Levinas.* Stanford, Calif.: Stanford University Press.

Phillips, D. Z. 1988. *Faith After Foundationalism.* London and New York: Routledge.

Placher, William. 1996. *The Domestication of Transcendence: How Modern Thinking About God Went Wrong.* Louisville: Westminster John Knox Press.

Plantinga, Alvin. 1967. *God and Other Minds: A Study of the Rational Justification of Belief in God.* Ithaca, N.Y.: Cornell University Press.

———. 1993a. *Warrant: The Current Debate.* New York and Oxford: Oxford University Press.

———. 1993b. *Warrant and Proper Function.* New York and Oxford: Oxford University Press.

———. 1998. *The Analytic Theist: An Alvin Plantinga Reader.* Ed. James F. Sennett. Grand Rapids: William B. Eerdmans.

———. 2000. *Warranted Christian Belief.* New York and Oxford: Oxford University Press.

Plantinga, Alvin, and Nicholas Wolterstorff, eds. 1983. *Faith and Rationality: Reason and Belief in God.* Notre Dame, Ind.: University of Notre Dame Press.

Plato. 1997. *Complete Works.* Ed. John M. Cooper. Indianapolis: Hackett.

Pojman, Louis P., and Paul Pojman, eds. 2008. *Environmental Ethics: Readings in Theory and Application,* 5th edition. Stamford: Thompson Wadsworth.

Popper, Karl. 1971. *The Open Society and Its Enemies,* 5th rev. edition, vols. 1 and 2. Princeton, N.J.: Princeton University Press.

Prosser, Brian T. 2002. "Conscientious Subjectivity in Kierkegaard and Levinas." *Continental Philosophy Review* 35: 397–422.

Prusak, Bernard G. 2000. "Translator's Introduction." In Janicaud et al. 2000, 3–15.

Purcell, Michael. 2006. *Levinas and Theology.* Cambridge: Cambridge University Press.

Putnam, Hilary. 2004. *Ethics Without Ontology.* Cambridge, Mass.: Harvard University Press.

———. 2008. *Jewish Philosophy as a Guide to Life: Rosenzweig, Buber, Levinas, Wittgenstein.* Bloomington: Indiana University Press.

Quinn, Philip L. 1998. "Kierkegaard's Christian Ethics." In Hannay and Marino 1998, 349–75.

Rawls, John. 2005. *Political Liberalism.* New York: Columbia University Press.

———. 1999. *A Theory of Justice,* rev. edition. Cambridge, Mass.: Belknap Press/Harvard University Press.

Rée, Jonathan, and Jane Chamberlain, eds. 1998. *Kierkegaard: A Critical Reader.* Oxford: Blackwell.

Renan, Ernest. 1991. *The Life of Jesus.* Amherst, N.Y.: Prometheus.

Ricœur, Paul. 1974. *The Conflict of Interpretations: Essays in Hermeneutics.* Ed. Don Ihde. Evanston, Ill.: Northwestern University Press.

———. 1981. *Hermeneutics and the Human Sciences: Essay on Language, Action, and Interpretation.* Ed. and trans. John B. Thompson. Cambridge: Cambridge University Press.

———. 2000. "Experience and Language in Religious Discourse." In Janicaud et al. 2000, 127–46.

Robbins, Jill. 1999. *Altered Reading: Levinas and Literature.* Chicago: University of Chicago Press.

Rolston, Holmes, III. 1992. "Challenges in Environmental Ethics." In Cooper and Palmer 1992, 135–46.

———. 2003. "Feeding People versus Saving Nature?" In Light and Rolston 2003, 451–62.

———. 2008. "Naturalizing Values: Organisms and Species." In Pojman and Pojman 2008, 107–20.

Romm, Joseph. 2008. "'The Cold Truth About Climate Change." Salon.com. Online at http://www.salon.com/news/feature/2008/02/27/global_warming_deniers/print.html. Accessed 21 May 2008.

Roochnik, David. 1990. *The Tragedy of Reason: Toward a Platonic Conception of Logos.* New York: Routledge.

———. 2003. *Beautiful City: The Dialectical Character of Plato's* Republic. Ithaca, N.Y.: Cornell University Press.

Rorty, Richard. 1979. *Philosophy and the Mirror of Nature.* Princeton, N.J.: Princeton University Press.

———. 1982. *Consequences of Pragmatism (Essays: 1972–1980).* Minneapolis: University of Minnesota Press.

———. 1989. *Contingency, Irony, and Solidarity.* Cambridge: Cambridge University Press.

———. 1991a. *Objectivity, Relativism, and Truth: Philosophical Papers Vol. 1.* Cambridge: Cambridge University Press.

———. 1991b. *Essays on Heidegger and Others: Philosophical Papers Vol. 2.* Cambridge: Cambridge University Press.

———. 1992. *The Linguistic Turn: Essays in Philosophical Method.* Chicago: University of Chicago Press.

———. 1996a. "Remarks on Deconstruction and Pragmatism." In *Deconstruction and Pragmatism.* In Mouffe 1996, 13–18.

———. 1996b. "Response to Simon Critchley." In Mouffe 1996, 41–46.

———. 1998a. *Achieving Our Country.* Cambridge, Mass.: Harvard University Press.

———. 1998b. "Justice as a Larger Loyalty." In *Cosmopolitics: Thinking and Feeling Beyond the Nation,* ed. Pheng Cheah and Bruce Robbins. Minneapolis and London: University of Minnesota Press, 45–58.

———. 1998c. *Truth and Progress: Philosophical Papers Vol. 3.* Cambridge: Cambridge University Press.

———. 1999. *Philosophy and Social Hope.* London: Penguin.

———. 2002. "Anticlericalism and Atheism." In *Religion After Metaphysics,* ed. Mark Wrathall. Cambridge: Cambridge University Press, 37–46.

———. 2003. "Religion in the Public Square: A Reconsideration." *Journal of Religious Ethics* 31, no. 1: 141–49.

———. 2004. "Philosophical Convictions." *The Nation* (June 14): 53–55.

———. 2006. *Take Care of Freedom and Truth Will Take Care of Itself: Interviews with Richard Rorty.* Ed. Eduardo Mendieta. Stanford, Calif.: Stanford University Press.

———. 2007. *Philosophy as Cultural Politics: Philosophical Papers Vol. 4.* Cambridge: Cambridge University Press.

Rorty, Richard, Derek Nystrom, and Kent Puckett. 2002. *Against Bosses, Against Oligarchies.* Chicago: Prickly Paradigm Press.

Rorty, Richard, and Pascal Engel. 2007. *What's the Use of Truth?* Ed. Patrick Savidan. Trans. William McCuaig. New York: Columbia University Press.

Rosenthal, Sandra B. 2003. "A Time for Being Ethical: Levinas and Pragmatism." *The Journal of Speculative Philosophy* 17, no. 3: 192–203.

Rousseau, Jean-Jacques. 1999. "Selections from *Confessions.*" In *The Norton Anthology of World Masterpieces,* 7th edition, vol. 2. Ed. Sarah Lawall and Maynard Mack. New York: W. W. Norton & Co., 427–37.

Rudd, Anthony. 1993. *Kierkegaard and the Limits of the Ethical.* Oxford: Clarendon Press.

Russell, Matheson. 2006. *Husserl: A Guide for the Perplexed.* London: Continuum.

Samaras, Thanassis. 2002. *Plato on Democracy.* New York: Peter Lang.

Sandel, Michael J., ed. 1984. *Liberalism and Its Critics.* New York: New York University Press.

———. 1998. *Liberalism and the Limits of Justice,* 2nd edition. Cambridge: Cambridge University Press.

———. 2006. *Public Philosophy: Essays on Morality and Politics.* Cambridge, Mass.: Harvard University Press.

———. 2009. *Justice: What's the Right Thing to Do?* New York: Farrar, Straus, and Giroux.

Sanders, John. 2007. *The God Who Risks,* 2nd edition. Downers Grove: InterVarsity Press.

Sartre, Jean-Paul. 1956. *Being and Nothingness.* Trans. Hazel E. Barnes. New York: Washington Square Press.

———. 1985. *Existentialism and Human Emotions.* New Jersey: Philosophical Library.

Saxonhouse, Arlene W. 1996. *Athenian Democracy: Modern Mythmakers and Ancient Theorists.* Notre Dame, Ind.: University of Notre Dame Press.

Schaeffer, Francis A. 1976. *How Should We Then Live? The Rise and Decline of Western Thought and Culture.* Old Tappan: Fleming H. Revell.

Scharlemann, Robert P., ed. 1992. *Negation and Theology.* Charlottesville: University Press of Virginia.

Schonbaumsfeld, Genia. 2007. *A Confusion of the Spheres: Kierkegaard and Wittgenstein on Philosophy and Religion.* Oxford and New York: Oxford University Press.

Schönfeld, Martin. "The Green Kant: Environmental Dynamics and Sustainable Policies." In Pojman and Pojman 2008, 49–59.

Schrader, George. 1968. "Kant and Kierkegaard on Duty and Inclination." *The Journal of Philosophy* 65, no. 21 (November): 688–701.

Schrijvers, Joeri. 2005. "Phenomenology, Liturgy, and Metaphysics: The Thought of Jean-Yves Lacoste." In Jonkers and Welten 2005, 207–25.

Sikora, R. I., and Brian Barry, eds. 1978. *Obligations to Future Generations.* Philadelphia: Temple University Press.

Silverman, Hugh J., ed. 1989. *Derrida and Deconstruction.* New York: Routledge.

Simmons, J. Aaron. 2005. "Review of *God in France.*" In *Bulletin de la Société Américaine de Philosophie de Langue Française* 15, no. 2 (Fall): 99–105.

———. 2006. "Finding Uses for Used-Up Words: Thinking *Weltanschauung* 'After' Heidegger." *Philosophy Today* 50, no. 2 (Summer): 156–69.

———. 2008. "Existential Appropriations: The Influence of Jean Wahl on Levinas's Reading of Kierkegaard." In Simmons and Wood 2008, 41–66.

———. 2009. "'Vision Without Image': A Levinasian Topology." *Southwest Philosophy Review* 25, no. 1: 23–29.

———. 2010. "'A Faith Without Triumph': Emmanuel Levinas and Prophetic Pragmatism." *Monokl: Special International Issue on Levinas* (Spring).

———. Forthcoming. "Richard Rorty: Kierkegaard in the Context of Neo-Pragmatism." In *Kierkegaard Research: Sources, Reception, and Resources. Vol. 11, Kierkegaard's Influence on Philosophy,* ed. Jon Stewart. Aldershot: Ashgate.

Simmons, J. Aaron, and David Wood, eds. 2008. *Kierkegaard and Levinas: Ethics, Politics, and Religion.* Bloomington: Indiana University Press.

Simmons, J. Aaron, and Diane Perpich. 2005. "Making Tomorrow Better than Today: Rorty's Dismissal of Levinasian Ethics." *Symposium* 9, no. 2 (Fall): 241–66.

Simmons, J. Aaron, and Nathan R. Kerr. 2009. "From Necessity to Hope: A Continental Perspective on Eschatology Without *Telos.*" *Heythrop Journal* 48 (2009): 1–18.

Simmons, William Paul. 1999. "The Third: Levinas's Theoretical Move from An-archical Ethics to the Realm of Justice and Politics." *Philosophy and Social Criticism* 25 (6): 85–106.

———. 2000. "Zionism, Place, and the Other: Toward a Levinasian International Relations." *Philosophy in the Contemporary World* 7, no. 1 (Spring): 21–25.

———. 2003. *An-archy and Justice: An Introduction to Emmanuel Levinas's Political Thought.* Lanham, Md.: Lexington.

Simpson, Evan, ed. 1987. *Anti-Foundationalism and Practical Reasoning: Conversations Between Hermeneutics and Analysis.* Edmonton: Academic Printing and Publishing.

Smith, James K. A. 1997. "How to Avoid Not Speaking: Attestations." In Olthuis 1997, 217–34.

―――. 2002. *Speech and Theology: Language and the Logic of the Incarnation*. London: Routledge.

Smith, Quentin. 1979. "Husserl's Theory of the Phenomenological Reduction in the *Logical Investigations*." *Philosophy and Phenomenological Research* 39, no. 3 (March): 433–37.

Sneller, Rico. 2005. "God as War: Derrida on Divine Violence." In Jonkers and Welten 2005, 143–64.

Solomon, Robert C. 1980. "General Introduction: What is Phenomenology." In *Phenomenology and Existentialism*, ed. Robert C. Solomon. Lanham, Md.: Rowman and Littlefield, 1–41.

Søltoft, Pia. "Anthropology and Ethics: The Connection Between Subjectivity and Intersubjectivity as the Basis of a Kierkegaardian Anthropology." In Houe, Marino, and Rossel 2000, 41–48.

Sosa, Ernest. 2007. *A Virtue Epistemology: Apt Belief and Reflective Knowledge Vol. I*. Oxford: Clarendon Press.

―――. 2009. *Reflective Knowledge: Apt Belief and Reflective Knowledge Vol. II*. Oxford: Clarendon Press.

Spielberg, Stephen, dir. 1993. *Schindler's List*. Amblin Entertainment and Universal Pictures.

Spotts, Peter N. 2007. "Earth Nears Tipping Point on Climate Change." *Christian Science Monitor*. 30 May. Online at http://www.csmonitor.com/2007/0530/p02s01-wogi.htm. Accessed 21 March 2008.

Stack, George J. 1975. *Kierkegaard's Existential Ethics*. University, Ala.: University of Alabama Press.

Staten, Henry. 1984. *Wittgenstein and Derrida*. Lincoln and London: University of Nebraska Press.

Stauffer, Jill, and Bettina Bergo, eds. 2009. *Nietzsche and Levinas: "After the Death of a Certain God."* New York: Columbia University Press.

Steeves, H. Peter, ed. 1999. *Animal Others: Ethics, Ontology, and Animal Life*. Albany: State University of New York Press.

―――. 2005. "Lost Dog, or, Levinas Faces the Animal." In *Figuring Animals: Essays on Animal Images in Art, Literature, Philosophy, and Popular Culture*, ed. Mary Sanders Pollock and Catherine Rainwater. New York: Palgrave Macmillan, 21–35.

Steinberg, Milton. 1960. "Kierkegaard and Judaism." In Milton Steinberg. *Anatomy of Faith*, ed. Arthur A. Cohen. New York: Harcourt, Brace, 130–52.

Stengren, George L. 1977. "Connatural Knowledge in Aquinas and Kierkegaardian Subjectivity." *Kierkegaardiana* 10: 182–89.

Sterba, James P. 2008. "Environmental Justice: Reconciling Anthropocentric and Nonanthropocentric Ethics." In Pojman and Pojman 2008, 252–64.

Stern, David S. 2003. "The Bind of Responsibility: Kierkegaard, Derrida, and the Akedah of Isaac." *Philosophy Today* 47, no. 1 (Spring): 34–43.

Stewart, Jon. 2003. *Kierkegaard's Relation to Hegel Reconsidered*. Cambridge: Cambridge University Press.

Stiltner, Brian. 1993. "Who Can Understand Abraham? The Relation of God and Morality in Kierkegaard and Aquinas." *Journal of Religious Ethics* 21, no. 2 (Fall): 221–45.

Stolle, Jeffrey. 2001. "Levinas and the *Akedah:* An Alternative to Kierkegaard." *Philosophy Today* 45, no. 2 (Summer): 132–43.

Stout, Jeffrey. 1988. *Ethics After Babel: The Languages of Morals and Their Discontents.* Princeton, N.J.: Princeton University Press.

———. 2004. *Democracy and Tradition.* Princeton, N.J.: Princeton University Press.

Strauss, David Friedrich. 1994. *The Life of Jesus Critically Examined.* Ed. Peter C. Hodgson. Trans. George Eliot. Mifflintown, Penn.: Sigler Press.

Talisse, Robert B. 2001. "A Pragmatist Critique of Richard Rorty's Hopeless Politics." *The Southern Journal of Philosophy* 39, no. 4: 611–26.

———. 2005. *Democracy After Liberalism: Pragmatism and Deliberative Politics.* New York and London: Routledge.

———. 2007. *A Pragmatist Philosophy of Democracy.* New York: Routledge.

Talisse, Robert B., and Scott F. Aikin. 2005. "Why Pragmatists Cannot Be Pluralists." *Transactions of the Charles S. Peirce Society* 41, no.1 (Winter): 101–18.

———. 2008. *Pragmatism: A Guide for the Perplexed.* London and New York: Continuum Press.

Taylor, Charles. 1987. "Overcoming Epistemology." In Baynes, Bohman, and McCarthy 1987, 464–88.

———. 1989. *The Sources of the Self: The Making of the Modern Identity.* Cambridge, Mass.: Harvard University Press.

Taylor, Mark C. 1981. "Sounds of Silence." In Perkins 1981b, 165–88.

———. 2000. *Journeys to Selfhood: Hegel and Kierkegaard.* New York: Fordham University Press.

Taylor, Paul. 1981. "Biocentric Egalitarianism." *Environmental Ethics* 3. As reprinted in Pojman and Pojman 2008, 139–54.

———. 1986. *Respect for Nature: A Theory of Environmental Ethics.* Princeton, N.J.: Princeton University Press.

Ten Boom, Corrie. 1971. *The Hiding Place.* New York: Bantam.

Theunissen, Michael. 1984. *The Other: Studies in the Social Ontology of Husserl, Heidegger, Sartre, and Buber.* Cambridge, Mass.: MIT Press.

Thomas, Emyr Vaughan. 1999. "From Detachment to Immersion: Wittgenstein and 'The Problem of Life.'" *Ratio* 12 (June): 195–209.

Thulstrup, Marie Milulová. 1988. "The Single Individual." In *Bibliotheca Kierkegaardiana, vol. 16: Some of Kierkegaard's Main Categories,* ed. Niels Thulstrup and Marie Milulová Thulstrup. Copenhagen: C. A. Reitzels Forlag, 9–25,

Thulstrup, Niels. 1980. *Kierkegaard's Relation to Hegel.* Trans. George L. Stengren. Princeton: Princeton University Press.

Treanor, Brian. 2001. "God and the Other Person: Levinas's Appropriation of Kierkegaard's Encounter with Otherness." *Proceedings of The American Catholic Philosophical Association: Person, Soul, and Immortality* 75: 313–24.

Trusted, Jennifer. 1992. "The Problem of Absolute Poverty: What Are Our Moral Obligations to the Destitute?" In Cooper and Palmer 1992, 13–27.

Vanheeswijck, Guido. 2005. "Every Man Has a God or an Idol: René Girard's View of Christianity and Religion." In Jonkers and Welten 2005, 68–95.

Van Til, Cornelius. 2003. *Christian Apologetics*, 2nd edition. Ed. William Edgar. Phillipsburg, N.J.: P&R Publishing.

Van Troostwijk, Chris Doude. 2005. "Phrasing God: Lyotard's Hidden Philosophy of Religion." Trans. Maarten Doude van Troostwijk. In Jonkers and Welten 2005, 165–85.

Vattimo, Gianni. 1997. *Beyond Interpretation: The Meaning of Hermeneutics for Philosophy*. Trans. David Webb. Stanford, Calif.: Stanford University Press.

———. 1999. *Belief*. Trans. Luca D'Isanto and David Webb. Stanford, Calif.: Stanford University Press.

———. 2002. *After Christianity*. Trans. Luca D'Isanto. New York: Columbia University Press.

———. 2004. *Nihilism and Emancipation: Ethics, Politics, and Law*. Ed. Santiago Zabala. Trans. William McCuaig. New York: Columbia University Press.

Vattimo, Gianni, and Richard Rorty. 2005. *The Future of Religion*. Ed. Santiago Zabala. New York: Columbia University Press.

Visker, Rudi. 1997. "The Cause of my Opposition to Levinas: A Clarification for Richard Rorty." *Ethical Perspectives* 4, no. 3 (October): 154–70.

Voparil, Christopher. 2004. "The Problem with Getting it Right: Richard Rorty and the Politics of Antirepresentationalism." *Philosophy and Social Criticism* 30, no. 2: 221–46.

———. 2006. *Richard Rorty: Politics and Vision*. Lanham, Md.: Rowman and Littlefield.

Wallis, Jim. 2005. *God's Politics: Why the Right Gets It Wrong and the Left Doesn't Get It*. San Francisco: HarperSanFrancisco.

Walsh, Sylvia. 1999. "Other-Worldliness in Kierkegaard's *Works of Love*—A Response." *Philosophical Investigations* 22, no. 1 (January): 80–85.

Walzer, Michael. 1977. *Just and Unjust Wars: A Moral Argument With Historical Illustrations*, 4th edition (2006). New York: Basic.

Ward, Graham. 1997. *The Postmodern God: A Theological Reader*. Oxford: Blackwell.

———. 2001. *The Blackwell Companion to Postmodern Theology*. Oxford: Blackwell.

Warnke, Georgia. 2003. "Rorty's Democratic Hermeneutics." In Guignon and Hiley 2003, 105–23.

Warren, Virginia L. 1982. "A Kierkegaardian Approach to Moral Philosophy: The Process of Moral Decision-Making." *Journal of Religious Ethics* 10, no. 2 (Fall): 221–37.

Weil, Simone, and Rachel Bespaloff. 2005. *War and the Iliad*. Trans. Mary McCarthy. New York: New York Review Books.

Weithman, Paul J., ed. 1997. *Religion and Contemporary Liberalism*. Notre Dame, Ind.: University of Notre Dame Press, 1997.

Welten, Ruud. 2005a. "God is Life: On Michel Henry's Arch-Christianity." In Jonkers and Welten 2005, 119–42.

———. 2005b. "The Paradox of God's Appearance: On Jean-Luc Marion." In Jonkers and Welten 2005, 186–206.

Wenz, Peter S. 2001. *Environmental Ethics Today*. New York and Oxford: Oxford University Press.

West, Cornel. 1989. *The American Evasion of Philosophy: A Genealogy of Pragmatism.* Madison: University of Wisconsin Press.

Weston, Michael. 1994. *Kierkegaard and Modern Continental Philosophy: An Introduction.* London: Routledge.

Westphal, Merold. 1991. *Kierkegaard's Critique of Reason and Society.* University Park: Pennsylvania State University Press.

———. 1992a. "Kierkegaard's Teleological Suspension of Religiousness B." In Connell and Evans 1992, 111–29.

———. 1992b. "Levinas, Kierkegaard, and the Theological Task." *Modern Theology* 8, no. 3 (July): 241–61.

———. 1995a. "Levinas's Teleological Suspension of the Religious." In *Ethics as First Philosophy: The Significance of Emmanuel Levinas for Philosophy, Literature, and Religion,* ed. Adriaan T. Peperzak. New York: Routledge, 151–60.

———. 1995b. "The Transparent Shadow: Kierkegaard and Levinas in Dialogue." In Matuštík and Westphal 1995, 265–81.

———. 1996. *Becoming a Self: A Reading of Kierkegaard's* Concluding Unscientific Postscript. West Lafayette, Ind.: Purdue University Press.

———. 1997. "Phenomenology and Existentialism." In *A Companion to Philosophy of Religion,* ed. Philip L. Quinn and Charles Taliaferro. Oxford: Blackwell, 143–49.

———, ed. 1999a. *Postmodern Philosophy and Christian Thought.* Bloomington: Indiana University Press.

———. 1999b. "Taking Plantinga Seriously: Advice to Christian Philosophers." *Faith and Philosophy* 16, no. 2 (April): 173–81.

———. 2000. "Commanded Love and Divine Transcendence in Levinas and Kierkegaard." In *The Face of the Other and the Trace of God: Essays on the Philosophy of Emmanuel Levinas,* ed. Jeffrey Bloechl. New York: Fordham University Press, 200–23.

———. 2001. *Overcoming Onto-Theology: Toward a Postmodern Christian Faith.* New York: Fordham University Press.

———. 2002. "Divine Excess: The God Who Comes After." In Caputo 2002, 258–76.

———. 2004. *Transcendence and Self-Transcendence: On God and the Soul.* Bloomington: Indiana University Press.

———. 2007. "Vision and Voice: Phenomenology and Theology in the Work of Jean-Luc Marion." In Long 2007, 117–38.

———. 2008a. "The Many Faces of Levinas as a Reader of Kierkegaard." In Simmons and Wood 2008, 21–40.

———. 2008b. *Levinas and Kierkegaard in Dialogue.* Bloomington: Indiana University Press.

Will, Frederick L. 1974. *Induction and Justification.* Ithaca, N.Y.: Cornell University Press.

Wirth, Jason. 2004. "Empty Community: Kierkegaard on Being with You." In *The New Kierkegaard,* ed. Elsebet Jegstrup. Bloomington: Indiana University Press, 214–23.

Wittgenstein, Ludwig. 1965. "The Lecture on Ethics." *The Philosophical Review* 74, no. 1 (January): 3–12.

———. 1974. *Tractatus Logico-Philosophicus.* Trans. D. F. Pears and B. F. McGuinness. London and New York: Routledge.

————. 1980. *Culture and Value*. Trans. Peter Winch. Chicago: University of Chicago Press.

————. 2001. *Philosophical Investigations*. Trans. G. E. M. Anscombe. Oxford: Blackwell.

Wolf, Susan. 1982. "Moral Saints." *The Journal of Philosophy* 79, no. 8 (August): 419–39.

Wolfe, Cary, ed. 2003. *Zoontologies: The Question of the Animal*. Minneapolis: University of Minnesota Press.

Wolin, Richard. 2004. *The Seduction of Unreason*. Princeton, N.J.: Princeton University Press.

Wolterstorff, Nicholas. 1983a. "Introduction." In Plantinga and Wolterstorff 1983, 1–15.

————. 1983b. "Can Belief in God be Rational if it has no Foundations?" In Plantinga and Wolterstorff 1983, 135–86.

————. 1984. *Reason Within the Bounds of Religion*, 2nd edition. Grand Rapids: William B. Eerdmans.

————. 1995. *Divine Discourse: Philosophical Reflections on the Claim that God Speaks*. Cambridge: Cambridge University Press.

————. 2003. "An Engagement with Rorty." *Journal of Religious Ethics* 31, no. 1 (Spring): 129–39.

Wordsworth, William. 2000. "Preface to *Lyrical Ballads*." In *The Norton Anthology of English Literature*, 7th edition, vol. 2. Ed. M. H. Abrams and Stephen Greenblatt. New York and London: W. W. Norton & Co., 238–39.

Wood, Allen W. 1990. *Hegel's Ethical Thought*. Cambridge: Cambridge University Press.

Wood, David. 2002. *Thinking After Heidegger*. Cambridge: Polity.

————. 2003. "What is Eco-Phenomenology?" In *Eco-Phenomenology: Back to the Earth Itself*, ed. Ted Toadvine and Charles Brown. Binghamton: State University of New York Press, 211–33.

————. 2005. *The Step Back: Ethics and Politics After Deconstruction*. Albany: State University of New York Press.

————. 2007. "Specters of Derrida: On the Way to Econstruction." In *EcoSpirit*, ed. Lauren Kearns and Catherine Keller. New York: Fordham University Press, 264–90.

Wood, W. Jay. 1999. "On the Uses and Advantages of an Epistemology for Life." In Westphal 1999a, 13–27.

Wrathall, Mark A., ed. 2003. *Religion After Metaphysics*. Cambridge: Cambridge University Press.

Wren, David J. 1981. "Abraham's Silence and the Logic of Faith." In Perkins 1981b, 152–164.

Wyschogrod, Edith. 1989. "Derrida, Levinas, and Violence." In Silverman 1989, 182–200.

————. 1990. *Saints and Postmodernism: Revisioning Moral Philosophy*. Chicago: University of Chicago Press.

————. 2000. *Emmanuel Levinas: The Problem of Ethical Metaphysics*, 2nd edition. New York: Fordham University Press.

————. 2006. *Crossover Queries: Dwelling with Negatives, Embodying Philosophy's Others*. New York: Fordham University Press.

Wyschogrod, Edith, Jean-Joseph Goux, and Eric Boynton, eds. 2002. *The Enigma of Gift and Sacrifice*. New York: Fordham University Press.

Zagzebski, Linda, ed. 1993. *Rational Faith: Catholic Responses to Reformed Epistemology*. Notre Dame, Ind.: University of Notre Dame Press.

———. 1996. *Virtues of the Mind: An Inquiry into the Nature of Virtue and the Ethical Founda-tions of Knowledge.* Cambridge: Cambridge University Press.

Zaillian, Steve. 1993. Screenplay to *Schindler's List.* Web-published at The Internet Movie Database: www.imsdb.com.

Žižek, Slavoj. 2000. *The Fragile Absolute—Or, Why the Christian Legacy is Worth Fighting For.* London and New York: Verso.

———. 2001. *On Belief.* London and New York: Routledge.

———. 2003. *The Puppet and the Dwarf: The Perverse Core of Christianity.* Cambridge, Mass.: MIT Press.

———. 2006. *The Parallax View.* Cambridge, Mass.: MIT Press.

Žižek, Slavoj, Eric L. Santner, and Kenneth Reinhard. 2005. *The Neighbor: Three Inquiries in Political Theology.* Chicago: University of Chicago Press.

INDEX

Abraham, 38–40, 42, 46–49, 52, 56–58, 60–64, 71, 74, 191, 293, 312n30; anxiety of, 64–66; ordeal of, 75, 97; and Sarah, 57; and silence, 73, 113, 137. *See also Akedah;* Isaac; sacrifice (sacrificing)

absolutism, 93, 122, 195, 265

action: activism, 8, 260, 265, 287, 337n21; habits of, 190

Aikin, Scott F., 330n1, 331n6

Ajzenstat, Oona, 227, 230, 232, 237, 252–54

Akedah, 39, 48, 56, 68–69, 74, 76, 80, 169, 314n6; and Jacques Derrida, 72–75; and Emmanuel Levinas, 69–71. *See also* Abraham; Isaac; Stolle, Jeffrey

Alston, William, 12, 226, 237, 243, 246, 252, 333n35, 334n37; on Christian experience, 333n35, 334n37 (*see also* experience)

alterity, 6, 8, 35, 56, 101, 108, 135, 144, 156, 162, 179; absolute, 9, 27, 29, 110, 116, 160, 273, 285; obligation to, 64, 86; of the Other, 105, 251, 333n31; relation/response to, 72, 74, 77, 88, 90, 92, 93, 97, 98, 105, 114, 120, 140, 178, 295. *See also* Other, the; *and under* encounter

Amesbury, Richard, 198–99

anthropocentrism, 258, 265, 267, 337n19; relational model of, 12, 259, 263, 270–71, 277–80

anxiety, 112, 212, 313n40. *See also under* Abraham; Kierkegaard, Søren

apologetics (apologetic), 157, 164–65, 205

aporia (aporetic), 73–74, 123–24, 166, 235–36

appearance, 103, 124, 137, 140, 143, 154, 156, 160, 163; distinction with reality,

25, 191, 306n7. *See also* phenomenology

Aquinas, Thomas, 45, 64, 151–52, 312n38, 313n40

arche, 271; an-archic, 71, 112, 123–24, 272. *See also* foundationalism (foundation, foundational)

Arendt, Hannah, 302, 308n22

argumentation, 228–29

Aristotle, 5–6, 44–45, 117

arrogance, 118, 145, 149, 200, 207, 214, 266, 276

atheism (atheistic), 3, 79, 109, 116, 118, 155, 164, 188, 195; new atheism, 1, 228. *See also* Harris, Sam; theism (theistic)

Audi, Robert, 12, 209, 226, 238, 241–43, 249, 252, 328n1. *See also* foundationalism (foundation, foundational), modest

Augustine, Saint, 152, 203

authority, appeals to, 19, 142, 143, 162–63, 202–203, 232–33

Ayer, A. J., 197–98

Baier, Annette, 151, 224

Beauvoir, Simone de, 4–5

belief: basic, 151, 241, 244–45, 247, 249; Christian, 244; nonbasic, 241, 249; religious, 162, 189–90, 192–93, 195, 198, 205, 208–209

Bernasconi, Robert, 111, 124–25, 325n12

Bible, 87, 157, 200

bi-directional relationality, 63, 80, 82, 100, 140, 143–44, 167–68, 174, 176, 188, 203, 210, 212, 221, 246, 270. *See also under* responsibility biocentrism (biocentric), 267–68

Blanshard, Brand, 37–38, 49–50, 52

Bonhoeffer, Dietrich, 65, 87, 172, 295–99, 302, 318n15

Burggraeve, Roger, 118, 125, 303

Butler, Judith, 8–9, 210, 231, 321n25

Cain, 61–62

calculation, 74, 221, 235–36, 262, 273, 275–76, 282, 297

Callicott, J. Baird, 335n10, 336n11

Caputo, John D., 6, 11–12, 135, 146, 148, 174, 233–34, 286, 289–91, 323n20, 327n7

Catholicism (Catholic), 188, 204; for atheists, 166, 182

certainty, 64–65, 71, 97, 122, 148, 151, 206, 242–43, 246, 249–50, 304, 313n41, 320n11; lack of, 52, 60, 65, 72, 164, 192, 195, 207, 289, 295, 331n14; uncertainty, 203–204, 335n6

charity, 118, 188, 217; after justice, 173, 215–18, 223, 303 (see also justice (just)); critical task of, 167–68, 210

Chrétien, Jean-Louis, 2, 6, 10, 15, 35, 130, 135, 143, 145–47. See also new phenomenology; prayer; theological turn

Christ (Jesus), 87, 97, 168–69, 172–73, 179, 191–92, 203–204, 255, 296, 318n15, 325n1, 327n16; commandment of, 172; as exemplar, 87–88; imitation of (imitatio Christi), 85–86, 170–71, 295; kenotic message of, 188. See also kenosis (kenotic)

Christianity (Christian), 77, 142, 145, 152, 160, 162, 165, 167, 175–77, 182, 188, 195, 201, 203–204, 206, 245, 247, 282, 296, 298; nihilistic, 173–76 (see also Vattimo, Gianni); political value of, 175–76, 180, 188; and postmodernism, 11, 164, 187

civil rights, 220, 331n14

Clanton, J. Caleb, 195, 209, 324nn2,5

climate change, 12, 257–59, 261–81; epistemic problem of, 264, 270, 278; ethico-political problem of, 260, 264–67, 269–70, 278 (see also ethico-political, the); tipping point, 262. See also environmental philosophy

Cohen, Richard, 21, 311n21, 314n6

community, 31, 105–106, 169, 181, 182, 215, 237, 246–47, 256, 269, 286, 334n38; death of, 262, 334n1; ethico-political, 32, 259, 273–76, 280 (see also ethico-political, the); ethico-religious, 274–75 (see also ethico-religious, the)

compassion, 111, 124, 286. See also passion (passionate)

comprehension, 97, 100, 103; difficulty of, 17, 51, 110, 151; overflow of, 103, 115, 251

conscience, 99, 109, 176; bad (guilty), 217, 290, 301

consciousness, 54, 78, 97, 112, 143; intentional, 106, 136–37, 160

contextuality (contextualism), 189, 191, 200, 245, 246

Continental philosophy, 2, 7, 47; cliquism of, 7; and ethics, 3, 5–6, 8–10, 12, 14, 15, 21, 36, 170, 172, 218, 220, 257, 285, 294; and political philosophy, 3, 7, 10, 284–88; of religion (see under philosophy of religion)

contingency, 189, 193; of existence, 19, 175, 177, 188; of language, 326n1; of truth, 203

Critchley, Simon, 6, 11, 14, 126–27, 227–28, 230, 232, 252–54, 308n27, 333n37

critique (criticism), 60, 75, 91, 114, 168, 173, 181, 210, 248, 287; fixed point for, 113–15, 119; political, 25, 36, 108, 113, 116–18, 125, 248; self-critique, 116, 130, 216

death, 51, 61, 65, 69, 85, 102, 112; being-toward, 145; of the other, 112; penalty, 216, 220. See also under Derrida, Jacques; God; metaphysics

decision, 171, 236–37, 275, 288, 298; undecidability, 171, 236–37, 297, 303. See also under ethico-political, the

deconstruction, 131, 236, 330n2

democracy (democratic), 130, 149, 167,
177, 180, 182, 188, 190, 210, 215–18,
220, 222–23, 225, 303; to come, 8,
129, 170, 179, 181, 283. *See also* liberalism (liberal; liberal state); priority;
and under Derrida, Jacques
Denmark, 210, 214, 218, 257
Derrida, Jacques, 2–7, 15, 35, 72–75, 86,
110, 116, 124, 135, 142–43, 145, 167,
169, 171, 181–82, 215–16, 231–32,
249–50, 256, 280, 288, 324n4; democracy to come, 123, 125, 129–30, 218,
280, 287 (*see also* democracy (democratic)); *différance*, 232–33, 331n12;
on epistemology, 232; *The Gift of
Death*, 72, 74, 129, 145; hospitality,
7–8, 15, 31; and justice, 148, 151, 170,
231, 235–37, 248–49, 289 (*see also* justice (just); law); the messianic, 130,
135, 144–45, 280 (*see also* eschatology
(eschatological, the eschaton)). *See
also* deconstruction; Rorty, Richard
(Rortian); *and under Akedah*
desire (desirable), 116, 128; for the infinite,
101, 109; metaphysical, 108, 124; for
moral guidance, 288, 290, 296
despair, 93–95, 97–98, 107
Dewey, John, 17, 23, 38, 194, 306nn5,6
diachrony (diachronic), 110, 259, 271–72,
277, 317n13
divine command theory, 45–49, 60, 75, 80,
107, 314n10, 315n22. *See also* Evans,
C. Stephen
Dooley, Mark, 27, 284–88, 291, 308n20
Drury, M. O'C., 198–99, 205

economics (economic), 7, 40, 137, 145,
279, 335n6
egalitarianism, environmental, 259, 266–
270, 278. *See also* environmental philosophy
ego, 120, 147, 273; absolute, 118, 120, 122;
alter-ego, 144
egoism (egoistic), 84, 88, 92, 93, 101, 110–
11, 117, 144, 145, 146, 173, 277–78,
318n15; species, 277, 278. *See also
under* Kierkegaard, Søren

emergency situation, 257, 262, 334n1;
meta-ethical, 12, 258, 279; requirements for, 258, 261
encounter, 108; with alterity, 100, 105,
109, 114, 273; face-to-face, 113, 248;
inaugural, 100, 115, 129. *See also
under* ethico-religious, the
Enlightenment, the, 24, 77, 119, 193, 235,
237, 238
environmental philosophy, 8, 257, 259,
265–68, 277; ecocentric, 267–68. *See
also* anthropocentrism; egalitarianism, environmental; *and under* fascism (fascist)
epistemology (epistemological), 11, 24,
115, 191, 209, 222, 226, 239, 247,
330n4; analytic, 226, 237; Reformed,
151, 200, 246, 330n4, 332n25; of
trust, 12, 142, 248, 151, 226, 253, 254.
See also certainty; foundationalism
(foundation, foundational); justification (justified, justificatory); knowledge; *and under* first philosophy
eschatology (eschatological, the eschaton), 119, 122, 123, 145, 177, 181,
255, 280–81; vision, 127. *See also* Derrida, Jacques; hope
ethico-political, the, 7, 9, 10, 88, 162, 225,
277, 279, 284, 287, 288, 292, 324n4;
decision, 236, 256, 276, 282, 331n14;
efficacy, 35, 170–71; exemplar, 87,
284, 295–302; existence, 3, 237, 304,
337n3; project / task, 177, 182, 231;
value, 275. *See also under* climate
change; community
ethico-religious, the, 39, 56, 61–62, 64,
66, 76, 79–80, 84, 88, 93, 99, 115,
129–30, 222; encounter, 39, 47, 106,
134, 140, 152, 158, 161, 169, 175, 204,
223–25, 231, 237, 240, 249–52, 256,
271, 290; existence, 209, 214; exposure, 114, 125, 237; relation, 77, 128,
271; sociality, 11, 274, 276 (*see also* sociality); struggle, 246; subjectivity,
75, 185, 212–13 (*see also* subjectivity);
task, 223; tension, 62. *See also* community

ethics (ethical), 59, 197; as ethical subjectivity, 82–83; as love, 83–86 (*see also*
love); theory, 12, 45, 59, 259, 263,
264, 266, 270, 277, 279, 338n11; as
universal normativity, 83; virtue,
253. *See also under* Continental philosophy; emergency situation; experience; Kierkegaard, Søren
ethnocentrism (ethnocentric), 31, 146,
180, 229, 306n9. *See also* Rorty,
Richard (Rortian)
Eucharist (Eucharistic), 157, 163, 178, 204;
subjectivity, 178
Europe, 211, 257
Evans, C. Stephen, 43, 45–48, 50, 56, 75,
81, 249, 310n11, 313n39, 314n10,
315n22, 330n4. *See also* divine command theory
evidence, 200, 227, 244, 332n23
exemplar. *See under* ethico-political, the
experience: ethical, 254; religious, 137–
38, 147–48, 195. *See also under* Alston,
William
exposure. *See under* ethico-religious, the;
Levinas, Emmanuel (Levinasian)

Face, the. *See* Levinas, Emmanuel (Levinasian); Other, the; *and under* encounter
faith, 87, 113–15, 143, 145, 148, 176, 192,
202–203, 205–206; Christian, 168,
195, 295, 327n7; knight of, 50, 59,
61, 63, 65, 205 (*see also under* Kierkegaard, Søren). *See also* Christianity
(Christian); fascism (fascist); postmodernism (postmodern); *and under*
struggle
fallibilism, 181, 243, 252. *See also* certainty
fascism (fascist), 215, 218, 220; eco-fascism,
268. *See also* National Socialism
feminism (feminist), 150, 305n2, 307n15,
327n7, 331n14
Ferreira, M. Jamie, 51, 81, 311n24
fideism (fideist), 38, 49, 51, 148, 237, 246,
332n25. *See also* faith
first philosophy, 6, 25, 32, 80, 114, 306n7;
epistemology as, 100, 109, 239;

ethics as, 90, 124, 237, 240, 271,
317n11
forgiveness, 163, 179, 284, 296, 300, 302
formalism, 15, 26, 30, 308n27; ethical, 218,
284, 288; political, 218, 288
Foucault, Michel, 7, 18, 125, 194, 306n5
foundationalism (foundation, foundational), 31, 123, 126, 175, 238, 248;
an-archic, 124; anti-foundationalism,
22, 24, 191, 239; deconstructive,
123, 163, 250; disciplinary, 239–41,
254; epistemic, 239–42, 254; loss
of, 192; metaphysical, 239–41, 243,
254; minimal, 226 (*see also* Alston,
William); modest, 12, 226, 242–43,
249–50, 289 (*see also* Audi, Robert);
post-foundationalism, 10, 12, 226,
252, 254; strong/classical, 148, 188,
242–44, 250; varieties of, 332n18;
weak, 226. *See also* arche; epistemology (epistemological)
freedom, 107–108, 112, 114, 122, 236
Freud, Sigmund (Freudian), 1, 176, 198,
225, 324n8:1. *See also* psychoanalysis
(psychoanalytic)
fundamentalism, 61–62, 312n33. *See also*
religion (religious)

Gadamer, Hans-Georg, 11, 67, 121, 233,
307n11. *See also* hermeneutics
Gellman, Jerome, 68, 312n32
generosity, 111, 169, 299
Geras, Norman, 302, 309n29
gift, 62–64, 66, 67, 78, 80, 85–86, 100, 145,
151, 179, 284–85; ethics as, 79, 100;
givenness, 145, 156, 160; from God,
60, 62, 64, 66, 67, 78, 80, 85, 140. *See
also* Marion, Jean-Luc; *and under* Derrida, Jacques; love
God, 1, 35, 45–48, 60–61, 73, 160, 166–68,
174, 182, 190, 194, 318n15; be-for(e)
God, 104, 212, 274, 292; before God,
46, 55, 57, 59, 60, 73, 75, 95–100,
104, 140, 205, 214, 237, 250, 309n5,
318n15; of the Bible, 155, 159–60; of
the book, 157, 174, 187–88; as *causa
sui*, 138; as creator, 201; death of, 12,

invitation, 87, 146, 149, 180, 216

irony (ironic), 17–18, 59, 98, 114, 127–28, 191, 254. *See also under* Rorty, Richard (Rortian)

Isaac, 38–40, 42, 47, 52, 56–58, 60–61, 63–64, 71, 312n30. *See also* Abraham; *Akedah*

Islam, 160, 162, 165, 175, 207, 247; and the Koran, 191; and postmodernism, 164

James, William, 189–90, 194, 199, 327n12

Janicaud, Dominique, 2, 11, 136, 139–43, 153–58, 164, 166, 190, 208, 230; his critique of Levinas, 140, 155, 159. *See also* new phenomenology; theological turn

Judaism (Jewish), 76–77, 79, 142–43, 145, 152, 160, 162, 165, 169, 175, 177–78, 182, 204, 207, 219, 247, 313n1; and postmodernism, 164. *See also* religion (religious); theism (theistic)

justice (just), 1, 6–7, 9, 15, 36, 68, 78, 84, 91, 113, 117–18, 125–26, 143, 145–46, 151, 170, 181, 204, 207, 210, 214–16, 220–22, 231, 234, 236, 280–81, 303–304, 331n14; and critique, 91, 113, 185, 277; ever-increasing, 10, 36, 145, 215–16, 218, 222, 255, 280–81; as fairness, 150 (*see also* Rawls, John); for all, 215, 280; for each, 215, 280; for the Other, 68, 125, 143, 204 (*see also* alterity); incompleteness of, 129–30, 219, 304; injustice, 126, 170, 173, 237; intergenerational, 277 (*see also* environmental philosophy); and law, 235–36, 249, 331, 334n38 (*see also* law). *See also under* Derrida, Jacques; Rorty, Richard (Rortian)

justification (justified, justificatory), 10, 24–25, 73–74, 80, 116, 123, 131, 149–50, 163, 190, 205, 209–10, 222, 225–26, 228–29, 232, 239–41, 246, 253. *See also* epistemology (epistemological); knowledge

Kant, Immanuel (Kantian, Kantianism), 5–6, 30, 59, 63, 74, 104, 110, 117–

18, 121, 124, 152, 181, 235, 293; and metaphysics, 118–20; *Moralität*, 42, 60, 66 (*see also* morality (moral))

Kearney, Richard, 177, 180, 218, 326n7. *See also kenosis* (kenotic)

kenosis (kenotic), 11, 146, 149, 166–68, 170, 173, 180, 204, 283, 318n15, 323n19; in Emmanuel Levinas, 177–78; subjectivity, 178–79; in Gianni Vattimo, 174, 176. *See also* God; Incarnation (incarnational)

Kierkegaard, Søren, 5, 36, 80, 231, 246, 282, 302; Anti-Climacus, 70, 81; attack on Christendom, 86, 164, 214; Johannes Climacus, 43, 51, 55, 75, 78, 82–83, 97, 124, 176, 201–203, 205–206, 322n10; *The Concept of Anxiety*, 81; *Corsair* affair, 211; egoism of, 52, 59, 79; and ethics, 38, 40, 44–45, 58–59, 67, 80–81, 88, 91, 310n18; faith, 38–40, 49, 51, 59, 80, 96, 123, 131; *Fear and Trembling*, 37–41, 43, 45, 47–49, 52, 57–58, 64–65, 67, 72, 74–75, 81–83, 93, 310n20; on Hegel, 4, 40–42, 44, 53, 56, 82, 194; individualism, 328n5; and Kant, 43–44; leveling, 212–13, 223; and Emmanuel Levinas, 218–23 (*see also under* Levinas, Emmanuel (Levinasian)); paradox, 51, 63, 309n3; particularity/singularity, 52, 54–56, 58; and politics, 285–86; *The Present Age*, 211–214, 257; rationality, 38, 50–52, 63; religion, 77, 212; and religious knowledge, 249–50; *The Sickness Unto Death*, 91–100; Johannes de Silentio, 39–40, 43, 45, 48–49, 56–59, 61–62, 67, 70, 74, 76, 83, 113, 201, 203, 313nn40,41; teleological suspension of the ethical, 45, 48, 62, 71, 203, 221, 311n26; transparency, 55, 89, 91, 96–100, 103, 107, 129, 140, 178, 210, 237, 250, 315n5, 318n15; on truth, 202–204; Judge William, 42–43, 45, 67, 81. *See also* Abraham; ethics (ethical); faith; Isaac; paradox (paradoxical); subjectivity

King, Martin Luther, Jr., 304

knowledge, 112, 114, 119, 247, 313n41; absolute, 121. *See also* epistemology (epistemological); justification (justified, justificatory)

Lacoste, Jean-Yves, 2, 6, 15, 130, 135, 145, 146, 147, 148, 153, 157, 178, 179, 231, 291, 323n17, 324n1. *See also* liturgy; new phenomenology; theological turn

language, 113, 205, 208, 222. *See also* Wittgenstein, Ludwig; *and under* contingency

law, 77, 168, 191, 216–17, 235–36, 286, 297, 331n14; of God, 67 (*see also* God); of logic, 319n11; love as, 167–68, 192 (*see also* love); moral, 43, 180, 310n10; natural, 333n34. *See also* Derrida, Jacques; justice (just); Rawls, John; Rorty, Richard (Rortian)

Lehrer, Keith, 151, 330n3, 333n37

Levinas, Emmanuel (Levinasian), 2–3, 5, 9, 32, 35–36, 80, 131, 142, 227, 252, 259, 282, 285; critique of Søren Kierkegaard, 37–38, 56, 58–59, 92; and ethics, 6, 9, 14, 75, 77, 126, 131, 227, 229–31; exposure, 70, 74–76, 91, 97, 100–107, 112, 114–16, 120, 129, 140, 178, 210, 250, 273 (*see also under* ethico-religious, the); the face, 9, 112–13, 119, 215, 248, 274–77; on God, 70–71, 79, 204; heteronomy, 274; on Husserl, 144; and methodology, 119; non-human ethics, 274; on ontology, 101–103; and the political, 214–20; Saying/Said, 103, 113; subjectivity, 108–13, 178; Talmudic writings, 80, 143, 157; temporality, 271–74; the third, 74, 78. *See also* charity; *kenosis* (kenotic); Rorty, Richard (Rortian); *and under Akedah*

liberalism (liberal, liberal state), 18, 29, 31, 116, 125, 126, 149, 177, 214–18, 222–23, 253, 254, 307n15, 316n1, 329n15; Christian, 172 (*see also* Christianity (Christian)); hope, 128 (*see also* hope); ironist, 17–18, 128 (*see also* irony (ironic)); motivational deficit of, 253 (*see also* Critchley, Simon); political liberalism, 2, 23, 149; postmodern bourgeois, 172, 229, 255, 302; self, 93, 110; utopia, 17, 18, 116, 125–29, 145, 222, 255, 256. *See also* Rawls, John; Rorty, Richard (Rortian)

Light, Andrew, 260–65. *See also* environmental philosophy

liturgy, 147, 148, 159, 179. *See also* Christianity (Christian); Lacoste, Jean-Yves; religion (religious)

Locke, John, 53, 93, 127, 232

love, 61–63, 65–66, 74–75, 85, 144, 146, 167–68, 182, 286, 315n23; commandment, 84–86, 88, 99, 100, 144, 168, 171; as gift, 145; of wisdom / wisdom of, 182; works of, 6, 39, 84, 146, 177. *See also under* ethics (ethical); God; law

MacIntyre, Alasdair, 49–50, 310n18, 321n25

Marion, Jean-Luc, 2, 6, 10, 15, 35, 123, 130, 135, 138, 142–45, 147, 151–52, 156, 204, 231; fourth reduction, 147; saturated phenomena, 123, 147, 151, 157, 204. *See also* gift; new phenomenology; phenomena (phenomenon); theological turn

Marx, Karl, 194, 227, 230, 283, 325n1

Merleau-Ponty, Maurice, 155–56, 159, 322n13

messianism. *See under* Derrida, Jacques

metaphysics, 17, 31, 101, 114, 125, 158, 187; critique of, 187, 189, 195; death / end of, 162, 175, 198; of presence, 233; scholastic, 187. *See also under* desire

metaphor, 110, 112, 194, 319n2, 327n15

method (methodology), 50, 124; phenomenological, 139–40, 155–56, 159–60, 163, 320n20, 322n14 (*see also* phenomenology); transcendental, 118–20, 123–25, 142, 320n17 (*see also* possibility) morality (moral), 24, 43, 45–46, 64, 119, 124–25, 293, 312n38, 335n7; certainty, 71, 75; codification of, 87–88; social, 39, 45, 49, 71, 77, 78, 83 (*see also* Hegel, G. W. F. (Hegelian)). *See also* ethics (ethical); *and under* Kant, Immanuel

National Socialism, 179, 298. *See also* fascism (fascist)
neighbor, 104, 168–69
neo-Pragmatism. *See under* Pragmatism
new phenomenology, 1, 6, 9, 10–11, 15, 25, 28, 36, 68, 82, 90, 118, 120, 122, 130, 133–34, 141, 144, 147, 153, 161, 163, 209, 237, 282, 323n19; political dimension of, 145. *See also* phenomenology; theological turn
Niebuhr, Reinhold, 172–73, 287, 297
Nietzsche, Friedrich (Nietzschean), 2, 4–5, 100, 118, 122, 148, 166, 174, 182, 188, 194, 225, 233, 246, 325n1; on truth, 194
nihilism, 174–75; moral, 38. *See also* Blanshard, Brand; Nietzsche, Friedrich (Nietzschean)
normativity, 7, 21, 44, 49, 75, 90, 111, 117, 316n2; universal, 44, 60, 83, 290
Nussbaum, Martha, 8–9, 315n1, 321n25, 336n17

objectivity, 105, 205, 240, 246, 296, 308n19, 312n38
obligation, 7, 71, 75, 112, 116, 126, 173, 190, 235, 274, 290; infinite, 11, 12, 74, 280, 295, 299; to future generations, 259, 279, 336n14 (*see also* environmental philosophy)
ontology, 90, 93, 97, 102–103, 109, 112, 115, 125, 144, 167, 205; of constitutive responsibility, 10, 12–13, 32, 35, 90, 91, 103–104, 108–109, 113, 116–18, 130, 134, 158, 162, 168–69, 173, 175, 177, 185, 189, 196, 204, 209, 211, 218–20, 237, 272, 282–83, 291; fundamental, 138; reductionism, 117–18; social, 316n2 (*see also* Gould,

Carol); strong/weak, 174–77 (*see also* Vattimo, Gianni)
onto-theology, 7, 138, 146, 161, 164–65, 187–88; critique of, 192–93, 195–96, 198–200. *See also* Westphal, Merold
Other, the: call of, 32, 78, 110, 140, 146, 179, 210, 237, 249, 274; face of, 15, 70, 71, 76, 119, 120, 144, 146, 170, 204, 215, 248, 251, 314n10, 320n19
Otherism, 8, 225–26, 231, 240–41, 246, 248–55, 257, 271, 274–77, 280, 284, 288–89, 292, 294, 302, 330n2; key tenets of, 224
Outka, Gene, 64, 81, 309n6, 312n37

paradox (paradoxical), 97, 105, 124, 129, 188, 192, 203–206, 212; Absolute, 206; de-paradoxicalization, 193. *See also* Kierkegaard, Søren; *and under* struggle
particularity, 39, 52–58, 154, 193, 216; of religious traditions, 157, 161. *See also* singularity
Pascal, Blaise (Pascalian), 117, 178
passion (passionate), 49, 51, 52, 63, 83, 97, 102, 196, 201–203, 211, 231. *See also* compassion
passivity, 78, 104, 110, 273
peace, 8, 111–12, 118, 125, 302–303, 319n30
Peperzak, Adriaan, 101, 114–15, 123, 165, 317n11, 319n3
Perpich, Diane, 129, 230–31, 248–49, 320n19
persuasion, 227–29, 252
phenomena (phenomenon): impossible, 138, 144; religious, 122, 137, 142–44, 147; saturated (*see under* Marion, Jean-Luc)
phenomenology, 1, 9, 159, 162, 164, 174, 230; of the inapparent, 139–40, 144; of the invisible, 124; political stakes of, 146; of religion, 163; as rigorous science, 137, 139, 155, 159, 160. *See also* appearance; Husserl, Edmund; method; new phenomenology; religion (religious); theological turn

philosophy of religion, 32, 151, 195, 206, 218, 226; Analytic, 136, 148–49; Continental, 1, 7, 10, 13, 15, 32, 82, 133, 148–49, 152, 158, 165, 227, 282–84, 321n5, 323n19, 325n11

Plantinga, Alvin, 12, 151, 226, 242–44, 246, 252; "Great Pumpkin" objection, 245; proper functionalism, 332n26. *See also* epistemology

Plato, 108, 317n12, 329n6

policy, public, 7, 15, 35, 190, 209, 257, 277, 279

political theory / philosophy, 15, 32, 35, 88, 149, 151, 185, 209, 220, 225, 288, 291. *See also under* Continental philosophy; Rorty, Richard (Rortian)

politics, going all the way down, 21, 90, 117, 201, 216, 221. *See also* democracy (democratic); liberalism (liberal, liberal state)

positivism. *See* Ayer, A. J.; *and under* Rorty, Richard (Rortian)

possibility: conditions of, 111, 118–19, 122, 124, 125, 152, 236; quasi-logical existential conditions of, 120, 122–23, 125, 142, 214, 221, 236, 290. *See also* impossibility (im-possible)

postmodernism (postmodern), 11, 174, 185, 188, 194–96, 207, 231–32, 234, 252, 324n7, 325n2, 327n7, 330nn3,4. *See also* faith; saints (saintly); *and under* God

power, 101, 107, 108, 111, 145, 178, 225; that established the self, 96–100; lack of, 55, 107; power play, 90, 162, 165, 225; of the world, 175–76

practice (praxis), 9, 114, 120

Pragmatism, 18, 191–92, 196, 285; environmental, 259–60 (see also environmental philosophy); neo-Pragmatism, 14, 22, 27, 129, 131, 135, 188–89, 306n6 (*see also* Rorty, Richard (Rortian))

prayer, 143, 147, 157, 163. *See also* Chrétien, Jean-Louis; religion (religious)

presuppositionalism (presuppositionalists), 159, 163, 230

priority: concerning ethics and politics, 236, 290; concerning ethics and religion, 71, 76; concerning God and the Other, 10, 35, 36, 39, 63, 67, 68, 78–79, 100, 143, 144, 180, 213 (*see also* God); of democracy to philosophy, 23, 235 (*see also* democracy (democratic))

promise, 129, 145, 179, 218; of God, 56, 58, 60. *See also* gift

psychoanalysis (psychoanalytic), 3, 113, 142, 248, 305n1:2, 319n11. *See also* Freud, Sigmund (Freudian)

Purcell, Michael, 178–79

Putnam, Hilary, 4–6, 9

quasi-logical existential conditions of possibility. *See under* possibility

quietism, 115, 173, 221, 280

race, 8, 52, 145, 150, 305nIntro:4

rationality (reason), 76–77, 97, 119, 124, 193, 225–26, 274, 333n33; public reason, 11, 16, 149, 150, 155, 208, 209, 328nn1,3 (*see also* Rawls, John); reason-giving, 225–26, 228

Rawls, John, 2, 38, 93, 127, 149–50, 155, 209, 235, 254, 293, 316n1; comprehensive doctrine, 208, 222; fact of reasonable pluralism, 225, 229; *Theory of Justice*, 23. *See also* justice (just); liberalism (liberal, liberal state); Rorty, Richard (Rortian)

reconstructive separatism, 11, 162–63

reconstructivism (reconstructed, reconstruction), 11, 160, 162, 164, 188, 190–92, 207–208

relativism, 20, 195, 200, 201, 246

religion (religious), 195, 199–200; commitments of, 190–91; determinate, 188, 204, 206–207; phenomenology of, 141, 142 (*see also* phenomenology); postmodern, 187; practice, 192; in the public square, 2, 10, 25, 149–50, 208–209, 221; as romance, 192; without religion, 133, 135, 187, 201. *See also* Christianity (Christian); ethico-religious, the; experience; God; Judaism (Jewish); theism (theistic)

responsibility, 73–74, 78, 80, 109, 127, 129, 151, 303; bi-directional, 10, 11, 39, 66, 152, 183, 256, 257, 275, 282; call to, 78; infinite, 170, 220, 298; intellectual, 190–91, 208; as lived reality, 119

revelation, 64, 71, 147, 163, 172, 204, 231, 312n33. *See also* Marion, Jean-Luc, saturated phenomena

Ricœur, Paul, 2, 120, 123, 145–47, 231, 280; post-Hegelian Kantianism, 120–22, 256

risk, 75, 97, 148, 195, 204–205, 251, 290; of faith, 296, 327n17

Rolston, Holmes, 265–66, 270, 277–79

Rorty, Richard (Rortian), 14, 32, 38, 79, 90, 101, 114, 116–17, 130–31, 133, 151, 161, 167–70–180, 188, 199, 220–21, 228, 254–55; critique of Emmanuel Levinas, 9–10, 14–15, 18–21, 26–30, 127–31; critique of positivism, 197; and democracy, 229–30; on Jacques Derrida, 15–16, 18–21, 26–27; on epistemology, 231; and ethics, 29–30, 307n10; on irony, 16–18, 127–28, 254 (*see also* irony (ironic)); and justice, 20, 23–24, 235–237 (*see also* justice (just)); on the Left, 21–22, 25, 307n15; and liberalism (*see* liberalism); metaphysics, 16, 19; and political theory, 22–25; public/private, 16–19, 26; on John Rawls, 23–24, 27 (*see also* Rawls, John); redescription, 17, 25–26, 126, 192, 307n17; relativism, 20; on religion, 22–26, 37, 155, 167, 189–93, 200, 205–207, 209; social hope, 17, 18, 31, 79, 128, 131, 188, 190, 235, 255–56; use of theory, 24; on Michael Walzer, 23–24 (*see also* Walzer, Michael). *See also* ethnocentrism (ethnocentric); Pragmatism, neo-Pragmatism

Rousseau, Jean-Jacques, 53, 55, 93, 127

Rudd, Anthony, 42, 44, 51, 310n18, 311n26

rupture, 51, 63, 93, 100, 103, 110, 115, 116, 145, 168, 215, 272, 280

sacrifice (sacrificing), 47, 59, 61, 63–65, 69, 71–72, 74–75, 85–87, 110–12, 125, 274, 315n23. *See also* Abraham; *Akedah;* Isaac

saint(s) (saintly), 50, 117, 170, 292, 338n10; postmodern, 12, 171, 284, 291–96, 298, 304; saintliness, 117. *See also* postmodernism (postmodern); Wolf, Susan; Wyschogrod, Edith

salvation, 174, 175, 187, 201, 213, 295

Sandel, Michael, 23, 316n1, 321n25

Sartre, Jean-Paul, 4–5, 21, 44, 112, 324n8:1

Saying/Said. *See under* Levinas, Emmanuel (Levinasian)

Schindler, Oskar (filmic depiction of), 301–303

Schleiermacher, Friedrich, 82, 121, 141

science (scientific), 200–201, 203, 221

scripture. *See* Bible

self (selfhood), 92, 98, 177, 211; despite-itself, 110

Sellars, Wilfrid, 125, 245–46, 320n16

separatism (separatist), 11, 159–60, 162, 188, 190, 208–209

Shakespeare, William, 303–304

silence. *See under* Abraham

sin, 22, 28, 85, 95–96. *See also* Christianity (Christian); religion (religious)

singularity, 17, 37, 39, 40, 44, 52, 54–58, 60, 62, 69, 72–73, 75, 88–89, 100, 126, 189, 201, 205, 216, 218, 293, 303. *See also* particularity

Sittlichkeit. See under Hegel, G. W. F.; morality (moral), social

skepticism, 151–52, 317n13

sociality, 32, 44, 46, 71, 90, 106, 127, 225, 304, 310n15, 316n2; non-human, 259. *See also under* ethico-religious, the

Socrates, 117, 283

speciesism (speciesist), 265–66, 277–78; restricted, 336n13

Stolle, Jeffrey, 71–72, 75. *See also Akedah*

struggle: of faith, 40, 65, 68–69, 97, 195, 198, 202–207, 222, 296 (*see also* faith); hermeneutic, 142, 232 (*see also* hermeneutics); with paradox, 189, 192,

204, 212 (*see also* paradox (para-doxical))
sub specie aeternitatis (under the aspect of eternity), 101, 193–94, 326n5
subjectivity, 35, 75, 80, 112, 125, 179, 203, 205–206, 211, 273; as for the other, 111; eucharistic, 178. *See also under* ethico-religious, the; Eucharist (Eucharistic); Levinas, Emmanuel (Levinasian)

Talmud, 69. *See also under* Levinas, Emmanuel (Levinasian)
Taylor, Charles, 238, 315n1
Taylor, Paul, 267, 321n25
telos (teleology), 49, 93, 187, 232, 280, 311n20; of the ethical, 41, 48, 49, 62, 76
temporality, 258, 271–72
Ten Boom, Betsie, 299–301
Ten Boom, Corrie, 299–301
testimony, 9, 152, 171, 333n35
theism (theistic), 118, 138, 174, 191, 194–95, 199, 292. *See also* atheism (athe-istic); Christianity (Christian); Juda-ism (Jewish); religion (religious)
theological turn, 11, 13, 15, 32, 82, 133, 135–36, 153, 157–58, 195, 283–84, 287, 315n1. *See also* new phenome-nology
theology, 138, 158–59, 162, 164; natural, 164, 187, 193, 206; negative, 232, 320n13, 331n12; post-liberal, 326n1; process, 327n7
theory (*theoria*), 9, 114, 120
totalization, 37, 54, 58, 92, 101, 127, 130
trace, the, 9, 103, 113, 156, 290, 317n13; of God, 71, 144, 251, 312n35 (*see also* God)
transcendence (transcendent), 6, 103, 118, 151, 155, 157, 160–61, 179, 193, 196, 204; phenomenology of, 123–24; transcendent externality, 194. *See also* method (methodology); phenome-nology
transparency. *See under* Kierkegaard, Søren
trauma (traumatic), 95, 110, 115, 215

trust (trusting), 113, 115, 120, 148, 151, 205, 224, 237, 246–47, 251–53, 256, 333n37; in God, 206. *See also under* epistemology (epistemological)
truth, 124, 143, 193, 246; absolute, 187, 193; correspondence theory of, 191. *See also* Nietzsche, Friedrich (Nietz-schean); *and under* contingency

utilitarianism (utilitarian), 19, 192, 216, 253
utopia, 123, 126, 128, 256, 283, 287. *See also under* liberalism (liberal, liberal state)

value theory, 265; holism, 267; instrumen-talism, 259, 273, 276, 278; intrinsic, 259. *See also* ethics (ethical)
Vattimo, Gianni, 15, 152, 166–67, 173–77, 187–88, 192, 195, 206, 208, 215, 245, 246, 323n19; on belief, 176. *See also* belief; *kenosis* (kenotic); Christianity (Christian); ontology
violence (violent), 107, 115–16, 118, 125, 129, 179, 209, 214–15, 298, 302, 305, 334n2
Virgin birth, 189, 191–92. *See also* Chris-tianity (Christian)
Voparil, Christopher, 25–26
Vries, Hent de, 2, 10, 135, 142, 157, 166; on Dominique Janicaud, 157–58

Walzer, Michael, 23–24, 235, 257–59, 261–62. *See also under* Rorty, Richard (Rortian)
war, 2, 111–12, 258; of all against all, 107, 112, 292. *See also* Hobbes, Thomas (Hobbesian)
we-intentions, 245–46, 255–56. *See also* Sellars, Wilfrid
West, Cornel, 195, 324nn2,5, 338n9
Westphal, Merold, 7, 42, 62–63, 65, 77, 87, 135, 173, 193, 204, 206, 221, 234, 237–38, 246, 251, 254, 309nn3,5, 310n8, 330n4, 333n34; Religiousness A, B, C, 86, 87
Wittgenstein, Ludwig, 63, 113, 118, 189,

J. AARON SIMMONS received his doctorate from Vanderbilt University and is Assistant Professor of Philosophy at Hendrix College. He specializes in Continental philosophy of religion and political philosophy, and is editor (with David Wood) of *Kierkegaard and Levinas: Ethics, Politics, and Religion* (Indiana University Press, 2008), as well as the author of numerous essays in such journals as *Philosophical Forum, Journal of Religious Ethics, Philosophy and Theology,* and *The Heythrop Journal.*